A Comprehensive Explanation of Holy Baptism and the Lord's Supper (1610)

A Comprehensive Explanation of Holy Baptism and the Lord's Supper (1610)

by

Johann Gerhard

translated by Rev. Elmer Hohle

edited by
Mr. David Berger,
Director of Library Services,
Concordia Seminary, St. Louis
and
Rev. James D. Heiser,
Pastor, Salem Lutheran Church
Malone, Texas

REPRISTINATION PRESS
MALONE, TEXAS

Hardcover edition published in 2000.
Softcover edition published in 2014.

REPRISTINATION PRESS
ROUTE 1, BOX 285
MALONE, TEXAS 76660

www.repristinationpress.com

ISBN 1-891469-66-5

TABLE OF CONTENTS

Preface (by Johann Gerhard) 11

I. CONCERNING HOLY BAPTISM

Chap. 1. Of the various ways the word Baptism is used
in the Holy Scriptures. 17
Chap. 2. Concerning the various names which are given
to the Sacrament of Baptism. 22
Chap. 3. How the Old Testament Foretells holy Baptism
with Sayings and Types... 25
Chap. 4. Concerning the Founder of holy Baptism. 31
Chap. 5. By whom should be and can holy Baptism be
Administered in the Christian Church? 34
Chap. 6. Whether a Baptism performed by one whose
teaching is errant or whose life is criminal is
indeed a true and efficacious Sacrament. 43
Chap. 7. Whether the Baptism of John was just as
powerful a Sacrament unto salvation as is the
Baptism of Christ's disciples. 49
Chap. 8. Concerning the external element or
matter of Baptism, which is natural water........ 60
Chap. 9 The water in holy Baptism is not lowly water,
but is formulated and combined
[with] God's Word. 64
Chap. 10. Wherein does the form or essence of holy
Baptism consist; that is, What does it actually
mean to Baptize? 70
Chap. 11. That Baptism may be performed not only by
immersion, but also by pouring on the water... 73
Chap. 12. Whether the outpouring of the water in
Baptism should occur once or more often;
also upon which part of the body it
should be poured. 77

Chap. 13. That holy Baptism is a powerful means
for rebirth [through which the Holy Spirit
regenerates people].. 81
Chap. 14. That holy Baptism is an powerful means
for renewal. 94
Chap. 15. What sort of reminders and meanings are
presented to us in holy Baptism. 99
Chap. 16. What constitutes the washing from sin
in Baptism...103
Chap. 17. Whether the power of holy Baptism extends
itself throughout the entire life of the person. 110
Chap. 18. That only living people are to be baptized. ...117
Chap. 19. Which adult people are to be baptized. 123
Chap. 20. That the little, minor children are not to be
excluded from holy Baptism. 131
Chap. 21. That only children of Christian parents
are to be baptized. 143
Chap. 22. Whether children who are conceived and
born of such parents who lie in fornication,
adultery, or other gross sins are to
be baptized. 150
Chap. 23. Whether also foundlings are to be baptized. .155
Chap. 24. Whether the children of Christian parents
are in God's covenant of grace and are saintly
prior to their Baptism. 157
Chap. 25. Whether the children who are baptized
believe. 163
Chap. 26. What position is to be taken concerning
unbaptized children who die either in womb
or before they are baptized. 176
Chap. 27. At what time should holy Baptism
is to be administered? 184
Chap. 28. Whether one should make use of Baptism
more than one time. 188
Chap. 29. At what cite should and may holy Baptism
be administered? 193

Chap. 30. Concerning the ceremonies that are generally
      used at Baptism. 197
Chap. 31. Concerning the specific ceremony of
      Holy Baptism. 200

II. CONCERNING THE HOLY SUPPER

Chap. 1 Concerning the names which are given
      this Sacrament in the Holy Scriptures. 211
Chap. 2 Concerning the passages and types of the
      Old Testament which prophesy
      about this Sacrament. 214
Chap. 3 By whom the Holy Supper was instituted
      and ordained. 221
Chap. 4 Through whom the administration of the
      Holy Supper is at present performed. 223
Chap. 5 Concerning the outward, visible elements
      which Christ used, and has ordained to be
      used, for this Sacrament. 227
Chap. 6 Whether also little, round pieces of bread
      may be used from the Holy Supper. 230
Chap. 7 Whether one should use leavened or
      unleavened bread for the Holy Supper. 233
Chap. 8 Whether it is necessary to mix the wine in the
      Holy Supper with water. 236
Chap . 9 Whether the consecrated wine is to be
      extended to all those who receive the
      consecrated bread in the Holy Supper. 241
Chap. 10   Why the Lord Christ specifically ordained
      bread and wine as the external elements of
      this Sacrament. 253
Chap. 11 That Christ's body and blood are truly
      present in the holy Supper. 257

Chap. 12 Whether one should steadfastly abide by the same meaning which the letter of the words of institution of the Holy Supper renders necessary. 271

Chap. 13 Concerning the consecration, through which the external elements are sanctified for this Holy Sacrament... 295

Chap. 14 Whether the outward (external) elements, namely bread and wine, lose their nature through the consecration and in essence are changed into Christ's body and blood. 300

Chap. 15 Concerning the purpose for which Christ made use of the breaking of bread in the Holy Supper. 310

Chap. 16 Whether the consecrated bread and chalice are to be given into the hands of the communicants, or whether instead the consecrated bread is to be laid into their mouths and they are to drink out of the consecrated chalice. 322

Chap. 17 Whether it is contrary to Christ's institution for only the priests to receive the consecrated bread and chalice in order thereby to help others.. 325

Chap. 18 Concerning the eating and drinking of the true body and blood of Christ in the holy Supper. 330

Chap. 19 That not only bread and wine, but also the true body and blood of Christ are consumed and received in the Holy Supper, and of what this same sacramental consumption (eating and drinking) consists. 332

Chap. 20 Whether the consecrated bread is to be lifted up [elevated] and locked into the little sacramental house [tabernacle]........................... 350

Chap. 21 Whether the consecrated bread is to be
      carried around in a procession. 355

Chap. 22 Whether one should adore the consecrated
      bread in the Holy Supper.....................................358

Chap. 23 To what purpose the Lord Christ has
      instituted the holy Supper and what kind of
      benefit the believers receive from a wholesome
      use of it. 363

Chap. 24 Whether the Lord Christ instituted the holy
      Supper so that under the bread and wine
      His true body and blood be sacrificed to
      God the Lord by the Priests. 374

Chap. 25 Whether the sacrifice of the Mass is an
      atoning sacrifice for sin and the
      punishment of sin..403

Chap. 26 Whether the Holy Supper is the kind of
      sacrifice through which spiritual and bodily
      benefits, yes, also deliverance from all needs,
      may be achieved. 408

Chap. 27 Whether the sacrifice of the Mass does any
      good for the dead in purgatory...........................411

Chap. 28 Whether certain Masses should or may be
      conducted to revere [adore] the deceased
      saints in order thereby to obtain their
      intercessions. 414

Chap. 29 That the holy Supper was instituted for
      Christians only and is to be offered
      only to them..417

Chap. 30 That only Christians who examine themselves
      are to be offered the holy Supper......................420

Chap. 31 Concerning the proper, wholesome
      preparation for [the partaking of]
      the Holy Supper. 428

Chap. 32 Whether the unworthy receive the true body
      and the true blood of Christ sacramentally.......437

Chap. 33 At what time the holy Supper was
           instituted by Christ, and when it is to be
           celebrated by us. 450
Chap. 34 How often one should avail one's self
           of the Supper. 455
Chap. 35 In what place this holy Supper should and
           can be administered. 459
Chap. 36 Concerning the ceremonies which are used
           at the administration of the holy Supper. 466

Deo perennis gloria
In sempiterna secula.

PREFACE.

ust how precious and heavenly a gift is set aside and ordained for the Church through the most worthy Sacraments of holy Baptism and the holy Lord's Supper can best be understood when we consider why God the Lord (to whom alone belongs the authority to institute the Sacraments, since only He can impart divine power to them) initiated these Sacraments, and [when we] consider what He desires to create and accomplish in the hearts of men through them. Even though various ultimate reasons might be put forth for this divine institution and ordinance, yet there chiefly appears to be a threefold reason for it. For, first of all, God the Lord established the holy Sacraments so that they should be blessed means through which forgiveness of sins and other heavenly benefits are placed before us.

Concerning holy Baptism, St. Peter says in Acts 2:38 that it occurs for the forgiveness of sin, and in 1 Pet. 3:21 that it makes us saved. St. Paul attests to it in Tit. 3:5 that it is a bath of rebirth and renewal of the Holy Spirit, and in Eph. 5:26 that Christ cleanses His Church through this water-bath in the Word. To this relates also the formality of the administration of this holy Sacrament; for, when the servants of Christ speak according to His command and ordinance: "I baptize you in the Name of the Father and the Son and the Holy Spirit," then, among other things, this indicates that God the Father takes on and takes up the baptized [person] as His dear child and heir; that Christ washes the baptized of his sin through His blood; and that the Holy Spirit desires to work the grace of rebirth and renewal in the baptized.

Christ Himself testifies concerning the holy Supper that in it He imparts to us His true body to eat and His true blood to drink. Now, since the very same body of Christ is given into death for us and the very same blood of Christ is poured out on the cross for us, it follows beyond contradiction that Christ imparts to us the blessed bread which is the fellowship of His body in the holy Supper (1 Cor. 10:16), and imparts to us the blessed cup, which is the fellowship of His blood, for that very same reason. He presents and offers with this administration all that His body and shed blood have acquired for us. So it appears sufficient that in the Sacraments of holy Baptism and the holy Supper forgiveness of sins, God's grace, and heavenly benefits are presented to us. Indeed, God the Lord allows His heavenly gifts to be presented to us also through the Word of the Gospel. (Rom. 1:16 – for it (the Gospel) is a power of God to make saved all who believe it. 1 Tim. 4:16 – **Have regard about yourself and about the doctrine, persevere in these points; for when you do that, you will make yourself saved and those who listen to you.**)

Again, since we humans are by nature besieged with doubt and often think, "Who knows if all that God the Lord promises in the Word of the Gospel actually occurs?," behold, even for the very purpose to quell our doubts and to lift us up from our weakness, the faithful God allows His heavenly gifts to be offered and presented through this holy Sacrament, especially to such an individual.

Thereupon, God the Lord instituted the holy Sacraments in such a way that they should be a blessed means through which faith is awakened in the heart of man, a blessed means through which that faith is increased and strengthened (whenever anyone does not deliberately set themselves in opposition to the Holy Spirit), [and] a blessed means through which we believe we may become recipients of the proffered heavenly gifts. Holy Baptism is a bath of rebirth, as Christ (John 3:5) and St. Paul (Tit. 3:5) testify. Now, no one can be born again without faith, John 1:12,13 – **As many as received Him, those He gave power to become God's children, those who believed on His name, who were born not from blood, nor from the will of the flesh, but from God.** From this it follows that the Holy Spirit works the faith for rebirth through holy Baptism. It washes and cleanses from sin, Acts 10:43 – **About Him** (Christ) **testify all the prophets, that through His name all who believe on Him shall receive the forgiveness of sin.** It follows that the Holy Spirit works forgiveness of sins through Baptism. Through holy Baptism, God the Lord sets up a covenant of grace with the person (1 Pet. 3:21). Now then, no one can please God without faith (Heb. 11:6). It follows that faith is effected through Baptism and [that] through the same a person is taken up into God's covenant of grace. Holy Baptism makes us saved (1 Pet. 3:21). Now, no one can become saved except through faith, Mark 16:16 – **Whoever does not believe, he will be damned**. However, from this it follows that the Holy Spirit effectively works faith unto salvation in the hearts of people through holy Baptism.

In no way can it be denied what then pertains to the holy Lord's Supper: It was instituted by Christ chiefly to strengthen faith. For how could Christ have strengthened our faith very much except He extend and impart to us [*ipsum redemptionis nostrae precium*] the actual cost of our redemption through which He earned forgiveness of sins and all heavenly benefits? So, since St. Paul admonishes [in] 1 Cor. 11:26 – **For as often as you eat from this bread and drink from this cup, you shall proclaim the Lord's death, etc.,** that is, thank Him for it from the heart; and, since Christ Himself says in the words of institution that we are to do such in remembrance of Him, it is quite evident that the holy Supper was instituted for us to uphold within ourselves and to further within ourselves the living and powerful remembrance of Christ's good deeds. Finally, the holy Sacraments were instituted that they should be seals through which the divine promises are strengthened and sealed in our hearts.

For in the same way that St. Paul writes in Rom. 4:11 that circumcision was a seal of the righteousness of faith, we also can speak in the same manner about the Sacraments of the New Testament, that they are seals of the divine promises which become our portion through faith.

St. Peter announces in 1 Pet. 3:21 that Baptism is the covenant of a good conscience with God. This could not be said of Baptism if the covenant of God's grace were not sealed and established for us through the same, especially since we could not calm our heart before Him nor have a quiet conscience until we are assured of this divine grace-covenant in our heart. Christ Himself verifies what pertains to the holy Lord's Supper; namely, that it is a New Testament in His blood which was poured out for us. With that [declaration] He adequately gives the understanding that through the fellowship of His body and blood we are assured that we are taken into the grace-covenant of God, and that we become recipients of all the gifts of this Supper through faith. To this can be related, justifiably so, the beautiful little verse, 1 John 5:8 – **And three there are that witness on earth: the Spirit and the water and the blood, and these three are together.** This text fits most closely if one understands "the Spirit" as the Word (which is the office of the Spirit, 2 Cor. 3:6), understands "the water" as holy Baptism (which is a blessed water-bath in the Word, Eph 5:26), and understands "the blood" as the holy Lord's Supper (in which Christ's body and blood are distributed). These three, namely, Spirit, water and blood, testify on earth of our salvation. That is to say, God the Lord has not only given us His holy Word, but also His holy Sacraments of Baptism and the Lord's Supper. Through these Sacraments, the Holy Spirit completely witnesses in our hearts and reassures us of the promises of salvation, just as the fathers, for these very reasons, often called the Sacraments pledges, tokens, seals [*arrhas, sigilla,* *signacula*] and visible signs of the invisible divine grace.

Thus, these are the three foremost ultimate purposes for which God the Lord instituted these holy Sacraments. (Add also thereto the final principal purposes [*fines minus principales*]: that the Sacraments are marks of the Church, the bond of public assembly, a model or type of spiritual matters, e.g., holy Baptism indicates the killing of the old man, Rom. 6:4, the holy Supper reminds us of brotherly love, 1 Cor. 10:7, and the like.) It can be adequately learned from these reasons what a precious, heavenly gift God has set aside and ordained for His Church in the holy Sacraments. But since this is such a great gift, it should then be so highly regarded by us that we not only use the holy Sacraments with inner thankfulness in true repentance and faith, but even more, that we also persistently uphold the pure doctrine of the Sacraments and zealously fight against every kind of falsification and perversion of the Sacraments' words of institution. Anyone who is named in a will as an heir of a magnificent legacy, in all fairness, will indeed hold in honor the instigator or testator of such a will. How much more is it not incumbent on us to show such honor to the words and Testament of Christ! This is already expressly clarified by John 8:31, **if we remain in His utterances, then we will be His true disciples,** and John 12:48, that **the Word which He has spoken to us will also finally judge us on that Day.**

Since, unfortunately, there has arisen much strife and fighting concerning both of these holy Sacraments among those who completely confess Christ and His Word, I, with the modest abilities God has proffered me, have drawn the pure doctrine of holy Baptism and of the holy Lord's Supper singularly and solely from the source of the divine Word. I have clarified the seemingly-contradictory points of the Scriptures. And, I give to others who are graced with higher gifts, guidance to deal with other articles of the Christian religion in such a fashion and manner that, according to my simple-minded thinking, it would wonderfully benefit the simple [folk].

Heldburg in Franken, den 1. September 1610

Johann Gerhard D.

CHAPTER 1

THE VARIOUS WAYS IN WHICH THE WORD 'BAPTISM' IS USED IN THE HOLY SCRIPTURES.

 he purpose for explaining this point is that a person might better understand the Bible verses in which 'Baptism' or 'baptizing' are considered. "To **baptize**" commonly means to wet or wash with water, and that occurs either by dipping into, immersing, pouring or sprinkling.

In 2 Kin. 5:14 Naaman stepped in and **baptized himself seven times in the Jordan**.

Mark 7:4 – **The Pharisees..., after they return from the market place, do not eat until they have washed themselves** (have baptized themselves)**, and they have adopted many other practices, such as washing** [Greek: βαπτισμους – to baptize] **drinking-vessels, jugs, brass pots and tables**.

Mark 7:4 – **You hold on to the traditions of the fathers about washing** (baptizing) **pitchers and cups**.

Luke 11:38 – **When the Pharisee saw that He** (Lord Christ) **didn't wash** (baptize in the Greek) **Himself, he marvelled**.

Hebrews 9:10 – (In the tabernacle, worship was conducted) **Only with food and drink and various baptisms** [βαπτισμοις διαφοροις—with various Levitical cleansings and sprinklings].

In metaphorical and figurative terms, "**Baptism**" means:

1. To be thrust into cross and temptation, yes, also into death. For in the same way anyone who is dipped into water and is baptized thinks of it in no other way than that he must all the more drown—yet ultimately be pulled out; so also when the "raging waters" [Psa. 124:5] of tribulations, temptations, and perils of death sweep over our souls, we, too, think that we shall all the more perish—and yet ultimately we shall be rescued through God's grace.

Mat. 20:22–23 – **Can you drink the cup which I must drink, and let yourself be baptized with the Baptism with which I must be baptized?** ("Cup" and "Baptism" here mean both cross and suffering.) **You will, indeed, drink of My cup, and be baptized with the Baptism with which I have been baptized,** etc.

Rom. 8:17 – **We are co-heirs with Christ, as we otherwise suffer along with...** (we too must drink from the "cross-cup" [German: *Kreuzbecher*] from which Christ drank). Mark 10:38–39 repeats this.

Luke 12:50 – **I must first let Myself be baptized with a Baptism** (I must first suffer and die. Christ prays [Psa. 69:2, 3, 15, 16]: **The water comes up over my soul. I sink in this deep, bottomless slime. I am in deep water and the flood wants to drown me. Rescue me from the deep water so that the flood waters do not drown me and the deep does not engulf me,** etc. In this case, Jesus is speaking of this Baptism).

2. Furthermore, **Baptism** signifies the outpouring of the singularly special gifts of the Spirit. For in the same way that they who were thus baptized were sprinkled and poured upon with water, so also in the early Church the distinctively unique gifts of the Spirit were richly poured out upon the apostles and other Christians.

Mat. 3:11 – **I baptize you with water for repentance** (says John). **He who comes after me will baptize you with the Holy Spirit and with fire.** (He will pour out over you the unique gifts of the Spirit in the form of fiery tongues—as then actually occurred on Pentecost.) Since John speaks *in futuro*, this appears to be the only meaning of his words, "He will baptize you with the Holy Spirit." Yet we do not reject the interpretation of those who regard this as John's making a distinction between the power and work of Christ in holy Baptism and John's own Baptism as a servant's work. While John baptizes with water, Christ baptizes with the Holy Spirit at the same time.

Mark 1:8 and Luke 3:16 repeat this.

John 1:33 – **Upon the One whom you see the Spirit descend and remain, the same is the One who baptizes with the Holy Spirit.** For all that, it appears as if this passage actually speaks about the universal gifts of the Spirit which the Lord Christ imparts through John and others of His baptizers.

Acts 1:5 – **John baptized with water; you, however,** (Christ is speaking to His disciples) **will be baptized with the Holy Spirit not long after this day.** (The fulfilling of this promise is described in my second chapter which follows.) Acts 11:16 repeats this again.

Here some also [take into consideration] what is written in Acts 19:4ff: **When they heard this, they let themselves be baptized in the Name of Jesus** (not as if they were being baptized again, but according to the explanation which immediately follows). **And when Paul laid his hands upon them, the Holy Spirit came upon them, and they spoke in tongues and prophesied.** About this, see under chapter 7 below.

3. The word "Baptism" is also used [in relation to] the deliverance of the children of Israel from the Egyptians through the Red Sea, which the Lord God carried out for them through Moses. This action is called a "Baptism" first and foremost because it was a type of our own Baptism. For just us the Israelites were led out of the land of Egypt through the Red Sea, so also we were rescued from spiritual enslavement to the hellish "Pharaoh" through the salvation-giving water of Baptism. Conversely, just as Pharaoh and his whole horde was drowned in the Red Sea, so also the Old Adam with all his lusting and doings is drowned in holy Baptism. Subsequently, this leading out of the Red Sea is called a Baptism because the Israelites became bound to faith and obedience through this wondrous action by God and by His servant Moses. So also, in similar fashion, we became obligated to a life of service and obedience to Christ our Savior through holy Baptism.

1 Cor. 10:1-2 – **Our fathers were all under the cloud.** (The column-of-smoke cloud [followed] behind the Israelites and came between the army of the Egyptians and the multitude of Israel, Exo. 14:19-20) **and all went through the sea, and were all baptized by Moses under the cloud and the sea.** (It reads in his language: they were baptized by Moses.)

As discussed in the foregoing, the word "to baptize" is used in a metaphorical sense. As a word substitute it is taken:

4. For the entire ministerium or office of John the Baptist. For while John did not just baptize, but also taught, yet his entire office is labeled the Baptism, since he was the first to administer this Sacrament in the New Testament, and since it is part of scriptural usage to indicate the whole by naming only a piece or a part of the whole.

In Mat. 21:25 Jesus asks the Pharisees: **From where came John's Baptism? Was it from heaven or from men?** (Did John teach and baptize because of his own good thinking or because of divine command?)

Mark 11:29, Luke 20:4 repeat this.

Acts 1:22 – **From the Baptism of John until the day He** (Christ) **was taken from us**, etc.

Acts 10:37 – **After the Baptism which John preached.**

Acts 18:25 – **Apollos knew only of the Baptism of John.** (He knew only of the preaching of John about the Messiah, who would soon establish Himself.)

Acts 19:3 – **On what were you baptized?** Paul asks those in Ephesus. The answer: **Upon John's Baptism.** (We know of no other teaching and Baptism than what John promoted. We know nothing of a visible outpouring of the Holy Spirit over those who are thus baptized.)

Originally and foremost, "to baptize" means to dip into water, or sprinkle with water, a person in the Name of the Father, and the Son, and the Holy Spirit so that the person is born-again, renewed, and becomes a partaker of salvation through such a water-bath. Relevant here are all the passages of the Bible in which this holy Sacrament of the New Testament is treated. Of these, many will be explored in the following chapter.

CHAPTER 2

CONCERNING THE VARIOUS NAMES
WHICH ARE GIVEN TO THE SACRAMENT OF
BAPTISM.

 hile this holy Sacrament of the New Testament is universally called Baptism, there are yet other names given to it in the holy Scriptures. It is also called:

1. A **Flood**, namely because the Flood [German: "sin-flood"], through which the world was punished in Gen. 6, 7, [and] 8, was a type of this Sacrament. For just as all sinful flesh on earth was annihilated in the Flood, and only godly Noah—along with a few others—was preserved in the ark, so also the sinful flesh in man is subdued and killed in holy Baptism. Conversely, the inner new man is born and preserved to eternal life.

Psa. 29:10 – **The Lord is enthroned to instigate a flood.** (God the Lord had promised in Gen. 9:11 that from henceforth a Flood which would destroy the world would never again occur. Therefore, this text must be interpreted to mean a spiritual flood. Some interpret it literally in the following way: that from God's command the waters sometimes pour down in such a way that one thinks a new Flood is coming. But the explanation of a "spiritual" Flood is preferable because St. Peter in his first epistle, ch. 3:21, testifies that the Flood is a type of Baptism.)

2. A **Waterbath in the Word,** "for Baptism is not just common water, but it is water seized by God's command and wrapped up with His Word. Without the Word the water is

plain water and no Baptism. But with the Word of God it is a Baptism, a grace-enriched water of life." [Small Catechism, Baptism:III]

Eph. 5:26 – Christ **cleansed** His fellowship **through the water bath in the Word**.

3. **Water,** not as if Baptism were common water, but rather, because the water is a vital element of Baptism. It is the external element through which the heavenly gifts in Baptism are imparted.

John 3:5 – **Unless a person is born out of the water and [the] Spirit, he cannot come into God's kingdom.**

Heb. 10:22 – **Bodily washed with clean water**.

1 John 5:6 and 8 – **This is He who comes with water and blood** (these are the two holy Sacraments, Baptism and the Lord's Supper, through which Christ imparts His blessings) **not with water only, but with water and blood. And there are three which witness upon earth: the Spirit** (in the holy office of the ministry, which is **the office of the Spirit,** 2 Cor. 3:6) **and the water** (in holy Baptism) **and the blood** (in the holy Supper).

Relevant to this are the prophecies of the Old Testament which refer to a clean and living water, [the subject dealt with] in chapter 3.

4. **A bath of rebirth and renewal,** for the Holy Spirit gives to man new birth and renewal unto eternal life through holy Baptism.

Tit. 3:5 – **In conformity with His mercy, He (God the Lord) saved us through the bath of rebirth and renewal of the Holy Spirit.**

5. A **circumcision without hands** occurs, for the circumcision in the Old Testament was a type for holy Baptism. Just as God the Lord established a covenant with the one who was circumcised (Gen. 17:10), so also Baptism is a covenant of a good conscience with God (1 Pet. 3:21). Just as the Lord God in the outward circumcision simultaneously also inwardly cut off the heart's foreskin, Deu. 30:6, so also

our sinful flesh is simultaneously also inwardly subdued and killed through the outward water of Baptism.

Col. 2:11 – **In whom** (Christ) **you also are circumcised with the circumcision without hands through the discarding of the sinful body of the flesh, namely with the circumcision of Christ, since you have been buried with Him through Baptism.**

CHAPTER 3

HOW THE OLD TESTAMENT FORETELLS HOLY BAPTISM WITH SAYINGS AND TYPES.

aptism is a holy Sacrament of the New Testament instituted by God Himself, since it is solely His domain to instigate and ordain the holy Sacraments as visible means of grace. Just as Amos 3:7 generally indicates that the Lord does nothing [without revealing] His secrets to His servants, the prophets, so then, it previously pleased Him also to permit passages about and types [of] this Sacrament [to] be directly proclaimed in the Old Testament. In keeping with the Old Testament style, the sayings which prophesy about holy Baptism are frequently couched in figurative words and must be clarified out of the New Testament.

Psa. 29:10 – **The Lord sits enthroned to initiate a flood.** (Why holy Baptism is called a flood was clarified in the previous chapter.)

Psa. 46:5 – **Yet the city of God shall remain exquisitely cheerful with its fountain; there are the holy dwellings of the most High.** (Within this City of God, the fountain of the Christian Church is also holy Baptism, through which we are washed from sin's filth.)

Psa. 103:5 – **Who makes your mouth happy, and you become young again like an eagle.** (We become young again and obtain new strength through rebirth, so that we rise up like eagles, Isa. 40:31. But then, holy Baptism is the bath of rebirth and renewal, Tit. 3:5.)

Isa. 44:3–4 – **Thus says the Lord: I will pour water upon the thirsty and streams upon the dry. I will pour**

My Spirit upon your seed and My blessing upon your descendants, so that they may grow like grass, like the willows in the water brooks. (In holy Baptism the Spirit of God is poured upon us, Tit. 3:5, which makes us fruitful for every good [work].)

Isa. 49:22 – **They (the people) will bring your sons here, and carry your daughters upon their shoulders.** (As with the Israelite children, this occurs in holy Baptism; the children are brought to Jesus through it, Mat. 19:13, Mark 10:13, Luke 18:15.)

Isa. 52:15 – **My servant will sprinkle many Gentiles.** (This sprinkling occurs also in holy Baptism through Christ's blood because we are washed [clean] from sin through it.)

Isa. 61:10 – **He (the Lord) has put on me garments of salvation and clothed me with the Robe of Righteousness** (Gal. 3:27: **For as many of you who are baptized, you have put on Christ**).

Eze. 16:9 – **I bathed you with water and washed away your blood.** (Through the water of holy Baptism, we are washed [clean] of our blood-red guilt of sin, Eph. 5:26.)

Eze. 36:25–26 – **I will sprinkle pure water over you, so that you become cleansed of all your uncleanness; And, I will give you a new heart and a new spirit, and take away from your flesh the stony heart and give you a heart of flesh** (Baptism is a **Bath of rebirth and renewal of the Holy Spirit**, Tit. 3:5).

Eze. 47:1, 5, 8, 9 – **a water flowed from under the threshold of the Temple. ... The water was too high and a man could not touch the ground ... When the water comes into the sea, the same will become healthy ... Yes, wherever its streams flow, all that moves and lives in it will live ... and all to whom this stream comes, shall become well and live.** (Just as the angel came down from heaven to Bethesda's pool in Jerusalem and stirred the water so that the first one to step in became healed from whatever epidemic plagued him, John 5:4, in the same way the living water, the Holy Spirit, John 7:38–39, sinks His power into the water of Baptism so that it serves us to our soul's health and life. Rev. 4:6 – **Before the throne there was a glassy sea like crystal.** Chap. 2:1–2 – **and he showed me a stream of living water, clear as crystal, which flowed from the throne of God and the Lamb, down the center of its narrow pathway.**)

Joel 3:23 [sic, v. 18] – **A spring will flow out of the house of the Lord, the stream of which will water the acacias** (holy Baptism waters and brings to life dried-up souls).

Mic. 7:19 – **The Lord will hurl all our sins into the depths of the ocean.** (This sea-of-grace is holy Baptism, Rev. 4:6, into which all sins are thrown and sunk.)

Zec. 13:1 – **At that time the house of David and the citizens of Jerusalem will have a free, open fountain against sin and uncleanness.**

The types of holy Baptism are drawn over to holy Baptism in the New Testament partly by the Holy Spirit Himself. To some extent, one can conclude that they can appropriately be compared to holy Baptism under some circumstances, even though these very same types are not all immediately transparent and clear.

Gen. 7 describes the Flood [German: "Sin-flood"], through which all flesh on earth perished. It is a type of Baptism, as perceived from Psa. 29:10. The comparison was shown in the previous chapter.

Gen. 8 reveals that Noah, along with a few others, was preserved in the ark during the time of the Flood. Also, [it reveals] how he let a raven fly out, which never returned; contrarily, a little dove returned to the box with an olive branch (v. 8). This is a type of holy Baptism.

1 Pet. 3:20–21 – **Through which** (Noah's ark) **a few, that is, eight souls, were kept by means of water; so also water now saves us in Baptism, which is signified by the former.** Just as only those who were in the ark were

kept alive through the Flood, while contrarily all the others perished, so also we may be preserved to eternal life only through the Sacrament of holy Baptism, since we become members of the Church through it. So also the hellish, black raven of the devil must abandon the baptized person; and conversely, the Holy Spirit comes upon him and brings peace and comfort to his conscience—just as at He descended upon Jesus in the form of a dove at His Baptism (Mat. 3:16, Mark 1:10, Luke 3:21–22, John 1:32).

In Gen. 17, God commands circumcision to Abraham and to his seed. Paul testifies in Col. 2:11–12 that this is a type and figure of holy Baptism. The comparison is referenced in the previous chapter.

Exo. 14 describes how the children of Israel were led through the Red Sea. Conversely, Pharaoh and all his hosts were drowned in it. This passage of the Israelites through the Red Sea is also a type of Baptism, as Paul describes it in 1 Cor. 10:2. The comparison is dealt with in chapters 1 and 3.

In Exo. 15:25, Moses sank a [piece of] wood into bitter water. The water turned sweet and refreshed the Israelites in the arid desert. In varying degrees, this could also be likened to Baptism, for Christ, the Tree of Life (Rev. 22:2), similarly sinks Himself with all His merits into the water of Baptism. Thereupon, it becomes a rich-in-grace Water of Life that is able to quench our soul's thirst.

In Exo. 17:6, the water springs out of the rock so that the Israelites could be quenched of thirst and be vitally sustained. To some extent, this can also be [a type of] Baptism since the Rock was Christ (1 Cor. 10:9). Out of Christ's side flowed blood and water (John 19:34), thereby signifying both Sacraments. Since all of Baptism's power originates from Christ's merit, we are shielded from eternal thirst through the water of Baptism.

In Exo. 30:18; 38:8; and 40:7, God directs Moses to craft a brass laver with brass feet, set it between the tabernacle and the altar, and place water in it so that Aaron and his sons might wash in it whenever they wanted to enter the tabernacle so that they might not die. To some degree this can also be [a type of] Baptism. For just as none of the priests was to enter the tabernacle back then unless he had first washed with this water, so also anyone who wants to enter the eternal tabernacle must first be washed from sin through holy Baptism.

In Lev. 14:6–7, God the Lord commanded that for a leper to be clean, one had to take a live bird along with cedar wood, scarlet wool and hyssop, and dip them in the blood of (another) bird slaughtered over flowing water. Then the one who was being cleansed of leprosy was sprinkled with this, etc. Now, just as the latter bird's blood mingled with the flowing water [and] made it a healing water through which the leper was cleansed, so also the blood of Christ makes the water of Baptism into such a grace-rich water that we might be cleansed from the leprosy of sin.

Leviticus 15 prescribes various cleansings through which the Israelites were washed of their outward uncleanness. The very same cleansings are called **various Baptisms** in Heb. 9:10 because they are a type of holy Baptism through which we are washed [clean] of all the uncleanness of sin.

In Num. 19:2, God commands that a red cow be slaughtered and totally burned. This burned cow's ashes were then mixed with flowing water to make a sprinkling-water which would purify the unclean. This sprinkling-water is also a model of holy Baptism, for the blood of Christ, which was roasted on the stem of the cross in hot love, is sunk with all its power into Baptism's water. Thus it becomes a wholesome sprinkling water through which we are washed from all uncleanness.

In 1 Kin. 7:23 Solomon made a huge cast sea in his temple since Moses in his day let a brass laver be made. It was for the specific purpose that the priests wash themselves in it whenever they wanted to go into the temple to perform offerings. This sea, or huge water tub (for the Hebrews call any large accumulation of water "a sea"), is also a type of holy Baptism. In Rev. 4:6 a glassy sea like unto crystal was before the throne of the Lamb.

In 2 Kin. 5:14, Naaman, upon the bidding of the prophet Elisha, washed himself in the Jordan, and was cleansed of his leprosy because of that. This is a type of holy Baptism, for Christ, the Head of the Church, let Himself be baptized in the Jordan (Mat. 3, Mark 1, Luke 3, John 1) and thereby He sanctified the Jordan and all other water so that it washes us from sin in holy Baptism.

CHAPTER 4

CONCERNING THE FOUNDER OF
HOLY BAPTISM.

s with all Sacraments, this Sacrament of Baptism was instituted by God Himself. For since God's grace and heavenly goods are offered and imparted through the Sacraments, no one but God the Lord can institute Sacraments, since He alone can give power and divine accomplishments to the Sacraments. That God the Lord is the Founder of holy Baptism, which He Himself instituted in the New Testament, becomes evident:

1. Because John, who first administered this Sacrament, was sent by God to baptize.

In Mat. 21:25, Christ asks the Pharisees if John's Baptism was from heaven or from men. (He thus teaches that John did not administer Baptism because of human opinion, nor was [he] sent by men to baptize; rather, that God commanded him to baptize, as can be deduced from the following mode of expression in Luke 15:21 – **I have sinned against heaven**; that is, against God who resides in heaven. So also here: John's Baptism was from heaven, that is, instituted and commanded by God, who resides in heaven.) This is repeated in Mark 11:29, Luke 20:4.

Luke 3:2, 3 – **The command came to John in the wilderness, and he came into the regions of the Jordan and preached the Baptism of repentance for the forgiveness of sins** (accordingly did John preach about Baptism because of God's command, and administered it because of God's command).

Luke 7:29,30 – **And all the people that heard him, [including] the publicans, gave God His due and let themselves be baptized with John's Baptism. But the Pharisees and scribes** [lit. Ger.= "Bible scholars"] **rejected God's counsel against themselves and did not let themselves be baptized by him.** (If John's Baptism was God's counsel, then he also must have had the command to baptize.)

In John 1:33, John says: **He who sent me to baptize with water,** etc.

2. Because Christ, through whom God has spoken to us (Heb. 1:1), and who has revealed the counsel of God concerning our salvation (John 1:18), openly repeated the divine institution of Baptism after His death and resurrection and commanded His disciples to baptize in the whole world, i.e., not just in the land of the Jews, but also the Gentiles.

Mat. 28:19 – **Therefore, go out and teach all nations and baptize them in the name of the Father and of the Son and of the Holy Spirit.**

There appears to be a contradiction here; namely, one does not read anywhere that John expressly received a command to baptize in the Name of the Father, the Son, and the Holy Spirit as the disciples received from Jesus. So, maybe John's Baptism was not instituted by God. ANSWER: Even though these words do not specifically mention that John, like the disciples, had outwardly received such a command to baptize, nevertheless, there is no doubt that he was driven to do it through an inner inspiration from the Holy Spirit, which the prophets and apostles regarded just as highly as they would an outward, oral command given to them by Christ. Thus, **1.** John the Baptist says in John 1:33 – He was sent to baptize with water. Now, "to baptize" means not only to pour water over someone, for the Word has to be present if it is to be called a Baptism. The Word is, so to speak, the soul of Baptism. Also, not just any word with water makes Baptism; rather, the special Word that a person pour out the water—or dip in water—in the name of the Father and the Son and the Holy Spirit. Since John was accordingly sent to baptize, he must indeed have received this Word of God. **2.** John also demonstrates from the prophet Isaiah in John 1:23 that he, in his entire office, undertook nothing (including his task of baptizing) from his own counsel or opinion. How, then, could he have baptized without a command from God? **3.** John also baptized for the forgiveness of sins (Mark 1:4)—Now, only God is able to forgive sins. Therefore, God the Lord must indeed have instituted the Baptism of John. Otherwise his Baptism would not have had the power to forgive sins.

CHAPTER 5

THROUGH WHOM SHOULD AND CAN HOLY BAPTISM BE ADMINISTERED IN THE CHRISTIAN CHURCH?

lthough God Himself instituted holy Baptism, yet He does not administer or perform it Himself without the instrumentality of people, for we could not endure His divine majesty and glory in the weakness of our flesh. Also Christ, as He traveled around during His days in the flesh here on earth, never baptized anyone (John 4:2), so that those who would have been baptized by Christ could think that they had received a better Baptism than those who were baptized by the apostles and others. So just as God the Lord does not reveal His counsel and will to us through Himself but through men, so also He administers Baptism not through Himself but through men, and it is just as powerful as if He Himself did the baptizing without intermediaries. The administration and performance of Baptism in an orderly way actually belongs to those whom God has placed in the office of the ministry; however, in case of an emergency, another baptized Christian may certainly administer this holy Sacrament.

I. That the orderly manner of administration and performance of holy Baptism therefore belongs to those who hold the office of the ministry becomes obvious:

1. Because the office to teach includes within itself the administration of the holy Sacraments. For since the Sacraments are visible signs of the grace which God promises in His Word, so also the performance [application] of the holy Sacraments belongs to those who are in the orderly calling of the ministry.

In Mat. 28:19, Christ says to His apostles: Therefore go and teach all people, **and baptize them in the name of the Father and the Son and the Holy Spirit.** (Here the apostles are simultaneously commanded to teach and baptize.)

Mark 16:15, 16 – **Go into all the world and preach the Gospel to every creature. Whoever believes and is baptized will be saved, etc.**

2. Because the apostles obediently followed this command of Christ not only to teach, but also baptize, therefore it is proper for teachers and preachers, as successors [*Nachfolgern*] of the apostles, not only to teach, but also to baptize.

John 3:22 – **Then Jesus came with His disciples into the Jewish country and carried on His business with them, and baptized.** (This will be clarified in a moment in the next verse.)

John 4:2 – **However, Jesus Himself did not baptize, rather His disciples.**

Acts 2:38, 41 – **Peter spoke to them** (his listeners): **Repent, and each of you let yourselves be baptized in the name of Jesus Christ. ... Those who gladly received the Word let themselves be baptized.**

Acts 8:12 – **But when they** (those in Samaria) **believed Philip's preaching about the kingdom of God and about the name of Jesus Christ, they let themselves be baptized, both men and women.**

In Acts 8:38, Philip baptized the chamberlain.

In Acts 9:19; 22:16, Ananias baptized Paul.

In Acts 10:48, Peter commands that those in Cornelius' house in Caesarea who had received the Holy Spirit be baptized. (In his language, it actually reads "Peter had commanded" [past perfect tense] that they should let themselves be baptized, which indeed can then be understood to mean that Peter himself baptized them.)

In Acts 16:15, Lydia, the seller of purple, is baptized (Undoubtedly by Silas or another of St. Paul's travel companions or by St. Paul himself. For what is written in 1 Cor. 1:14 ff.—that St. Paul baptized no one but Crispus, Gaius, and the household of Stephanus—is not to be understood concerning every place in general, but only that St. Paul baptized "no one else" in Corinth).

In Acts 16:33, the jailer at Philippi was baptized (also by St. Paul himself).

In Acts 18:8 Crispus is baptized (by St. Paul, as learned from 1 Cor. 1:14), also many Corinthians.

In 1 Cor. 1:14, Paul baptized Crispus and Gaius, [and] in v. 16, Stephanus' household domestics.

3. Because John, who was the first in the New Testament to administer this holy Sacrament, simultaneously taught and baptized. Here are relevant all the passages in which it is announced that John baptized.

Mat. 3:5, 6 – **Then** [people] **came to him** (to John) **from the city of Jerusalem and the entire Jewish country, and all the countries around the Jordan, and had themselves baptized by him, etc.** This is repeated in Mark 1:5, Luke 3:7.

In Mat. 3:16, Mark 1:9, Luke 3:21, [and] John 1:33 he baptizes Christ.

Mark 1:4 – **John was in the wilderness; he baptized and preached about Baptism.**

In Luke 3:12 he baptized Publicans; repeated in ch. 7:29.

In John 1:28; 10:40 he baptized in Bethabara.

In John 3:23 he baptized by Aenon close by Salim.

Acts 1:5; 11:16; 19:4 – John baptized with water, etc.

Subsequently, passages in which the Baptism of John is assumed: In Mat. 3:7 many Pharisees and Sadducees came to the Baptism of John.

Mat. 21:25; Mark 11:30; Luke 20:40 – **The Baptism of John, was it from heaven,** etc.?

Mark 1:4; Luke 3:13 – **John preached about Baptism to repentance.**

Luke 7:29, Acts 1:22, 10:37, 13:24, 18:25, [and] 19:3–4 also assume the Baptism of John.

Finally, passages in which John is called the Baptist; for this occurs because he was the first to perform this holy Sacrament of Baptism.

Mat. 3:1 – At that time came John **the Baptist**, etc. This name is also given to him in: Mat. 11:12; 14:28; 16:14; 17:13; Mark 6:14, 24, 25; Luke 7:20, 28, 33; 9:19.

[Even] as now John, the first servant of the New Testament, simultaneously taught and baptized, so, also, it applies to the [other] servants of the New Testament in that they not only taught but also baptized.

4. Because teachers and preachers are set as housekeepers over the divine mysteries; therefore, it is also appropriate, according to the common order, that they also administer and impart the same.

1 Cor. 4:1 – **Therefore let everyone regard us thusly: as servants of Christ and housekeepers over God's mysteries.**

1 Tim. 3:5 – **So if someone does not know how to direct his own house, how will he take care of the people of God** (how will he present them with teaching and Sacrament)?

Tit. 1:7 – **A Bishop – as a housekeeper for God.**

5. Because circumcision, which was a type of Baptism, was performed in an orderly manner through the teachers and priests. Gen. 17:23–24 – Abraham performed the circumcision of himself and everyone in his house that had a male name. In Gen. 21:4 he circumcised Isaac. In Jos. 5:3 Joshua circumcised the children of Israel. In 1 Macc. 2:46 the priest Matathias circumcised the children that were yet uncircumcised.

Here again there appears to be a contradiction, in that St. Paul says in 1 Cor. 1:17 – **Christ did not send me to baptize, rather to preach the Gospel,** as if the Apostle Paul was sent only to teach and not to baptize at the same time. Thus it appears that the performance of Baptism does not intrinsically and in an orderly manner belong to the office of the ministry. ANSWER: This is not to be understood in the sense that St. Paul did not actually hold the office of an apostle to administer holy Baptism, for then he would have done an injustice in that he baptized Crispus, Gaius and the household of Stephanus in 1 Cor. 1:14, 16. Rather, it has to be understood in a comparative manner: Paul was primarily sent to preach the Gospel of Christ in all the world, which requires higher gifts of the Spirit than to baptize. For the Sacraments can also be performed through such persons who are not affected with such high gifts of the Spirit. The power and the efficaciousness of the Sacraments do not derive from the worthiness of the servant; rather, singularly and alone from God the Lord. He is the Baptizer who gives power to holy Baptism as it is administered in His Name.

II. Even though, for the sake of good order, holy Baptism should be administered by the servants of the Word so that everything proceeds honorably and orderly (1 Cor. 14:40), yet in case of an outward emergency where a person cannot find a servant of the Church available, and the child would otherwise die without Baptism, another fellow-baptized Christian may indeed administer this holy Sacrament. This, then, is indicated:

1. Because holy Baptism is the only means through which children conceived and born in sin can become re-born and become heirs of eternal life. So that we, as much as in us lies, do not let salvation slip from them in such situations of extreme emergency, holy Baptism by other Christians should and must be provided them. There is nothing that flies in the face of God's express command in such action.

John 3:5 – **Truly, truly I say to you: unless a person is born out of water and Spirit, he cannot come into the kingdom of God** (compare this with Gen. 17:4 – **When a boy is not circumcised on the foreskin of his flesh, that soul shall be rooted out from his people because he forsook My covenant.** In light of this, since this Sacrament [Baptism] is so extremely necessary as the sole means of rebirth [for children], one should not deny it to any child whenever one has available the essential pieces of this Sacrament, namely,

water and the Word. Now, it is not an essential ingredient
of Baptism that the Baptizer be a preacher. Rather, the order in this matter should and must be determined by the
emergency).

2. Because circumcision, in place of which Baptism
came to pass [and] which was also the means through which
children in the Old Testament were received into God's
covenant, was at times performed by women.

Exo. 4:25 – **As he** (Moses) **was on his way to an
inn, the Lord met him and wanted to kill him** (He let him
suddenly come down with a deadly illness because he had
neglected to circumcise his little son), **Then Zipporah took
a stone** (a rock knife, Jos. 5:2, whetted sharp as a stone, Psa.
89:44) **and circumcised her son's foreskin, and touched
Moses' feet with it and said: You are a bridegroom of
blood to me** (I had to circumcise my child. It cost blood for
you to be my bridegroom and husband... for she circumcised
her son reluctantly).

1 Macc. 1:63 – **The women who circumcised their
children were killed, as commanded by Antiochus.**

2 Macc. 6:10 – **Two women were led forth because
they had circumcised their sons, etc.**

3. Because in case of an emergency a fellow Christian
can comfort and instruct another with the Gospel. How much
more is he allowed, when confronted with the most severe
emergency, to administer holy Baptism.

In Rom. 16:3, **Priscilla** is mentioned as St. Paul's
helper in Christ Jesus. (The reason she is called that is written in Acts 18:26—since she diligently presented the way of
God to Apollos, she no doubt did this for others, too.)

In 2 Tim. 3:15 Timothy was instructed in the holy
Scriptures from childhood on by his **grandmother Lois** and
his **mother Eunice,** cf. chap. 1, v. 5 of the same epistle.

From this we conclude [that] it takes greater gifts of
the Spirit for a person to teach and instruct than for a person
to baptize, as St. Paul corroborates in 1 Cor. 1:14. So, since

women can, in case of an emergency, teach and instruct, how much more should they also be allowed to baptize [in case of an emergency]. Here certain examples can be presented which show that from the feminine gender certain ones were made prophetesses. There was, for example, **Deborah** (Jud. 4:4f.); **Hulda** (2 Kin. 22:14); **Hannah** (Luke 2:36); **the daughter of Philip** (Acts 21:9). So also the passages which witness that believing wives are also **fellow heirs of the grace of life** (1 Pet. 3:7), who are consequently **made kings and priests before God** (Rev. 1:6; 5:10; 1 Pet. 2:9; and many more).

Here again, [are] apparent contradictions:

1. That the divine power for rebirth is not even tied to this Sacrament. So one should not let fellow Christians—and especially women—administer this Sacrament, since God can also rebirth a person without this Sacrament. ANSWER: Even though God the Lord is not shackled to this Sacrament so that He could not perform rebirth without [Baptism] (with the result, then, in Christendom of not making the sacrilegious judgment concerning unbaptized children that they are damned—discussion of this will follow in proper order in chapter 26), nevertheless, we still are tied to this Sacrament. Thus we should not neglect it whenever a person has access to it, even if only to the essential parts of it. For Christ's command is explicit in that He says, John 3:5 – **Unless a person is born out of water and Spirit, he cannot come into the kingdom of God.**

2. That Baptism belongs rightly to the public office of the ministry; therefore, it should not be performed by others. ANSWER: Even though the order and proper mode according to which Baptism is to be performed is by the teachers, yet it cannot be concluded that in case of an utter emergency an ordinary Christian should be forbidden to administer this Sacrament, since the aforementioned order is not a vital part of the Sacrament. An effective instrumental cause does not enter into the essence of the matter [*causa efficiens instrumentalis non ingreditur rei essentiam*]. Also, nothing occurs in such a case that is contrary to God's express command, since God has nowhere commanded that in case of an emergency a fellow Christian should not be allowed to baptize. Consequently, as teaching essentially belongs to the office of the ministry, yet in case of an emergency, when no teacher is available—such as at the time of the plague, during protracted sieges, and other [military] defeats—another ordinary Christian may indeed teach, comfort, and instruct. So, according to the public order, holy Baptism should be performed by the preacher. However, if no preacher is available in case of an extreme emergency, another Christian should and may baptize.

3. That the example of Zipporah is inapplicable to this matter, since she rashly performed the circumcision in anger; also, since Moses was opposed to it. From this it would follow that Baptism could be performed by someone else in the presence of an ordained preacher. ANSWER: Although Zipporah performed the circumcision in anger, yet because the essential elements [actions] were present, it was a proper circumcision. To this also add the further evidence that God backed off from Moses, i.e., He warded off the sudden fatal illness from him, and He was no longer wrathful because the circumcision had been performed. Thus, this is how we turn this argument around: just as God held this circumcision to be a proper one—one that was performed out of anger, without forethought, by this woman—how much more is it a valid Baptism when administered devotionally by believing women? What pertains to Moses' presence is, in this case, not to be regarded as a "presence," for an unexpected fatal illness had befallen Moses so that he himself could not perform the circumcision. Again, we turn the argument around: Since it was a proper circumcision which Zipporah performed in the presence of Moses, how much more is it a valid Baptism in case of an emergency and in the absence of a man when it is performed by a woman?

4. Because St. Paul says in 1 Cor. 14:34 – **Let your women keep silent in public, for it should not be allowed that they speak.** Further, in 1 Tim. 2:12 -**But I do not permit a woman to teach ...** so if they are not to teach, they should also not baptize. ANSWER: The keeping silence of which St. Paul speaks concerns such women who have not been properly instructed and still want to learn, as is to be understood from the indicated context (1 Cor. 14:35 and also in 1 Tim. 2:11). The correct answer is that Paul is here speaking of the public order as it is to be observed in the Church. So we also say that a woman is allowed neither to teach nor baptize, but it is an entirely different matter in the case of an emergency. This order should not and cannot prescribe for such an emergency. **It stands as evil for the women to speak in the congregation** (1 Cor. 14:36). Therefore, he is speaking of such a situation where a woman wants to teach in open assembly and in the presence of men.

5. Since a woman or some other common Christian is permitted to administer Baptism in case of an emergency, it would then follow that the holy Sacrament of the Lord's Supper can be administered by someone other than a preacher. ANSWER: There is a complete difference here, for holy Baptism is the sacrament of initiation [*sacramentum initiationes*] through which little children become members of Christ and heirs of eternal life. But the Lord's Supper is not such an absolutely necessary Sacrament to the extent that a person, in case of an emergency, could not be kept in the faith to eternal life without it. Furthermore, the spiritual reception of Christ's body and blood, which is absolutely necessary for salvation, can take place also without the sacramental reception. However, for the little children there is no other means through which we may bring them to Christ and to eternal life except through the Sacrament of holy Baptism.

CHAPTER 6

WHETHER A BAPTISM PERFORMED BY ONE WHOSE TEACHING IS ERRANT OR WHOSE LIFE IS CRIMINAL IS INDEED A TRUE AND EFFICACIOUS SACRAMENT.

arying answers concerning this question must be given since it inquires both about the teaching and the life of the one who baptizes.

I. Whenever the Baptism of a false teacher is questioned regarding whether it is a true, efficacious Baptism, it must be answered with this distinction: Some false teachers falsify the vital parts of holy Baptism, as when some use something else than water, or those who do not baptize in the Name of the Father and the Son and the Holy Spirit. Some, however, permit the vital elements of Baptism to remain, steadfastly maintain them, and simply falsify other portions of divine teaching. As pertaining to the former, such a Baptism is not a true and efficacious Sacrament. So then, that those who are baptized by such must, when they come to the true Church, first be baptized—since they did not receive a true Baptism—we substantiate on the following basis:

In Mat. 28:19 Christ commands that one should baptize in the Name of the Father and the Son and the Holy Spirit. In Eph. 5:26 Baptism is called **a water bath in the Word**. From this it is to be deduced that the essential parts of holy Baptism are water and the Word. Whenever these parts are mutilated or changed, something departs from the essential parts of holy Baptism. Therefore it cannot be a proper Baptism.

Yet is should be noted concerning this, that if and when a servant [officiant] secretly harbors in his heart a false delusion about the proper parts of holy Baptism, while the Church which he serves upholds the orthodox parts, in such case a true and efficacious Baptism would be administered by such a servant. For the holy Sacraments are gifts of the Church which the secret, hidden error of a servant cannot take away from Baptism as long as he at least keeps the essential parts of the [Sacrament] and does not change anything concerning the outward element of water or the Word.

As pertaining to others who steadfastly uphold the essential parts of Baptism, and yet falsify other chief parts of the Christian religion, they perform a true and efficacious Baptism. This we substantiate as follows:

1. Whenever the essential parts of Baptism are kept, there a true Baptism is administered. This is clearly self-evident, since to the total entity of everything belongs nothing more than its essential parts. Since, then, the essential parts of Baptism are upheld in this case, therefore it is a proper and total Baptism.

Mat. 28:19, Eph. 5:26 – Baptism is **a water bath in the Word**.

2. The circumcision which Moses' wife, Zipporah, performed, was a true circumcision. Yet it is easy to overlook that Zipporah, who was born a Gentile, was not yet at that time orthodox in every part of the true religion. In Exo. 4:25, 26 Zipporah circumcised her little son. Because of this, God eased up on Moses.

3. The prophets in the Old Testament often reproved the gruesome idolatries and errors of the Levitical priests who administered the Sacrament of circumcision in an orderly fashion. But one never reads that they taught that those who were circumcised by such idolatrous, erring priests were to be circumcised anew. They never admonished them not to circumcise. Therefore, they must have practiced true circumcision.

Eze. 16:20, 21 – **You took your sons and daughters which you begat for Me** (who through the Sacrament of circumcision were received into My Covenant as My children) **and offered them to be gobbled up** (by false gods). **That you slaughtered My children and let them be burned up.** This is repeated in chap. 23:37.

4. As Christ sojourned here on earth during His days in the flesh, He never once cast aside the circumcision of the Levitical priests, even though He frequently faulted them for many errors.

Mat. 23:2, 3 – **The Scribes and Pharisees sit upon Moses' seat. Everything then which they tell you to practice, do and practice it.** (In so far as they sit on the seat of Moses, i.e., teach what Moses commanded them to teach, and inasmuch as they also offer the Sacraments in the manner which God, through Moses, commanded them to be offered, you are to follow their teaching and utilize their Sacraments. Under the same Sacrament was included also circumcision.) John 7:22 – **Moses therefore gave you circumcision, not that it came from Moses, but from the fathers,** etc.

Here, again, there appears to be a contradiction: That since heretics are not true members of Christ and the Church, they cannot properly offer the Sacraments as gifts of Christ and the Church. ANSWER: Even though the false teachers are no longer members of Christ and the true Church on account of their obstinate errors, yet this does not [prevent them from administering] a true Baptism in that they simply uphold the essential parts of it. For they simply lend God the Lord their mouth and hand; it is God who baptizes and can work effectually through the service of these perverted teachers. As long as the false teachers uphold Christ's Word and institution, to that degree they are still external members of the Church even though they are separated from the spiritual body of Christ because of their errors. In the same way, God the Lord can gather a handful of believing adults through the preaching of those who do not in all points teach the true pure Word of God, [but] rather mix in human trifles and their own dreams (as happened during the time of Elijah when God preserved seven thousand souls who did not bow their knees to Baal, 1 Kin. 19:18, even though everything was directed by Baalish priests and only the prophet Elijah remained [faithful] v. 10), so also God can gather a Church from minor children through the Sacrament performed by such as who are not orthodox in all parts [of doctrine], but simply uphold the essential parts of Baptism.

II. Concerning the Baptism of another one whose life is sinful and reprehensible, teachers and preachers should rigidly apply themselves that they be non-culpable (1 Tim. 3:2), and irreproachable (Tit. 1:7). Yet, if it ever occurs that a godless servant baptizes, one should not for that reason regard his Baptism as empty and powerless if indeed he [the officiant] upheld unsullied the essential elements of Baptism, [a statement] which is [herewith] substantiated:

1. When everything that belongs to this Sacrament is present, then this Sacrament is complete and effectual. What belongs to the essence of holy Baptism is retained in such a case.

In Mat. 28:19 [and] Eph. 5:26 Baptism is a **water bath in the Word** (where water and the Word are retained, a true Baptism is administered).

2. The prophets and Christ accused the priests, Pharisees, and scribes of great vices, as one can see now and then in the prophets and evangelists, especially in Isa. 28:7, Jer. 5:31, Eze. 24:2, etc., [and] Mat. 23:1 ff. Even so, one does not read that they regarded their circumcision as invalid and [so] rejected it.

Mat. 23:2,3 – **The Scribes and Pharisees sit upon Moses' seat. All that they then say you should observe, that observe and do,** etc.

3. In the performance of this Sacrament, the servant is merely a simple tool of God who does not baptize in his own name but in the Name and by the command of the Father and of the Son and of the Holy Spirit. So, as the servant's worthiness gives nothing to the Baptism, so also the servant's unworthiness does not at all take away from the Baptism.

Mat. 28:19 – **Baptize them in the Name of the Father and the Son and the Holy Spirit.**

1 Cor. 3:7 – **So it is neither he who plants, nor he who pours [water] on something, rather God gives the growth.**

1 Cor. 4:1 – **Let every person regard us in this way, namely, as servants of Christ and housekeepers over God's mysteries.**

Relevant here is what John repeats so often—that he baptizes with water (Mat. 3:6, Mark 1:8, Luke 3:12, John 1:26)—as if he meant to say [that] he merely lent God his hand to pour out water; it is God who gives power to his Baptism.

Here [is] an apparent contradiction: that [if] the godless servants do not themselves have the Holy Spirit, how can they proffer the gifts of the Spirit to others through Baptism? ANSWER: The servants of the Church are not here dealing from their own power or their own opinion. Rather, they baptize as God's stand-in and God baptizes through them, just as Christ baptized through His disciples (John 4:2). For, just as God is effectual also through the Word of those who themselves are not converted and not God-fearing (for the Word is and remains a power of God for salvation to those who believe it, Rom. 1:16, whether it be conveyed by the pious or by the evil), so also nothing is taken from the essence or the power of the Sacrament of Baptism if the servant who performs it is godless. Does not the living power remain within the seed even though it is sown into the ground by a rogue? Is it not always a seal, be it stamped with a gold signet or with an iron signet? Does it take away or add to the power of water if it is guided into garden furrows via silver or via wooden conduits? It is God who baptizes and gives Baptism its power; the worthiness or the unworthiness of the servant neither hinders nor furthers such. **Should their** (mankind's) **unbelief nullify** (or gainsay) **faith in God? Far from it! (**Rom. 3:3, 4).

CHAPTER 7

WHETHER THE BAPTISM OF JOHN
WAS JUST AS POWERFUL AS A SACRAMENT UNTO SALVATION
AS IS THE BAPTISM OF CHRIST'S DISCIPLES.

o understand properly this question one must be aware that the "Baptism of John," which John performed, and the "Baptism of Christ's disciples," which Christ's disciples performed, are labeled that way even though neither John nor the disciples of Christ ever baptized for themselves on their own authority and without God's command. So we say concerning this Baptism of John that it was just as much a holy Sacrament of the New Testament as was the Baptism of Christ's disciples; and furthermore, that the Holy Spirit was just as effectual for rebirth, renewal, and eternal salvation through John's Baptism as through the Baptism of Christ's disciples. This we also substantiate:

1. Just as the disciples baptized by God's command with water in the Name of the Father and the Son and the Holy Spirit, so also John baptized not out of his own discretion but by God's command, as indicated above in chap. 4, sec. 1. He also baptized in the Name of the one true God, as will be proven later on. Indeed, he also used the external element that was used in the apostolic Baptism, namely, natural water. How, then, can it be a different Sacrament?

Mat. 3:11, Mark 1:8, Luke 3:16, John 1:26,31, Acts 1:5 – **I baptize you with water, etc**.

In Mat. 3:6 and 16, Mark 1:5, Luke 3:21, [and] John 10:40, John baptizes in the Jordan.

In John 3:23 he baptizes **at Aenon near Salim because there was much water there.**

2. Just as God the Lord was effectual for rebirth and forgiveness through the Baptism of the apostles, so also He performed these works through John's Baptism.

Mark 1:4, Luke 3:3 – **John baptized and preached about the Baptism of repentance for the forgiveness of sins.** (Precisely the same form of speech is used concerning the apostolic Baptism. Acts 2:38 – **Let each one be baptized in the name of Jesus Christ for the forgiveness of sins.** In Acts 22:16 Ananias says to Paul: **Let yourself be baptized and wash away your sins.**)

In Mat. 3:7 [and] Luke 3:7, John says to the Pharisees who had come to him and let themselves be baptized: **You generation of vipers, who tipped you off that you might escape the future wrath?** From this it can be seen that one could escape the future wrath of God through the Baptism of John, which could not happen without the forgiveness of sins.

In Luke 7:30 Christ says that the Pharisees and Scribes, who would not allow themselves to be baptized by John, **scorned the wrath of God that was against them.** It thus follows that it was God's gracious counsel and will to receive them into grace and life through the holy Baptism of John.

Also pertinent is that Zacharias in Luke 1:77 says John would give to the people of God **knowledge of salvation, which exists through the forgiveness of sins.** This forgiveness of sins is experienced not only through the teaching of the Gospel, which John promoted alongside the teaching of the Law; rather, also through the Baptism of the repentant. His Baptism was no less a means of forgiveness of sins and salvation than was his teaching of the Gospel.

John 3:5 – **Unless one is born out of the water and the Spirit, he cannot come into the kingdom of God.** (Here Christ prescribes the same Baptism which was in use at that time for rebirth and the opening up of the heavenly kingdom; a diligent examination of evangelical history reveals that only John's Baptism was in vogue at that time.)

In Acts 18:25, it is written of Apollos that He **spoke with a fervent spirit**; and yet, it is next announced that he **only knew about the Baptism of John**.

In John 1:37, it appears that Peter was baptized by John. [Peter] writes concerning such Baptism of [John] in 1 Pet. 3:21 – **Which** (water) **now also saves us through Baptism**; consequently, the Baptism of John must also have been effectual for salvation.

At this point it must be remembered—what is not at all denied—that at times through the laying on of hands, along with the apostolic Baptism, special gifts of the Spirit, such as prophecy and speaking in tongues, etc., were given (Acts 8:16; 19:5, 6). But it cannot be concluded from this account that John's Baptism is not a Sacrament like the apostolic Baptism; or, that it was not quite as effectual for salvation; or, not to mention the fact that it was not actually through Baptism but through the laying on of hands that these special gifts were given to the baptized; or, that not all thus baptized by the apostles became recipients of these special gifts. So the distinction between the special and the common gifts of the Spirit (the common being necessary for everyone's salvation) are easily discerned, since John obviously did not lay hands upon those he baptized so that they might receive the special gifts of the Spirit (which were to be given first after the Ascension and the glorification of Christ, John 7:39). Still, his Baptism was effectual for forgiveness of sins, rebirth, and salvation.

3. If John's Baptism is not a Sacrament like the Baptism which the apostles of Christ administered, and which these days is performed by their successors [*Nachfolger*], then it follows that our Head, Christ, received a different Baptism from that which we, His members, received. Also, this assumption removes the glorious comfort which the beloved ancients take from the Baptism of Christ, in that they say (and not improperly so): Christ, with the touching of His most holy body in the water of holy Baptism, sanctified water for this Sacrament. He also came to Baptism as the Lamb of God on whom was laid the sins of the entire world. As our stand-in, He let Himself be washed from sin and placed into the water of holy Baptism all of His merits and righteousness so that we might thereby become clothed as with a garment of salvation.

In Mat. 3:13, Mark 1:9, Luke 3:21, [and] John 1:33, Jesus came to the Jordan and let Himself be baptized of John.

1 Cor. 12:13 – **Through one Spirit we are all baptized to one body,** in which Christ is the Head (Eph. 1:22).

4. It would further appear from this [point #3 above] that the holy apostles, most of whom were baptized by John, had received a different Baptism than what they now administered to others and what we receive in our day, even though it is stated:

Eph. 4:4–6 – **One body and one Spirit, as you are also called to the one and same hope of your calling. One Lord, one faith, one Baptism, one God and Father of us all.** (Just as all Christians in the New Testament are one body, just as they all receive one Spirit, just as all have one hope of life, just as there is for them one faith, one Lord, one God and Father, so they also have one Baptism.)

John 3:22, 23 – **After this came Jesus and His disciples into the Jewish Land, and carried on His business with them and baptized. John, however, also still baptized at Aenon near by Salim, for there was much water there, and they came there and let themselves be baptized.** From this, it is obvious that John's and Christ's disciples both baptized at the same time. But if John's Baptism was to be only a preparation for Jesus' Baptism, why was it necessary for them to baptize simultaneously? Would it not have been better to direct those who wanted to be baptized directly to Christ, i.e., to the apostolic Baptism?

[Relevant here] is what is apparent from John 1:37 and 41: that some of the disciples of Christ were formerly in the school of John [and] undoubtedly they were baptized by him. But one does not read that later on they were baptized anew.

Here, again, [are] apparent contradictions:

1. That John did not have such an express command to baptize as did the disciples [of Christ] later on; therefore, his and theirs are not the same Sacrament. This has been answered in chapter 4 above.

2. That John did not baptize in the Name of the Father and the Son and the Holy Spirit—as did the apostles—but, rather, in the Name of Him who would come after him, i.e., in the Name of Christ (Acts 19:4); therefore, both Baptisms cannot be of the same form, or be one and the same Sacrament. ANSWER: **1.** Even though it is nowhere expressly revealed in the Scriptures that John baptized in the Name of the Father and of the Son and of the Holy Spirit, yet there is no doubt that John in the performance of his Baptism called upon the Name and baptized in the Name of the One who sent him to baptize; that One, however, is the One true God, One in essence and Triune in Person (John 1:33). For we should not and cannot think that John poured out water or dipped in water without the Word—since that would not have been a Baptism, but simply an ordinary water bath—as the Word is the foremost part in Baptism. Rather, he administered his Baptism in the Name of the One by whom he was sent to baptize. That One is the One true God: Father, Son, and Holy Spirit. **2.** As, therefore, there existed one teaching of John and the apostles, they also performed one and the same Sacrament, since the Sacraments are seals through which the teaching is affirmed, though later on—as the apostles baptized after Christ's Ascension—there was brighter illumination of doctrine and greater measure of grace. One can indeed extract from the Gospel of John of what John the Baptist's teaching consisted. He taught that God sent His

Son and gave everything into His hand (John 3:34, 35); that this Son of God was the Lamb of God who carried the entire world's sin (John 1:29, 36)—through which he clarifies all the types of Old Testament offerings as pointing to Christ; further, that God gave the Spirit to the Son not according to measure (John 3:34). John baptized in this true Name of God. He affirmed his teaching about Christ's person and good deeds through the routine of Baptism. **3.** The apostles also baptized before Christ's Ascension (John 3:22; 4:2) and, indeed, even during the time John still baptized. Now about this there is no express revelation that the disciples baptized in the Name of the Father and the Son and the Holy Spirit. However, who could therefore say that they baptized without the Word or that they used a different form of Baptism? Concerning how and for what they baptized, one must likewise take that from the teaching [of] their Lord and Master, Christ. He likewise had taught, like John, that God sent His Son into the world so that all who believed in Him would be saved (John 3:16); that the Son came down from heaven and willingly allowed Himself to be lifted onto the timber-trunk of the cross, so that all who believe on Him would be saved (vv. 14,15); that the Holy Spirit rebirths us to everlasting life through the water of Baptism (v. 5). On this teaching, the disciples of Christ baptized; but then, there is no difference between this and John's teaching. **4.** In John 3:26, it is revealed that it upset the disciples of John that Christ, through His disciples, baptized. That's why they brought it up to their master, John, with these words: **Master, He who was beside you the other side of the Jordan—the One about whom you testify—see, He baptizes, and everybody is coming to Him.** Had Jesus Christ's disciples baptized differently than their master John, they certainly would not have kept quiet about it [especially at this moment of disgruntlement]. **5.** What is pertinent to the point of Acts 19:4—from which it appears as if John baptized upon the coming Christ but the apostles upon Him who had already made Himself known—is hereupon easily answered. For there it does not speak so much about the words which John used at his Baptisms, but rather about [the content of] his sermon: **John baptized with the Baptism of repentance, and said to the people that they should believe on Him who would come after him, that is, on Jesus who is the Christ.** And whether John ever baptized upon the coming Messiah, that is not to be drawn from Christ's becoming man (according to which He already had made Himself known); but rather [he baptized] upon His office, and, furthermore, upon His suffering and death. Now, in the same way, the disciples of Christ also baptized upon the coming Messiah before Christ's suffering; and yet, there is no other Sacrament which the disciples administered before or after the sufferings of Christ. To summarize: As there is but one faith for the fathers who placed their hope upon the coming Messiah, and for us who believe on Him who has finally made Himself known, so also there is but one Baptism, which John and the disciples of Christ performed before Christ's suffering, and which the apostles performed after Christ's sufferings. **6.** Furthermore, John, as Christ evermore established Himself in His office with teaching and wondrous deeds, then no longer taught: "He comes after me"; rather, **He has appeared in your midst** (John 1:26). So then, without doubt he would no longer have baptized [in the Name of] the coming Messiah, but rather in the Name of the One who appeared more and more, and with his Baptism led the Bride, so to speak, in order to present her to the heavenly Bridegroom (John 3:29). **7.** Finally, even as John baptized upon Christ (Acts 19:4), or upon the Name of the Lord Jesus (v. 5), so also it is said concerning the apostolic Baptism of St. Paul (Gal. 3:27), that they were baptized **upon Christ** or **upon the Name of Christ,** as Peter says in Acts 2:38; [furthermore], in the "Name of Christ" or "the Anointed," the total Trinity is comprehended as God the Father, who anointed the Son; God the Son, who was anointed; [and] God the Holy Spirit, with whom the Son was anointed without measure.

3. That John says in Mat. 3:11, Mark 1:8, Luke 3:16, John 1:26 and 33, that he baptizes with water, but Christ with the Holy Spirit. From this it appears to follow that the Holy Spirit's gracious works were absent in the Baptism of John. ANSWER: **1.** Provided such were the case—that John here is speaking about the common gifts of the Spirit which are necessary for every Christian's salvation and are still imparted through Baptism to this day—one still may not thereby conclude that the Holy Spirit was not effectual through the Baptism of John, for he preached the Baptism of repentance for the forgiveness of sins (Mark 1:4). Instead, he is distinguishing between the chief cause, through which the heavenly gifts spring forth in Baptism, and the *instrumental* cause or servant, through which the outward Baptism is performed. In similar fashion, St. Paul makes a distinction in 1 Cor. 3:6 between the one who plants and waters and the one who gives the growth. **2.** When we, however, properly view the text [in point 4, above] and compare it with other references in the Scriptures, then one discovers that John here is not speaking of the common gifts of the Spirit, but about the very special gifts which were poured out upon the apostles and their followers on Pentecost and upon certain Christians in the early Church. Such becomes obvious because, first of all, John is speaking of the future [*in futuro*]; "He will baptize with the Holy Spirit" is understood as occurring after His transfiguration and ascension. John 7:39 – **The Spirit was not yet present**, that is, the special gifts of the Spirit were not yet poured out, **because Jesus was not yet transfigured**. Comparison with the following references also demonstrates this: In Mat. 3:11 it is written this way: **He will baptize you with the Holy Spirit and with fire**, [a promise which] was fulfilled on Pentecost Day (Acts 2:3) when the divided tongues were observed by the apostles, as if they were afire, while the Holy Spirit sat down over each of them. In Acts 1:4, 5, Christ Himself gives us a glorious clarification of these passages. He commands His apostles **that they not leave Jerusalem, but rather wait upon the promise of the Father, which you have heard (said He) from Me,** and then adds: **For John baptized with water; you, however, will be baptized with the Holy Spirit not long after this day.** Here we have from the mouth of Christ the interpretation of what it means to be baptized with the Holy Spirit; namely, it means to receive the special [extraordinary] gifts of the Spirit. St. Peter explains these words in Acts 11:15,16 with equal beauty – **However, as I then began to speak,** he says, **the Holy Spirit fell upon them, in the same way He fell on us at the first beginning. Then I remembered the Word of the Lord as He said: John baptized with water, you, however, will be baptized with the Holy Spirit.**

4. That those who were thus baptized by John found it necessary to be baptized again with Christ's Baptism, as seems apparent from Acts 19:4, 5, 6. For there the Ephesians who had been baptized into John's Baptism were baptized anew by St. Paul. Therefore, it must follow that John's Baptism and the apostles' Baptism did not have the same power and effect. ANSWER: **1.** We do not wish at this time to sharply dispute whether some who were baptized by John also afterwards were again baptized by the apostles, for 8,000 Jews were converted and baptized in Acts 2:4 and 4:4. Of these, some possibly had previously been baptized by John. But, it cannot be allowed that after being baptized by John it was necessary for rebirth and salvation to be again baptized by the apostles. **2.** To say nothing of the following: Nowhere does one read that those disciples who, as soon as John's Baptism died off [ceased], came over to Christ from John's school, in which they had been baptized, [to be] baptized anew. It is written in Acts 18:25 concerning Apollos that he knew only of the Baptism of John, and yet it is not recorded that he was baptized again; rather, he was only "intensely instructed." **3.** If it was so necessary to receive the apostles' Baptism after John's Baptism, how could St. Paul say in

Eph. 4:5 that there is one Baptism of the New Testament? **4.** At one time both John's and Christ's disciples baptized simultaneously, as can be seen from John 3:22, 23. But if John's Baptism was simply a preparation for the apostles' Baptism, why did he not quit baptizing as soon as the apostles began? **5.** The point [meaning] of Acts 19:4, 5, 6 is somewhat difficult and can't be clarified in the same way. Some understand that which is portrayed in v. 5 (the Ephesians let themselves be baptized into the Name of Jesus) to indicate that they were not baptized anew with water by St. Paul; rather, that they, through the laying on of hands, received the unusual (special) gifts of the Spirit, as defined in v. 6. But then, it is not [unusual] in the Scriptures that the self-same outpouring of the special gifts of the Spirit are called a Baptism, as indicated in chapters 1 and 2 above. **6.** But before we proceed to a conclusive interpretation of the point, we must note that the Ephesians, who were only baptized with the Baptism of John, are called **Believers** (v. 2) and **disciples of Christ** (v. 1). But no one can believe and be a disciple of Christ without the grace of the Spirit, 1 Cor. 12:3 – **No one can call Jesus his Lord except through the Holy Spirit.** Consequently, since these Ephesians who were baptized by John were believers and disciples of Christ, it would, of course, follow that the Holy Spirit was in them and effective in them through the Baptism of John! **7.** Hereupon we [move on] to interpret the texts—As Paul found certain disciples in Ephesus, he asked them (v. 2) if they had received the Holy Spirit; that is, [if they] had they received the visible gifts of the Spirit, as it is to be understood from v. 6. To this, then, they replied, **We have never heard whether there is a Holy Spirit**, that is, whether such special and wonderful gifts of the Spirit are imparted to believers—just as John [writes] in John 7:39: **The Holy Spirit was not yet present**. The Apostle further asks in v. 3 – **Upon whom are you baptized**, as if he wanted to say, by whom and how have you then been baptized? They answered, **on John's Baptism**, that is, with the Baptism of

John. Thereupon St. Paul takes the opportunity to speak of the distinction between the gifts of the Spirit as imparted through John's Baptism and those that were imparted through the laying on of hands by the apostles. **John,** he says, **baptized with the Baptism of Repentance** (literally in the Greek it reads as follows: John indeed had baptized with the Baptism of repentance, so as not to keep out from it the forgiveness of sin, as it appears in Mark 1:4). This is followed by v. 5 – **As they heard this** (meaning those to whom John had preached about Baptism) **they let themselves be baptized in the Name of the Lord Jesus.** Paul also describes in these verses (4 and 5) the procedure and manner of how John baptized: he first preached to the people that they should believe on Him who should come after him—on Jesus, who is the Christ or Messiah—and thereupon those who heard and believed this proclamation let themselves be baptized of John into the Name of Jesus. This interpretation is in keeping with the Greek text in that both of the little words μεν and δε: "one the one hand" and "but" in v. 4 and v. 5 answer each other.*

---

* Translator's note: μεν with δε generally occurs seldom in the N.T. Greek text, but occur rather frequently in Acts. This last sentence by Gerhard leaves me puzzled, since I find in my Nestle Greek New Testament that the μεν is omitted in vv. 4 and 5 of Acts 19. Possibly Gerhard is regarding it as an anacoluthon, with the contrast supplied from the context.

CHAPTER 8

CONCERNING THE EXTERNAL ELEMENT OR MATTER OF BAPTISM, WHICH IS NATURAL WATER.

p to now [the following have been dealt with]: the effective principal and ministerial cause of Baptism [*de causa efficiente principali et ministeriali baptismi*]; the instigator and institutor of holy Baptism, who is God Father, Son and Holy Spirit; [and] the servants through whom this Sacrament should and can be administered. Hereupon follows the matter [*materie*] of Baptism, which is natural water. If, indeed, God the Lord is wondrous in His works and His counsel inscrutable, then one cannot indeed unreasonably scrutinize and ask: Why did it please the Lord God that water should even be used in this high, holy Sacrament? The following reasons thus come to mind:

1. The types and prophecies of the Old Testament, especially the Levitical cleansings, are thereby fulfilled; regarding this [subject] cf. chapter 3 above.

2. Since this Sacrament of Baptism for rebirth and salvation is of such high importance, God the Lord willed to ordain for it such an external element to which mankind could have access at all times and in all places.

3. Also through the water is portrayed the inner workings of the Holy Spirit which He performs in, with, and through Baptism. For as natural water normally washes and cleanses the body, so also through the power of the divine Word the water of holy Baptism, which is apprehended in that Word, becomes a saving means through which the spiritual uncleanness of sin of body and soul is washed away.

4. Just as the Holy Spirit hovered over the waters of the first creation and in the same way [thereby] made them fruitful, (Gen. 1 and 2), so also God the Lord once more ordained the water for the regeneration [rebirth], which is at the same time the "other" creation [ἀνάκτισις, "new creation"], and which through the power of the Spirit is made into a saving means of rebirth and renewal.

That now holy Baptism shall take place in, through, and with water, and therefore no man is permitted to change the external element and substitute something in its place, we substantiate thus:

1. Because John, who first administered the Sacrament by command of God, baptized with nothing but water.

Mat. 3:11, Mark 1:8, Luke 3:16, John 1:26, 31 – **I baptize with water**; Acts 1:5; 11:16 – **John baptized with water.**

In Mat. 3:6, 13, 16; Mark 1:5, 9; Luke 3:3, 21; John 10:40, he baptized in the Jordan.

In John 3:23 he baptized at Aenon, near by Salim, **for there was much water there** (so that one doesn't think that only the water of the Jordan was sanctified for Baptism).

2. Because the holy apostles never baptized differently than through and with water, both prior to and after Christ's passion.

Acts 8:36, 38 – **And as they** (Philip and the chamberlain) **went down the road, they came upon some water. And the chamberlain said: See, there is water, what hinders that I let myself be baptized? And** (they) **stepped off into the water, both Philip and the chamberlain, and he baptized him.**

Acts 10:47 – **Then Peter answered: May anyone forbid the water that these might be baptized, etc.?**

3. Because the word "baptize" actually means to wet [sprinkle] or wash with water, as is indicated above in ch. 1, sec. 1. [Even if] it is [sometimes] applied to other matters, such as occurs in figurative terms, none of the actual meaning of the word is thereby confused. To this [principle] apply all the passages about this holy Sacrament in which the word "baptize" or "Baptism" is used.

4. Because Baptism is called "water" or a "water-bath" in the Word, as shown above in chap. 2, sec. 2 and 3. [It is called that] because the water is the material or external element in holy Baptism.

5. Because Christ was baptized in the Jordan and thereby simultaneously sanctified the Jordan's and all other water for Baptism.

In Mat. 3:16, Mark 1:9, Luke 3:21, [and] John 1:32, Jesus is baptized by John in the Jordan.

6. Because the blood and water which flowed from the side of Christ on the cross signify both the Sacrament of Baptism and of the holy Supper. A Church is gathered for the Lord Christ through these Sacraments, and a spiritual bride is led to Him, just as a rib was once taken from the side of Adam and through it Eve was fashioned for him in Gen. 2:22.

John 19:34 – **The one soldier opened His side with a spear, and immediately blood and water came out.**

From all this it is apparent that it is necessary that water be used for holy Baptism. But, in this nothing is implied that the water [must] be warm or cold, that it be taken from a well or stream or sea, for none of these deprive the water of its essence. Whether, however, such water must first be prepared for Baptism with an exorcism [*exorcismus*] or confirmed through an oath, nothing can be found in God's Word about that. Rather, we see much more that John the Baptist and the apostles brought common water to Baptism.

Here again, [is] an apparent contradiction, the one which was indicated in chapter 5 above: It is a proper Baptism when an ordinary Christian administers Baptism in case of an emergency; from this it seems to follow that it is also a valid Baptism when, in case of an emergency, a different element than water is brought to Baptism. ANSWER: There is a vast difference between these two cases. For a servant who baptizes is not a vital part of Baptism; the efficient cause, especially the ministerial efficient cause, never enters the essence of that subject [*causa efficiens, präsertim ministerialis nunquam ingreditur rei essentiam*], but the water is matter and an essential part of holy Baptism. Therefore, someone other than an ordained servant of the Church may baptize in case of an emergency. However, there should not and may not be brought to Baptism a different external element than water, for one of the essential parts of Baptism would be altered in such a case.

CHAPTER 9

THE WATER IN HOLY BAPTISM IS NOT LOWLY WATER, BUT IS FORMULATED AND COMBINED [WITH] GOD'S WORD.

 ven though the water which is used for holy Baptism continues to retain its natural essence and natural attributes after Baptism, nevertheless it is not just lowly [plain] water, but it is formulated in God's Word and combined with God's Word. Thus it is a powerful means through which the Holy Trinity works powerfully: the Father takes on the one who is baptized as His dear child; the Son washes him of his sins with His blood; the Holy Spirit regenerates and renews him for everlasting life.

From this we conclude:

1. That not only is the water a vital element of Baptism, but also the Word which gives the water this power for regeneration, renewal, and salvation. For, the water would be common and ordinary water without the Word; also, it could never, ever have such heavenly power.

Mat. 28:19 – Go forth and teach all people **and baptize them in the Name of the Father and the Son and the Holy Spirit.** From this it is seen that the Name of the Father and the Son and Holy Spirit is to be called upon at the Baptism and over the baptized. For we should not look at these words casually, but rather thoughtfully, as to what they contain. When, therefore, the baptizer says, I baptize you in the Name of the Father and the Son and the Holy Spirit, he thereby indicates: **1.** That Baptism is not a human statute or ordinance; rather, [it is] an endowment from the true God. It is a holy Sacrament which God Himself instituted, who is One in essence. **2.** That the baptizer did not arbitrarily perform this Sacrament at his own discretion, but rather in God's stead as His householder and servant. When he baptizes in the Name of God the Father, God the Son, and God the Holy Spirit, it is as if the Father, Son and Holy Spirit did the baptizing. 2 Cor. 5:20 – **So we are proclaimers in Christ's stead, for God admonishes through us. So we plead then in Christ's stead, etc. 3.** That when the Name of the Father, the Son, and the Holy Spirit is invoked over this water, the same One desires to be effective and fulfill His promise in this child who is being baptized. **4.** That this water is no longer simply lowly water. Rather, it is such a water through which the entire Holy Trinity would be effective, and also is effectual. For when the servant says, I baptize you in the Name of the Father, the Son, and the Holy Spirit, it means so very much: I testify herewith that through this Sacrament you [the person being baptized] are being received into God's covenant of grace; that God the Father takes you as His child; that the Son washes you from sins with His blood and clothes you with His righteousness; that the Holy Spirit regenerates and renews you to everlasting life. **5.** That the child being baptized, who from now on is taken up into God's covenant, herewith becomes obligated to confess from His Word the One true God, to honor and call upon Him, [and] also under the troops of Christ—who instituted this Sacrament of Baptism—to strive against the devil and all his doings and ways.

All this is encompassed in these words when the baptizer says: I baptize you in the Name of the Father and the Son and the Holy Spirit. We can bring forth other references from the Scriptures for a better clarification of these words.

In Exo. 5:23 Moses speaks to Pharaoh in the name of the Lord.

In Deu. 18:7, the Levites serve in the Name of the Lord.

Deu. 18:20 – **When a prophet presumes to speak in My Name that which I have not commanded him to speak,** etc.

1 Sam. 17:45 – **I come to you in the Name of the Lord of Sabaoth.**

2 Sam. 6:18 – **David blessed the people in the Name of the Lord.**

Mat. 18:20 – **Where two or three are gathered together in My Name,** etc.

Mark 9:39 – **they did deeds in Christ's Name.**

Luke 9:48 – **Whoever receives the child in My Name,** etc.

John 16:23 – **If you petition something of the Father in My Name,** etc.

From these and similar references in Scripture, it can be seen that to do or say something in the name of God means to do or say something on God's command, in God's place, with true invocation of God, by God's power, in genuine trust in God, to God's glory, etc.

Consequently, since the baptismal water is poured out in the name of the Father, the Son, and the Holy Spirit, it no longer is plain ordinary water; rather, it is formulated with God's command and wrapped up in God's Word and is a divine, passive agent [instrument of God].

In Eph. 5:26 St. Paul calls Baptism a **water bath in the Word.**

2. Further, since the Name of God is nothing other than God Himself (Psa. 48:11 – **God, as Your Name, so also is Your glory** [fame]; 2 Chr. 14:11 – **We rely upon You, and in Your Name we have come against this horde**), and as the Name of the Father and the Son and the Holy Spirit are through Christ's ordinance and institution, it further follows that the entire Holy Trinity is present at Baptism and also effectually works through the same.

Mat. 28:19 – **And be baptized in the Name of the Father and the Son and the Holy Spirit.** (Whenever you perform Baptism upon My command and according to the divine order, then it is not just an outward ceremony or an external water bath; rather, it has in it the activity of God's grace, with God the Father, God the Son, and God the Holy Spirit present. The Father, for My sake as the Mediator, takes the little child being baptized up into grace. I wash him from sins, I endow him with and make as his own, all My merits and blessings. The Holy Spirit is effectual through rebirth and renewal so that the baptized also is a child of God, a true disciple of Christ, a temple and habitation of the Holy Spirit.)

3. Because the Holy Spirit is the third Person of the Godhead, and Baptism is performed not just in the name of the Father and in the name of the Son but also in the name of the Holy Spirit, it also follows that the Holy Spirit is effectual in, with, and through the water of Baptism, that God here offers all those who are thus baptized the gift of the Holy Spirit, and also that the Holy Spirit desires to work faith, rebirth, and renewal in all who do not willfully resist. Additionally, the covenant of God's grace is sealed within their hearts.

John 3:5 – **Unless one is born out of water and the Spirit, he cannot come into the kingdom of God.** (The Holy Spirit is present with the water of Baptism and effectually makes it into a blessed means of regeneration [rebirth].)

2 Cor. 1:21–22 – **It is God, however, who strengthens us along with you in Christ, and who anointed us and sealed us and gave into our hearts the deposit of the Spirit.**

Eph. 1:13 – **Through whom you also were sealed with the Holy Spirit as the Promise, who is the deposit of our inheritance unto our redemption, etc.**

Eph. 4:30 – **And don't sadden the Holy Spirit, with whom you are sealed for the day of your redemption** [deliverance].

Here are pertinent all the passages which testify that the Holy Spirit will be given to the children of God, for such occurs not only through the Word of the Gospel, but also through the Sacrament of Baptism.

4. Because the Son of God in the fullness of time took upon Himself a true human nature and united Himself with it with an indissoluble link. Thus it further follows that He is present at Baptism not only according to His divinity, but also according to His assumed human nature. And especially the blood of Christ is not to be excluded from holy Baptism: **1.** because the Son of God's true human nature also assumed flesh and blood, in which, with which, and through which His human nature now performs all His works; **2.** because the power of holy Baptism arises and springs forth from the merits of Christ and from the shedding of His blood as it occurred on the timber-trunk of the cross; **3.** because in holy Baptism we were washed from sins through the blood of Christ; **4.** because we were baptized into Christ's death. Now, however, Christ's death also includes His shedding of blood.

John 19:34 – Blood and water flowed out from Christ's side on the cross. (Through this both Sacraments of the New Testament are designated. Their power and effectiveness come from the death of Christ.)

Rom. 6:3, 4 – **Don't you know that all who like us have been baptized into Jesus Christ were baptized into His death? Thus we also were buried with Him through Baptism into His death,** etc.

Gal. 3:27 – **As many of you who have been baptized, you have put on Christ.**

1 John 1:7 – **The blood of Jesus Christ His Son** (the Son of God) **makes us clean from all sin.**

Here, again, [is] an apparent contradiction, that since the Holy Trinity instituted this Sacrament, therefore it may not be said that the Holy Trinity is an essential element of holy Baptism. ANSWER: Even though God the Father, Son, and Holy Spirit is the founder and institutor of holy Baptism, yet such does not preclude that on account of that one can say: the Holy Trinity is the other essential element of holy Baptism, since God the Lord in the words of institution revealed Himself to this end and promised the following—that He wants to be effectual with all His richly gracious deeds through Baptism. Is it not also true that Christ is the founder and institutor of the holy Supper? Even so, He Himself with His body and blood is also the most high and worthy food of the same—just as on the stem of the cross He simultaneously was the High Priest and the Offering.

CHAPTER 10

WHEREIN DOES THE FORM OR ESSENCE OF HOLY BAPTISM CONSIST, THAT IS, WHAT DOES IT ACTUALLY MEAN TO BAPTIZE?

 o baptize actually means to pour water upon, or dip into water, in the Name of the Father, the Son, and the Holy Spirit. For one can clearly see from the institution of this Sacrament that it is not enough to invoke the Name of the Father, the Son, and the Holy Spirit beside and over the water. Rather, the Baptism must also take place; that is, that the person must be sprinkled with, or be dipped into, such baptismal water. On the other hand, it is not enough to merely pour on water or dip into water. On its own and for its own sake such does not make a Baptism. Rather, such must take place in the Name of the Father, the Son, and the Holy Spirit.

Mat. 28:19 – Go forth into all the world and teach all people **and baptize them in the Name of the Father and the Son and the Holy Spirit.**

From this it can readily be concluded: **1.** That these words are not to be altered, much less omitted; rather, Baptism must thus be performed as Christ ordained and instituted it. **2.** That it is not a valid Baptism when these words are changed, since it abandons Christ's institution in such a case, just as it no longer is a valid Baptism when one uses a different external element in place of water. How much less will it be a Baptism when these words: **In the Name of the Father and the Son and the Holy Spirit** are sacrilegiously changed? **3.** That the baptismal water, when it is not poured onto the person, does not in any way possess a hidden, heavenly power in and of itself. For none of the Sacraments has a use other than God's institution [*nihil enim habet rationem sacramenti extra usum a Deo institutum*]. When the baptismal water is poured upon the person in the Name of the Father, and the Son, and the Holy Spirit, it is then a divine water. When, however, it is no longer used to this end for which it was instituted by God, then it has no more special power or effect than any other common water.

Here, again, [are] apparent contradictions:

1. That when one states that one should never baptize except in the Name of the Father and the Son and the Holy Spirit, a secret, hidden power—and in fact, any magic you wish [*magica quaedum vis*]—is ascribed to the words. ANSWER: **1.** We do not hereby in any way ascribe to the outward sound and resonance [clang and peal] of these words a secret power so that through the same the baptismal water is made into a means of regeneration. Rather, we teach and confess herewith that true disciples of Christ, with genuine Christian simplicity, want to remain true to His Word and institution. John 8:31 – **As you remain in My words, so shall you be My legitimate disciples;** John 10:27 – **My sheep hear My voice,** etc. **2.** Even though the baptismal water is made to be a blessed bath of rebirth solely and only through the gracious working of the entire Trinity, nevertheless, Christ has bound us to these words through His institution and has promised to perform such great works of grace when we simple-mindedly and persistently keep to the words of institution as obedient students [disciples]. **3.** And even though nothing might depart from the essence of holy Baptism even though one baptized in the name of the Holy Trinity and did not necessarily narrate all three Persons by name and in order, we still steadfastly say and teach that one should not use any form or words for Baptism than what Christ Himself prescribed for us. Without doubt, the divine wisdom of Christ had reasons enough even to name all three

Persons and to baptize in the name of all three Persons. Of all the reasons, not the least is that all three Persons and each One individually perform marvelous works of grace upon the baptized child: the Father takes him on as His child; Christ as His disciple and brother; the Holy Spirit as His temple and habitation.

2. That in Acts 2:38; 10:48, it is mentioned that the apostles baptized in the name of the Lord Jesus, therefore one may also use this formula for Baptism. ANSWER: 1. It is not to be assumed that the beloved disciples would diverge from the words of institution which were prescribed for them by the Lord Christ. 2. Accordingly, nothing in these words describes what sort of baptismal formula the apostles used. Rather, what is indicated through them is that they baptized upon Christ's command and Word; that they performed the Baptism in the faith, teaching, confession, and thereby—so to speak—united their baptismal candidates with Christ; that the baptized—now united with Christ—should solely confess Him as the Messiah, Mediator and Savior; that they should serve to the best of their ability the One into whose death they were baptized (Rom. 6:3). They should do this in similar fashion as St. Paul says about the Israelites in 1 Cor. 10:2: They were **baptized into Moses**, i.e., they were led by Moses through the Red Sea (which passing-through was a type of Baptism) and thereby were united with Moses so that they should believe and follow what he presented to them by the command of God. 3. Furthermore, the name of Christ encompasses the entire Holy Trinity, for Christ is called an Anointed One. Subsequently, in this name is comprehended the Father, who anointed Christ; the Son, who was anointed according to His human nature; the Holy Spirit, with whom He was anointed and endowed without measure. Therefore, when the apostles baptized in the name of the Father, and the Son, and the Holy Spirit, St. Luke briefly summarizes this with these words and says they baptized in Christ's name.

CHAPTER 11

THAT BAPTISM MAY BE PERFORMED NOT ONLY BY IMMERSION, BUT ALSO BY POURING ON THE WATER.

hen holy Baptism is performed in the name of the Father and the Son and the Holy Spirit, it is one and the same whether the child to be baptized is immersed or has the water poured on it. And since today pouring is the practice in the Christian Church, one should stay with the current practice and not wantonly deviate from this practice out of one's own discretion. That Baptism may also be performed in the name of the Father and the Son and the Holy Spirit through pouring, we indicate thusly:

1. Because "baptize" generically means to sprinkle and wash with water, it occurs either through immersion or through pouring, as already indicated by the examples above in ch. 1.

2. Because the word "Baptism" is used for the visible outpouring of the special gifts of the Spirit, as was also indicated in ch. 1, sec. 2, it follows that pouring also constitutes a Baptism.

Joel 3:1 – **And after this I will pour out My Spirit over all flesh, etc.** This was fulfilled as the apostles were baptized with the Holy Spirit on Pentecost (Acts 1:5; 2:17; 11:16).

3. Because the word "baptize" is used for the passage of the children of Israel through the Red Sea, though they were nevertheless not immersed in it.

1 Cor. 10:2 – And (the children of Israel) **were all baptized into Moses with the cloud and with the sea** (water).

4. Because Baptism is called a water bath. Now then, the word "**bathing**" or "**washing**" is used not only when the entire body is immersed and bathed, but also when the washing is performed with pouring and sprinkling.

In Eph. 5:26, Baptism is called **a water bath in the Word**.

Tit. 3:5 – **the bath of regeneration and renewal of the Holy Spirit**.

In these passages Baptism is called a washing [bath], but that washing may be performed through pouring is obvious:

Exo. 2:5 – **And the daughter of Pharaoh went down and wanted to bathe in the water** (not that she had totally stepped in; rather, she washed her feet in the stream).

Exo. 30:18 – **You shall make a brass hand basin with a brass foot** [stand] **in order to wash, etc.** (They did not completely dip their entire body into it; rather, they washed their hands and feet in it, v. 19.)

2 Sam. 11:2 – **From the roof David saw a woman wash herself**.

1 Kin. 22:38 – **They washed the wagon by the pool of Samaria.**

Psa. 6:7 – **I sprinkle my bed with tears** (I wash it with tears).

John 9:7 – **Go over to the pool of Siloam and wash yourself.**

5. Because without doubt, John the Baptizer also baptized that way, i.e., by pouring water over the heads of those he wanted to baptize. For since John openly baptized in the Jordan, it is not credible that he completely immersed his baptismal candidates into the water. Further, that they would be immersed in the Jordan with their clothes on seems unlikely. That the same huge horde of men and women, who, without distinction, came to John's Baptism, would strip down naked to be totally immersed in the Jordan is even more preposterous. It is most highly plausible, then, that they stood on the shore of the Jordan, or stepped in at the edge, and [that] John thus poured water over their heads.

Mat. 3:5, Mark 1:5 – There went out to him (John) [people] **from the city of Jerusalem and the entire Jewish country and all the country on the Jordan, and let themselves be baptized of him in the Jordan, etc.**

Mat. 3:16, Mark 1:10 – **And when Jesus had been baptized, He immediately stepped out of the water.**

6. Because the holy apostles and others in the first apostolic Church also baptized by pouring out water.

In Acts 2:41, three thousand men are baptized in one day (and it is not recorded that they went out to some stream and there were totally immersed).

In Acts 16:15, Lydia and her entire household (or household domestics) were baptized. (Here, of course, it is unbelievable that they all were immersed [dipped into] water—either clothed or naked.)

In Acts 18:8, Crispus and his entire household were baptized.

In Acts 22:16, Ananias says to Paul: **Get up and let yourself be baptized and wash away your sins, etc.** (That Paul, however, was baptized indoors in the same home in which he was a guest is to be surmised from Acts 9:18, 19. But how can one substantiate that in the haste of [the occasion] there could have been provided so much water and such a large tub that St. Paul could be totally immersed into the water?)

In 1 Cor. 1:16, St. Paul baptized the house domestics of Stephanus.

Here, again, [are] apparent contradictions:

1. That the word "to baptize" derives from immersion [dipping into]; therefore, it is necessary that holy Baptism be performed with immersion. ANSWER: Although "to baptize" comes from "to immerse," yet this does not prevent that it should also mean to sprinkle the water in general. The same thing occurs through immersion or sprinkling, just as it has been indicated above. Beyond that, even if the German word "to baptize" [*taufen*] means totally and solely "to immerse," it still shall be sufficient for the matter that one can prove that the Greek word βαπτίζειν, which Christ used in instituting Baptism, means both "to dip into" and "to sprinkle."

2. That how we are baptized into Christ's death and how we are buried with Him in death is better signified by immersion than through sprinkling (Rom 6:3, 4); also, the drowning and killing of our old Adam in holy Baptism [is better signified by immersion]. ANSWER: 1. Holy Baptism was never even instituted in order to signify this or that; rather, much more that it should be a powerful means through which God the Holy Spirit wants to effect rebirth and renewal. 2. The Holy Spirit can accomplish this work and end result through baptismal water either when it is poured out or when the person is immersed in it—just so long as it is a water bath in the Word. 3. However, we do not object if one seeks various implications of Baptism's water; just so one does not hold or allege that therein consists the essence of holy Baptism. Rather, he [should] allow Baptism to remain a powerful means of rebirth and renewal, and only thereafter search for signifying meanings. As, then, immersion signifies that we become buried with Christ in His death, and that the old Adam becomes drowned in Baptism, so also sprinkling can signify that we are sprinkled with Christ's blood in holy Baptism (1 Pet. 1 and 2), and become washed of all sins (1 John 1:8). The pouring can signify that the Holy Spirit is richly poured out with His gifts (Tit. 3:6). 4. As also immersion draws on the type of the Flood [sin-flood], in which all flesh was drowned (1 Pet. 3:21), so also pouring and sprinkling draws on the figure of the Covenant which God established with the Israelites when they were sprinkled with the blood of the offerings (Exo. 24:8).

CHAPTER 12

WHETHER THE OUTPOURING OF THE WATER IN HOLY BAPTISM SHOULD OCCUR ONCE OR MORE OFTEN; ALSO, UPON WHICH PART OF THE BODY IT SHOULD BE POURED.

ust as it makes no difference whether the person baptized is totally immersed or has water poured on him—so long as he is bathed with water in the name of the Father, the Son, and the Holy Spirit—so also it makes no difference whether the pouring happens one time or three times, nor whether the one being baptized is drenched with water totally or [only] on a particular portion of the body. This we also demonstrate:

1. Neither the institution nor other Scripture references give any consideration to the thought whether one should pour three times or entirely dip in the person. Rather, Christ speaks generically: **Baptize.**

Mat. 28:19 – **Therefore go out and teach all nations and baptize them**, etc.

2. At all times there is a distinction to be made about the holy Sacraments between the presentation of the inherent heavenly benefits through the means of the external elements, and the manner and mode of that presentation. The former is essential and cannot be omitted, but the latter is an *adiaphoron* or intermediate thing [*Mittelding*] and may be changed at times, just so long as the presentation itself remains as it has been ordained by God.

In Mat. 26, Mark 14, Luke 22, [and] I Cor. 11, the institution of the holy Lord's Supper is described, wherein

Christ commands that in and with the bread His body is to be distributed and eaten, and in and with the wine His blood is to be distributed and drunk. This distribution—this eating and drinking—must steadfastly remain in the holy Lord's Supper. But, whether those who go to the Lord's Supper have it [the bread] given to them in the hands or placed in their mouths, whether the bread is broken before or after the blessing, whether the communicants drink themselves or have the chalice held for them, it matters not. So also here in the holy Baptism, it is necessary that the person being baptized is wetted in the name of the Father, and the Son, and the Holy Spirit. However, whether this should take place through immersion or through pouring, even whether one should pour once or more times, [there is] no express command from Jesus concerning [the matter].

3. Holy Baptism has not been instituted for the purpose of washing away the outward uncleanness of the body, nor on account of this necessity: that the body is to be washed several times. Rather, it is to be a bath of rebirth and renewal. Therefore, it is enough that one simply pour onto one part of the body, just as the bread and wine in the holy Lord's Supper are not to be received for the purpose of satisfying bodily hunger and thirst with it, on account of which it would be necessary that one receive much bread and wine.

1 Pet. 3:21 – **Which** (the water) **now also saves us through Baptism, through which is signified, not the putting off of dirt** [filth] **from the flesh** (note that the water of Baptism is not used to clean the body), **rather, the covenant of a good conscience with God through the resurrection of Jesus Christ.**

Since one has no express command from God as to whether the water in Baptism is to be poured upon [applied] once or more times, also whether such is to be poured over the entire body, one should, therefore, [on the basis of these practices] not instigate schisms and divisions; rather, in regard to this matter, one should adhere to the practice of the Christian Church in each locale. And, since our practice is to pour water three times over the head of the one being baptized, one should discreetly abide by the same custom.

Here, again, [are] apparent contradictions:

1. That it is better to pour on the water one time, since the unity of the divine way is thereby demonstrated. ANSWER: We must once more reiterate that God did not establish Baptism primarily in order to signify this or that, but rather, that it be a water bath in the Word for rebirth and renewal. If this is first established as the reason, then one may subsequently seek meanings, but such that do not fly in the face of the rule of faith. Just as when the pouring occurs only once, the unity of the divine way can thus be indicated, so also when the pouring occurs three times, the holy Trinity of Persons is indicated. (Also, since we are totally buried with Christ through Baptism into His death, so one might also say that the threefold pouring signifies that Christ remained in His grave for three days—though that's stretching it a bit.)

2. That the rebirth and renewal involves the whole person; therefore, it necessarily appears that also the whole body should be drenched with water. ANSWER: The rebirth and renewal by the Holy Spirit can indeed be accomplished in and on the total person even when the baptismal water is not poured over the entire body, since the power for rebirth is also not secretly hidden and concealed in the baptismal water—as common water possesses the natural power to clean the body. Rather, the power of rebirth is and remains totally and solely the possession of the Holy Spirit; yet He desires to perform the same through the water of Baptism as through a means ordained by Himself. It may conveniently be [noted here], for better understanding, that the power of circumcision (which was replaced by Baptism in the New Testament, Col. 2:11) was for the good of the entire person and was nevertheless performed through the external circumcising of only one part of the body, namely the foreskin.

CHAPTER 13

THAT HOLY BAPTISM IS AN EFFECTUAL MEANS THROUGH WHICH THE HOLY SPIRIT REGENERATES PEOPLE.

ntil now we've dealt with the Founder, the external element, and the form of holy Baptism. Hereupon follows its benefit and effect, since the water in holy Baptism is not lowly water, but rather the water formulated in God's command and combined with God's Word (as was indicated above). That is why it is no longer used for the purpose of removing filth from the body, as ordinary water usually does (1 Pet. 3:21); rather, it is a divine means and passive agent, sanctified by the Word of God and set apart for this outstanding benefit from all other water, so that with and through the same [this water] the entire Holy Trinity is effective for eternal life in those who are baptized. Consequently, the first benefit and result of holy Baptism is that it regenerates [re-births] the person.

John 3:5 – **Unless one is born out of the water and the Spirit, he cannot come into the kingdom of God.**

Tit. 3:5 – **According to His mercy He saved us through the bath of rebirth and renewing of the Holy Spirit.**

Pertinent here is that, according to Eze. 47:9, water that was flowing out from the threshold of the Temple made alive and healthy everything that it touched, which is a type of holy Baptism.

From this benefit of holy Baptism comes forth [originates], and yes, to it also belongs the following:

1. That the Holy Spirit works faith in the heart of the child being baptized. For since Baptism is (as previously stated) a bath of regeneration and is (as will follow later) an effectual means for the forgiveness of sin, [that is] for sonship with God and for eternal life, so also must faith be ignited and awakened through holy Baptism (understand that this refers to the hearts of those who do not stubbornly resist the working of the Holy Spirit), since the entire Scripture testifies that no one can be regenerated or receive forgiveness of sins, nor become a child of God or inherit eternal salvation without faith. On account of that, Baptism is not ordinary water, but the Word of God is also present, making it the means through which people are regenerated.

John 17:20 – **I petition for those who will believe on Me through their word.**

Rom. 10:17 – **So faith comes from the sermon** (from the hearing)**, but the proclamation** (the hearing) **comes through the Word of God.** Cf. 1 Pet. 1:23.

[The matter of] the faith of baptized children will be dealt with more extensively later, as will also the related question of why it is that not all who are baptized thus then become recipients of true faith and salvation.

2. That holy Baptism is an effectual means through which the Holy Spirit works forgiveness of sins. Relevant here, first of all, are the Old Testament types, such as the Flood [sin-flood] (Gen. 7); the various Levitical cleansings (Lev. 15); the sprinkling with the water in which were mixed the ashes of the red cow (Num. 19); [and] the cleansing of Naaman from leprosy in the Jordan (2 Kin. 5). For just as the same water served them for bodily cleansing, so also Baptism washes us from spiritual uncleanness. Subsequently, also relevant are the prophecies of the Old Testament, as God the Lord says.

Eze. 16:9 – **I washed away your blood,** etc.

Eze. 36:25 – **I will sprinkle clean** [pure] **water over you so that you become cleansed of all your uncleanness,** etc.

Mic. 7:19 – **He will . . . hurl all our sins into the depths of the sea.**

Zec. 13:1 – **At that time the house of David and the citizens of Jerusalem will have a free-flowing fountain against sin and impurity.**

To this pertains in particular the following New Testament passages:

Mark 1:4, Luke 3:3 – **John preached the Baptism of repentance for the forgiveness of sins.**

Acts 3:38 – **Peter said to them, Repent and each of you let yourselves be baptized into the Name of Jesus Christ unto the forgiveness of sins,** etc.

In Acts 22:16 – Ananias says to Paul: **Get up and let yourself be baptized and wash away your sins,** etc.

Rom. 6:3 – **Don't you know that all who like us have been baptized into Jesus Christ have been baptized into His death?** Through Baptism we are implanted into Christ in such a way that we receive the power of His death with such certainty as if we ourselves had suffered for our sins.

2 Cor. 5:14 – **Since One died for all, thus they all have died.**

1 Cor. 6:11 – **You have been washed off through the Name of the Lord Jesus and through the Spirit of our God** (in holy Baptism).

Eph. 5:26–27 – **Christ has cleansed her** (the fellowship [of the Church]) **through the water bath in the Word, in order to present to Himself a fellowship which is glorious, which does not have a spot or wrinkle, nor any such thing,** etc.

1 Pet. 1:2 – (The ones called) **according to the foreknowledge of God the Father, through the sanctification of the Spirit, to obedience and to the sprinkling of the blood of Christ.** (The sprinkling of the blood of Christ occurs in the Word of the Gospel, and in the holy Sacraments, and so also in Baptism, for the forgiveness of sins.)

1 John 1:7 – **The blood of Jesus Christ, His Son** (the Son of God) **makes us clean of all sin.** (This blood of Christ is sprinkled over us in holy Baptism, and we are washed clean by it.)

Also rightly included [in this context] is that in Mat. 3:7 [and] Luke 3:7, John the Baptizer testifies that one can flee the wrath of God through the reception of Baptism; but then no one can flee the wrath of God unless for the sake of Christ his sins are forgiven him.

3. That God establishes a covenant of grace with us in holy Baptism, which, however, consists of the forgiveness of sins and the bequeathing of the Holy Spirit—both of which occur in Baptism, Jer. 31:31, 33, 34 – **See, the time is coming when I will make a new covenant with the house of Israel and with the house of Jacob. And this will be the covenant which I will make with the house of Israel, says the Lord: I will give My law in their heart and write it in their soul, and they shall be My people. Thus I will be their God.—I will forgive them their iniquity and never again remember their sin.** That God the Lord now in holy Baptism establishes a covenant of grace with us, we indicate thus:

In Gen. 17:10 God establishes a covenant of grace with Abraham and his seed through circumcision and thereby promises that He will be God (and gracious Father) to Abraham and his seed. But now circumcision was a type of our Baptism, and Baptism in the New Testament came into being for the same purpose (Col. 2:11).

In Exo. 24:8, Moses sprinkles the Israelite people with the blood of the offering and says: **See, this is the blood of the covenant which the Lord makes with you.** (So also are we sprinkled with the blood of Christ through holy Baptism, 1 Pet. 1:2, and washed of sin (1 John 1:7), so that we become recipients of God's covenant of grace.)

1 Pet. 3:21 – **Which** (water) **now also saves us in Baptism, which is signified through the same** (the water of the Flood), **not the taking off of dirt from the flesh, rather the covenant of a good conscience with God through the resurrection of Jesus Christ.** (In the Greek it is written ἐπερώτημα, which means question [inquiry] and answer [reply]—as is customary in the closing of legal contracts and

covenants. One party asks [inquires], the other party answers [responds], and from this the covenant is concluded. This word [ἐπερώτημα] is also used by the 70 translators of the Old Testament [i.e., the Septuagint] when they want to say that a person in certain situations asked for answers from God's mouth. St. Peter draws from this [reference] when he labels Baptism such a question [appeal], and teaches thereby that in Baptism we can be assured of God's grace and thus henceforth can have a good conscience.)

1 John 5:6 – **This is the One who comes with water and blood, Jesus Christ; not with water alone, but with water, blood, etc.** (As Christ comes to us through the water of Baptism, Baptism will always be the means through which we become recipients of Christ's merits and are taken up [received] into God's covenant of grace.)

1 John 5:8 – **Three are the witnesses on earth: The Spirit and the water and the blood, and these three are together** (God the Holy Spirit witnesses through the Word—which is the office of the Spirit—that we have been taken up into His covenant of grace, and He empowers this covenant with the two seals of Baptism and the holy Lord's Supper).

4. That we put on Christ and like unto beautiful garments, are clothed with His righteousness.

Isa. 61:10 – **He** (the Lord) **has clothed me with garments of salvation and dressed me with the robe of righteousness, etc.** (That this takes place in holy Baptism is attested to by the following little verse from Gal: 3:27 – **As many of you as have been baptized have put on Christ.**)

1 Cor. 12:13 – **Through one Spirit we have all been baptized into one body** (of which body Christ is the Head, Eph. 1:22. We all become partakers of Christ's righteousness through holy Baptism and, through the Holy Spirit, members of Christ.)

5. That through holy Baptism we are taken on [accepted] as children of God, which follows from the preceding; for those who become born of God are children of God (John 1:13); those who believe in Jesus are children of God (v. 12); those whose sin is forgiven are God's children (Mat. 9:2); those who are taken into God's covenant of grace are children of God (Lev. 26:11, Isa. 52:11, 2 Cor. 6:18); those who are clothed with Christ's righteousness please God the Lord as His dear children (Rom. 5:1). In particular, the following little verse belongs here:

Gal. 3:26, 27 – **You are all the children of God through faith in Christ Jesus. For as many of you who have been baptized have put on Christ.** (Again St. Paul here shows that the baptized Galatians are children of God and indicates as proof of this fact that in their Baptism they had put on Christ.)

6. That the Holy Spirit saves us through Baptism, which follows once more from the foregoing, for regeneration [rebirth] takes place for eternal life (Jam. 1:18, 21). **Whosoever believes on the Son has eternal life, etc.** (John 3:36). Where there is forgiveness of sins, there is life and salvation (Psa. 32:1). Whoever is in God's covenant of grace is an heir of life (2 Cor. 6:16). Whoever has the Son has eternal life (1 John 5:12). **If we then are children, we are also heirs, namely, God's heirs and fellow-heirs with Christ** (Rom. 8:17). In particular, the following verses pertain here:

In Gen. 8:18 at the time of the Flood, a few were kept alive in the Ark. St. Peter applies this [event] to holy Baptism (1 Pet. 3:21), through which we are kept alive for eternal life.

In Eze. 47:9 the prophet sees water flowing out from the Temple's threshold, through which everything that is touched by it is made alive.

Mark 16:16 – **Whoever believes and is baptized, will be saved, etc.**

John 3:5 – **Unless one is born out of the water and the Spirit, he cannot come into the kingdom of God** (From this contrarily follows the opposite point [*a contrario sensu*], that whoever is born again out of water and the Spirit, such a one will enter into the kingdom of heaven).

Tit. 3:5 – **According to His mercy He** (God the Lord) **saved us through the bath of rebirth and renewal of the Holy Spirit.**

1 Pet. 3:21 – The water in holy Baptism saves us. (It is a beneficial means through which the Holy Spirit saves us, even as St. Paul says in 1 Tim. 4:16 – **If you do such** [persevere in doctrine], **you yourself will be saved and those who listen to you,** since the Gospel is mainly a power of God for the salvation of all who believe it, Rom. 1:16. The Word of God thus implanted in us can save our souls, Jam. 1:21.)

From this, it can be correctly concluded that in and at the Baptism of Christ heaven opened over Him (Mat. 3:16, Mark 1:10, Luke 3:21). Thereby is indicated that through holy Baptism the locked door of heaven is again opened for us by the Holy Spirit, so that we who once by nature, because of inherited sin, were children of wrath (Eph. 2:3), and subjugated to eternal death, have now become children of God and heirs of eternal life through Baptism. See, all these great, inexpressible benefits are included in that single word when the Holy Spirit says that Baptism is a bath of rebirth.

Here, again, [are] apparent contradictions:

1. That holy Baptism actually is not an effectual means for rebirth; rather, the water of holy Baptism only signifies what is worked by the Holy Spirit in only certain ones in Baptism; and therefore also: as water washes away the uncleanness of the body, so the Holy Spirit washes from the uncleanness of sin through Christ's blood. ANSWER: **1.** The water of holy Baptism is not just a sign by which is symbolized rebirth and the washing away of sin; rather, it is an effectual means through which the Holy Spirit washes sin away. The Holy Spirit is and remains at all times the principal cause [*causa principalis*], the chief cause who works the rebirth and washes from sin. The water in Baptism, since it is combined with the Word of God and thus is no longer base [common, plain] water, is the instrumental cause [*causa*

instrumentalis]—the means and passive agent—through which the Holy Spirit performs His gracious work. **2.** Therefore one should not view the baptismal water in Baptism according to its natural powers and properties; rather, one should look upon it as a divine water, since the Word of God is present and since it is simultaneously colored with Christ's blood. **3.** St. Peter expressly testifies in 1 Pet. 3:21 that the water in holy Baptism is not used for the removal of dirt from the flesh. How can one then say that the essence of holy Baptism and the official sacramental mission [*officium sacramentale*]—the sacramental working of the baptismal water—consists of such an analogy: that as water washes the body of uncleanness, so also Christ's blood washes the soul from sin? **4.** In the institution of holy Baptism, this analogy or meaning is not intended; rather, Christ commands to baptize in the name of the Father and of the Son and of the Holy Spirit (Mat. 28:19); He binds the name of the Father and of the Son and of the Holy Spirit (which is to be spoken thusly) with the water in Baptism, and thereto He adds the promise that Baptism will be an effectual means for salvation (Mark 16:16). **5.** The Scriptures also nowhere say that the water in holy Baptism symbolizes the rebirth and cleansing from sin; rather, much more it says that we are reborn from the water and the Spirit (John 3:5); that the water bath in the Word cleanses us (Eph. 5:26); that through this bath of rebirth, God saves us (Tit. 3:5); that Baptism saves us (1 Pet. 3:2). We learn from this that the work of Baptism's water is not to signify rebirth and cleansing from sin, but, rather, to effectually work the same; to wit, the instrument [*instrumentaliter scilicet*], as a means and agent appointed for this by God. **6.** Also, if the cleansing from sin is merely signified by baptismal water, then one must not only pour it upon the head, as happens in our churches, but the entire body must be thoroughly bathed with it and cleansed so that the significance might be that much stronger. **7.** It would also follow then (if one maintained that the essence of holy Baptism consists of this significance) that the Scripture nowhere speaks with actual clear words about the essence and power of Baptism; rather, all the passages must first be interpreted through this same analogy, or worse yet, be perverted. **8.** To say nothing [of the fact] that the significances and representations actually belong to the Old Testament—which were shadows of that which was in the future, but the body itself is in Christ (Col. 2:17). And again, Heb. 10:1 – **The Law had the shadow of the future good things, not the essence of the actual benefits. 9.** All the types and passages which point to Baptism or speak of it do not ascribe to it a mere significance; rather, they testify that it is an effectual means through which forgiveness of sins and salvation are bequeathed to us. The Sin-flood signifies not only the end of all flesh—it was a means through which God destroyed all flesh. So also this holy "Sin-flood" [Baptism] not only signifies the forgiveness of sins and the death of the old Adam, but it is an effectual means to that end. The Levitical baths were a means to bodily cleansing; the water which flowed forth from the threshold of the Temple signified not only health and life; rather, it made everything healthy and alive. The washing in the Jordan signified not only that Naaman would be cleansed of leprosy; rather, it was a means through which God effectually cleansed Naaman from leprosy. Had he not washed off in the Jordan, he certainly would not have become clean, and [one could cite many] other types. **10.** And, so that we might conclude, one should not deny the Sacraments that which is ascribed to them by the Word. But now, the Word ascribes to Baptism that it not only signifies the heavenly blessings; rather, that it is an effectual means through which God works faith, forgiveness of sins and salvation in our hearts (Rom. 1:16, 10:17, Jam. 1:21, etc.). Therefore, one should not deny [that] the Sacraments are a visible Word and visible sign of grace which God promises in His Word; yes, that they are also saving means and instruments through which God's grace is offered, received, and sealed.

2. That the children of believing Christians are actually already in the covenant of God's grace by virtue of their parents' Baptism, since God the Lord promised in Gen. 17:7 that He would be our God and our seed's God. Therefore, the children are not taken up into God's covenant through Baptism; rather, Baptism is only a sign and seal of what has already happened for them. ANSWER: **1.** The children thus born from believing parents are no less by nature children of wrath than any other (Eph. 2:3). They are conceived and born in sin (Psa. 51:7). They are sired out of unclean seed (Job 14:4). They are flesh from flesh (John 3:6). How, then, can they be in God's covenant of grace? More on this point follows further [in the next section]. **2.** What pertains to the previous point is that a gracious promise of God is described in it, namely: How God desires to take up into His covenant of grace Abraham and his seed—and even more so in the New Testament—those who share Abraham's faith, [as well as] their children, not merely without means or only because of their being born physically from believing parents; rather, He desires to do so through circumcision in the Old Testament and through Baptism in the New Testament, as is additionally pointed out in v. 10 – **This however is My covenant which you should keep between Me and you and your seed after you: all who are male among you shall be circumcised.** And in v. 14 is added the warning: **Whenever a lad is not circumcised on the foreskin of his flesh, that soul shall be rooted out from My people, since he has neglected My covenant. 3.** In Acts 2:39 this point is marvelously [and] succinctly clarified for us: **Repent**, says St. Peter, v. 38, **and each of you let yourself be baptized, etc.** He adds to this in v. 39 – **For this promise is to you and to your children, etc.** If, prior to their circumcision, the children of believing Jews in the Old Testament, and if, prior to their Baptism, the children of believing parents in the New Testament were already in the covenant of God, how, then, could St. Peter

exhort them to be baptized, since this promise [would have] already been fulfilled in them? **4.** This promise of God thus extends no further than that the children of the believers are herewith given this marvelous advantage: that they in their childhood years should be admitted to the Sacrament of Circumcision in the Old Testament and holy Baptism in the New Testament, which advantage the children of unbelievers do not have, as will be more extensively elaborated on at the appropriate place.

3. If holy Baptism is an effectual means of regeneration [rebirth], then it should follow that all who merely receive Baptism are all regenerated; but, that isn't possible, else Baptism would be beneficial *ex opere operato*, for the sake of the completed action, even when there is no faith in the heart of the baptized [person]. ANSWER: **1.** Obviously God the Lord wants to perform regeneration in all who are baptized. Yes, He indeed performs it in all those who do not stubbornly resist His gracious performance. Accordingly, since the under-aged little children do not aspire against the Holy Spirit, it is obviously certain and true that they all become reborn. **2.** From this it cannot be concluded, however, that Baptism also without faith is beneficial, since it is at the same time the means through which God the Holy Spirit works faith in the hearts of little under-aged children, as previously indicated. Therefore, it remains certain that no Sacrament—and thus also Baptism—is beneficial without faith. **3.** At the same time, it must not be denied that faith is worked and increased through the Word as well as out of the Sacrament. Just as it is in Heb. 4:2 -**The Word of the preacher did not help those who heard but did not believe it,** and yet it remains a blessed means through which God the Lord desires to work faith (Rom. 1:16; 10:17). Also, the holy Sacrament of Baptism benefits nothing without faith, and, at the same time, it is a blessed means through which God the Holy Spirit wants to ignite and increase faith in all who do not willfully resist.

4. At times there are some baptized who already are regenerate, like the chamberlain who is baptized in Acts 8:38, who, by all counts, believed with his whole heart and, accordingly, was already born again. In Acts 10:47, certain ones are baptized upon whom the Holy Spirit had already fallen. Therefore, Baptism cannot be a means for rebirth. ANSWER: Although these and others already were reborn before they were baptized, nevertheless Baptism loses nothing by not [serving as] a bath of rebirth. Furthermore, this can be demonstrated with the example of the divine Word, for the divine Word is heard by many who already are regenerated, and yet it remains a blessed means through it all, since we can be regenerated through the incorruptible Seed (Jam. 1:18). Just as faith and the gifts of the Spirit are increased in the regenerate through the hearing of the divine Word, similarly such takes place in and with them through holy Baptism, to say nothing of [the fact] that Baptism is a divine signet through which rebirth and other divine gifts are sealed within them.

5. The example of Simon, the magician, who was baptized but was not regenerated (Acts 8:23) attests that not all who are thus baptized are at the same time reborn. From this it certainly follows that Baptism is not a bath of rebirth. ANSWER: That not all the washed ones, when they are baptized, obtain rebirth and salvation occurs as a result of their resisting the work of the Holy Spirit; and they hinder the Holy Spirit in His gracious work through their hypocrisy, as Simon also did. From this, however, there is no way one can conclude that holy Baptism of and for itself is not a means of regeneration, or that the under-age children (who then do not resist the Holy Spirit) should not be reborn in holy Baptism. If the Word happens not to work faith and salvation effectually in everyone [who hears it], should it therefore [be] disqualified as a means through which God the Lord works faith and salvation?

6. Many are baptized in childhood, who thereafter, when they are grown, grossly sin. Such have not been regenerated because in 1 John 3:9 it is written – **Whatever is born of God does not sin, for His seed abides in him and cannot sin because he is born of God.** ANSWER: This does not mean that such who received Baptism in childhood were not born again; rather, that they have lost the grace of God and the Holy Spirit because of sins against conscience. For the rebirth and renewal of holy Baptism is made available to forgive, to subdue the Old Man with his evil lusts and sin, which is not totally removed from the flesh. A person is also renewed by the Holy Spirit so that he should strive against the flesh, fight off the evil lusts, and also strive in a steadfast campaign against the indwelling sin that still remains. When, however, such a reborn and renewed person willfully follows the lusts of the flesh and lives according to the flesh, then he loses the grace of God, the gracious indwelling of the Holy Spirit and eternal life, as should be apparent on this point and extensively clarify the little verse introduced from John [1 John 3:9].

CHAPTER 14

THAT HOLY BAPTISM IS A POWERFUL [EFFECTUAL] MEANS FOR RENEWAL.

 person is not only reborn through holy Baptism (that is, that his sins are forgiven and he becomes a child of God and an heir of eternal life); rather, he also is renewed; that is, he is given the Holy Spirit who begins to renew the understanding, the will, and all the forces of body and soul so that the lost image of God begins to be renewed in the person so that the spirit henceforth strives against the flesh to overcome it and constrain it. All this is so that sin does not rule in the person but, on the contrary, may be forcefully withstood. Yet, it is to be noted that this renewal is not immediately completed; rather, sin remains in the flesh, but it is not reckoned for damnation. Also, its powerful supremacy is taken away. (More about this will follow later. First it is to be demonstrated that a person is renewed through Baptism.)

In Tit. 3:5, Baptism is expressly called not only a bath of rebirth, but also of **the renewal of the Holy Spirit**. This very same renewal occurs **in the inner man** (2 Cor. 4:16), in the spirit of the mind (Eph. 4:23), through which the old man is taken off and the new put on, **who is renewed for knowledge according to the image of Him who made him** (Col. 3:10).

One would like to apply here what is written in Psa. 103:5 – *renovabitur ut aquilae juventus tua*, **who makes your mouth happy, and you again become young like an eagle.**

From this renewal follows, yea, also pertains to it:

1. The laying aside of the sinful flesh. For to be renewed is nothing else than to lay aside the sinful flesh, that is, to muffle and subdue sin so that it no longer rules and that the flesh no longer controls and has the upper hand.

In Gen. 7:21 all flesh was destroyed in the Flood. This is a type of holy Baptism, which is a spiritual Flood (Psa. 29:10). Through it the flesh is subdued and killed.

In Gen. 17:10 God commands Abraham [to observe the practice of] circumcision. God clipped off the foreskin of the heart through it (Deu. 30:6, Rom. 2:28). Now, circumcision is a type of Baptism, through which the inward, spiritual circumcision occurs in the same manner.

In Exo. 14:28 Pharaoh and all his men drown in the Red Sea so that the children of Israel could safely go through. This signifies Baptism, in which the old Adam with all sin and evil lusts and with a host of vices [*execitu vitiorum*] must go down [perish].

Particularly the verse from Col. 2:11 is relevant here – **In whom** (in Christ) **you also are circumcised with the circumcision without hands through the laying aside of the sinful body of the flesh, namely with the circumcision of Christ.**

2. That we are buried with Christ through Baptism into death; for that is nothing other than that our old man is crucified with Christ, put to death and laid in the grave in and through Baptism, so that the resurrection of the new man (that is, the spiritual resurrection of Christ within us, i.e., renewal) follows.

Rom. 6:3–4, 6 – **Don't you know that all of us who are baptized in Christ are baptized in His death? So we are indeed buried with Him through Baptism in death, so that just as Christ was awakened from the dead through the glory of the Father, so also should we walk in a new life. Since we know that our old man is crucified with Him so that the sinful body perish, that we henceforth no longer serve sin.**

Col. 2:11, 12 – **In whom** (in Christ) **you also are circumcised without hands through the laying aside of the sinful life in the flesh, namely, with the circumcision of Christ, in that you are buried with Him through Baptism, etc.**

3. That the Holy Spirit is given in and through Baptism, whose work is rebirth and renewal (Tit. 3:5 – **Through the bath of rebirth and renewal of the Holy Spirit**). He also is the pledge [deposit] of our inheritance and the seal by which the rebirth, the covenant of God, and the promise of eternal life are sealed into the heart of the one being baptized (2 Cor. 1:21–22, Eph. 1:13–14; 4:30).

Mat. 3:16, Mark 1:10, Luke 3:21, John 1:32: As Christ is baptized, the Holy Spirit travels down upon Him in the form of a dove. Among other things, this signifies that those who thus are baptized should receive the Holy Spirit, though not in such full measure as Christ.

In Acts 2:38 Peter says to his hearers, the Jews – **Repent and let each of you have himself be baptized upon the name of Jesus Christ for the forgiveness of sins. Thus you will receive the gift of the Holy Spirit.**

4. That Christ is put on in holy Baptism. For such takes place not only for rebirth so that we are made to share [in] all His benefits, merits and righteousness, and thus through Him become children of God and heirs of eternal life, but it also takes place for renewal, that He lives in the heart through faith (Eph. 3:17), and lives in us (Gal. 2:20), that is, works the fruits of the Spirit. Thus, this is the new man which we put on (Col 3:10), namely – **heartfelt compassion, friendliness, humility, gentleness, patience, love, etc.,** as it is indeed explained in v. 12 and 14. However, that Christ is put on in such a way not only for rebirth, but also for renewal, St. Paul clearly teaches in Rom. 13:4.

Gal. 3:27 – **As many of you who have been baptized have put on Christ.**

5. That we are taken into God's covenant through

Baptism (1 Pet. 3:21), for this covenant encompasses within itself not only rebirth, but also renewal and sanctification.

Jer. 31:31; 33:34 – **Look! The time is coming, says the Lord, in which I will make a new covenant with the house of Israel and with the house of Judah. This shall be the covenant: I will give My Law into their hearts and write it in their mind** (this is renewal). **I will forgive them their iniquity and never again remember their sin** (this is rebirth).

Eze. 36:25–26 – **I will sprinkle pure water over you so that you will become purified from all your uncleanness** (this is rebirth). **I will give you a new heart and a new spirit, and will take away from your flesh the stony heart and give you a heart of flesh** (this is renewal).

6. In summary: Here pertain all the passages which affirm that we become reborn through Baptism, for rebirth and renewal are indissolubly linked [inextricably intertwined] with one another (Tit. 3:5); that faith is ignited through holy Baptism, for the heart is cleansed through such faith (Acts 15:9) and true faith is active in love (Gal. 5:6); that we become washed from sin through Baptism, for the gift of the Holy Spirit is indissolubly linked with this forgiveness of sins (1 Cor. 6:11); that we become children of God and heirs of eternal life through Baptism, since this also naturally encompasses sanctification, Heb. 12:14 – **Apart from which** (sanctification) **no one will see the Lord**.

Here, again, [is] the apparent contradiction that some are baptized who already are renewed while also others are baptized who definitely are not renewed. Indeed, after being baptized, all are inclusively admonished to renew themselves (Col. 3:10, Eph. 4:23); and it is expressly written in 2 Cor. 4:16 that the inward man be renewed from day to day. From this it would follow that Baptism is not a bath of renewal. ANSWER: To this it is even more appropriate to respond than to the objections in the previous chapter, for 1. Even though there be certain ones who are already renewed, it does not follow that Baptism should not be a bath of renewal for them, since the gifts of the Spirit, and thus also renewal, are effectually increased in it. **2.** Even though some are indeed not renewed through Baptism, nevertheless, that still does not negate Baptism's power to renew; for these very same people resist the gracious workings of the Holy Spirit (as He usually does work through Baptism, and also desires to work in them) through their unbelief, stubborn [deliberate] evil and godlessness, just as the Word of God is not effectual in all who hear it and yet remains a powerfully effectual means through which God desires to renew us. 3. Even though baptized persons are admonished to daily continue in sanctification and renewal, it still does not follow that they should not be renewed and sanctified in holy Baptism; rather, it only follows from this that renewal in holy Baptism is not so totally complete that daily growth and increase is no longer necessary, as will be more fully dealt with later. St. Paul speaks very clearly, 2 Cor. 7:1 – **Since then, dearly beloved, we have such a promise, let us then cleanse ourselves of all splotches of the flesh and of the spirit, in the fear of God.** He teaches with this that daily cleansing and renewal is nothing else than a continuation, a growth, and increase in sanctification; but then, that which is continued must already have begun.

CHAPTER 15

WHAT SORT OF REMINDERS AND MEANINGS ARE PRESENTED TO US IN HOLY BAPTISM.

lthough holy Baptism was instituted by God the Lord chiefly for the reason that it be a bath of rebirth and renewal for eternal life (and thus be regarded as a powerful means and not as a plain [common] sign of heavenly gifts), yet it is not improper to consider the various remembrances and meanings to which Baptism *minus principaliter* [i.e., incidentally] at the same time provides parallels. It is not improper just so long as a person stays under the guidance of the holy Scripture and does not claim that Baptism was instituted solely or chiefly for the sake of such remembrances or claim that the entire essence of and power of Baptism consists of such remembrances and meanings.

1. Baptism reminds us "that the old Adam in us, through daily contrition and repentance, should be drowned and die with all sin and evil lusts, and once more a new man daily come forth and rise up who lives before God forever in righteousness and purity." (Small Catechism) For in the same way, the little baptismal candidate is dipped into the water or is poured upon with water, so that it appears as if one is going to drown him and yet afterward pulls him forth alive; so also should the old man in the baptized and reborn person even more daily drown and be drowned. In contrast, the new man should come to the fore and be in control of [the conduct of] living [one's life].

Rom. 6:3–5 – **Don't you know, that all who like we are baptized in Jesus Christ, are baptized in His death.**

So we indeed are buried with Him through Baptism in death, so that just as Christ did rise from the dead through the glory of the Father, so should we also then walk in a new life. But since we along with Him have been—so to speak—planted to death, so also we shall similarly be resurrected.

Col. 2:12 – **Inasmuch as you have been buried with Him** (Christ) **through Baptism,** etc.

2. That we are washed from sin through holy Baptism. For just as common, natural water usually washes the body from all uncleanness, so also the water in holy Baptism—since it is encompassed in the Word of God and the entire holy Trinity wants to work through the same—is thus a powerful means through which we are washed of all uncleanness of sins and become snow-white. Pertinent here also is that Christ's blood not be locked out [excluded] from holy Baptism. Rather, Christ is present [in Baptism] as God and Man. He actually and certainly sprinkles and washes us with His blood as we are sprinkled with the water.

Eze. 36:25 – **I will sprinkle clean water over you so that you become cleansed of all your uncleanness.**

1 Pet. 1:2 – The chosen ones, etc. **to obedience and for sprinkling with the blood of Christ.**

1 John 1:7 – **The blood of Jesus Christ, His Son** (the Son of God) **makes us clean from all sin.**

Heb. 10:22 – **Thus let us come near with genuine hearts, sprinkled in our hearts,** etc.

3. That we shall finally be delivered from every evil and be made partakers of eternal glory. For just as it appears with the dipping in or pouring upon as if one wanted to drown the little baptismal candidate and yet thereafter pull him out again, so also—even though we indeed must be poured on with a Baptism of crosses and be dipped into the waters of tribulation—God the Lord commits Himself in Baptism that He, in a certain time, will pull us out again and bring us to the glory of everlasting life.

2 Sam. 22:17, Psa. 18:17 – **The Lord pulled me out of huge waters.**

Psa. 32:6 – **When great flood waters came, they did not reach them** (the saints).

Psa. 69:15–16 – **That I was rescued ... out of the deep water. That the water flood did not drown me,** etc.

Psa. 144:7 – **Rescue me from huge waters,** etc.

4. Since God the Lord establishes a covenant of grace with us in Baptism, we are thereby reminded that we, as spiritual warriors in the troops of Christ, are to fight against the devil and all his ways and works. We are not to overstep the charter boundaries of the divine covenant; rather much more, we should campaign to the bloody end and be prepared in direst need to shed our blood for Christ's sake, even as He poured out His blood so that we, in Baptism, might be washed from sin and be taken up into God's covenant.

Here listen to St. Paul in 1 Cor. 1:13 – **Have you been baptized in the name of Paul?** (As if he wanted to say: "You should not label yourselves 'Paulish,' since you have not been baptized unto me; rather, you should call yourselves after Christ, upon whom you have been baptized and into whose covenant you have been taken up.")

1 Pet. 3:21 – Baptism is **a covenant of a good conscience with God through the resurrection of Jesus Christ.** (Since through Baptism we have been taken up into God's covenant and have been enrolled in His spiritual knights, we should also then **practice a good knighthood, that we believe and maintain a good conscience, 1 Tim 1:18–19.**)

5. Since we all have received the same Baptism and no one has a better Baptism than another, this should be an admonition to us for brotherly love and unity, that we should be eager to maintain the unity in the Spirit. Since no one has a better Word or Sacrament than another, and since we also become one spiritual body through Baptism, therefore we should always be unified as members.

1 Cor. 12:13, 20 – **For we are through one Spirit all baptized into one body,** etc. **Now then, the members are many, but the body is one.**

Eph. 4:3, 4, 5 – **Work hard at keeping the unity in the Spirit through the bond of peace. One body and one Spirit, as you also are called upon a single hope of your calling. One Lord, one faith, one Baptism.**

CHAPTER 16

WHAT CONSTITUTES THE WASHING FROM SIN IN HOLY BAPTISM.

 t was demonstrated above in chapters 13 and 14 that Baptism is a powerful [effectual] means for rebirth and renewal. The forgiveness of sins belongs to rebirth; the putting to death of the sinful flesh and the making alive of the spirit applies to renewal. What pertains to rebirth and the forgiveness of sins is that it is totally accomplished, so that **no longer are those condemned who are in Christ Jesus** (Rom. 8:1). But that which pertains to renewal is not so completely accomplished that one no longer needs to be renewed daily. Rather, it is begun in Baptism [and] continues throughout one's entire life as one subdues the activity of the flesh through the Spirit. It will finally be completely accomplished in eternal life. When it is accordingly asked what sort of salutary [wholesome] means and medicine Baptism is against sin, that is to be answered: 1. *Peccatum remittitur in baptismo, ita ut non imputetur*: sin is forgiven in holy Baptism so that it is no longer imputed. 2. *Peccatum et vetus Adam in baptismo mortificatur, ut non regnet*: the sinful flesh or old Adam is put to death so that it no longer rules. But this killing is not constituted in such a way that henceforth the evil lusts are totally obliterated or no longer are considered sinful in [and] of themselves; rather, they no longer rule [dominate].

However, [the fact] that renewal in Baptism is not complete to the point that sin is ripped out of the flesh root and vein, so that it is no longer present, we indicate thusly:

1. After being baptized, the evil lusts or inherited sin

still remains stuck in the flesh of those who are baptized. It is truly sin, even though it is striven against by the power of the Spirit to keep it from breaking out in open, gross sins, a point which will be elaborated on later in its proper place.

Rom. 7:7–9, 18 – **But I did not recognize sin, except through the Law. For I would have known nothing about lust had not the Law said: Do not let yourself lust. But then sin took the command as an excuse to give rise to all kinds of lust in me. For without the Law sin was dead,** etc. **For I know that in me, that is in my flesh, lives nothing good.** (St. Paul obviously was baptized and born again. Nevertheless, he laments that sin resided in his flesh.)

Pertinent here [is] that all saints petition for forgiveness of sins (Psa. 32:6). Christ taught His disciples—who indeed were baptized —to pray: **And forgive us our debts** (Mat. 6:12). **If we say we have no sin, we lead ourselves astray and the truth is not in us,** 1 John 1:8, since evil lust is a sin which continually sticks to us and makes us indolent (Heb. 12:1). Therefore, it is not that sin is expunged in holy Baptism so that it no longer should adhere to the heart; rather, forgiveness consists in this, (*non-imp.*) *imputatione*, that sin is no longer imputed against one.

2. Baptized Christians are admonished that they should strive against the sin in their flesh, and in the Spirit they should daily renew their minds. If, then, sin were root and vein totally eradicated through Baptism, why would it be necessary to be concerned with and battle against it as if it might sprout up again and flourish? Also, why would it be necessary to be daily renewed?

Rom. 6:6, 12, 14 – **Since we know that our old man is crucified with Him** (Christ), **so that the sinful body cease, that we henceforth do not serve sin. ... So then do not let sin have control over your mortal body to carry out its lusts in obedience to sin. ... For sin will not be able to rule over you since you are not under the Law but under grace.**

Rom. 8:12–13 – **So then we are debtors ..., not to the flesh that we live after the flesh. For if you live according to the flesh, you will have to die.**

In 1 Cor. 6:11, St. Paul testifies about the baptized Corinthians that they have been washed off; in 1 Cor. 5:7 he states that they are unleavened and admonishes them at the same time to sweep out the old leaven, and states in 2 Cor. 7:1 that they should cleanse themselves of all spots of the flesh and spirit and proceed with sanctification.

2 Cor. 4:16 – **The inward man is renewed from day to day.**

Eph. 4:23–24 – **But renew yourselves in the spirit of your mind and put on the new man who is created after God in true stewardship of righteousness and holiness.** (Of course, the Ephesians had put on Christ through Baptism no less than the Galatians did (3:27); even so, he admonishes them that they should put on the new man in the same way as he also admonishes the baptized Romans to put on the Lord Christ, Rom. 13:14.)

Col. 3:9–10 – **Take off the old man with his works and put on the new who is renewed in knowledge according to the image of Him who created him.**

3. If sin were completely expunged in Baptism to the point that it no longer exists, how is it that the baptized children sometimes are overtaken with illness, yes, even die soon after being baptized before they come to their years of discretion? Furthermore, from whence do the actual sins of the baptized originate if the inherited sin has indeed been expunged? How would a Christian authority be able to punish a perpetrator upon his converting and letting himself be baptized if indeed sin were uprooted through Baptism? Therefore, it holds true that God remits the sin and the eternal punishment of sin, yet the sin remains stuck in the flesh, and God has reserved for Himself according to His counsel and will to visit temporal punishment upon some certain sins either by Himself or *via* the government.

Rom. 5:14 – **Death ruled from Adam until Moses, also over those who had not sinned with the same transgression as Adam,** etc.

Rom. 6:23 – **Death is sin's wages.**

Rom. 8:10 – **Since however Christ is in you, so the body is indeed dead on account of sin; the spirit, however, is life on account of righteousness.**

4. Children born of reborn [regenerated] parents are no less conceived and born in sin, as was indicated above in chap. 13, point of contention #2, and as will be thoroughly expounded later in its proper sequence and place; but how could that be if in Baptism sin, with all its roots, were eradicated from the reborn parents?

Job 14:4 – **Who will find a clean person among them since they all are unclean** (since they all are sired from unclean seed)?

Psa. 51:7 – **Look, I have been sired from sinful seed and my mother conceived me in sin.**

John 3:6 – **What is born from flesh is flesh,** etc.

Eph. 2:3 – **And** (we) **were also children of wrath from nature, just like also all the others.**

Here, again, [is an] apparent contradiction, that the types and passages which deal with the power of Baptism appear to indicate that sin is totally expunged from the one baptized and is uprooted from its very foundation, just as the sinful flesh is removed through circumcision (Col. 2:11); the sinful people were truly drowned in the Flood and in the Red Sea(Psa. 29:10, 1 Cor. 10:2); Naaman was completely cleansed of his leprosy in the Jordan (2 Kin. 5:14); the sick, blind, lame and gaunt were truly made well in the pool of Bethesda (John 5:4); the man born blind was rescued from all blindness in the pool of Siloam (John 9:7); thus also we were cleansed in Baptism (Eph. 5:26); sin is taken away, expunged, extinguished (Isa. 44:22); that we become white as snow (Psa. 51:9); that there no longer remains any blemish or spot (Song of Songs 4:7, Eph. 5:27). From all these [examples] it appears that sin is totally expunged. ANSWER: **1.** It has been previously clearly indicated that sin continues to remain resident in the flesh of the baptized (Rom. 7:18); that renewal has to increase day by day in the life of the baptized (2 Cor. 4:16). Therefore, one cannot say that sin is completely expunged in Baptism and that renewal is immediately complete. **2.** Accordingly, sin is viewed in two ways. First *ratione materialis*, that is to say, how it is contrary to the Law of God, how it is a corruption of nature, etc.; [and alternately] *ratione formalis seu reatus*, how it makes us guilty of damnation before God. When one speaks of sin *respectu sui formalis*, how it truly makes us guilty of damnation before God, then it is certain that in this regard it is totally forgiven, canceled, washed away and taken away in Baptism so that it is no longer reckoned for damnation to him who strives against it, since there is no longer any condemnation to those who are in Christ Jesus (Rom. 8:1). However, when we speak of sin *ratione materialis*, that is to say, how it is contrary to the Law of God, then the Scripture and the personal experience of each regenerated person testifies that sin still remains in the flesh after Baptism (Rom. 7:23); yet it is no longer as mighty and powerful as before, but, rather, the evil lusts are weakened so that a baptized Christian can strive against them through the Spirit. **3.** When one diligently takes note of this distinction, then one can that much the better understand these quoted Scripture references. For what is stated there—that God cancels, takes away, washes away, cleanses us from, does not remember our sins—all pertains to the *remissionem* or (*non-imp.*) *imputationem peccati* [remission or non-imputation of sins] in which God does not want to impute sin against us; much more would He rather cover us with the grace-mantle of His mercy for the sake of Christ's merits, for that is how the forgiveness of sins is described in Psa. 32:1, 2 – **Blessed is he who is forgiven transgressions, whose sins are covered. Blessed the person to whom the Lord does not impute his misdeeds, etc.** This is what St. Paul indicates and further clarifies in 2 Cor. 5:19 – **God was in Christ and reconciled the world with Himself and did not impute its sin against it,** etc. Since then this (*non-imp.*) *imputio peccati* is so genuine and powerful—as if not a single stain or spot is present throughout, as if the person never did anything evil, as if from now on he is totally pure (note: that is why it is called an expiation, a washing off and taking away of sin)—yet it still remains true that, also after Baptism and the forgiveness of sin, evil lust still resides in the flesh. **4.** For note that St. Paul says in Rom. 8:1 that there is nothing damnable to him who finds himself in Christ Jesus, [in spite of the fact] that he himself most certainly understands and complains, as in the previous chapter (7:17), that sin lives within him. How is this to be resolved? In this manner: Even though sin still resides and rails within the flesh, nevertheless it can no longer condemn reborn people as they confess their indwelling and clinging sin, repent of it, petition for, and hope through Christ for forgiveness, and mightily contend against it so that it [will] no longer rule. Also, St. Paul says in 1 Cor. 5:7 that the Corinthians are unleavened, and yet at the same time admonishes them to sweep out [get rid of] the old leaven. In 1 John 1:7, John says that the blood of Jesus Christ makes us clean of all sin, yet immediately in v. 8 he adds on: **If we say we have no sin we deceive ourselves,** etc. Also Christ says in John 13:10: **Whoever is washed ..., he is totally clean;** and yet next to it is written that such a one must still wash his feet, that is, contend against evil lusts and affections. **5.** Consequently, forgiveness of sins does not consist in this, that God uproots it root and vein; rather, He covers it, does not impute it. Through this forgiveness comes also the slaying of the sinful flesh and the making alive of the spirit, that is, renewal. However, this renewal is not completely fulfilled, as was extensively demonstrated above, because of what is written in Song of Songs 4:7 and Eph. 5:27, that the regenerate have no stain or spot. It is to be understood about any such spots which make one unworthy before God *actu*, in deed, and would [therefore] be reckoned for condemnation, that in eternal life all spots will be completely obliterated [at] the source and taken away.

Whatever further passages and apparent claims are put forth [regarding] that through the forgiveness of sin God the Lord totally uproots sin with all its veins and roots, and that nothing sinful remains in the regenerate so that if God were to deal with them in His strict righteousness He could find nothing of which to impute against them ..., these matters will all be clarified in the Article about Justification, where they actually belong.

CHAPTER 17

WHETHER THE POWER OF HOLY BAPTISM EXTENDS ITSELF THROUGHOUT THE ENTIRE LIFE OF THE PERSON.

lthough there still remain other questions about the power and working of holy Baptism (beside this very one and the others we have already dealt with), nevertheless they do not belong here but rather to the article concerning the holy Sacraments in which the power and working of the same are dealt with in general: [Are] the benefits of the Sacraments *ex opere operato*, solely because of the accomplished action even though there is no faith or new beginning within the heart? In certain Sacraments [is] a *character indelebilis*, a non-extinguishable sign, imprinted onto the soul, and the administration of the same Sacrament need not be repeated because of that [character]? [Are] the Sacraments effectual means of God's grace and the forgiveness of sins or merely outward signs? These questions do not really belong here, since they pertain not only to the power of holy Baptism but to the power of all the Sacraments. Therefore, we will deal here only with this subject: that a baptized Christian has and retains the comfort of his Baptism for his entire life; though he might at times sin, through true repentance he possesses an established recourse to the grace-covenant of God. We prove this as follows:

1. God establishes a covenant of grace with us in holy Baptism and commits Himself that He desires to be our gracious God and Father, as was clearly indicated above in chapter 13, #3. Now, such an everlasting covenant of grace is never completely withdrawn on account of our disobedience; rather, we always have access to it through contrition and repentance.

In Gen. 17:7, God speaks about the covenant of grace in circumcision: **I will establish My covenant between Me and you and your seed who will follow after you, that it be an everlasting covenant,** etc. ([Now that] holy Baptism has come as a replacement for circumcision (Col. 2:11), therefore it must also be an everlasting covenant.)

Exo. 6:5 – **I have remembered My covenant.**

Lev. 26:9 – **I will keep My covenant for you.**

Lev. 26:44 – **They do not disgust Me so ..., that I will no longer keep My covenant with them, for I am the Lord God.**

Num. 18:19 – **This shall be an everlasting, incorruptible covenant before the Lord to you and along with your seed.** (In Hebrew it reads a 'salt' covenant, for just as salt keeps meat from spoiling, so also this covenant will be incorruptible.)

Deu. 4:31 – **God will never forget the covenant that He swore to your fathers.**

Deu. 7:9 – **Thus you shall now know that the Lord your God is a faithful God who faithfully and mercifully keeps His covenant [with] those who love Him and keep His commandments for a thousand generations** (or when they repent after sinning).

1 Kin. 8:23 – **You** (the Lord) **who keep the covenant and compassion for Your servants who live before You with their whole heart.**

2 Kin. 13:23 – **The Lord turned to them for the sake of His covenant with Abraham, Isaac, and Jacob,** etc.

Neh. 1:5 – **O Lord, God from heaven, great and terrifying God, who maintains His covenant [with] and compassion [for] those who love You and keep Your commands...** (In v. 6 [Nehemiah] acknowledges the sin of the Israelites and yet puts his trust in the covenant; therefore, through repentance there is again a return to the covenant of God). [The same idea] is repeated in ch. 9:32 and also in Dan. 9:4.

Isa. 54:10 – **For mountains will give way and hills shall fall down, but My grace shall never give way and the covenant of My peace shall not collapse, says the Lord who has mercy on you.**

Isa. 55:3 – **For I will make an eternal covenant with you, namely the sure grace to David.**

Jer. 32:40 – **I will make an eternal covenant with him.**

Jer. 33:20, 21 – **Thus says the Lord: If My covenant with day and night quits so that day and night no longer come at [the appointed] time, then My covenant with My servant David will also cease,** etc.

Eze. 16:60 – **But I will reflect on My covenant which I made with you during your youth, and I will establish an eternal covenant with you.**

Eze. 37:26 – **I will make a covenant of peace with them which shall be an eternal covenant with them,** etc.

Hos. 2:19 – **I will betroth Myself to you eternally,** etc.

Rom. 3:3, 4 – **Should their** (mankind's) **unbelief negate God's faithfulness? Far from it. Much more it remains so that God is true and men are false,** etc.

Rom. 11:29 – **God cannot regret His gifts and calling.**

2 Tim. 2:13 – **Were we not to believe, yet He remains true. He cannot betray Himself.**

Here [it is pertinent to state] that God again calls back fallen mankind and reminds them that through genuine repentance they should turn around to the covenant of grace.

Jer. 3:12 – **Turn back you rebellious Israel, says the Lord, then I will not set My countenance against you,** etc.

2. Just as the believing Israelites comforted themselves throughout their entire life because of their circumcision, so also may all Christians comfort themselves for the entire time of their lives because of their Baptism. For no less than in circumcision [does] God the Lord establish a covenant of grace with us in Baptism.

1 Sam. 14:6 – **And Jonathan said to his weapons carrier: Come let us go over to the lair of these uncircumcised.** (We are in God's covenant of grace, they are not. Therefore God will help us, etc.)

In 1 Sam. 17:26, 36, David says: **For who is this uncircumcised Philistine who mocks the offspring of the living God? So shall this uncircumcised Philistine now be just like one of them,** etc.

3. The example of believers in the New Testament testifies that their baptismal promise comforted them also after falling into sin, as they were converted back around through true repentance.

The Corinthians were spotted with various sins, yet St. Paul directs them to their Baptism, 1 Cor. 6:11 – **You are washed** (understand, through holy Baptism). 1 Cor. 12:13 – **For we have through one Spirit all been baptized to one Body.** (Herewith the apostle reminds them of their baptismal promise, that they should genuinely turn to God and thus again be taken up into the covenant of grace, etc.)

The Galatians also had no insignificant failures; nevertheless, St. Paul comforts them with their Baptism, Gal. 3:27 – **For as many of you who have been baptized have put on Christ.**

St. Peter had grossly sinned and had denied Christ; nevertheless, after his conversion, he comforted himself with his Baptism, 1 Pet. 3:21 – **Baptism saves us** (he includes himself).

4. Thus the holy Scriptures also speak about the working of Baptism in *präterito, präsenti et futuro* [in the past, present, and future], so that we are taught that the power and working of Baptism [are] not to be seen only in the twinkling-of-an-eye moment [when] we are baptized, but stretch out over an entire lifetime.

Tit. 3:5 – **According to His mercy He did save us through the bath of rebirth** (for thus the *präteritum* is written in the Greek text, by-gone time [past tense]), etc.

1 Pet. 3:21 – **Baptism saves us** (here it speaks in *präsenti*, about the present time [in the present tense]).

Mark 16:16 – **Whoever believes and is baptized will go to heaven** (here it speaks *in futuro*, about the future time [future tense]), etc.

Relevant here is what is written in Rom. 6:3: we are baptized unto Christ's death. On that account, the power of Baptism is based on the death of Christ. Now, however, Christ did not only pay for past, but also for future, sins with His death, 1 John 1:7 – **The blood of Jesus Christ ... makes us clean from all sins.** Therefore, holy Baptism must indeed also be able to give us comfort when we fall into sin. Thus it is written in Tit. 3:5 that Baptism is a bath of renewal; it is begun in Baptism, but it endures for a lifetime.

5. If, however, the power of Baptism did not extend through all of life, it would follow that Christians who fell into sin would have to be regarded as not being baptized; that hypocrites who in Baptism hinder the gracious workings of the Holy Spirit would have to be baptized again; that Baptism [should be] reserved for the final hour of death—and similar additional absurd [conclusions].

Here follow some apparent contradictions:

1. That baptized Christian cannot be damned; they can do anything they want since the covenant of God is eternally established in Baptism. ANSWER: There are two classifications of sins: certain ones occur out of the weakness of the flesh, including the inward evil lusts, sinful thoughts, etc.; others occur out of an evil premeditation and against the witness of conscience. Pertaining to the former sort of sin, such people remain regenerate in this life and do not forfeit the grace of God, for the regenerate daily confess, repent and petition for forgiveness for Christ's sake. They daily strive against lusts through the power of the Spirit.

Daily they become perfected and long for the complete purity of eternal life (Rom. 8:23). Concerning the latter sort of sin, such people may not continue with the grace of God and the indwelling of the Holy Spirit, because if reborn people willingly sin out of premeditation and against conscience, they thereby lose God's grace and break the covenant of their Baptism; yet, from God's [perspective], the covenant of grace established in Baptism is not entirely lifted (Rom. 3:3). Rather, such fallen sinners can again be received into the same through true repentance.

2. That in Heb. 6:4 and 6 it is written: **For it is impossible that those who once were enlightened**, etc. ... **If they fall away** etc. ... **that they should again be renewed unto repentance;** from this it appears to follow that many are locked out from the way of repentance and from the covenant of Baptism after they fall into sin. ANSWER: The apostle is here actually not speaking in general about all sins against conscience, [but] rather about the sin against the Holy Spirit, which will not be forgiven in this or in the future world (Mat. 12:32). The entire context surrounding this text [Hebrews 6] supports this and will be further elaborated upon in its proper place; for he speaks of those **who were once enlightened and have tasted the heavenly gift and became recipients of the Holy Spirit and have tasted the benevolent Word of God and the power of the future world, if they fall away and themselves again crucify the Son of God and hold Him up to scorn,** etc. (v. 4, 5, 6); that is, they again tread against the testimony of their hearts and away from the acknowledged truth. They slander Christ and His Word in opposition to the witness of their own hearts. That, however, is indeed the sin against the Holy Spirit and will not be forgiven—not because, in case they were to repent, God would plainly and simply deny His grace; but rather, because such persons will never more be converted since they reject the means by which the Holy Spirit would convert them.

3. If the covenant which God establishes in holy Baptism is an everlasting covenant, then it must follow that after falling into sin a person need not repent. ANSWER: We, of course, violate the covenant of God on our part [and] thus forfeit the benefits of this covenant, but God on His side remains unmoved. He does not renounce Himself (2 Tim. 2:13). If we are again to become recipients of the benefits of the covenant, then we must genuinely repent, as the entire Scriptures direct fallen Christians to do. This very necessity for repentance after falling into sin does not indicate that God on His side has totally nullified the covenant, but rather, that we on our part have violated the covenant and thus forfeited the benefits of the covenant. Consequently, the urgency is that we approach God through true repentance, preceded by true confession and heartfelt regret over sin, and comfort ourselves with the grace of God and the merits of Christ (of which we became recipients in Baptism), and thus again be assimilated into the covenant.

CHAPTER 18

THAT ONLY LIVING PEOPLE ARE TO BE BAPTIZED.

hus far, all the *causis* of Baptism have been comprehensively dealt with: **1.** Concerning the *causa efficiente*—who instituted holy Baptism? Through whom should and can this holy Sacrament be administered? In case of an emergency, may an ordinary Christian baptize? If Baptism is administered by one culpable in teaching or life, is it a true and effectual Sacrament? Was the Baptism of John just as effective a Sacrament for salvation as the Baptism of Christ's disciples? **2.** Concerning the *materie*, which is the external element in Baptism, namely, natural water; that also this baptismal water is not lowly water, but rather that it is constituted with God's Word. **3.** Concerning the *forma*, [that is], what it actually means to baptize; whether Baptism can also be administered through the pouring on of the water; whether this pouring takes place once or several times; whether just a part of the body can be poured upon, or whether it is necessary that the entire body be drenched. **4.** Concerning the *fine* and the *effectu*, i.e., whether Baptism is a powerful [effectual] means for rebirth [and] whether it is also a means for renewal; what sort of remembrances and meanings are portrayed in holy Baptism. How the forgiving of sins is procured in holy Baptism; whether the power of Baptism extends through the entire life of a Christian. So far all these points have been comprehensively dealt with. Hereupon now follows *objectum baptismi*, [i.e.], who is to be baptized, since here likewise various sorts of questions do arise. First of all, we say that Baptism is for all living persons;

thus, what is not human and, further, is not alive, may not and should not be baptized.

We support this [assertion] as follows:

1. Only people were thought of in the institution of holy Baptism. Therefore, nothing must be cut away from this piece of divine ordinance.

Mat. 28:19: – **Therefore, go out and teach all nations and baptize them,** etc.

2. St. John the Baptizer and the apostle, also others, when they baptized in the first churches, baptized no one but living people.

Mat. 3:5, Mark 1:5, Luke 3:7 – **There went out to him** (John) **the city of Jerusalem and all the lands on the Jordan, and let themselves be baptized;** (that is, all the residents of the city of Jerusalem and the surrounding lands came to his Baptism, as it is declared in Luke 3:7), etc. He baptized publicans (Luke 3:12), soldiers (v. 14), Pharisees and Sadducees (Mat. 3:7). But nowhere will one find that he baptized something other than living people.

The apostles baptized 3,000 souls (that is living people) (Acts 2:41); men and women of Samaria (8:13); Simeon (v. 13), the chamberlain from the land of the Moors (v. 38); Paul (Acts 9:18); many believers from Caesarea (Acts 10:47); Lydia and her entire household (Acts 16:15); the jail master and all his [household] (v. 33); Crispus, his entire household, and many of the Corinthians (Acts 18:8); the household servants of Stephanus (1 Cor. 1:16). But nothing is found that they baptized something other than living people.

3. Just as God has revealed Himself in His Word solely for the sake of people, so also He has instituted the holy Sacraments only for the sake of people; that's why they should be administered wholly and solely for them.

In Gen. 17:12, circumcision is instituted for living people only.

In Exo. 12:4, the Easter lamb [Passover lamb] is instituted for the Israelites only.

In Mat. 26:26, Mark 14:22, Luke 22:19, [and] 1 Cor. 11:23, the Lord's Supper is instituted for living people only. So then, it must also be said about holy Baptism that is was instituted solely for living people and is to be extended only to such.

4. The power and working of holy Baptism pertains only to living people. They alone can become regenerated and renewed—not deceased people, or other things which have neither life nor soul.

From this, it may be concluded that [the following are] not to be baptized:

1. Bells and altars, for they have neither life nor soul. Also, they cannot be reborn or renewed.*

2. Deceased people, for they have already passed on. For Baptism was not instituted for them, nor can they be reborn through it.

3. The children who still are in their mother's womb, for since they have not yet been born into this life naturally, they also cannot be reborn. Nor is it appropriate to baptize pregnant wives with the intention that it will benefit such children who are still enclosed in the womb, since the Sacraments must be extended to each person individually in order to benefit someone. Nor is it adequate that the child might be partially born into this world; rather, the bodily birth must occur completely before the spiritual rebirth ensues: *Non potest quisquam renasci, antequam sit natus.*

4. The same for a monstrosity which does not have human form, but proceeds from a mixing of human and animal species: *ex concubitu bestiali nata.*** It is a totally different situation with such deformed births in which for example a limb is mangled, a limb is missing, or deformed with similar disfigurations.

5. It is also superstitious [practice] that certain feminine coral flax, diapers, or other little cloths are permitted

---

* Such 'Baptisms' the Reformers identified as one of the Papal abuses (e.g. Treatise on the Power and Primacy of the Pope, § 73).

** Whether such births actually occur is another matter. Ed.

to be baptized alongside, with the intention that the same coral, diapers and cloths have imparted to them a special power for good health, for the working and power of Baptism pertains only to people.

Here, again, [are] some apparent points of contention:

1. That just as the baptismal water is an effectual means for rebirth and renewal, so also much more it will possess a power to sanctify the bells and bestow bodily health to people. ANSWER: The power for rebirth and renewal is not somehow secretly and invisibly hidden away in Baptism's water [in the sense that] the power to cool off [refresh] is in rose-water, the power to expel is in carbonated water, the power to cleanse is in common water; rather, the Holy Spirit alone works rebirth and renewal. The water in Baptism is merely a means and instrument with which and through which the Holy Spirit is willing to be effectual. Therefore, it is superstitious that a person use the baptismal water for a different purpose than that for which God has ordained it, or that one ascribe to it a different power than that which is ascribed to it in God's Word, or that one sprinkle other creatures with it for sanctification other than those whom God has commanded us to baptize. If one wants to ascribe to the water of Baptism a unique power apart from God's Word, or if one wants to employ it for a different purpose, then that would be a sin against God's command since He forbids [us] to take His name in vain.

2. That St. Paul says in 1 Cor. 15:29 – **For what are those doing who allow themselves to be baptized on behalf of the dead if above all else the dead do not arise? Why do they allow themselves to be baptized on behalf of the dead?** From this, it appears to follow that in previous times the dead also were baptized. ANSWER: We have to admit that this is a difficult section and that there are differing interpretations over it. **1.** Initially one wants to conclude from this that one should also baptize the dead, just as this was the practice of some in the early Church, which can be perceived from the 3. *concil carthagin* [the Third Council of Carthage]. However, this flies in the face of the reasons already concluded above. It also does not agree with the words of the apostle. For he does not say, since the dead do not arise, why does one baptize the dead, rather: **what are those doing who usually let themselves be baptized** ὑπέρ των νεκρων, **over the dead. 2.** Some have attempted to conclude from this that one may baptize a living person for a dead one, that is, that it redounds to the good and benefit of the dead. But this also contradicts the Scriptures, which testify that the righteous lives [by] his faith (Hab. 2:4, Rom. 1:17, Gal. 3:11, Heb. 10:38). **3.** Some understand it thus: that the practice of baptizing the dead indeed did not please St. Paul, but he used it against them as an argument for the resurrection of the dead, just as one might direct something against someone in a debate, even though one does not himself condone the idea, *dicunt non factum, sed finem facti probari ab apostolo.* This [explanation] also seems to be somewhat forced, for St. Paul permits the custom which he mentions here to remain in its worth or worthlessness; if it had been an erroneous practice, he certainly would have castigated the Corinthians on account of it. **4.** Some understand here that the dead are those who were deathly ill and drawing their last breath, for in former times it was the practice to withhold Baptism until this point so that they not disobey the covenant of Baptism later. Such were called *clinici*, as is apparent from Epiphaneus (*haeres.* 28) and Augustine (*de civit. Dei*, Book 20, Chapter 9). However, this interpretation does not agree very well with the words of the apostle, for he is speaking of those who allow themselves to be baptized over the dead. **5.** Others interpret the words of the apostle with the same usage as of the Jews who formerly washed clean and bathed the bodies of the deceased prior to their being laid to rest in the earth. This custom continued with the Christians in the early church, as is apparent in Acts 9:37. But this also does not make enough of a difference, for St. Paul speaks here not about what those do who baptize the dead or [literally] wash them; rather, he speaks about Baptism over the dead. **6.** Some understand the text simply and generally as St. Paul herewith viewing the end result of holy Baptism: that we are buried along with Christ into His death, so that we also share in His resurrection (Rom. 6:4, 5), as if the apostle should be saying: If the dead do not rise, why do you let yourself be baptized in order that through it the old Adam be killed and you come to share in the resurrection? **7.** But this next answer comes closest to [the meaning of] the text: That the term "the dead" is meant to be understood as [indicating] the bodies of the deceased which are lying in their graves; that St. Paul is here referring to the practice, which was customary in the early church, of the *catechumeni* or newly converted Christians allowing themselves to be baptized in the cemetery over the graves as a witness [to the fact] that they believed in the resurrection of the dead, and as a witness [to the fact] that they were prepared to give up their lives for the Christian religion.

CHAPTER 19

WHICH ADULT PEOPLE ARE TO BE BAPTIZED.

ince all people are either still in their childhood or have since arrived at the age of discretion, the distinction between kinds of persons must be dealt with in order to perceive and know on which people holy Baptism is to be bestowed. As pertaining to adults, we say that men and women are to be baptized without distinction as to Jew or Gentile [and] without distinction as to gender. Yet, we say that they are first to be instructed in the chief parts of the Christian religion and that with their public confession they testify that they adopt the Christian faith. This answer regarding the Baptism of adults encompasses three parts:

First, that Baptism in the New Testament is no longer solely for the Jews, but is also instituted for the Gentiles, which we demonstrate [as follows]:

1. From the institution of holy Baptism, for there Christ specifically has the Gentiles in mind.

Mat. 28:19 – **Therefore go forth and teach all nations and baptize them** (as if He wanted to say [that] until now John, and you along with him, have baptized in the land of the Jews. From now on go into all the world, teach, and baptize all who will receive your Word, be they Jews or Gentiles), etc.

2. From the example of the apostles who, without distinction, baptized Jews and Gentiles after Christ's ascension.

In Acts 2:38–45, three thousand are baptized at one time. (St. Peter did not precisely ask whether there were also some Gentiles among them on that occasion, even though most of them—though not all—were Jews.)

In Acts 8:12, the Samaritans are baptized; in v. 13 Simon; in v. 38, the chamberlain from the land of the Moors; in Acts 10:48, those from Caesarea; in 16:15, Lydia and her household; in v. 33, the master jailer in Philippi and all his [household]; in 18:8, Crispus, his household, and many Corinthians; in 1 Cor. 1:16, Crispus, Gaius, Stephanus' household; in 1 Cor. 12:13, the Corinthians; in Gal. 3:27, the Galatians; etc. (But these were all descendants of Gentiles.)

3. Since the Gentiles are called into the kingdom of Christ and the distinction between Jews and Gentiles has from [then] on been lifted in the New Testament.

Rom. 10:12 – **There is no difference here between Jews and Gentiles; there is simultaneously one Lord for all,** etc.

1 Cor. 1:24 – **To those, however, who are called, both Jews and Greeks, we preach Christ,** etc.

Gal. 3:28: **Here there is no Jew nor Greek,** etc., **for you are altogether one in Christ Jesus.**

Eph. 2:14–15 – **He** (Christ) **is our Peace, who out of both made one and broke down the fence which was in between, in that He through His flesh removed the enmity—namely the Law—which was undergirded with regulations,** etc.

Here are pertinent all the passages of the Old and New Testament which deal with and proclaim the calling of the Gentiles. (At the proper place this [subject] will be dealt with more fully.) For since the Gentiles have been called to the fellowship of the kingdom of Christ and to its heavenly blessings, they must not be excluded from the Sacraments of the New Testament.

Here again is an apparent conflict, that circumcision was commanded for the Jews in times past: I will establish a covenant with you and with your seed after you, God says to Abraham in Gen. 17:10; therefore, holy Baptism—which came to replace circumcision (Col. 2:11)—also applies only to the Jews. ANSWER: Even though God's covenant of grace in the circumcision applied principally to the Jews, yet the Gentiles were never excluded from it if they were willing to receive circumcision. In Exo. 12:48–49 God makes the following ordinance: **If a stranger resides beside you and desires to observe the Lord's Passover, he shall circumcise every male, then let him prepare,** etc. **The same Law applies to the indigenous resident and to the foreigner who lives among you.** This [passage] testifies as an example that those in the Old Testament who converted to the true God of Israel and received circumcision were not few in number. How much more now shall not the difference between Jews and Gentiles in the New Testament be totally removed, since the fence or the wall of separation is completely broken down through Christ's death, and since from now on the common calling has gone out to all the Gentiles in the entire world—as was previously demonstrated. Accordingly, St. Paul explains it magnificently (Rom. 9), that not all who are from Israel and are children according to the flesh are true Israelites, that is, are not children of God; rather, the children of promise are counted as the seed (vv. 6, 7, 8, etc.). For that reason, then, the Jews are broken off through their unbelief (Rom. 11:20), [whereas] the Gentiles—who were wild olive trees—have been grafted into, and made participants in, the root and sap of the olive tree beneath them (v. 17).

The second part of the answer consists in this, that men and women are to be baptized in the New Testament without distinction of sex, a [position] which we prove as follows:

1. From the institution of Christ, who commanded without distinction that all Gentiles are to be baptized as they are simply taught and confess Christ. Consequently women are not excluded.

Mat. 28:19 – **Therefore go forth and teach all nations and baptize them,** etc.

2. Since St. John and the holy apostles baptized male and female persons without distinction.

Mat. 3:5, Mark 1:5 – **There went out to him** (John) **the city of Jerusalem and the entire land of Judah, and all the lands by the Jordan** (that is, all people, as it is clarified in Luke 3:7 [and] 7:29, without a doubt including also women).

In Acts 2:41, three thousand souls were baptized; in Acts 8:12, men and women of Samaria; in Acts 16:15, Lydia, the seller of purple, and her entire household; in v. 33, the master jailer and all his [household]; in Acts 18:8, Crispus and his entire household and many of the Corinthians; in 1 Cor. 1:16, the household of Stephanus, all were baptized.

3. Since St. Paul expressly testifies that men and women are to be baptized without distinction in the New Testament.

Gal. 3:27–28 – **For as many of you who have been baptized have put on Christ. Here is no Jew nor Greek, here is no slave nor free-born citizen, here is no man nor woman, for you are altogether** [totally] **one in Christ Jesus.**

4. Since it is commonly written that Christ cleanses His fellowship or Church through Baptism. But then, also women belong to Christian churches, 1 Pet. 3:7 – **As joint heirs of the grace of life.**

Eph. 4:5 – **One Lord, one faith, one Baptism** (Those who confess and call upon one Lord, hold one confession of faith, [and] should also be washed with one Baptism).

Eph. 5:25–26 – **Just as Christ also loved the fellowship** [Church] ... **and has cleansed her through the water bath in the Word.**

[It is pertinent to note here] that women are just as much in need of this blessed bath as are the men, since they are born **flesh of flesh** (John 3:6). If everything that pertains to the essential elements of Baptism happens for them [women], they too are not excluded from the grace of rebirth and renewal; hence, Baptism, which is the means thereto, should also not be denied them.

Here, again, [are] some apparent points of contention: that circumcision in the Old Testament was instituted only for the boys and men (Gen. 17:10); but now holy Baptism has taken the place of circumcision (Col. 2:16). ANSWER: **1.** The institution of circumcision was expressly intended for the little boys (Gen. 17:10, 12, 14); consequently the women are excluded. However, everyone in general is commanded to be baptized in the institution of Baptism. **2.** This distinction between men and women is lifted in the New Testament, as far as it pertains to holy Baptism (Gal. 3:28). **3.** Also the essential [procedures] of circumcision do not take place for women, but the essential elements of Baptism present a different circumstance. **4.** Even though the women of the Old Testament did not receive this Sacrament upon their own flesh, nevertheless they were not excluded from God's covenant of grace; rather, they benefited from it because the men among them were circumcised (Gen. 17:7–9).

The third part of the answer about the question of baptizing adults requires that, prior to being baptized, all adults, of necessity, must first be instructed in the Christian religion and openly confess that they are devoted to it from the heart. This we demonstrate:

1. From the institution of Christ, which commands first to teach and then to baptize.

Mat. 28:19 – **Therefore go forth and teach all nations and baptize them**, etc.

Mark 16:15–16 – **Go into all the world and preach the Gospel to all creatures. Whoever believes and is baptized will be saved.**

2. From the example of St. John and the apostles, who always first taught their hearers and thereafter baptized them.

Mat. 3:1, 2, Luke 3:3 – **At that time came John the Baptizer and preached in the wilderness of the Judean** land and said: Repent, etc. (after this it first occurred that he baptized).

In Acts 2:38, Peter first preaches repentance before he baptizes the three thousand souls.

In Acts 8:12, the Samaritans were first preached to, after [which] they were baptized.

In Acts 8:13, Simon first becomes a believer, then he lets himself be baptized.

In Acts 8:38, as the chamberlain wanted to be baptized, Philip first asked him if he believed with his whole heart.

In Acts 9:17, Paul is first instructed by Ananias, and then baptized.

In Acts 10:44–47 the believers in Caesarea listen to the Word, then they are baptized.

In Acts 16: 14–15, Lydia first listens to the Word, then she is baptized.

In Acts 16:32–33, the master jailer in Philippi and his household are first told the Word of the Lord, then they become baptized.

In Acts 18:8, the Corinthians who become baptized first become believers through the Word.

3. [According to] the type of circumcision, even as Abraham first instructed the adults in his home concerning the meaning of this ceremony, so also adults must first be instructed before they become sprinkled with holy Baptism.

Gen. 18:19 – **For I know** (says God about Abraham)**, he will command his children and his house after him that they hold to the ways of the Lord and do what is right and good,** etc.

Even more so, God commands that they should instruct their grown-up children about the Sacrament of the Passover lamb and in its significance, Exo. 12:26, 27 – **And when your children will say to you: What sort of service do you have there? You shall say: It is the Paschal-Offering of the Lord who passed over the Children of Israel in Egypt, in which He plagued the Egyptians and rescued our homes.**

4. From the example of proclaiming the divine Word, [we note that just as] one should no longer preach the Word to those who slander it and [reject] it, even less should one offer the holy Sacraments to them against their will.

Mat. 7:6 – **You should not give something sacred to the dogs, and your pearls you should not hurl in front of the sows.**

Mat. 10:14 – **And wherever someone won't accept you nor listen to your discourse, then go out from their homes or cities and shake the dust from your feet.** This [directive] is repeated in Mark 6:11 [and] Luke 9:5.

In Acts 13:46, 51, Paul and Barnabas say to the Jews – **The Word of God had to be first spoken to you; but now that you have pushed it from you and regard yourself unworthy of eternal life, see then that we turn ourselves to the Gentiles. They, however, shook the dust from their feet on account of them, etc.**

Here, again, [are] apparent points of contention:

1. That in Mark 1:4 it says – **John, who was in the wilderness, baptized and preached about Baptism and repentance;** from this it appears to follow that John baptized first and thereafter preached. ANSWER: **1.** Who would let himself be baptized by John if he were not first instructed concerning the reason for this new ceremony of Baptism? **2.** That's why we say that St. Mark was not even considering the order here—whether John taught first or baptized first; rather, he wanted to describe the entire ministry or official function of John. **3.** The evangelist Mark is an *abbreviator Matthäi*. He briefly formulated what Matthew described with detail and comprehension. But Matthew clearly testifies that John first proclaimed and thereafter baptized. **4.** The evangelist Luke expressly indicates that he desired to write in an orderly fashion the history of the New Testament (Luke 1:3). But, in the same way he testifies that John preached first, thereafter he baptized (Luke 3:3, 7, 12).

2. That God the Lord wants that all men be helped (1 Tim. 2:4); thus it apparently follows that everyone is to be baptized without distinction and without stipulation. ANSWER: It is indeed God's most sincere intention that all men be helped to salvation. But He does not simply desire such apart from all means, but rather with the stipulation that they turn to Him. Consequently it is stated to that end in the apostolic verselet: **Who** (God) **desires that all men be helped and that they come to the knowledge of the truth.** God the Lord wants to bring [a person] to such a knowledge of the truth through the Word and the holy Sacraments in conjunction with the operative power of the Holy Spirit. Those who then deliberately despise this counsel of God on behalf of their salvation (Luke 7:30), and strive against the Holy Spirit (Acts 7:51), God does not want to make them saved against their will or pull them up to heaven by their hair. Indeed, He would rather punish those who despise His grace with the loss of His Word and Sacraments. For just as one should not toss pearls and sacred things before those who are like dogs and sows (Mat. 7:6), but [should] commit [such people] to the righteous judgment of God (since God is not pleased by a service done unwillingly), so also it might not please Him that one make people partake of the Sacraments through coercion.

CHAPTER 20

THAT THE LITTLE MINOR CHILDREN ARE CERTAINLY NOT TO BE EXCLUDED FROM HOLY BAPTISM.

he Sacrament of holy Baptism is instituted not only for adults who can publicly make confession, but also for the little minor children who most certainly are not to be excluded from this Sacrament. (However, what sort of children may and should be baptized will be clarified later in various chapters. For now, we want to show that the little minor children are to be baptized.)

1. Such, of course, becomes apparent from Christ's institution, where He generally commands Baptism of the Gentiles; yes, He even adds the word "all" to indicate that no distinction as to nationality, gender, or age is to be observed in offering Baptism. Rather, the children may and should also be baptized if the parents believe. The apostles demonstrate this in that they baptized believers along with their entire household.

Mat. 28:19 – **Therefore go forth and teach all nations and baptize them**, etc.

2. Children are no less in need of holy Baptism than the adults; indeed, children need it more than the older folks, for one can deal with them [adults] through the proclamation of the divine Word. The children, however, cannot be washed of the inherited sin into which they are born through any other means (under normal circumstances) than through holy Baptism.

John 3:5–6 – **Unless someone is born out of the water and Spirit, he cannot come into the kingdom of**

God. **What is born from flesh, that is flesh, and what is born from the Spirit, that is Spirit.** (The children are flesh born from flesh; if they are to enter eternal life, they must be born again. But there is no other means for rebirth than holy Baptism. The Word of God is also a means for rebirth, but God deals through it only with the adults, with the informed.)

Here are pertinent all the passages about inherited sin: that the children are conceived and born in sin (Psa. 51:7) out of unclean seed (Job 14:4); that sin rules over them, even though they have not yet committed actual sins (Rom. 5:14), since they are by nature children of wrath (Eph. 2:3). In this extreme calamity (misery and distress) they either have to remain eternally, or simply and solely be rescued from it through holy Baptism.

3. God the Lord commanded to bring also the children to Him and has promised He wants also to be the God of our seed and graciously to receive the children thus brought to Him.

Gen. 17:7 – **So that I be your God and your seed after you** (not merely to that end without any means, but rather when the *sacramentum initiationi* [*sacrament of initiation*]—circumcision in the Old Testament and Baptism in the New—is performed upon our seed or children. Therefore, it is immediately stated in v. 10 – **This however is My covenant: ... all who are male among you shall be circumcised).**

Mat. 18:14 – **So also it is not the desire of your Father in heaven that any of these little ones be lost.**

Mat. 19:13–15 – **Children were brought to Him** (Christ), **that He lay hands on them and pray. The disciples, however, renounced them. But Jesus said: allow the children, and restrain them not, to come to Me, for such are the kingdom of God. And [He] laid the hands on them and moved away from there.** In Mark 10:14 [and] Luke 18:16, this is further recounted and elaborated upon: **Truly I say to you: whoever does not receive the**

kingdom of God as a child, he will not come into it (these children are called τα Βρέφη [Luke 18:15], that is, young little children who were also brought or carried to the Lord Christ, προσέφερον αὐτῶ [Mark 10:14]. Therefore, without any doubt, these were tiny, under-aged children whom Christ wants to have brought to Him. One is not to exclude such from Baptism in the New Testament any more than such were excluded from circumcision [in the Old Testament]. The motive is this: If a person excluded a child in the Old Testament from circumcision, then one would simultaneously have excluded him from God's grace, which is apparent from Gen. 17:14; so also, if a child in the New Testament were to be excluded from Baptism, he would be excluded from Christ and His grace at the same time, [John 3:5].).*

Acts 2:38, 39 – **Repent and each one of you let yourself be baptized upon the name Jesus Christ, etc. For the promise is yours and your children's, and all who are far off, whom God will call.** (Upon those to whom the promise is extended, the same are to be received into God's covenant through Baptism. But then, the promise is extended not only to the adults, but also to their children. Hence, the children of the believers are also to be baptized. And it is to be noted that the same promise St. Peter is calling to mind here was commonly remembered in reference to the "seed," under which was included also the minor children as they were received into God's covenant through circumcision in the Old Testament. Peter wishes to say: So also the minor children in the New Testament are to be received into the covenant through Baptism.)

4. Since the little children have access to all the boon and blessings of holy Baptism, therefore they should also not be denied Baptism.

In Tit. 3:5, Baptism is a bath of rebirth and renewal of the Holy Spirit. (So then, all those who are born into this

---

* The word *ausschliessen* translated "to exclude" literally means "to lock out."

world can now be reborn out of water and Spirit, John 3:5.)

Relevant here are all the passages which speak of the efficacy and working of holy Baptism, as they are cited above in chapters 13 and 14: how the Holy Spirit works faith through Baptism; forgives sin; receives us into the covenant of grace; cloaks us with Christ's righteousness; makes us children of God and heirs of eternal life; [and] further, that the Holy Spirit renews us through Baptism. These blessings are also completely necessary for little children and since God the Lord commits Himself in His Word to the end that He desires to work this also in little children, one should not withhold from them the means which God the Lord has ordained for that [purpose].

5. The types and prophecies of the Old Testament demonstrate that children are not to be excluded from Baptism.

In Gen. 17:12, God also commands boys only eight days old to be circumcised. (Now then, in the New Testament Baptism has come in its place, Col. 2:11; as certain children were received into God's covenant through circumcision, so also now these [are received] through holy Baptism.)

In Exo. 14:22, the children of Israel go through the Red Sea. This passage is a type of holy Baptism (1 Cor. 10:2); at that time there were many children among the people of Israel. Exo. 12:37 – **Six hundred thousand men on foot, not counting the children.**

Isa. 49:22 – **So shall they** (the people) **bring your sons here in their arms and carry your daughters here upon their shoulders.**

6. It was also the practice of the apostles that when a head of house became a believer, the entire household was baptized—in which households, without a doubt, there were children.

In Acts 16:15, Lydia and her entire household are baptized.

In Acts 16:33, the head jailer lets himself be baptized and all of his [household] along with him.

In 1 Cor. 1:16, St. Paul baptized the household of Stephanus.

7. Since holy Baptism is such a water bath in the Word through which each and every member of the Church should and can be cleansed from sin, it would follow either that the children are not to become members of the Church, or that if they are [to become members], that Baptism is not to be denied them.

Eph. 5:25, 26, 27 – **Just as Christ also did love the fellowship and did give Himself for her in order to sanctify her and has cleansed her through the water bath in the Word, in order that He might present her to Himself as a fellowship which is glorious,** etc. (Which Christ loved and for which He gave Himself into death. He also wants to cleanse her through the water bath in the Word, i.e., through Baptism, so that she becomes a recipient of the very same merits which He won for her through His death. Now then, Christ did not only love and give Himself into death for adults, but also for the little children. Therefore the little children must also be baptized.)

Here belong also other passages which in general speak about Baptism.

1 Cor. 12:13 – **Through one Spirit we have all been baptized to one Body,** etc.

Gal. 3:27 – **For as many of you who are baptized, you have put on Christ.**

In 1 Pet. 3:21 Baptism saves us. (Whoever wanted to survive the Flood had to go into the ark. Thus, whoever wants to be preserved for salvation has to be baptized.)

Here, again, many points of contention are brought forth, such as:

1. That one does not have a divine command that children are to be baptized. ANSWER: [It is] true that the specific word to baptize "children" is not written in the Scriptures, but the Baptism of children can be shown from the Scriptures with good, verifiable proof, which actually has already been done. It is especially proper on this question to take note of the following three hypotheses: first, that the children are conceived and born in sin and are by nature children of wrath; for another, that God the Lord has no desire that they perish; rather, He wants them brought to Him; third, that no other means exists through which children can be reborn to eternal life, except, of course, Baptism. If these three points can be shown from divine Scripture, as [they] easily and thoroughly can be, then it follows from having no other means that the children are to be baptized. Indeed, nowhere is it specifically written in the Scriptures, according to the letter, that women are to be baptized, but one can on good grounds conclude it from the Scriptures. Indeed, the same proofs which lead to the conclusion that women are to be baptized also [support] the Baptism of children.

2. That Christ first commands to teach and thereafter to baptize (Mat. 28:19); but now, [since] children cannot be taught and instructed, one should not baptize them. ANSWER: Christ is here above all speaking of a situation where a new Church is to be established, as the holy apostles at that time were sent with Baptism to the entire world, and so also to the Gentiles who knew less than nothing about this Sacrament; in such a situation, teaching and instruction obviously must precede it. But since the holy apostles baptized the entire household when the head of house became a believer, thereby providing an interpretation of this command of Christ, so should we also do, and baptize, along with believing parents, their children. This can be demonstrated with the type of circumcision. As God commanded Abraham in Gen. 17:10 to circumcise all males in his household, there is no doubt that Abraham first instructed the adult males about it; however, when his son Isaac was born, he did not wait until Isaac attained the age of discretion; rather, he circumcised him as soon as he was eight days old (Gen. 21:4). Beyond that, it stands written in the Greek text μαθητεύσατε, [that is], "make Me disciples."

Such does not take place only through the proclamation of the divine Word, but also through holy Baptism, since it is the *sacramentum initiationis*, the door to God's Church; just as Christ directly establishes both of these means for this: Go into all the world, [and] make disciples; [in other words] gather to Me a Church. By what means? **1.** Baptize **2.** Teach them to keep what I have commanded you.

3. That Christ, in John 3:5 – **Unless then one is born out of water and the Spirit, he cannot come into the kingdom of God**—is referring only to adults because He is speaking with Nicodemus, himself an old man; therefore, this [statement] may not be applied to children. ANSWER: Christ is speaking here in general about all people and testifies that they all need rebirth if they are to be saved. This is not only evident from the tone of these words, where Christ says in general: **Unless one becomes born of the water and Spirit, he cannot come into the kingdom of God,** but also from the subsequent words, where Christ adds: **What is born from flesh, that is flesh**, as if He wanted to say: This is the reason that indeed all mankind needs to be reborn by the water and the Spirit, since by nature [all] are born flesh from flesh. That is why heaven is closed to them (1 Cor. 15:50 – **Flesh and blood cannot inherit the kingdom of God**), unless they are born again from the Holy Spirit through Baptism. Who would then say that these words, "what is born from flesh, that is flesh," do not apply to little children? Since it is never as an adult, but as a little child, that one is born flesh of flesh, therefore what Christ says in the foregoing verse: **Unless one is born from the water and Spirit, he cannot come into the kingdom of God**, must indeed be applied to little children.

4. That the children of believing parents are holy and pure; therefore, they do not first have to be washed from sin in Baptism. ANSWER: That all mankind is conceived and born in sin should have become clear as sunshine already from the exposition under the topic of inherited sin. What pertains to the children who are born of believing parents will be dealt with later in a special chapter and it will be shown that they are children of wrath no less than others (Eph. 2:3); no less conceived from unclean seed (Job 14:4); no less conceived and born in sin (Psa. 51:7). Therefore, it is of necessity that they become reborn through holy Baptism if they are to enter the kingdom of God. Note above what has already been dealt with about this in Chapter 13, Point of Contention #2.

5. That the children who were brought to Jesus in Mat. 19:13, Mark 10:14, and Luke 18:15 were actually grown up and, furthermore, had already been circumcised on the eighth day. Therefore, one cannot prove from this that our under-age children are to be baptized. ANSWER: **1.** St. Luke calls these children τα Βρέφη in ch. 18:15. In the holy Scriptures, this Greek word at all times defines a delicate, under-aged, and (most of the time) suckling [nursing] child. In Luke 1:41, 44, the fetal child in its mother's uterus is called Βρέφος; in Luke 2:12 and 16, a Child lying in a manger is also called thus; in Acts 7:19, the Israelites, when first born, are called Βρέφη; and in 1 Pet. 2:2, as newly born children [are called] ὡς ἀρτινέννητα Βρέφη. Moreover, the evangelists testify that these children were brought to the Lord Christ, or were carried to Him in arms; consequently, they could not have been very big. **2.** What pertains to these children having been circumcised must not present a hindrance in the light of this command and promise of Christ to our bringing our children to Him through Baptism. For we conclude the following: Since Christ commands in general that the children are to be brought to Him, and since He also promises that He wants to receive them and bless them, the children most certainly must not be denied Baptism, since it is the only means through which they may be brought to the Lord Christ.

6. That circumcision had to take place precisely on the eighth day (Gen. 17:12). So then, since it may be shown that children in the New Testament are to be baptized from the fact that children in the Old Testament were circumcised, it must then follow that they should also be baptized precisely on the eighth day. ANSWER: There is a marked distinction here, for God the Lord expressly ordained that the children had to be circumcised precisely on the eighth day; and with good reason, so that perhaps the delicate children not die from pain during the circumcision. However, such danger does not exist in the Baptism of the New Testament, so Baptism is not precisely tied to a particular day. Hence, one makes reasonable haste with his children to this valuable saving means of rebirth, and it remains irrefutably true that just as the children in the Old Testament were received into God's covenant through circumcision, so also the children in the New Testament are received [into] God's covenant through holy Baptism, if they are otherwise to be reborn to eternal life. There is one Founder of circumcision and Baptism. There is the same necessity and the same effect in both Sacraments. Therefore, just as the children back then were not excluded from circumcision, no less are the children here in the New Testament to be excluded from Baptism; otherwise the grace of God in the New Testament would be more intensely restricted than in the Old.

7. That the Lord Christ was baptized when He was thirty years old in Mat. 3:16, Luke 3:21 etc.; and now Christ is portrayed for us as our example to follow, that we are to learn from Him (Mat. 11:29) and that we follow after Him (Mat. 16:24). From this it must follow that we ought to defer Baptism until we are older. ANSWER: **1.** Christ was baptized when He was about 30 years old. From this it would follow that were Christ prescribing a regulation for us with this example, then one should let himself be baptized at age 30, and not as soon as he reaches the age of adult discretion. **2.** Christ was obviously not baptized in childhood because at that time the Sacrament of Baptism had not yet been instituted, in that John, who was the first baptizer, had not begun baptizing much before the time Christ actually began to preach.

3. What's more, Christ was immediately circumcised in His youth, but now Baptism has come to replace circumcision (Col. 2:11). **4.** Christ did not need to be baptized for His own Person since He was totally holy and pure; rather, He let Himself be baptized in order to sanctify our Baptism and to make it a blessed bath for rebirth. But the little children are conceived and born in sin. Therefore, one should hasten to baptize them so that, as far as it depends on us, we do not deprive them of their rebirth and salvation. **5.** All of Christ's words and deeds are, of course, presented for our learning; yet, we should not follow all of His examples without distinction, since at times that would be impossible [and] also because at times we lack the reason for doing a particular thing Christ did and performed. **6.** The holy apostles baptized the entire household of believing heads-of-households, as was briefly indicated previously; but who could believe that all of those were over thirty years of age?

    8. The holy Sacraments are of no benefit without faith. Little children do not believe since they cannot hear the Word of God or understand it (Rom. 10:17). Hence, also Baptism does not benefit them. ANSWER: Although by nature the little children do not believe, yet God wants to awaken faith in them through the Sacrament of holy Baptism, since faith is also a blessing which others receive from this holy Sacrament, as was indicated above. Therefore we turn this last [point] around: children do not believe or understand of themselves according to their corrupted nature, and so they must be brought to Baptism if they are to believe and be saved. The Word of God does not help the hearers if they do not believe (Heb. 4:2); and yet it is an effectual means through which God wants to work faith (John 17:20 [and] Rom. 10:17), and understanding in the hearts of those who do not deliberately strive against the Holy Spirit (Acts 7:51). Further, the Sacrament of holy Baptism avails nothing without faith; yet it is an effectual means through which God the Lord desires to work faith, rebirth, forgiveness of sins and salvation in all those who do not deliberately strive against this sanctification, as was indicated above in chapter 13. But whether it can be said of baptized children, that they can in no way believe, this matter will be exhaustively dealt with later.

9. God establishes a covenant of grace with us in holy Baptism (1 Pet. 3:21). Now then, it is required for a covenant that both participating parties know what is contained in it and that promises are made by both sides. Consequently, since the children do not understand the terms of this covenant, they should also not be baptized. ANSWER: **1.** Was not circumcision likewise a covenant of God (Gen. 17:10)? Likewise the lads, even though only eight days old, were circumcised. In the same way, one could say that since they did not understand the covenant of God one should also not have circumcised them. **2.** It is necessary, of course, with human beings that when a covenant is established, each part is well understood and each article is willingly agreed to. However, God the Lord occasionally establishes His covenant with mindless creatures, [to wit], Gen. 9:9–10 – **Behold** (God says to Noah and his sons) **I establish a covenant with you and with your seed after you, and with all living animals beside you, with birds, with cattle and all living creatures upon earth with you, with all that went into the ark, with all kinds of creatures that are on the earth.** So then, if God can establish His covenant with mindless creatures, how much more can He do that with under-aged children in whom, even though they do not yet use their reason, the Holy Spirit is nevertheless effectual, regenerates and renews them, as will be shown later on. **3.** Not to mention additionally that at times, also among human beings, covenants are established with minor children which are ratified on their behalf by their parents or guardians; so Christ is the advocate for the little children in the same way (1 John 2:1). He expressly says: **Let the little children come to me and detain them not, for such are the kingdom of**

God (Mat. 19:14, Mark 10:14, Luke 18:16). What Christ has long ago answered on behalf of the little children, sponsors repeat at Baptism in the same manner. (More on this later.)

CHAPTER 21

THAT ONLY CHILDREN OF CHRISTIAN PARENTS ARE TO BE BAPTIZED.

hat has been said up to now, that also little children are to be baptized, should not be understood to mean that all children are to be indiscriminately baptized. Rather, it is appropriate only that the children of Christian parents come to holy Baptism.

Under the designation "children of Christian parents" is to be understood:

1. Those who are born from Christian parents where both father and mother are members of the Christian Church; that is, they confess the Christian religion, hear the Word and use the Sacraments, even if at times they might not truly believe and be in the household of the elect.

In Gen. 17:7, God promises that He wants to be the God of Abraham and his seed. (On the strength of this promise Abraham not only circumcised Ishmael, who was only thirteen years old [v. 25], but thereafter also Isaac, when he was only eight days old [Gen. 21:4]. Also, in the New Testament, we Christians are no longer strangers to the testament of promise [Eph. 2:12]; rather, we have come near [to it] [v. 13]. Hence, the same promise applies also to us and, on the strength of the same, we may, and should, not only have our grown children baptized, but also the small, minor children, since God promises He wants to be the God of our seed.)

Acts 2:38–39 – **Repent and each of you let yourselves be baptized upon the name Jesus Christ**, etc. **For this promise is yours and your children's.** (It is to be noted here that St. Peter concludes from this that the Jews should let themselves be baptized since the promise applies to them and their children. It also follows that since Christians in the New Testament likewise became recipients of this promise that their children, too, should and may be baptized.)

Acts 3:25 – **You are the children of the prophets and the covenant which God made with your fathers,** etc.

1 Cor. 5:12 – **For what concern to me are those on the outside, that I should judge them?** (Here St. Paul makes a distinction between those who are in the Church and those who are outside the Church of God. Those who are in the Church, along with their children, receive not only the Word, but also the Sacraments, as special blessings of the Church. But concerning those who are on the outside, who were not born into the lap of the Church, he says: **For what concern to me are those on the outside, that I should judge them? —But God will judge those who are on the outside,** etc. [v. 13].)

1 Cor. 7:14 – **For the unbelieving husband is sanctified through the wife, and the unbelieving wife becomes sanctified through the husband; otherwise your children would be unclean, but now they are holy.** (This sanctification of the children born of Christian parents is not just a worldly purity, as if only children born of Christian parents were to be regarded as legitimately and honorably born, as opposed to heathen and unbelieving children as unrighteous, since also outside God's Church the distinction was made between the legitimately born and bastards. Nor is it an inner holiness of heart and spirit, as if the children of believing parents were holy and regenerate already from the mother's womb, since they are conceived and born in sin no less than others. Rather, this is a *sanctitas ecclesiastica*, an ecclesiastical holiness; that, namely, such children are to be regarded as clean even though only one of the parents is a Christian and the other is an unbeliever. In other words, they are to be regarded as having been born within the Church and thus having an access to holy Baptism as the *sacramento initiationis*. The others, however, who are born

of such parents who are both unbelievers, are to be regarded as unclean, that is, the promise of God does not apply to them: I will be your God and the God of your seed. Therefore, they cannot be permitted to be baptized the same as the children of Christians; rather, they must first, when they are grown, be instructed and confess their faith. Apparently, however, in a manner of speaking, the children of believers were [designated] as clean and the children of unbelievers as unclean, taking a cue from the Levitical Law, where certain ones had to remain outside the Israelite camp because of their uncleanness. So, then, the children of non-Christians are not to be immediately received into the Christian Church—of which the Israelite camp was a type—through holy Baptism. Rather, they are first to be instructed.)

Eph. 2:11–14 – **Think about this, that you, while you still were Gentiles** [heathen] **according to the flesh and were called uncircumcised, etc. That you were at the same time without Christ, strangers and outcasts from the citizenship of Israel and alien to the testament of promise. Thus you had no hope and were without God in the world. Now, however, you who are in Christ Jesus and once were distant have now become near through the blood of Christ. For He is our peace, who made one out of both and broke down the fence that was in between.** (Since in the New Testament the distinction between Jew and Gentile has from now on been lifted, so also from now on the children of believing Gentiles are included in the promise in which God the Lord says: I will be your God and the God of your seed.)

2. Accordingly, under the designation of children of Christians is to be understood those whose father or mother is a member of the Christian Church, even though both parents do not confess the Christian faith, and such children should not be denied holy Baptism.

1 Cor. 7:12–14 – **Should a brother have an unbelieving wife and she is pleased to live with him, he**

should not divorce from her. And should a wife have an unbelieving husband and it pleases him to live with her, she should not divorce from him. For the unbelieving husband becomes sanctified through the wife and the unbelieving wife becomes sanctified through the husband, otherwise your children would become unclean; now, however, they are holy. (The Corinthians were asking St. Paul if a believing spouse might in good conscience live with an unbelieving spouse. The apostle affirms such and adds thereto that the unbelieving spouse becomes sanctified through the other, as all things are pure for the pure [Tit. 1:15]. So a non-Christian spouse is pure for a Christian spouse, and the Christian may remain with the spouse without sinning. Later it is asked about children who are conceived in a marriage between a Christian spouse and a non-Christian whether they are to be regarded as holy or unclean; that is, whether they are to be regarded as children of Christians or children of heathen? The apostle answers that they are not to be regarded as unclean [and] one should not exclude them from the Church as children of heathen; rather, one should regard them as being holy for the sake of the Christian spouse, that is, as being born into the Church, and no less allow them to be baptized than the children whose parents are both Christians.)

3. The children whose parents converted from heathendom or from Judaism, even though they were conceived in heathendom, are to be regarded as children of Christians.

Relevant here are the passages which testify that the apostles baptized the converted Christians along with their entire household, as these are recounted in chap. 19, # 6. For from [these examples] one sees that they regarded also such as children of Christians.

4. Those who are taken in by Christian parents and adopted [are also to be regarded as children of Christians]. For in the same way that we become God's children through the νοθεσίαν or *adoptionem*—in that God through His only-born

Son, Christ, takes us on as children—so also those whom Christian parents [adopt] are to be regarded as their true children. Here also belong those Christian parents who receive parental authority and guardianship [over children] through proper channels and solemnly promise that on behalf of them [the original parents] henceforth diligently to rear and instruct the children in the Christian faith.

Acts 2:38–39 – **Repent and let each of you be baptized upon the name of Jesus Christ,** etc. **For the promise is to you and your children and to all who are far off, whom God our Lord will call hereto.** (Here St. Peter testifies to the divine promise also upon those who—even though their birth is still far off—will yet be called hereto by God the Lord through His wondrous governance and through His proper means; as one can see that sometimes in legitimate wars the children of heathen are brought into the parental authority of Christians and are [thus] given access to holy Baptism.)

Here, again, [are] some apparent points of contention:

1. That in general all children are spotted with inherited sin and because of that are all children of wrath (Eph. 2:3); therefore one should not make such a distinction between them that one permits children of Christians an entry to Baptism, but barricade [obstruct] the others. ANSWER: It is quite obvious that not only the children of Jews, Turks, and heathen, but also the children of Christians, are conceived and born in sin, as will be established later on. But, there still remains the distinction that certain children are born within the circular wall [the fellowship circle] of the Church, while others are born outside the same. Therefore, certain ones have an entry to Baptism, but the others must first be instructed. Certain ones, since they are born of Christian parents, also belong to the promise: I will be your God and the God of your seed. But the others, since they are born from parents who are outside the Church, are regarded as unclean, as the Apostle says in 1 Cor. 7:14;

that is, as long as they and their parents do not embrace the Christian faith, this promise of God does not apply to them, nor the grace-covenant, nor holy Baptism; rather, they are strangers to the testament of promise (Eph. 2:12).

2. That in such a case the children of heathen [parents] are apparently being punished innocently for the sake of their parents; yet God the Lord says in Eze. 18:20 – **The son shall not carry the crime of the father.** ANSWER: The misdeed of the parents does not harm the children if they themselves are innocent or convert to God. But the children are not innocent in this case, but, just like the parents, lack in faith. If they convert to Christianity in their years of discretion, they obviously do not bear the transgression of their fathers. However, this [issue] will be dealt with in greater detail in the article concerning eternal election of grace: Whether the means of salvation—which also include Baptism—are closer to one person than to another so that he has an [easier] access to the same than another, as one must then admit that the children of Christians have the advantage that they may immediately be baptized in their childhood years and thus become saved, as opposed to the children of non-Christians, who must first be instructed in their adult years before they may be allowed access to Baptism.

3. That St. Paul attests in 1 Tim. 5:8 that there are many who are more scandalous than the heathen living among Christians. Consequently, one should not make a distinction between the children of Christians and children of non-Christians regarding this question. ANSWER: Even though sometimes the parents, because of their unchristian life, are more scandalous than the heathen, yet they have received Baptism in their childhood. They were received up into the lap of the Christian Church through their Baptism, and even though they do not benefit from the blessings which God the Lord promised them in the grace-covenant of holy Baptism because of their lack of faith and because of their godlessness, nevertheless, the covenant remains intact from God's [side], so that they (if they truly turn back to God [repent]) do not need any other Baptism and do not need another covenant. Furthermore, their children also still benefit from the same covenant and have it better than the children of non-Christians who are strangers to the testament of promise (Eph. 2:12).

CHAPTER 22

WHETHER THE CHILDREN WHO ARE CONCEIVED AND BORN OF SUCH PARENTS WHO LIE IN FORNICATION, ADULTERY, OR OTHER GROSS SINS ARE TO BE BAPTIZED.

hen it was stated in the previous chapter that only the children of Christians are to be baptized, that is not to be understood to mean that only those children are to be baptized whose parents are true Christians and genuine children of God. Rather, one understands by the name "Christian" all those who confess the Christian faith, appear [show up] for the Word and the holy Sacraments, even though they do not evidence the fruits of true faith and thereby demonstrate that they are not true members of Christ and are not numbered among the elect. From this it is apparent that these children who are conceived in adultery or fornication are to be baptized, which we verify by the following:

1. The privilege [to be baptized] for the children of Christians is not grounded on the piety or worth of the parents, but rather upon the promise of God that He wants to be our God and the God of our seed. Therefore, this prerogative is not extinguished in any way if the parents are godless.

In Gen. 17:7, God says to Abraham, I want to be your God and your seed's after you.

Acts 2:39 – **For the promise is yours and your children's.**

2. Although the parents of such children fall into outward sin and deprive themselves of the blessings of the covenant which God established with them in holy Baptism, the established covenant still remains valid from God's perspective. Hence, also the children of such parents are still to be regarded as children of the covenant. Pertinent here are the testimonies which demonstrate that God the Lord establishes a grace-covenant with us in holy Baptism, as is discussed above in chap. 13, #3; then also the same testimonies which show that from God's point of view the same covenant is not completely canceled because of our disobedience, as discussed in chapter 17, #1.

3. Just as in the Old Testament the very children who were conceived in whoredom or adultery, or whose parents were otherwise godless, were also circumcised, so in the New Testament the children of such parents should no less be baptized, since holy Baptism has come in place of circumcision.

In Jud. 11:1, Jephthah was the child of a whore and was circumcised just the same. This conclusion is based on the fact that the Spirit of the Lord came over him (v. 29); and that the elders of Gilead elected him their head (v. 8); [and] also that he is included with the saints in Heb. 11:32.

In 2 Sam. 12:23, David says of the very child he adulterously conceived with Bathsheba – **I will indeed go to him.** From this it is easily concluded that he had been taken up into God's covenant through circumcision.

In 1 Kin. 14:1, Abijah is remembered, whose parents, Jeroboam and his wife, were both godless, since Jeroboam made golden calves in Bethel and Dan by which he caused the entire nation to sin (1 Kin. 12:28, 29, 30). Even though God gave him warning through Word and signs, he did not turn from his evil ways (1 Kin. 13:33). Even so, the son of Jeroboam, Abijah, was circumcised, as is apparent from 1 Kin. 14:13, where the prophet Ahijah refers to this child when he speaks to the wife of Jeroboam, stating that something good has been found before the Lord God of Israel in the house of Jeroboam.

Here, again, [are] apparent points of contention:

1. That God the Lord ordained in Deu. 23:2 that no child of a harlot should come into the fellowship of the Lord. From this it follows that they should not be circumcised or baptized and thus be taken up into the fellowship of the Lord. ANSWER: To come into the fellowship of the Lord does not mean here to become a true member of the Church; rather, something else is to be understood by this, which we substantiate as follows: In v. 1, God commands that no one who has been mutilated or is a eunuch is to come into the fellowship of the Lord. If from this it is to be understood that they are to be blocked from hearing the Word and from usage of the Sacraments, then it would follow that none of these can be saved. However, in no way can such be stated, since in Isa. 56:3–5 the Lord says to the eunuch: **The eunuch should not say: see, I am a dried up tree, for whoever** (among the eunuchs) **keeps My Sabbath and chooses what pleases Me, and steadfastly embraces My covenant, him I will give within My house and My walls a place and a better name than sons and daughters—an everlasting name I will give him which shall never go away.** In Deu. 23:3, God the Lord in the same way ordains: **The Ammonites and the Moabites should not come into the fellowship of the Lord, also unto the tenth generation; rather, they shall never come in.** This, however, cannot be understood in the sense that the Ammonites and Moabites were barred from entry into the Church because of this—since Ruth was a Moabite (Ruth 1:22). She is listed in the ancestral register of Christ (Mat. 1:5). And, concerning such strangers who converted to the true God of Israel, [there is a general statement] in Isa. 56:6, 7 – **And the children of strangers who have put themselves to the Lord to serve Him and to love His Name, so that they are His servants,** etc., **the same I will bring to My holy mountain and will gladden them in My house of prayer,** etc. Accordingly, one may say that [the words] "they should not come into the fellowship of the Lord" can in no way be understood to mean that in all matters they are excluded from entry to the Word and the Sacraments. Rather, [they are] understood to mean that [such individuals] are not to be placed in any public offices. Instead, they are to lead a private life among the people of God. That, however, Jephthah—who was a child of adultery—was made head over the people of Gilead is something out of the ordinary, to which the fellowship ordinance does not apply (Jud. 11:1 and 8). Some would say about the [expression], "that they should not come into the fellowship of the Lord," that it should be understood to say that they did not have the right to intermarry with the people of Israel. Be that as it may, it still is only a Levitical ceremonial law, binding only the Israelites of the Old Testament.

2. That God the Lord threatens the disobedient in Deu. 28:18 (the fruit of their bodies shall be cursed); therefore, one should not permit their children to be baptized. ANSWER: **1.** It has been shown that the children of godless parents were to be circumcised; therefore, they cannot be excluded from the Baptism of the New Testament. **2.** God the Lord promised that the children should not bear the transgression of their parents (Eze. 18:20). But how could children who are born into the Church be more terribly punished for the transgressions of their parents than by not having access to holy Baptism? **3.** Since this divine threat is directed in general against all disobedient children, it would follow that the children of all godless parents are thereby cursed and eternally damned if one takes this threat to mean an eternal curse. But how does that [square up with] the examples of pious children who were born of godless parents? Abijah was a pious, blessed child, though his father Jeroboam was a godless and idolatrous man. Hezekiah was a pious man, and yet his father Ahaz was godless. Josiah was a just, righteous king, and yet his father Amon was evil and godless. **4.** Consequently, the divine threat of Exo. 20:5, that God visits the transgression of the fathers upon the children to the third and fourth generation, has a two-fold meaning:

First, when the children also are godless and walk in the footsteps of their parents. Next, distinguishing between eternal and temporal punishment, this threat must also be understood to mean that such children are either unfruitful—which was regarded as a curse by the Jewish people—or that they simply have an accursed life and are unfortunate.

3. That in the Book of Wisdom 3:18–19 it is stated concerning the children of adulterers – **If they die soon, they have no hope, nor comfort at the time of judgment. For the unrighteous receive an evil end.** From this, it would follow that it is inexcusable to baptize the children of adulterers since they obviously have no hope. ANSWER: **1.** That book is not in the canon [of holy Scripture]; that is, it is not numbered among those [books] about which one can be certain that it came into being through the inspiration of the Holy Spirit, written by the prophets. **2.** Also, the crafter of this book does not desire that without distinction all children of harlots and adulterers are to be damned, for this flies in the face of the example of Jephthah and other believers. **3.** Rather, the sage here speaks of such children as they are in general; for if they are not brought up in the nurture and admonition of the Lord by their parents (Eph. 6:4), they grow up in their inborn evil. That is why it comes about that they generally go the way of godlessness and eventually perish.

CHAPTER 23

WHETHER ALSO FOUNDLINGS ARE TO BE BAPTIZED.

oncerning such children, it is also to be concluded that Baptism is not to be denied them. And, even though at times a little note is lying beside the child which announces it already has been baptized, one should nonetheless still baptize it.

1. Since the Sacrament of holy Baptism is so necessary for salvation, we should never, inasmuch as it depends on us, neglect any child in this regard.

John 3:5 – **Unless one is born out of water and Spirit, he cannot come into the kingdom of God.**

2. Since also a little note is not to be relied on in such a serious matter, one should [do] no less [than] proceed with the Baptism of such a foundling. Otherwise, after they are grown, they will waver in constant doubt whether they also have been baptized.

Here again an apparent point of contention, that on the assumption such children already have been baptized, one should baptize them conditionally and indeed in such a manner: "In case you have never been baptized, I baptize you in the name of the Father and the Son and the Holy Spirit." ANSWER: With such a method, the Baptism of such children would become even more uncertain than before, for if it ever wishes to know, it won't know whether it has been baptized or not. Therefore it is stated: *Non potest dici iteratum, quod nescitur esse factum*—one cannot say that such children have been baptized twice since one does not have any certain grounds and reliable witnesses. Hereupon, it can be further concluded that when women administer an emergency Baptism and later admit they do not remember with what words or with what sort of external element they did the baptizing, such children are, without any further thought, to be baptized in the presence of other devout Christians.

CHAPTER 24

WHETHER THE CHILDREN OF CHRISTIAN PARENTS ARE IN GOD'S COVENANT OF GRACE AND ARE SAINTLY PRIOR TO THEIR BAPTISM.

 lthough the children of Christians have an advantage (are privileged) over children of heathen, in that they may and should be baptized before they are instructed in the Christian religion and while still children; nevertheless, one should not think that they are in God's covenant of grace prior to their Baptism and are saintly because they are born of believing parents. Rather, they are by nature just as much children of wrath as the children of non-Christians; therefore, they are in need of holy Baptism so that they may be reborn to eternal life through it. We substantiate this:

1. From all the testimonies which speak about inherited [original] sin; for they extend universally over all mankind. Therefore, the children of believing parents are not to be excluded, as if they were not conceived and born in sin. But, since they are conceived and born in sin, they may not be considered to be in the covenant of God's grace and saintly on account of being born from believing parents.

Job 14:4 – **Who can find a clean person among them, since none are clean?** (Since they are all conceived out of unclean seed.)

Job 15:14–16 – **What is a man who is born of a woman that he should be pure and righteous? See, among His saints none is without blame, and the heavens are not pure before Him. How much more a man who is an** abomination and vile, who slurps down unrighteousness like water. (The tiny children in the mother's womb are nurtured with sinful blood and also drink in sin like water.)

John 3:6 – **What is born from flesh, that is flesh.** (Now, the children of Christians are indeed also born of flesh, since the siring of children occurs not according to the inward man, but according to the outward man. Therefore, they indeed also are flesh.)

Rom. 5:16 – **Therefore, since through one man sin has come into the world** (that is, upon all mankind) **and death through sin, and thus death permeated itself into all mankind since they all have sinned.**

2. From the very passages which in particular indicate that the children of believing Christians are conceived and born in sin.

In Gen. 5:3, Adam sired a son after his own exact likeness. (Adam had been created in perfect righteousness and holiness, but he lost such an image of God through sin; therefore, he subsequently sired children after his own image, which were now pathetically spoiled through sin.)

In Gen. 8:21, after the Flood there were none left except the children of devout Noah; even so, God the Lord says: **The thoughts of the human heart are evil from youth on.**

In Psa. 51:7, David says: **See, I have been sired from sinful seed, and my mother conceived me in sin** (even though David had pious parents, 1 Sam. 16:1).

Eph. 2:3 – **We also were children of wrath by nature, just as the others.** (Here St. Paul includes himself, even though he was born an Israelite, 2 Cor. 11:22.)

3. From the same witnesses which show that not birth, but rather rebirth, produces children of God.

In Mat. 3:9, John the Baptizer says to the Pharisees: **Do not even think to say among yourselves: We have Abraham for [our] father**, etc.

John 1:12–13 – **As many as received Him, those He gave power to become God's children, who believed on**

His name; who are born not from blood, nor from the will of the flesh, nor from the will of a man, rather from God.

John 3:3 – **Unless one is born anew, he cannot see the kingdom of God.**

In John 8:34, as the Jews brag that they were Abraham's seed, Jesus answers them: **Whoever does sin, he is the servant of sin** (teaching them thereby that they were servants of sin by nature, sold under sin [Rom. 7:14]).

Rom. 9:6–8 – **For not all who are from Israel are Israelites; also, not all who are Abraham's seed are also children, etc. Those who are children after the flesh are not God's children; rather, the children of promise are counted as seed.**

4. From the same testimonies which speak of the efficacy and effect of holy Baptism, that it is a bath of rebirth and renewal; for since also Christian children must be reborn and renewed in holy Baptism, it follows that they are not reborn, nor holy [sanctified], nor in God's covenant of grace prior to their Baptism. The very same testimonies about the efficacy and effect of Baptism were presented above in chapters 13 and 14.

Here, again, [are] apparent points of contention:

1. That God the Lord promises in Gen. 17:7 that He wants to be our God and the God of our seed; from this it appears to follow that by all rights the children of believing parents are also in the grace-covenant of God and sanctified prior to their Baptism. ANSWER: This little verse is clarified above in chapter 13, point of contention #2, and shows that God the Lord indeed graciously promises that He wants to be our children's God, but that they nevertheless have to be presented to Him and received into His grace-covenant through the ordinary means of Baptism. In the same manner, as in the earlier times of the Old Testament, it was necessary that the children of the Israelites had to be received into God's covenant through circumcision, so also, from our perspective, there must always be a means through which we become recipients of God's grace and His promised blessings. Thus also in this case, if the children are to become recipients of these rich-in-grace promises of God, the ordained means of the Sacrament of holy Baptism must be applied to that end. By force of this promise, they have an entry to the covenant, but are not actually in the covenant. [*Vi hujus promissionis habent aditum ad foedus, non autem sunt actu in foedere.*]

2. That St. Paul says in 1 Cor. 7:14 – **Now then they** (your children) **are holy,** [but] writing, in contrast, about the children of the unbelievers that they are unclean; from this it appears to follow that the children of Christians are holy from the womb, also without Baptism. ANSWER: This little verse was likewise clarified in chap. 20, sec. #1, and it was shown that this is not to be understood as referring to the inner holiness of the heart, since St. Paul himself adds that an unbelieving spouse is sanctified from the other [believing] spouse—which can in no fashion be applied to the inner holiness of the heart. Rather, this must here be understood to mean the *sanctitas ecclesiastica,* that the children born of parents where only one is a believer are to be regarded no less "holy" (that is, born into the Church and having access to holy Baptism) than those who are born when both parents are believing Christians.

3. That St. Paul says in Rom. 11:16 – **If the beginning** [first dough] **is holy, the dough also is holy, and if the root is holy, the branches also are holy.** From this, it apparently follows that the children of believing parents are also, by nature, believing and holy. ANSWER: The apostle especially wants to indicate that God the Lord had not completely rejected the people of Israel (Rom. 11:2). He proves this from God's covenant of grace, which God not only made with the fathers of the Jews, but also established it with their descendants. He brings forth the argument with figurative words in two allegories: **If the beginning** [first] **is holy, the dough also is holy; if the root is holy, the branches**

also are holy. With the first figure, the apostle draws upon the command of God (cf. Exo. 23:19, Lev. 23:10, Num. 15:19), with which the Israelites were bound [obligated] to bring the first-fruits into the house of the Lord. Through this *oblationem primitiarum*, the remaining fruits were sanctified so that they were clean and allowed to take nourishment. The apostle signifies the holy Patriarchs and fathers [by] "first-fruits." By "dough" he [refers to] the descendants; in so many words, he wants to say that since the fathers of the Jews were holy (that is, they were especially chosen to be a people of God's possession to whom also occurred the promise of the Messiah) so also the descendants shall be holy. Thus, the promise of the Messiah will also apply to them, provided that they simply seized the Messiah in true faith. That these matters are to be thus understood is supported by the entire chapter, especially in v. 20, in which St. Paul expressly testifies: The Jews are broken off because of their unbelief. From all which it is apparent that in no way may [such holiness] be understood to refer here to the inner holiness of the spirit and heart; otherwise, it would then follow that, in general, all the children of Jews would be included in the covenant of God's grace by nature. Rather, it [such holiness] is to be understood as referring only to *ecclesiastica sanctitas*, that the promise of the Messiah also applies to them and they have an entry to the covenant of God's grace.

4. That Christ says in Mark 10:14 – **Permit the children to come to Me, and forbid them not, for such are the kingdom of God.** From this it appears to follow that the children are by nature holy and heirs of eternal life. ANSWER: Obviously, the children are to be brought to the Lord Christ so that they receive His heavenly blessings; but that is precisely what occurs through holy Baptism, which is the *sacramentum initiationis*, the ordained means through which the children are permitted to be reborn and renewed and to put on the Lord Christ (Gal. 3:27)—not to mention that these children already had been received into the covenant of God through circumcision, and thus Christ justly received them.

CHAPTER 25

WHETHER THE CHILDREN WHO ARE BAPTIZED BELIEVE.

mong other apparent grounds for denying Baptism to little children, not the least of them is that holy Baptism does not benefit little children because they do not believe. We have already given answer to this above in chapter 19, point of contention #8—that, indeed, little children by nature do not have faith and do not bring faith to Baptism. Yet God the Lord wants to awaken the same in their hearts through the Sacrament of holy Baptism, since, along with other effects, God ignites faith in and through Baptism, as was demonstrated in chapter 13, # 1. That children who were taken up into the grace-covenant of God through the Sacrament of circumcision in the Old Testament and through holy Baptism in the New Testament, truly believed, we substantiate thusly:

1. Because the Scriptures expressly ascribe faith to them:

Mat. 18:6 – **But whoever vexes one of these smallest ones who believe on Me, for him it would be better if,** etc.

Mark 10:15 – **Whoever does not receive the kingdom of God as a little child, he will not come into it.** (We receive the kingdom of God only for the sake of Christ through faith; if we are to receive it as little children, [children] must certainly also be believers.) This is repeated in Luke 18:17.

2. Since the attributes and workings of faith are ascribed to little children.

Psa. 8:3, Mat. 21:16 – **Out of the mouths of young children (minors) and sucklings you have ordered forth**

praise. (No one can properly praise God unless it proceeds from a true faith, without which all prayer and praise becomes sinful.)

Psa. 22:10 – **You became my Confidence when I still was on my mother's breast.**

In Psa. 71:6 David says: **I have relied on You, beginning in the womb.**

Psa. 115:13, 14 – **He** (the Lord) **blesses those who fear the Lord, both small and big. The Lord bless you even more and more, you and your children.**

1 John 2:[13],14 – **I write to you children, for you know the Father.** (John here indicates three classes: fathers, youths, and children; therefore, by children he is not thinking of [young] adults, but rather of tender, small 'kids.' He testifies concerning them that they know the Father, which is an attribute of faith.)

1 John 5:4 – **For everything that is born of God overcomes the world, and our faith is the victory which has overcome the world.** (But now the baptized little children are born from God [John 1:13]; therefore, they also believe and overcome the world through faith.)

Rev. 11:18 – **Those who fear Your Name, the small and the big.**

Rev. 19:5 – **Praise our God, all His servants and those who fear Him, both small and large (great).**

3. Since the baptized little children please the Lord, they have become righteous, as it also is stated: **But without faith it is impossible to please God** (Heb. 11:6); and only through faith in Christ do we become righteous [justified] (Rom. 3:22, Gal. 2:16, [and] Eph. 2:5).

In Mat. 19:13–15, Mark 10:13–15, [and] Luke 18:15–16, as the children were brought to the Lord Christ, He hugged them, laid His hands on them, and blessed them; hence they indeed must have pleased Him. Yes, the Lord Christ even scolds the disciples because they wanted to bar those who brought these children to Him.

[It is pertinent to note here] that in 1 Kin. 14:13 the prophet says of Ahijah, the son of Jeroboam, that the Lord found some good in him; therefore, it must indeed have pleased God.

4. Because the baptized children are saved; but now, one cannot become saved in any other way than through faith in Christ, John 3:18, 36 – Anyone who believes on Him (the Son of God), **will not be condemned; whoever does not believe is already condemned,** etc. **Whoever believes in the Son, he has eternal life. Whoever does not believe in the Son, he will not see life, rather the wrath of God remains on him.** In John 14:6, Christ says: **No one comes to the Father except through Me;** Mark 16:16 – **Whoever does not believe, he will be damned.** Acts 4:12 – **And in no other is there salvation, nor has there been given another Name to people, through which we should become saved,** except only the name "Jesus Christ." 1 John 5:12 – **Whoever does not have the Son of God, he does not have life.** In sum, the entire Scripture testifies that we can only become saved through Christ; furthermore, only through faith can we be in Christ and become recipients of His merits (Eph. 3:17). There the matter must rest: either the little baptized children are eternally excluded from the kingdom of God, or else they become recipients of Christ's merits through faith.

In 2 Sam. 12:23, as David's child (sired with Bathsheba) dies, he says – **Can I fetch him again? I will indeed go to him, for he will not return again to me.** (Had David been in doubt as to this little child's salvation, he would not have said [that] he is going to go to him. Some, of course, claim that the child was not circumcised, since in v. 18 it is written that he died upon the seventh day and circumcision was to first take place on the eighth day (Gen. 17:14). However, it is closer to the meaning of the text that one understand the seventh day to refer to the days after which Nathan had come to David and reminded him of his sins. Now then, it is not likely that Nathan came to David with his proclamation of repentance on the very day the child was born.)

In Mat. 19:14, Mark 10:14, [and] Luke 18:16, Christ says: **Let the little children come to me and bar them not, for of such is the kingdom of God.**

Rev. 20:12 – **And I saw the dead, both big and small, stand before God, and the books were opened and another book was opened, which is the Life** (Also the little children are written into the book of Life), etc.

5. Since holy Baptism is an effectual means through which the Holy Spirit rebirths the baptized, washes away sins, takes them up into God's covenant, clothes them in the righteousness of Christ, and makes them children of God, as indicated above in chapter 13. But all this does not take place with the person if he does not believe. What St. Paul writes is especially relevant here:

Gal. 3:26–27 – **For you are all God's children through faith in Christ Jesus. For as many of you who have been baptized have put on Christ.** (Those who put on Christ in Baptism are children of God through faith in Jesus. The children put on Christ through Baptism and in Baptism; therefore, they are children of God through faith. If they are children of God through faith, who would or could say they do not believe?)

6. Because also the circumcised children in the Old Testament were believers and were saved through faith.

In Gen. 17:7, God promises that He wants to establish the sort of covenant with Abraham through circumcision where He would be his God and the God of his seed. (It follows that He was also the God of the circumcised children; that is, He was their gracious Father who remembered them all here [in this life] with His grace, and there [in eternity] He remembered them with eternal salvation. That such is the meaning of this promise is to be concluded from the following verses: Lev. 26:9,11,12 – **I will keep My covenant with you. I will make My residence among you, and My soul shall** not reject you. And (I) will walk among you and be your God; thus you shall be My people. Jer. 31:33–34 – **Rather this shall be the covenant that I will make with the house of Israel, etc.: You shall be My people, thus will I be your God. For I will forgive you your iniquity and no more remember your sins.** It is appropriate here [to refer to] what Jesus concludes from this in Mat. 22:31–32 – **But have you not read about the resurrection from the dead, which has been told you by God** when He says: **I am the God of Abraham, and the God of Isaac, and the God of Jacob? But God is not a God of the dead, rather of the living.** In the same way we conclude concerning the circumcised children—since through circumcision this promise applies to them—that God also became their God. Thus, they indeed will be preserved unto eternal life through faith.)

Rom. 4:11 – Abraham received the sign of circumcision as a seal for the righteousness of faith. (If circumcision was to be a seal for the righteousness of faith, then, indeed, also the circumcised children must have been believers; otherwise this Sacrament could not have contained the seal of the righteousness of faith.)

Here, again, [are] apparent points of contention:

1. That those children whom Christ placed in the midst of the disciples and testified concerning their faith were actually somewhat [mature] and were capable of speaking (since Christ called them to Himself) (Mat. 18:2), and since He speaks of children who actually could be offended (v. 6); therefore, the conclusion cannot be drawn from this that the very tiny little children can believe. ANSWER: Doesn't David say in Psa. 8:3, and Christ in Mat. 21:16, that God has prepared Himself praise out of the mouths of young children and sucklings? Doesn't Christ say of such children who are carried to Him in arms that such are the Kingdom of God (Mat. 19:14, Mark 10:14, Luke 18:15)? How, then, can the little children be regarded as unbelieving? **2.** Even though the child which Christ placed in the midst of the apostles was somewhat grown, there yet is (as pertains to understanding the article of faith) no difference between him and the tiny, minor children, since this child could no more give an account of his faith than the other minors. **3.** What Christ here says: **Unless you repent and become as the children, you will not come into the heavenly kingdom** (Mat. 18:3), He elsewhere applies to the tiny, minor, little children: **Whoever does not receive the kingdom of God as a little child, he will not enter into it** (Mark 10:15). Also, who wants to exclude from it [the kingdom of God] the very tiny, little children? In v. 10–11 the Lord Christ says – **See to it that none of you despise one of these little ones, for I tell you their angels in heaven at all times see the countenance of My Father in heaven; for the Son of Man is come to make saved what is lost;** therefore, we conclude that Christ is speaking of the tiny little children in general (whether circumcised or baptized) and verifies concerning them that they believe, which also is self-evident from the words: **whoever vexes one of these teeny ones who believe in Me**, etc. (v. 6). Thus, Christ [uses] the example of this child's situation to speak in general of the tiny, little children. **4.** Furthermore, Christ demands that we should repent and become like the children if we have any thought of entering the Kingdom of God. But if the children did not believe, must the believing old people become like the unbelieving children—not to mention that the children will not be saved if they do not believe? **5.** Furthermore, if the minor children are to be excluded and not understood to be included under the term of "these little ones," then it would follow that they must first become like grown-up children or be lost eternally—which is absurd. **6.** And why would Christ portray grown children and not minors as an example of simplicity in matters of faith and true humility, since experience attests that evil continually increases in children? [Cf.] 1 Cor. 14:20: **In regard to evil, be children. 7.** As to the [pretext] that Christ is speaking of such children who could be offended (Mat. 18:6), but [that] little minor children cannot be offended, rather only the adults, we reply in this way: In God's judgment, it is also an offense when someone thinks of doing something over which someone could be offended (even though the actual deed of the offense does not occur) since God looks more upon the will and intention than what actually occurs in deed against the person. For this, I give you clear example [in] Mat. 16:23: **Heave yourself from Me, Satan, Jesus says to Peter; you are an offense to Me.** How so? Was Christ irritated because of an actual deed by Peter? Far from it, for Christ speaks thus because Peter carried on with irritating talk through which others might be offended.

2. That the little children become righteous and saved solely by being credited with the righteousness of Christ apart from any personal faith. ANSWER: The entire Scripture testifies that the merits of Christ are received in no other way than through faith, not to mention that it is impossible to please God without faith (Heb. 11:6), let alone to be received into eternal life. In general, St. Paul concludes concerning this [matter] in Rom. 3:28: **Thus we hold then that a man becomes righteous without the works of the Law —only through faith.** [It] also appears from this that every time something is offered to many, yet not all receive it; so a distinction has to be found why of those who are offered a gift, some receive it and others despise and reject it. Thus, God the Lord offers His grace, forgiveness of sins, and eternal life to all people through the Word and the holy Sacraments. That not all become recipients of the same [is because] not all accept the offered gifts. From this it necessarily follows that the tiny baptized little children believe, or else must eternally forfeit all the gifts that are offered them in Baptism.

3. That maybe the little children are baptized on the faith of their parents or the Christian Church, since God promises in Gen. 17:7 that He wants to be our God, and since the Lord Christ forgave the paralytic because He looked upon the faith of those who brought him (Mat. 9:2). ANSWER: **1.** It is stated, as written by the prophet in Hab. 2:4 – **For the righteous lives by his faith,** which verselet is repeated in Rom. 1:17, Gal. 3:11, [and] Heb. 10:38. Therefore, each person must believe for himself if he is to be righteous and be saved, Rom. 4:5 – **But to the one who is not occupied with works, rather believes on Him who makes righteous the godless, to him his faith will be accounted for righteousness.** Thus, each person who would become righteous must have his own faith. **2.** Just as the unbelief of parents does not damage the children's salvation, so also the parents cannot give the children salvation with their own faith. Rather, it is written: **The righteousness of the righteous shall be over [credited to] him, and the unrighteousness of the unrighteous shall be over [charged against] him** (Eze. 18:20). **3.** Just as the children must be reborn again for themselves through holy Baptism if they are to enter the kingdom of God (John 3:3, 5), so also they must believe for themselves, since rebirth and salvation cannot take place without their own faith. **4.** Also, just as no one can consume bodily food for another person in order to achieve benefit and nourishment for [that person], so also each must eat Christ's flesh and drink His blood for himself if he is to have salvation (John 6:54). **5.** That the promise of Gen. 17:7 requires faith and in no way excludes it is expressly taught by St. Paul, Gal. 3:7–9 – **So you recognize it then that those who believe are the children of Abraham. The Scriptures, however, had already foreseen that God makes the Gentiles righteous through faith. Therefore it proclaims to Abraham: In you shall all the Gentiles be blessed. Thus then those who believe shall be blessed with believing Abraham.** Indeed, he also teaches this in Rom. 9:6, 7, 8 – **For not all are Israelites who are from Israel, nor are all who come from Abraham's seed necessarily [his] children,** etc. **That is, those who are children ac-**

cording to the flesh are not God's children; rather the children of promise are counted as seed. Therefore, the fulfillment of this promise to Abraham is in no way to be interpreted to mean that Abraham's seed became righteous and saved without individual faith. **6.** Concerning the paralytic in Mat. 9:1, he received the forgiveness of sins through his own individual faith, and not simply through the faith of his stretcher-bearers; for had he not believed that Jesus could and would help him, he would not have allowed himself to be carried to Jesus. Also, since Christ also calls him His son, how can one say he had no faith, since obviously we become children of God only through faith (John 1:12)? **7.** Consequently, we conclude that even though the faith of a stranger can provide bodily blessings (also with prayer it could happen that another might be given individual faith), that for righteousness and salvation each individual must believe with his own heart (Rom. 10:11). Thus, the children are first presented before the Lord Christ through sponsors and other members of the Christian Church, but then Christ gives them an individual faith in and through the Sacrament of holy Baptism through which they become righteous and saved.

    4. Because the children cannot use their judgment, so also they cannot believe, since faith [involves] knowledge, assent, and confidence, to the working of which trust belongs reason. ANSWER: **1.** The power of the Holy Spirit to work faith in us is thus in no way allied with [tied to] human reason, as if God in no way could work or maintain faith if the person did not use his reason. **2.** Yes, reason far more hinders faith than it could produce it, Rom. 8:7 – **For to be fleshly minded is an enmity against God.** 1 Cor. 2:14 – **The natural man perceives nothing from the Spirit of God, it is a foolishness to him, and he cannot recognize it,** etc., 2 Cor. 10:5 – **And take captive all reason under the obedience to Christ. 3.** Even though we do not understand what all takes place with faith in the tiny, little children, yet we should hold the Word of God in such reverence that we [do] not deny what it so clearly witnesses to regarding the faith of little children. **4.** Even though a person does not use his reason while sleeping, who dare say that faith then ceases in his heart and that Christ no longer lives in his heart through faith? (Eph. 3:17) Many times, also, the adult Christians lose their reason with insanity (especially at the time of death it often [occurs] that reason can no longer think), but who dare say that from then on faith ceases? **5.** Christ says in John 3:8 – **The wind blows wherever it wants to, and you indeed hear its whistling; but you do not know from where it comes and where it is going. So also is everyone who is reborn from out of the Spirit.** He hereby teaches us that as regards rebirth and the gracious working of the Holy Spirit, it is not crafted in such a fashion that we might be able to understand it with our reason. **6.** Did not John the Baptizer become filled with the Holy Spirit while in his mother's womb (Luke 1:15), so that he also gave a little hop in the womb as the mother of the Lord Christ entered the house of Zacharias? (v. 41); even so, John used no more of his reason for this than any other little child could. **7.** Does not God the Lord say in Hos. 2:21,22 that the corn, wine, and oil during the famine immediately [cry] to the earth, the earth cries to the heavens, and the heavens call upon God the Lord? Does not David say in Psa. 104 that the young lions seek food from God with their roaring? Does not Job 39:3 say that the young ravens call upon God when they have nothing to eat, which David repeats in Psa. 147:9? Does not St. Paul say in Rom. 8:22 that the creature yearns to become free from servitude to the perishable nature? We do not hear the crying and calling of these creatures, but God hears it; how much less should we conclude that the little children do not believe because we cannot hear nor understand it [their faith]? God testifies concerning their faith; He sees and understands more than we humans.

    5. Because faith comes from preaching (from hearing it) (Rom. 10:17); but then tiny, little children cannot hear the Word, nor understand it. Therefore, they will also not believe. ANSWER: **1.** God can also speak with mindless creatures. How much more will He be able to speak with the tiny, little children so that they can hear and understand? **Hear you heavens and earth; receive it in the ear** (Deu. 32:1, Isa. 1:2 and others). **2.** For not only is the Word of God the imperishable seed from which we become reborn (1 Pet. 1:23), but also holy Baptism is a bath of rebirth (John 3:5 [and] Tit. 3:5). So, then, the Word of God is not the sole saving means through which we come to faith, but also holy Baptism. **3.** Not only is faith effected and sealed in holy Baptism, but [Baptism] is also the means through which the Holy Spirit wants to ignite faith in the heart of anyone who does not deliberately resist Him; just as the Word is a means through which faith is awakened and later also increased and strengthened. **4.** Even though the tiny, little children in their minor years do not day by day increase in knowledge of the article of faith, as do the adults who have been instructed by the Word, yet no one would want to deny them all the things about faith concerning which the above applied passages clearly testify.

6. When the little children grow up and begin to speak, they are unable to give any answers about the articles of faith; hence they must not have received faith in Baptism. ANSWER: **1.** Was not John filled with the Holy Spirit in his mother's womb? (Luke 1:15) Even so, he still had to be instructed when he later came to his years of discretion. Yes, he clearly witnesses (John 1:31) that he did not recognize the Messiah in person in the early years of his ministry—whom he, of course, identified by jumping in his mother's womb (Luke 1:41). **2.** If the [adults] are not able to remember their faith in the risen Christ while they are sleeping or are out of their mind, so that they themselves cannot even confess with their mouths, how may one conclude that the little children do not believe because they do not confess their faith? **3.** God alone scrutinizes the hearts of mankind and can best see what is in them (2 Chr. 6:30). The self-same God expressly testifies in His Word that the baptized little children believe. We should much more believe this testimony from the divine Word than all that which our foolish reason brings to this subject.

7. Wherever there is true faith, it also produces the fruits of good works, Jam. 2:18 – **Show me your faith with your works;** but one sees no good works which the tiny little children have done, hence they do not believe. ANSWER: **1.** The good works and fruits of faith will not be outwardly seen at all times; rather, at times they remain inward and are revealed only to God, as [for example] the heart in the midst of severe illness longs for God, even though the tongue is unable to move; [or] as one desires from the heart to obey God the Lord in all things, even though at times he does not have strength to [carry out] the good [intention] (Rom. 7:15). **2.** Are not those good works and fruits of faith where the Scripture attests that God has ordained praise for Himself out of the mouths of young children and sucklings (Psa. 8:3); that they overcome the world? (1 John 5:4) **3.** One also does not see the fruits of inherited sin in [little children]; yet who would deny that they were conceived and born in sin because of this? (Psa. 51:7) Does not the power to bear good fruit remain in a fruit tree in the middle of winter? Should not faith be in the hearts of little children even though they have not yet demonstrated it with outward fruit? **4.** As pertaining to the passage from James, it is actually dealing with adult Christians, and hypocrites in particular, who boasted much about faith and yet did not demonstrate the same with good works.*

8. Godfathers or sponsors are used at the Baptism of little children; [they] answer in the stead of the child that it believes; therefore, the children are possibly baptized on the faith of the sponsors. ANSWER: This practice of using

---

* Thus it is irrelevant to the issue at hand. Ed.

godfathers at the Baptism was neither instituted by Christ nor practiced by the apostles. Rather, it was thus introduced by the gracious, good intentions of the Christian Church, as will be dealt with later in more detail. When these godfathers answer on behalf of the child that it believes in God, Father, Son and Holy Spirit, they are doing nothing more than repeating the comforting saying of Christ in Mark 10:15 – **Let the little children come to me and prevent them not, for of such is the kingdom of God.** Also, with this it is shown in whose Name the little child will be baptized. But in no way should it be concluded from the approaching of the baptismal sponsors that the baptized little children do not have their own faith. Rather, they bring the little child to Christ through their prayer, so that He may rebirth it through holy Baptism, awaken faith in it, and receive it into the everlasting grace-covenant of God.

CHAPTER 26

WHAT POSITION IS TO BE TAKEN CONCERNING THE UNBAPTIZED CHILDREN WHO DIE EITHER IN THE WOMB OR BEFORE THEY ARE BAPTIZED.

 ometimes it tragically happens that little children either die in the womb (and that which was to be the source of their life becomes their tomb) or yet, through an unexpected accident, they are ripped out of the land of the living before they can be brought to holy Baptism. Therefore, the question is asked: How are these children to be regarded? Are they indeed to be excluded from eternal life and the fellowship of all the angels and the elect, or not? First of all, we make a distinction between the little children who are born within heathendom outside the Christian Church and the children of Christian parents, who are born within the encircling wall of the Church. Concerning the former, we say with St. Paul 1 Cor. 5:12 – **For what do I have to do with those who are outside, that I should judge them? Do you not judge those who are inside? But God will judge those who are outside.** But as to the children of the Christians, we say that Christian parents who are just should hasten to bring them to Baptism as an ordained means for rebirth, and that those who are found to be dilatory in this, so that their little children die without Baptism because of their neglect or disdain, will because of this someday have to render a severe accounting to God the Lord in that they despised the counsel of God against [the best interests of] themselves and their children (Luke 7:30). At the same time, one should not wantonly damn or exclude from the fellowship of eternal life the children of Christians who, before they can be brought to Baptism, die in the mother's womb or are ripped away through an unexpected accident. What pertains to children who die in their mother's womb is obvious, as follows:

1. That they cannot be regarded as despisers of holy Baptism since Baptism is a bath of rebirth (John 3:5, Tit. 3:5), for what is supposed to be reborn must first be born. Now, such children never achieved birth; [therefore], how could one have brought them to Baptism and rebirth?

2. When children in the Old Testament died before they reached eight days, they had not been circumcised, since circumcision had to occur on the eighth day (Gen. 17:12). As, then, such children who died before the eighth day (and thus without circumcision) cannot be regarded as despisers of the divine ordinance or have the threat of v. 14 applied to them, so also the little children who die in their mother's womb (and hence without Baptism) can in no way be regarded as despising the divine ordinance. Since they are not despisers of Baptism, it can be said of them: *Non privatio sed contemtus sacramentorum damnat*, that is, not the lack of, but rather the despising of [contempt for], the sacrament is damnable.

3. Furthermore, through the prayer of their parents and the Church (which in public prays for all the pregnant women), such children have been commended to God the Lord. Therefore, you need not doubt that God (according to His gracious promise about answering prayer, which He has demonstrated throughout Scripture) has heard you in this matter. And what could not occur through the ordained means of holy Baptism, He has accomplished for these children in an extraordinary manner without means through His Holy Spirit. That He can do this He has demonstrated with the example of John the Baptizer, who was filled with the Holy Spirit in his mother's womb (Luke 1:15) and who testified to Christ by jumping (v. 41).

4. That we also have no occasion to doubt the gracious will of God in such a situation, He has clearly shown by His promise in Gen. 17:7. He wants to be our God and the God of our seed. The word "seed" is to be especially noted, since it includes also the little children who are still enclosed in their mothers' womb.

5. Yes, that is also why our Lord and Savior desired to be conceived in a mother's womb (Mat. 1:20, Luke 1:31 [and] 2:21), so that He might thereby indicate that He wanted to be the Redeemer and Savior of children in the womb. Where they are unable to attain the objective of receiving holy Baptism as an ordained means for rebirth, He wants to be effectual in them through His grace.

Regarding the little children who through an abrupt death are ripped away before they can come to Baptism, one should not wantonly judge them either, nor exclude them from eternal salvation.

1. Since they similarly do without Baptism not out of neglect but out of plight [affliction], therefore the divine threats of Gen. 17:14 [and] John 3:5 should in no way be applied to them.

2. Since they likewise also are commended to God the Lord by the prayer of their parents and the Church (which publicly prays for all sucklings), there can be no doubt that He will have heard such prayers. Here apply all the testimonies which witness to the power of prayer and to the certainty of its being heard.

3. So that we need not have doubts about the gracious will of God on this point, He has graciously offered [these assurances] to us.

Gen. 17:7 – **So that I be your God and the God of your seed after you.**

Mat. 18:14 – **Thus it is not the will of your Father in heaven that any of these little one be lost.**

Mat. 18:14, Mark 10:14, Luke 18:16 – **Let the little children come to Me and restrain them not, for such are the kingdom of God.**

John 6:37 – **Whoever comes to Me, him I will not reject.**

But since these children in these circumstances cannot be brought to God the Lord through the ordained means of holy Baptism, there is no doubt that God will, in remembrance of His promises, receive these children who are thus presented and commended to Him.

4. God the Lord is not bound to means in the same way that we human beings are so that He cannot help through His divine power without means.* For in the same way as we humans are bound to means as pertains to the external affairs of this life, so also in matters pertaining to eternal life we are bound to the Word and the holy Sacraments; contrarily, as God the Lord is not at all bound to means in outward matters (since He can maintain the life of man without food [and] give health again without physicians) so also in matters pertaining to eternal life, He is not bound to the means which He Himself has ordained. Thus, He can make a person saved without [using] them.

5. Since the examples testify that the little Israelite children were saved without circumcision in case of emergencies, [the same is true of Baptism], since Baptism has come in place of circumcision.

In Exo. 1:22, Pharaoh commanded all his people to throw the infant Israelite boys into the water as soon as they were born; but who would, on account of the fact that they were not circumcised, exclude these tender martyrs from eternal life?

In Jos. 5:5, it is mentioned that none of the little children born during the forty years of wandering in the wilderness were circumcised, because they had to be continually on the move. If, however, there had been any danger that these uncircumcised little children would on

---

* That is, unlike human beings, who depend on external means, God is not thus limited. He is able to act without external means. Ed.

that account have been eternally damned, no set of adverse circumstances would have hindered Moses [from taking the time to circumcise them].

In 1 Macc. 1:51, 60, 63–64 [Apocrypha], it is mentioned that the tyrant Antiochus forbade circumcision: he murdered all who held to God's Law; he killed the women who had their children circumcised; he had the parents strangled in their homes and hanged the children—from all which it can be seen that many children were murdered before they could be circumcised; but who would want to damn [them] because of this, in that they are far more [deserving] to be regarded as martyrs?

In Mat. 2:16, Herod allowed to be murdered all the children in and around Bethlehem who were two years and under. Without doubt, among these were certain ones who had not yet attained eight days of age and thus died without circumcision. But who would on account of that exclude them from God's kingdom? Much rather they are blessed little souls, quite secure little ones, little diamonds of the martyrs [*beatae animulae, parvuli integelluli, Martyrumque gemmulae*].

6. Since the examples testify that in cases of emergency certain ones were saved without Baptism, how much less should one make judgments about the tender little children who are presented before the Lord through a believing prayer?

In Luke 23:43, Christ promises the malefactor on the cross that he would be with Him in Paradise. And yet this malefactor [was never] baptized. Therefore, cases of emergency must be excepted from the rule of John 3:5.

Pertinent here is that in the early church many tiny children and catechumens were murdered by the tyrants before they could come to Baptism. But who would condemn them? Also applicable here is that Christ, [in addition to saying in] Mark 16:16: **Whoever believes and is baptized, he will be saved,** [also] says: **whoever does not believe, he will be damned.** That the Lord Christ in this additional statement does not mention Baptism shows without a doubt that He wanted to indicate that holy Baptism was not that essential for salvation, and also that, in case of an emergency, someone [would or could] be saved without [Baptism].

Here, again, are some apparent points of contention:

1. That Baptism is the ordained means for rebirth (Tit. 3:5), through which we are cleansed from sin (Eph. 5:26) and become saved (1 Pet. 3:21). Accordingly, when such children are not baptized, it is to be feared that they are not reborn, nor washed from sin, nor saved. ANSWER: Holy Baptism is indeed the ordained means for rebirth, the washing from sin, and being saved; therefore, it is in no way to be despised or neglected. But God the Lord can also work the same in an extraordinary manner and in the absence of the ordained means, even though He normally uses the ordained means. He has bound us to the means so that we should not despise or neglect them; Himself and His power, however, He has not bound to the means to such an extent that He could not work without them. Furthermore, [there are] many examples to be recalled in the Scriptures in which God kept certain people alive without food and drink, also returning them to health again without a physician. Thus we must allow ourselves to be satisfied that God converted Paul through a voice from heaven while he still was snorting with threats and murders against the disciples of the Lord (Acts 9:1, 4). We must allow it despite the fact that the ordained means of conversion are the hearing of the divine Word which God has placed in the mouths of His servants (Rom. 10:18), and through which He wants to be effectual in those who do not resist the Holy Spirit (Acts 7:51) and who do not scorn the counsel of God against themselves [i.e., to their own detriment] (Luke 7:30).

2. That God the Lord threatens with great seriousness in Gen. 17:14 – **Whenever a young boy is not circumcised on the foreskin of his flesh, his soul must be uprooted from out of his people**; and also concerning Baptism in John

3:5 – **Unless one is born out of water and Spirit, he cannot come into the kingdom of God.** It apparently follows that the uncircumcised and unbaptized little children are, for all practical purposes, damned. ANSWER: **1.** These grounds and examples here presented in no way apply to those who miss out on the holy Sacraments not from scorn, but because of an emergency. **2.** Although the regulation and ordinance of God still holds, yet, just as with other regulations, an emergency is excepted. **3.** Also, the severe threat of Gen. 17:14 is not to be universally applied to all the little children who die uncircumcised, since at times one parent, in opposition to the other parent, prevented the circumcision (Exo. 4:25). Rather, it applies to adults who neglect the circumcision on their own flesh out of scorn, and then to the children who defect and completely turn from the nation of Israel to the Gentiles and discontinue circumcision, as many did at the time of Antiochus (1 Macc. 1:54). **4.** It should especially be noted that this clarification and summary of the words of this text can be proven, for it is located near [the words]: a young lad who is not thus circumcised, his soul shall be uprooted, etc., because this action discontinued My covenant; or as it actually reads in the Hebrew language, **because this has circumvented, overstepped and scorned My covenant. 5.** Thus [as regards] Christ's words about the necessity of holy Baptism in John 3:5, this verse is to be understood in the same way as referring to the common ordinance, so that nothing be taken away from the power of God, the the extraordinary power and action of God [*extrordinariae potentiae et actioni Dei*], that He cannot in such cases of emergency effect rebirth without means.

3. That maybe such unbaptized little children have a special place where there is neither woe nor weal, a place where they do not behold the lovely fellowship of angels and the elect, but neither are they tortured with the hellish flames. ANSWER: **1.** Nowhere does the Scripture mention such a place. Rather, it portrays the contrast of heaven and hell in all cases, eternal life and eternal death, God's kingdom and Satan's kingdom, the fellowship of the blessed elect and the fellowship of the damned, salvation and damnation, without anything in between. **2.** In the light of how the Scriptures, without any middle ground, contrastingly portray believers and unbelievers, members of Christ and members of the devil, good and evil, devout and godless—between [any of] these it knows of no tertium or third place. **3.** Accordingly, one should not claim or invent such a strange place for unbaptized children [on the basis] of the opinion of one's own reason, but rather remain with the guidance of the Scriptures. **4.** Also, what kind of place would it be where there is neither weal nor woe? Further, it would be punishment and agony enough just to be eternally separated from God and the holy angels, from all fellowship with the elect, and from the view of loved ones. Without God's grace and presence there is no weal; with God's grace there is no woe! Without the angels and the association with the elect there is no blessed nor eternal life. **5.** It is to be noted at this point that all that has been presented up to now is to be understood as applying to the children of Christians. Regarding the children of heathen who are born outside the Church, it is written in 1 John 5:12: **Whoever does not have the Son of God, he does not have life,** and in Rom. 5:12: **So then, just as through one man sin came into the world, and death through sin.** At the same time, however, there will be a big distinction among those who are excluded from the kingdom of God, Luke 12:47, 48: **The servant, however, who knows the Lord's will but did not prepare himself, nor did according to His will, he will have to suffer many whiplashes. But he who did not know, yet did what is deserving of the whiplashes, will have to suffer few whiplashes.**

CHAPTER 27

AT WHAT TIME SHOULD HOLY BAPTISM BE ADMINISTERED?

y now the essential points have been dealt with concerning the benefit and the effect [of Baptism]; concerning the persons who may and should baptize, or be baptized. At this time there still remains certain details about this worthy Sacrament to consider: first, regarding time; then, place; and finally, outward ceremonies. Concerning the time when holy Baptism should and can be administered:

1. It was indeed the practice in the early church to baptize twice a year; namely, at Easter and then also on Pentecost. However, there is no definite time specified for holy Baptism in God's Word. Thus, it is not to be confined to any certain time.

Gal. 4:10–11 – **You observe days and months, and festivals and seasons. I fear for you that I may have worked on you for nothing.**

Col. 2:16 – **Thus let no one lay it on your conscience concerning food, or drink, or designated festivals, or new moons or Sabbaths.**

2. Since holy Baptism is the ordained means through which the children become regenerated to eternal life, it is thus right and proper for their parents to hasten with them to their Baptism so that they do not neglect their children's Baptism and later on find themselves in severe anxiety because of their [neglect].

John 3:5 – **So unless one becomes born out of water and Spirit, he cannot come into the kingdom of God.**

3. Since also the hour of death is uncertain and often a person is unexpectedly torn away from the land of the living through sudden illness, it is thus not advisable to postpone holy Baptism until the end of life. Indeed, the holy apostles baptized as soon as people became believers and professed the Christian faith. Nowhere do you find that they ever postponed Baptism until the hour of death.

In Acts 2:41, three thousand souls were baptized as soon as they became believers.

Acts 8:12–13 – **When they** (those from Samaria) **then believed Philip's preaching concerning the kingdom of God and concerning the name Jesus Christ, they let themselves be baptized—both men and children. Then Simon also came to faith and let himself be baptized.**

Acts 8:37 – **If you believe with your whole heart,** Philip says to the chamberlain from the land of the Moors, **then it is quite appropriate that you be baptized.**

In Acts 9:19, Paul lets himself be baptized soon after his conversion.

In Acts 10:47, those at Caesarea were baptized as soon as they had received the Holy Spirit.

In Acts 16:15, Lydia was baptized as soon as she became a believer.

In Acts 16:33, the head jailer and his household were immediately baptized when they believed Paul's proclamation.

In Acts 18:8, Crispus, his entire household, and many Corinthians became believers and let themselves be baptized soon after.

4. Since Baptism is also a holy Sacrament which should be dealt with with respect and devotion, it would indeed be appropriate if Baptism would be administered in the forenoon in public assembly with many Christians [present]; a prayer from a sober heart and mouth is usually more ardent and devotional, although (since no divine command exists concerning this matter) one cannot strongly force the issue.

1 Cor. 14:40 – **Let everything take place honorably and orderly.**

Here, again, [are] apparent points of contention:

1. That circumcision was administered on the eighth day (Gen. 17:10); but now holy Baptism has come in place of circumcision (Col. 2:11); therefore, it must similarly be administered on the eighth day. ANSWER: This apparent "proof" has by all counts been answered in chapter 19, point of contention #6. In a nutshell, it stated: **1.** In the Old Testament, circumcision was expressly bound to the eighth day by command of God, but no similar command exists concerning Baptism in the New Testament. **2.** That circumcision was even administered on the eighth day took place so that the tender little children might first gain a little strength to withstand the pain of circumcision. But no such danger exists with Baptism in the New Testament, not to mention the mystery and meaning that [would be] withheld from us for these eight days. **3.** Furthermore, the Levitical distinctions of days, food, and other ceremonies have been removed for us in the New Testament. Thus, we also in this matter justly exercise the freedom which Christ has dearly purchased for us, Gal. 5:1 – **So then hold your ground in the freedom with which Christ has freed us, and don't let yourselves be captured again in the yoke of slavery.**

2. Since in holy Baptism we are totally washed clean of sin, it would thus be better to postpone it until the hour of death so that we thus do not sin anew one more time and lose the blessings of holy Baptism. ANSWER: **1.** It has been demonstrated in chapter 17 that the efficacy of holy Baptism extends itself throughout [one's] entire lifetime. Therefore, this is reason enough not to postpone Baptism until the hour of death. **2.** For the same covenant of grace which God establishes with us in holy Baptism remains unrevoked from God's perspective. Therefore our access to it remains open at all times through genuine repentance and conversion. **3.** Nowhere does one read that the believers postponed

Baptism until the last hour of death. **4.** Not to mention that sin and the flesh are not totally eradicated, roots and veins, in holy Baptism; [therefore], we must thereafter struggle against them following Baptism and must daily petition for forgiveness of sins. This issue was extensively dealt with above in chapter 16.

CHAPTER 28

WHETHER ONE SHOULD MAKE USE OF BAPTISM MORE THAN ONE TIME.

 he time has come now also to address the particulars of this question, namely, if a Christian should let himself be baptized more than one time, just as we do not make use of the most worthy Lord's Supper only one time; rather, we avail ourselves of it as many times as we need consolation in the face of sin. To reply to this question, that the holy Sacrament of Baptism is to be employed no more than one time, the [following arguments apply]:

1. Since it is not mentioned or required in the institution of holy Baptism that one should employ [administer] holy Baptism more than once. As the Lord Christ instituted His holy Lord's Supper, He expressly commanded that one should not use it one time, [but] rather often and many times, Luke 22:19 – **Do this in memory of Me**; 1 Cor. 11:25, 26 – **Do such, as often as you drink it in memory of Me. For as often you eat of this bread, etc.** But concerning holy Baptism, one does not have any similar Word or command of God that it is to be used often.

Mat. 28:19 – Therefore go forth and teach all nations **and baptize them in the name of the Father and the Son and the Holy Spirit.**

2. Since one can find no example where the apostles ever baptized a believing Christian more than once. Relevant here is the example of all those who were baptized by the apostles (Acts 2:38; 8:12, 13, 38; 9:17; 19:44, 47; 16:13, 15; 18:8; 1 Cor. 1:14–16). Of none of these does one read that they were baptized again.

3. Since circumcision in the Old Testament was never put to use more than one time, and one nowhere finds that an Israelite was circumcised twice. Now then, holy Baptism has come to replace circumcision.

Col. 2:11 – **In whom** (in Christ) **you also have been circumcised with the circumcision without-hands, etc.**

4. Since holy Baptism is a *sacramentum initiationis*, the kind of Sacrament through which we are inducted into Christendom; but it is necessary to come to Christianity only once. Baptism is also the means for rebirth (John 3:5, Tit. 3:5); but then, just as we become born only once to this life, rebirth through holy Baptism is necessary only one time. Furthermore, God establishes a covenant of grace with us through Baptism. From God's perspective, this covenant remains unrevoked. Accordingly, repetition of Baptism is not necessary. Pertinent here are the passages taken from chapters 13 and 14 above, which witness to the efficacy and working of holy Baptism. They also prove that the efficacy of Baptism extends throughout all of one's life. (Note ch. 17 above concerning this matter.) Finally, holy Baptism testifies of God's gracious will toward us in this way: since His gracious will [is] immutable (Rom. 11:29), therefore Baptism should not be repeated. However, because our faith becomes weak at times, therefore it must be strengthened through the use of holy Communion. Just as a natural man is born only one time, but thereafter must be frequently nurtured and fed, so also it is adequate that we be reborn through Baptism once, but thereafter we must be frequently fed for eternal life with Christ's body and blood.

5. We become buried with Christ into death through Baptism. And now that Christ died and was buried only one time, so also we should be baptized only one time.

Rom. 6:3–4,9 – **Don't you know that all of us who are baptized in Jesus Christ, are baptized into His death? Thus we are indeed buried with Him into death, in order that just as Christ is risen from death through the glory**

of the Father, so we also should conduct ourselves in newness of life, etc. ... And [we] know that Christ arose from the dead, henceforth no longer dies; from now on death no longer will rule over Him.

Here, again, are some apparent points of contention:

1. That those who were baptized by John were later on baptized one more time by the apostles (Acts 19:4, 5, 6). ANSWER: [This subject] has been extensively dealt with above in chapter 7, point of contention #4.

2. That circumcision was repeated, for God the Lord commanded Joshua in Jos. 5:2 – **Make yourself knives of stone and circumcise again the children of Israel one more time;** hence Baptism, as that which came to replace circumcision (Col. 2:11) may also be repeated. ANSWER: In no way is it the meaning of the divine command in this text that those who had already been circumcised should be circumcised a second time. Rather, because circumcision had been neglected during the forty years in the wilderness, God the Lord commanded that Joshua should circumcise to a man all those who had been born during this time, as is apparent from the text (v. 4). This is the circumstance under which Joshua circumcised all the males of the people who had come out from Egypt: Of those who left Egypt, all the warriors died in the wilderness along the way (v. 5). For all the people who left Egypt were circumcised; but all the people who were born in the wilderness along the way after they left Egypt were not circumcised (v. 6). For the children of Israel wandered forty years in the wilderness until all the male warriors who had come out of Egypt perished (v. 7). Joshua circumcised the very children who had arisen in their place, for they had foreskins and had not been circumcised *en route.*

3. That we are baptized for the forgiveness of sins (Acts 2:38); but now we often need forgiveness of sins [and] therefore must let ourselves be baptized more than once. ANSWER: Even though we have a daily need for the forgiveness of sins, it does not follow we should even seek or receive forgiveness of sins by such a repetitious means. Rather, God the Lord establishes a covenant of grace with us in holy Baptism which consists of this: that God no longer will remember our sins any more (Jer. 31:34). We can comfort ourselves throughout life with this promise and grace-covenant, and [whenever] we, through sins, deprive ourselves of the blessings of this covenant, the way and entrance still remains open to us. Through repentance and conversion, we are able to obtain God's grace and forgiveness again. Consequently, it is not necessary to re-establish this grace-covenant by being baptized again since, from God's perspective, it [this grace-covenant] remains irrevocable at all times.

4. In holy Baptism, God simultaneously betroths Himself to us (Hos. 2:19) and endows us with the *arrham*, the pledge or engagement gift of the Holy Spirit (2 Cor. 1:22, Eph. 1:14). But sin is spiritual adultery, as the Scriptures and prophets attest again and again. Now, just as adultery rips apart the marital covenant, so also this covenant gets torn apart through sin, so that those who are conscience-stricken because of their sin require a new Baptism. ANSWER: When one person of the married [couple] falls into adultery, and the innocent party is willing to continue living with him, in such a situation no new betrothal or wedding is required. Only the following is required: that the fallen party confess his sins, humbly plead for pardon, and promise amendment of life. Thus God the Lord has declared in His Word: When we, after falling into sin, in true contrition and repentance confess our spiritual adultery and divorce, He will receive us again into grace and pardon our sin for the sake of Christ, our Bridegroom, our High Priest, and our Advocate (1 John 2:1). That also no new wedding via holy Baptism is required is shown by the beautiful promises of God, which read:

Jer. 3:1, 12, 13 – **If a man divorces his wife and she departs from him and takes another man, should he take** her back again? Is [it] not then true that the land has become polluted? You, however, have whored around with many paramours; yet the Lord says, Come back to Me. Turn back again rebellious Israel, says the Lord; thus I will not set My countenance against you, for I am merciful [compassionate], says the Lord, and I will not be angry with you forever. Simply confess your iniquity, that you have sinned against the Lord your God, and have run back and forth between all the strange gods under all the green trees, etc., Eze. 16:60, 61 – But I will remember My covenant which I have made at the time of your youth. Then you will remember your ways and be ashamed of yourself, etc.

CHAPTER 29

AT WHAT SITE SHOULD AND MAY HOLY
BAPTISM BE ADMINISTERED?

oncerning where and at what place holy Baptism should be administered, there is no express command given in the divine holy Scriptures. Nevertheless, it is a fine, praiseworthy practice that this worthy Sacrament be administered in the public assembly of Christians, and thus in the Church.

1. Because this holy Sacrament is a visible Word and a seal of that which is promised in the Word, [the proclamation of which] is performed in public assembly.

1 Cor. 14:26,34 – **When you come together, then one has a Psalm, one has a teaching, one has tongues, one has revelation, one has exegesis; let it all take place for improvement. Let your women be silent among the fellowship.**

2. Because the Sacrament of the holy Supper is performed in public assembly, holy Baptism is therefore to be regarded in the same way.

1 Cor. 11:20,33 – **When you then come together, doesn't one observe the Lord's Supper there? Therefore, my beloved brothers, when you come together to eat, wait for each other.**

3. Because the [observance] of this Sacrament calls for a fervent prayer, and prayer is much more effectual if many of you sit together.

Mat. 18:19, 20 – **Furthermore I say to you: where two among you become one on earth for the purpose of [offering] a petition, [it] will be meted out to them** from My Father in heaven. For where two or three are gathered in My name, there I am among them.

4. Since it is useful that a baptized person [in case of] doubt have sure evidence of his holy Baptism, therefore it is beneficial that there be many witnesses at the Baptism.

Num. 35:30, Deu. 17:6; 19:15, Heb. 10:28 – **In the mouth of two or three witnesses the matter shall be established.**

But at the same time, the administration of Baptism is in no way bound to the public assembly of Christians to such an extent that one dare not, in the absence [of such an assembly], baptize in a home in case of an emergency. [This contention] is substantiated thusly:

1. In the institution of Baptism, no certain place is assumed.

Mat. 28:19 – **Therefore go forth and teach all nations and baptize them, etc.**

2. The holy apostles did not use any special place for Baptism; rather, they baptized in every place where they were given the opportunity.

In Acts 2:41, three thousand souls are baptized under the open sky.

In Acts 8:38, the chamberlain from the land of the Moors was baptized in water which they happened upon along the road.

In Acts 9:19, Paul is baptized in the house in which Ananias lived.

In Acts 10:47,48, the believers in Caesarea were baptized in the home of Cornelius.

In Acts 16:15, Lydia, along with her whole household, is baptized with water.

In Acts 16:33, the head jailer, along with his own [family], is baptized in the jailhouse.

[Also] relevant is [the fact] that John baptized under the open skies outside of the Temple along the Jordan and at Aenon in Salim (Mat. 3:6, 16; Mark 1:5, 9; Luke 3:21; John 3:23; 10:40).

3. In case of emergency, the common order, which the Christian Church usually follows, is suspended, since the order of administration of the holy Sacraments is there to serve and not to command.

1 Cor. 14:40 – **Let everything take place honorably and orderly.** (In so far as an emergency does not force one to deviate from human ordinances, the distinction must steadfastly remain. One is not allowed to deviate from God's ordinance, for example, [by using] something else in Baptism besides water; but from ecclesiastical ordinances one may indeed deviate in case of emergencies.)

4. In the New Testament, the Divine Service is no longer [restricted] to a certain location as in the Old Testament; rather, God wants to be present with His grace in all places where people gather in His name and call upon Him.

Mat. 18:20 – **Where two or three are gathered together in My name, there I am among them.**

John 4:21 – **The time is coming when you will pray to the Father neither on this mountain nor at Jerusalem.**

1 Tim. 2:8 – **So then I want that men pray in every place**, etc.

5. Since circumcision, in whose place Baptism has come (Col. 2:11), was similarly administered at times in private homes, to say nothing of all the other places where circumcision is mentioned, and yet it is not expressly stated that it took place in the tent of the covenant [the Tabernacle] or the Temple. Thus obviously [circumcision] was performed in private homes. So we will allow ourselves to be content with those cases where we clearly know that the circumcision was performed at a home.

Exo. 4:24–25 – **And as he** (Moses) **was in the shelter, the Lord came towards him and wanted to kill him. Then Zipporah took a stone and cut her son's foreskin,** etc.

In 1 Macc. 1:63 [and] 2 Macc. 6:10, it is recorded that at the time of the rebellion instigated by Antiochus, certain women circumcised their children. This [action] most certainly occurred in private homes, because it would never have been allowed in an open assembly and also because a mother who had just given birth had to be confined for thirty-three days if she bore a boy, Lev. 2:4 [sic, Lev. 12:4], or sixty-six days if she bore a girl.

[In] Luke 1:59 Zacharias' little son is circumcised; however, that it took place in Zacharias' home is to be deduced since Elizabeth was present for it. According to the Law of Moses, she still had to be confined at that time.

Here, again, [are] apparent points of contention: that the administration of Baptism [properly] belongs to the office of preaching; [and because] the proclamation of the divine Word is to be done in the common assembly, therefore holy Baptism also should not be performed anywhere else. ANSWER: **1.** Obviously preaching and Baptism are to be thus regarded according to the general ordinances. **2.** However, in case of an emergency one may indeed deviate from this ordinance, since thereby nothing is done in opposition to any express command of God. **3.** Accordingly, just as one speaks comfort from God's word to the ill also in a home [and] imparts to them absolution and the holy Supper, so also one may and should, in case of an emergency, administer holy Baptism in a private home, so that (inasmuch as it depends on us) the little children do not lose out on the ordained means for rebirth.

CHAPTER 30

CONCERNING THE CEREMONIES THAT ARE
GENERALLY USED AT BAPTISM.

fter having dealt with time and place, namely, at what time and at which place holy Baptism should be administered, it [is appropriate] to conclude by considering (albeit briefly) the ceremonies, that is, the external pomp which is practiced in the administration of holy Baptism. Since these ceremonies are performed through no command of God, but rather have been established by people solely for the sake of profitability and good commemoration, there is little one can present from God's Word about such ceremonies. To speak in generalities, we say of them:

1. That neither the essence nor the efficacy of holy Baptism consists in such ceremonial usage, but only in this: that in accordance with Christ's command and the apostolic example, water is poured over the person in the name of the Father and the Son and the Holy Spirit.

Mat. 28:19 – Therefore go forth and teach all nations **and baptize them in the name of the Father and the Son and the Holy Spirit.**

Therefore, it is best that holy Baptism be administered purely and simply according to this institution of Christ, without a huge multitude of ceremonies, as the holy apostles have given us precedent with their example. They, without great pomp, baptized people in the name of the Father and the Son and the Holy Spirit (Acts 2:28; 8:12-13, 38; 9:19; 10:47; 16:15, 33; 18:8). Also, there is the danger among the masses that many ceremonies, especially when they are not directed at edifying, will cause [people] to take their eyes off of the chief part of Baptism and let their gaze be directed at the ceremonies. [There is the further danger] that such current external ceremonies [may] be regarded as necessary and ascribed divine efficacy, and that the symbolism and types which belong to the Old Testament [may] be pulled into the New Testament, etc.

 2. The ceremonies which are retained in the administration of holy Baptism should be directed towards edification; that is, that they particularly present to the eyes the worth and efficacy of holy Baptism and awaken a healthy respect towards this high and worthy Sacrament among the simple and naïve.

 1 Cor. 14:26, 40 – **Let everything happen for improvement. Let everything take place honorably and orderly.**

 3. The very same ceremonies which were used by the early church are directed towards edification and do not contradict the faith and thus are justly retained. And, even though contentious [people] press to have them removed, one reasonably retains them in Christian freedom. Again, when they are presented as needful and a part of the divine service, one rightly lets them remain because of the same Christian freedom.

 Gal. 5:1,13 – **So continually stand in the freedom with which Christ has freed us, and don't let yourself be captured again in the yoke of slavery. You, however, dear brothers, are called to freedom, etc.**

 Col. 2:16 – **Thus let no one lay it on your conscience over food or drink, or over designated festivals, or new moons, or Sabbaths, etc.**

 The ceremonies which flow in opposition to God's Word, or are simply ungodly or childish, as well as those to which are ascribed a special efficacy or necessity apart from the Word of God [and] which do not serve for edification—portraying holy Baptism as an external spectacle that doesn't serve a devotional purpose—are justly uprooted. Also [justly uprooted are such practices as] exorcising the baptismal water with special exorcism [*exorcismis*], blowing under the baby's eyes, putting salt in the mouth, putting spittle in the nose and ears and saying: **Ephatha, be opened**, anointing the breast and shoulders with oil, smearing the forehead with chrism, imparting milk and honey into the mouth, etc., and ascribing to each and all of these things a special efficacy. All these things are in part superstition, in part foolish, and totally irrelevant for edification—especially the exorcism of the baptismal water.

1 Tim. 4:4,5 – **For all creation of God is good and not reprehensible if it is received with thanksgiving, for it is sanctified through the Word of God and prayer.**

CHAPTER 31

CONCERNING THE SPECIFIC CEREMONY OF HOLY BAPTISM.

lthough it is easy to conclude from the foregoing regulations what is be regarded as the ceremony of holy Baptism, we still want especially to deal with one [ceremony] in particular for the sake of better order. This constitutes holy Baptism:

1. According to God's Word, our only help from the great harm and extreme misery into which we people have tumbled through the Fall of our first parents is through Christ. By His obedience and satisfaction, He again won [for us] God's grace, righteousness, and eternal life and these merits of Christ are offered, imparted, and received in holy Baptism as a bath of rebirth and renewal. This instruction and remembrance is rightly [properly] retained in holy Baptism to awaken devotion in those standing [in attendance at the Baptism].

Col. 3:16 – **Let the Word of Christ live richly among you in all wisdom.**

It is relevant [to note] here that John also reminded his listeners who wanted to be baptized of these [points]: that by nature they were evil trees on whose roots the axe has already been laid; that they were going to be chopped down and heaved into the fire (Mat. 3:10); that their physical birth from Abraham would not rescue them from this calamity (v. 9); that Christ is God's Lamb who carries the world's sins (John 1:29); and that he baptized for the forgiveness of sins (Mark 1:4).

In Acts 8:37, Philip asks the chamberlain from the land of the Moors prior to his Baptism if he believed with his whole heart that Jesus Christ is God's Son.

2. That the little baptismal candidate be brought before the Lord Christ through the **Our Father** and other beneficial little prayers, and God be called upon that He would, in accordance with His promise, be present in this act with His gracious working to impart the eternal blessing of the heavenly bath to the little baptismal candidate; that He would, through the same saving Flood, drown in him [the candidate] all that is inborn from Adam and all that he himself has additionally done. These little prayers are also properly retained in the administration of Baptism.

Luke 3:21 – **And it happened that as all the people let themselves be baptized – and Jesus also was baptized and prayed, etc.**

1 Tim. 4:5 – **For it** (the creation of God) **is sanctified through the Word of God and prayer.**

Here belongs [the fact] that Christ commanded the little children to be brought to Him (Mat. 19:14, Mark 10:14, Luke 18:15); for such occurs through believing prayer and sighing.

3. That little children are given a name in holy Baptism is also properly retained in the administration of Baptism. For, first of all, the baptized child can be reminded of [his] Baptism throughout his entire lifetime by his name; his name can also be for him a continual monument and witness to holy Baptism at all times, and especially in times of anxiety.

Gen. 3:20 – **And Adam called his wife Eve, because she was a mother of all the living.** As Adam, after the Fall, received the evangelical promise about the woman-seed that would trample the head of the hellish snake, he named his wife *Hevam*, or "the living one." He wanted to indicate by this that, from the heart, he rejoiced in, and comforted himself with, the fact that God the Lord had by grace received them—who had fallen into eternal death—and had given them the promise of life for the sake of the Messiah. Also, there is no doubt that both Adam and Eve were reminded of this divine blessing and promise with the name "Eve" every time they were severely tempted. Thus also Christians should daily remember the divine covenant of grace by the name which they received in Baptism. Here also other examples could be drawn upon by which to remember divine blessings.

Accordingly, also in prior times, children were given names in circumcision, but now holy Baptism has come in place of circumcision (Col. 2:11).

In Luke 1:59-60, 63, the little son of Zachariah is named **John** in his circumcision.

Luke 2:21 – **And when it was the eighth day, that the child was circumcised, His name was called Jesus, etc.**

In the third place, this ὀνομαθεσία or communication of the new name in holy Baptism gives a comfort to the baptized that they are registered by name in the Book of Life, that they have become God's children, true disciples of Christ, temples of the Holy Spirit, and heirs of eternal life.

Luke 10:20 – **But you rejoice that your name is written in heaven.**

Phi. 4:3 – **Whose names are in the Book of Life.**

Rev. 2:17 – **He who overcomes, to him I will give to eat of the hidden manna and give him a good testimony, and with the testimony write a new name which no one will recognize other than the one who receives it.**

Rev. 3:5 – **He who overcomes, he will be clothed with white clothing, and I will not expunge from the Book of Life,** etc.

Rev. 13:8 – **The names that are not written in the living Book of the Lamb, etc.,** repeated in chapter 17:8.

Finally, this name gives the baptized a constant reminder that their names have been recorded as spiritual soldiers among the troops of Christ in holy Baptism, that they should campaign against the devil, the world, and the sinful flesh in knightly fashion.

Rom. 6:4 – **Thus we are indeed buried with Him** (Christ) **through Baptism into death, so that in the same way Christ has been awakened from death through the glory of the Father, so also we should live in a new life.**

4. That the sign of the cross is made over the forehead and the breast of the little child, such may also have a beneficial meaning; namely, that the little baptismal candidate is counted as one of those who believe on the crucified Christ; yes, also, that the old man is crucified along with Christ in and through holy Baptism (Rom. 6:6). Nevertheless, the delusion must not be added that the sign of the cross in and of itself possesses special powers against the devil; rather, it must remain a reminder and meaningful sign.

In Gen. 48:14 when Jacob wanted to bless both sons of Joseph, Ephraim and Manasseh, he similarly made a cross over them with his hands, since he laid his hands over them cross-wise. By this, without a doubt, the Patriarch reminded himself of the cross of Christ—as he then gloriously prophesies about Christ in the following chapter 49 (v. 10, 11, 12), and later adds in v. 18: **Lord I wait upon Your Salvation.** Therefore, it is written in Heb. 11:21, through faith, Jacob blessed both sons of Joseph.

In Eze. 9:4, God the Lord commands the people of Jerusalem, who were sighing and complaining concerning the atrocities therein, to sign themselves with the sign "T" on the forehead. This also appears to parallel [the sign] in Rev. 7:3 where the servants of God are sealed on the foreheads. It was indicated through this sign that they set all their hopes on the crucified Christ and gloried only in the cross of the Lord Jesus Christ (Gal. 6:14); for, the "T" in former times was actually drawn like a cross †.

5. That through exorcism or through oath of renunciation, the devil is mandated in the name of the Father and the Son and the Holy Spirit to depart from the child who is being baptized. Here it is to be particularly noted that this ceremony should not be regarded as an essential and necessary part of holy Baptism; also, that in no way is the child to be regarded as being physically possessed by the devil; finally, that one should not hold the position that through these words the child is even totally finished with the kingdom of the devil and his power. Rather, this sworn renunciation is to be understood in no other way than as a reminder and testimony of: [1] the spiritual servitude of the little children in the kingdom of the devil; [2] the great misery in which the children are stuck because of inherited sin; [3] the power [efficacy] of holy Baptism by which people are taken out of the kingdom of the devil and placed into Christ's kingdom; [4] the continual combat and victory which Christ daily makes available for opposing the devil's kingdom through the office of the ministry and the Word. To this may be applied all the testimonies which elsewhere deal in greater detail with inherited sin and the efficacy of holy Baptism.

But since the words actually seem to say that the child is completely freed from the power of the devil, it is to be noted here that the Christian Church has the right and the power to proclaim by means of other Scripture-based words the doctrine of inherited sin, of the strength and kingdom of Satan, and of the efficacy of holy Baptism; also, with unanimous agreement, to completely do away with this renunciation of the devil by oath. Or, otherwise, if it is retained for the sake of the weak, it would be beneficial and necessary to present in public assembly, frequently and clearly, the proper understanding of this [oath] so that all superstition concerning the necessity of the exorcism, the bodily possession by the devil, and the special power of such words would be completely expunged from the hearts of the hearers, since in no way can it be denied that the declaration of exorcism sounds better than the words themselves.

On the other hand, when dealing with those who err in many other aspects of Christian doctrine, and whose reason for pursuing the abolition of the exorcism is that the children of Christians are supposedly already holy and already in God's covenant before Baptism, in such a case it is right to oppose them and in no way agree to the abolition, because that [course] runs counter to Christian freedom and counter to the pure doctrine of inherited sin. Also, no one should abolish these ceremonies on his own without the unanimous agreement of the Church; rather, in this, as in other matters concerning things "neither here nor there" [*adiaphora*], follow in harmony with the practice of the Christian Church.

Gal. 2:4–5 – **When however certain false brothers by infiltration had sneaked themselves in along side of our proclamation of freedom, which we have in Christ Jesus, in order to enslave us, we did not relent for one moment to be subject to them so that the truth of the Gospel would persevere among you.**

Gal. 5:1 – **So continue in the freedom with which Christ has freed us, etc.**

6. That the use of godfathers or baptismal sponsors at holy Baptism must not and should not be wantonly cast aside, since the office of such sponsors is as follows:

First of all, that they bring the little children to the Lord Christ and petition Him on their behalf that He would look upon them with the eyes of His mercy and receive them into the grace-covenant of holy Baptism.

Mat. 19:13, Mark 10:13, Luke 18:15 – **Little children were brought to Him** (the Lord Jesus) **so that He might lay hands upon them and pray**, etc.

Next, that they testify and reiterate in Christ's stead that the baptized little children believe and that they are heirs of the kingdom of God.

Mat. 19:14, Mark 10:14, Luke 18:16 – **Let the little children come to Me and detain them not, for such are the kingdom of God.**

Thirdly, that today or tomorrow [on any given day] they may give witness to the little children of their Baptism, so that a baptized Christian may all the better extinguish the fiery arrows of the devil.

Num. 34:30, Deu. 17:6; 19:15, Heb. 10:28 – **In the mouth of two or three witnesses the matter shall be verified.**

Fourthly, that in case of the death of the parents they take the children and rear them in the fear of God, just as they publicly promise in the presence of God and the Church.

Eph. 6:4 – **You fathers—raise up your children in the discipline and admonition of the Lord.**

Herewith it should be remembered, even though it does not subtract anything from holy Baptism whether the sponsors are godly or godless, that one should at the same time ask pious, God-fearing people, who adhere to the true religion, [to participate in] this holy and worthy action, so that one is not seen as approving of false teaching or godless living, 1 The. 5:22 – **Avoid every appearance of evil;** also, that one might with a clearer conscience commit the children, in the event of one's death, to being reared in the true religion and godliness.

7. That the baptizer lays his hand upon the forehead of the little child and prays also should not be tossed aside, for the holy patriarchs, prophets, and apostles used this ceremony in holy observances and blessings—a matter dealt with elsewhere. Here in particular the following testimonies fit in:

Mat. 19:13, 15 – **Little children were brought to Him** (the Lord Jesus), **that He might lay hands on them and pray, etc. And [He] laid hands on them and went away from there.** This is repeated in Mark 10:16.

In Acts 9:17, Ananias lays hands on Paul prior to baptizing him.

8. That the sponsors renounce the devil and all his works and all his ways in the child's stead, [but], on the other hand, confess the true faith in God the Father, God the Son, and God the Holy Spirit—this is also an unobjectionable ceremony. For since the little baptismal candidate is taken up into Christ's troops, he must obligate himself to strive against the devil because the total holy Trinity has received the person who is baptized into the grace-covenant. So, he must repeatedly obligate himself to knowledge, confession, and service of the true God.

In Mat. 3:8, John proclaims to those who came to his Baptism: **Go forth, do proper fruits of repentance.** In Luke 3:8 it is repeated.

In Luke 3:10, 12, 14, he tells the people, the tax-collectors, and the soldiers how they are to conduct themselves in service to God after receiving Baptism.

9. That the little, baptized child is dressed with a white shirt, so that it is visually evident [symbolized] that in its Baptism it is dressed with the righteousness of Christ, as with a garment of salvation; also that it should henceforth beware not to spot such a white dress with blood-red sins.

Gal. 3:27 – **For as many of you who are baptized have put on Christ** [have dressed yourselves with Christ].

10. Finally, the baptizer rightly so thanks God for such grace and speaks the blessing over the baptized child. With this the entire action is concluded.

Num. 6:22–27 – **And the Lord spoke with Moses and said: Speak to Aaron and his sons and say: Thus you should say to the children of Israel when you bless them: The Lord bless you and protect you. The Lord let His face shine over you, and be gracious. The Lord lift His face over you and give you peace. For you should lay My name upon the children of Israel that I bless them.**

Mark 10:16 – **And He** (the Lord Jesus) **took them up in His arms and laid the hands on them and blessed them.**

Herewith we conclude also this chapter about the ceremonies of holy Baptism, in particular, as well as the entire tract concerning the Sacrament of holy Baptism. From the bottom of our hearts, we thank God the Lord for all His benefits and especially for those which He has shown us in the grace-covenant of Baptism. And, we fervently and totally commend ourselves into His fatherly reign and protection. Amen.

Part II:
The Sacrament of the Altar

CHAPTER 1

CONCERNING THE NAMES WHICH HOLY SCRIPTURE GIVES TO THIS SACRAMENT.

n the previous volume, we have dealt with the first Sacrament of the New Testament, namely, holy Baptism. In this volume we shall consider the other Sacrament of the New Testament. For just as we are born again through the Sacrament of holy Baptism, so also we are nurtured for eternal life through the Sacrament of this holy Supper. Just as we were taken into God's covenant of grace through the former Sacrament, so also through the latter Sacrament we are preserved in the very same covenant of grace. Just as the Holy Spirit awakens faith in us through the former, so also He strengthens and increases it through the latter. Just as circumcision typifies the former, so the Passover [paschal] lamb of the Old Testament typifies the latter. Next, we shall consider by what names this Sacrament of the holy Supper is called in the holy Scriptures. There we find the following names:

1. It is called **the Lord's Supper**, because it was instituted and celebrated by our Lord Christ in the night after supper.

1 Cor. 11:20 – **When you come together, don't you keep the Lord's Supper?** (That St. Paul is not speaking here of the agape meal, which the first church observed in public, i.e., open assembly, but rather of the Sacrament of the true body and blood of Christ, becomes apparent from v. 23, in which the apostle opposes the inwardly disruptive misuse of Christ's institution.) He refers also to the Sacrament in the following instances.

2. It is also called **the Supper** precisely for the sake of the obvious reason.

1 Cor. 11:21 – **For when one celebrates the Supper, each one eats his own first,** etc. (The Corinthians felt that since Christ first instituted this holy Sacrament after the evening meal, they could not properly celebrate the Lord's Supper if they did not first hold a meal.)

3. It is called **the Lord's table** and **the Lord's cup** since we, as recipients, are fed through the same with the Lord Christ's body and blood, and with this heavenly meal we appear as guests of the Lord Christ. According to standard usage of such terminology in the Scriptures, **table** is understood to mean the meal itself.

1 Cor. 10:21 – **You cannot drink of the Lord's cup and at the same time drink of the devil's cup. You cannot simultaneously be a participant of the Lord's Table and the devil's table.**

4. It is called **the fellowship of the body and blood of Christ,** since in this Sacrament we receive not only the bread and wine, but also, at the same time, the true body and blood of Christ.

1 Cor. 10:16 – **The blessed cup which we bless, is it not the communion with Christ's blood; the bread which we break, is it not the communion with Christ's body?**

5. This Sacrament is called **the New Testament,** since it was especially instituted by Christ shortly before His death and thereby imparts to the Christian the highest of all legacies, namely, forgiveness of sins, life and salvation. Here we find all the necessary ingredients of what constitutes a proper testament. The testator is Christ, who established this testament shortly before His death; and with precise words He declares herewith (so to speak) His last will. It also enumerates the treasures which it dispenses: namely, the forgiveness of sins, through which God's grace, life and salvation are inextricably intertwined. To this is attached the seal of these promises; namely, the true body and the true blood of Christ are sacramentally tied together with the bread and wine as a visible sign. Further, there is the testimony of the holy apostles as notaries [L. *notarii*] and summoned witnesses.

Mat. 26:28 and Mark 14:24 – **This is My blood of the New Testament.** Luke 22:20; 1 Cor. 11:25 – **This cup is the New Testament in My blood.**

6. Finally, it is also called **the breaking of bread,** mainly because the custom of bread-breaking was once part of the ceremony through which the blessed bread was prepared in advance for distribution.

Acts 2:42,46 – **They remained steadfast in the apostles' teaching and in fellowship and in breaking bread and in prayer. And they were daily and constantly of one mind with each other in the Temple and broke bread back and forth in homes.**

Acts 20:7 – **On a certain Sabbath as the disciples came together to break bread, Paul preached to them,** etc. (While we do not completely reject the view of those who regard this breaking of bread as a regular meal—as the expression is also more commonly used in other places, including Luke 24:35 and Acts 27:35 – yet in these contexts it seems more likely that the bread-breaking is to be understood as the [Lord's] Supper, since the texts refer to first the teaching, then the prayers.)

1 Cor. 10:16 – **The bread which we break, is it not the communion of the body of Christ?**

CHAPTER 2

CONCERNING THE SAYINGS AND TYPES OF THE OLD TESTAMENT WHICH IN ADVANCE FORETELL THIS SACRAMENT.

 ust as the Sacrament of holy Baptism was foretold in the Old Testament with sayings and types, so also one can rightly affirm that certain sayings and types of the Old Testament point to this Sacrament of the body and blood of Christ. First of all, accordingly, the following passages are relevant here:

Psa. 23:5 – **You prepare for me a table in the face of my enemies.** This passage can be applied to the Lord's Supper inasmuch as Christ the Good Shepherd (John. 10:12) refreshes our souls (Psa. 23:3), grazes us on green meadows, and leads us to fresh water (v. 2).

Psa. 111:1–5 – **I thank the Lord with a total heart within the counsel of the godly and within the fellowship.** (As often as we eat of this bread and drink of this cup in the holy Supper, we should proclaim the Lord's death, that is, thank Him for this in public assembly [1 Cor. 11:26].)

V. 2 – **Great are the works of the Lord; whoever takes note of them, has sheer delight [joy] in them.**

V. 3 – **What He ordains, that is praiseworthy and glorious, and His righteousness abides forever.** (The holy Supper is also such an ordinance and institution of Christ in which He shows His great goodness.)

V. 4 – **He, the gracious and compassionate Lord, has instituted a remembrance of His wonders.** (That's why the holy Supper has been instituted by

Christ, that we should remember how He redeemed us through His goodness.)

V. 5 – **He gives food to those who fear Him.** (Whoever wants to partake beneficially of this precious, worthy food in the holy Supper must come to it in the true fear of God.)

He remembers His covenant forever. (We were indeed taken up into the grace-covenant of God through holy Baptism, but we often fall from it again through sin. Therefore, Christ has instituted His holy Supper so that we are reassured of the gracious forgiveness of sin and are taken up again into the very same covenant.)

Pro. 9:1–6 – **Wisdom builds her house and erects seven columns.** (The Wisdom of God is Christ [1 Cor. 1:24]; His house is the Christian Church [1 Tim. 3:15]; the seven columns are the merits of Christ upon which this house is established: on His birth, circumcision, holy life, suffering, death, resurrection and ascension into heaven [Acts 5:5]). **She** [Wisdom] **slaughtered her cattle and carried forth her wine and prepared her table.** (Christ, the Lamb of God slaughtered for us on the cross, has for a holy Supper prepared this table.) **And she sent out her maidens to invite from the top of the palace of the city: whoever is foolish, get over here. And to the fools she said: Come, live on my bread and drink the wine which I serve to you. Forsake the foolish ways, thus you will live,** etc. (This passage speaks in general of the blessings of the Gospel, through which we are fed and nurtured unto eternal life. What is more, the passage is not improperly applied specifically to the holy Supper, in which we, with bread and wine, are enriched with the body and blood of Christ.)

Isa. 25:6 – **And on this mountain the Lord of Sabaoth shall prepare a meal for all nations; a meal of pure wine, of fat, of marrow** [choice meat]**, of wine in which there are no dregs.** (In all this, the prophet is actually speaking of the spiritual meal which God the Lord has prepared in the holy Gospel for grace-hungry souls. But since the holy Supper is a seal which is attached to the Gospel promise, one can rightly apply this text to it.)

Pertinent here are the figures and types of the Old Testament which point to this holy Sacrament. Let it herewith be noted that not all types are equally clear; rather, some come closer and are clearer and more graceful. In particular, the figure of the Easter [Passover] Lamb and the heavenly bread [manna] in the wilderness, which are justly to be applied one to the other. We would recount, in an orderly and consecutive manner, all the figures which in one fashion or the other may be applied here.

In Gen. 2:9–10 God the Lord placed the Tree of Life in the middle of Paradise. **And there went out from Eden a stream to water the garden.** Through the fruits of this tree, the first people could have been sustained in the imperishable and continuing bloom of youth. However, through the Fall into sin, they and their offspring were trapped in death, so that from now on the way to this Tree of Life is closed off (Gen. 3:24). So you see, God the Lord established for the Church a different Tree of Life in the garden of Paradise: Christ is the true Timber of Life, whose leaves serve for healing (Rev. 22:2). The very same gives us His flesh to eat and His blood to drink in the holy Supper; otherwise, we would have no life in us, John 6:53–55: His flesh is the true food and His blood is the true drink. Whoever eats His flesh and drinks His blood has eternal life.

Gen. 14:18–19 – **But Melchizedek, the King of Salem, brought forth bread and wine, and he was a priest of the Most High God. And he blessed him** (Abraham) **and said: Blessed be you, Abram, by the Highest God, who owns heaven and earth.** (This Melchizedek is a type of the eternal High Priest, Christ [Heb. 7:1–3ff.]. Just as Melchizedek once brought forth bread and wine to refresh Abraham and his soldiers, so also Christ gives us with the bread and wine His true body and blood to eat and drink so that we thereby are refreshed in our spiritual hunger and thirst.)

Exo. 12 describes the institution of the other Sacrament of the Old Testament, namely the Easter Lamb [Passover], which may rightly be applied to the Sacrament of the holy Supper. First of all, just as the Israelites in their Sacrament ate the Passover lamb and smeared its blood on both posts and the top beam of the doorway, v. 4,7, **So also we have an Easter Lamb** [Paschal Lamb]**, that is Christ, offered for us**, 1 Cor 5:7, whose true body we eat and blood we drink in the holy Supper. Secondly, just as this Sacrament of the little Passover lamb was a constant sign of remembrance before the eyes of the Israelites that God the Lord spared their first-born in the Exodus from Egypt (v. 27), so also we should proclaim the death of Christ in and by the reception of the holy Lord's Supper (1 Cor. 11:26); that is, we are to be reminded that through the death of Christ we have been rescued from the slavery of the Pharaoh from hell; and from the heart we are to thank the Lord Christ for this. Thirdly, just as an uncircumcised person was not to eat of the Passover lamb (v. 48), so also no unbaptized heathen should be admitted to the holy Lord's Supper. Finally, just as the Israelites had to eat the Passover lamb with special ceremonies, so also the person who eats of this bread and drinks of this cup should first examine himself (1 Cor. 11:28). Just as they had to eat the little Passover lamb with bitter spices [herbs] and with unleavened bread (v. 8), so should our old Adam be salted away through genuine repentance (Mark 9:49). Also, the old yeast of evil must be swept away (1 Cor. 5:7–8), if we are to participate worthily in the holy Supper.

In Exo. 16:15, God allows manna to fall from heaven so that the Israelites were fed. God the Lord also let water flow out of the rock so that the children of Israel were given drink in the desert. Christ relates this event to Himself in John 6:49–51 – **Your fathers ate manna in the wilderness and died. This is the bread that comes from heaven, so that** whoever eats of it does not die. I am the living Bread come from heaven; whoever will eat of this bread, he will live in eternity; and the bread I will give is My flesh, which I will give for the life of the world. In a similar vein, St. Paul clarifies this type in 1 Cor. 10:3, 4 – Our fathers did all eat the same spiritual food and did all drink the same spiritual drink; but they drank from the spiritual Rock that followed along, which was Christ. Just as the children of Israel in the desert were fed with this heavenly bread and miraculously given to drink with the water from out of the rock, so also are we fed in the holy Supper with the living Bread that came from heaven, that is with Christ's flesh, and given drink with His holy blood, which flows from His wounds, so that our souls do not languish or die from spiritual hunger and thirst in the desert wasteland of this world. Just as the manna and the water out of the rock were clear testimony to divine grace, so also Christ has demonstrated His marvelous blessings to us in the institution of the holy Lord's Supper. Just as the manna had a lovely taste (Exo. 16:31), so also the spiritual nourishment of Christ in the holy Supper is especially sweet-tasting to a soul hungry for grace. In the same way that all the Israelites publicly ate of the manna (1 Cor. 10:3), so all believing Christians have a holy Lord's Supper in which they together all receive Christ's body and blood. In the same way that the manna became spoiled for those who, in opposition to God's command, saved it for the next day (Exo. 16:20), so—though of itself Christ's body is imperishable, immortal, and filled with life-giving Spirit—indeed for those who unworthily eat Christ's body and drink His blood, it redounds to them for judgment (1 Cor. 11:29). In the same way that the people ceased to gather manna on the seventh day (Exo. 16:23), even so—after the completion of the days of labor in this life when begins the eternal Sabbath (Isa. 66:23)—Christ will from then on no longer deal with us through Word and Sacrament. Rather, we will see Him face to face (2 Cor. 13:12).

In Exo. 24:8, Moses takes the blood of the slaughtered offering and sprinkles the people with it and says: **See, this is the blood of the covenant which the Lord makes with you**, etc. Just as the Israelites at that time were, on the basis of these words, taken up into the covenant of God through the sprinkling of the offering blood, which was a type of Christ, so also Christ says in the institution of the holy Lord's Supper: **Take, drink, this is My blood of the New Testament** (Mat. 26:28, Mark 14:24), as if He wants to say: I establish a new covenant with you which is verified and sealed with My own blood. As often as you then drink this My blood of the New Testament in the holy Lord's Supper, you can absolutely reassure yourselves that you are in the new grace-covenant of God.

In Exo. 25:30 God commands that in the tabernacle the exhibition [show] bread be placed before Him on the table at all times. These exhibition breads are a type of the holy Supper, in which the Bread of Life (Christ) is presented to us, not for the purpose of viewing it but rather for the purpose of eating it, so that thereby we may see and taste just how amiable and gracious the Lord really is (Psa. 24:9). In the Old Testament only the priests were allowed to eat of this exhibition bread (Mat. 12:4, Mark 2:26). However, in the New Testament Christ has made all of us kings and priests before God (Rev. 1:6), so that we all may eat of this Bread of life. Just as the priest Abimelech did not want to give the servants of David to eat of the exhibition bread until he was informed that they were sanctified (1 Sam. 21:5), so also the unholy and godless should not be permitted to attend the holy Supper; rather, it should be called *sancta sanctis* [*holy of holies*].

In 1 Kin. 19:6, 8, the angel brings the prophet Elijah bread and a canister of water in the desert. Through the power of that nourishment the prophet remained on God's Mt. Horeb for forty days and forty nights. (Christ feeds us in the holy Supper with His body and blood so that in the power of such nourishment we may safely pilgrimage through the desert of this world and arrive at the heavenly Jerusalem, of which God's Mt. Horeb is a type.)

In 2 Kin. 2:13, as Elijah rides up to heaven, he placed his mantle over Elisha. (Some of the fathers point to this as meaning that Christ, after His Ascension into heaven, in similar fashion extends to us in the Lord's Supper His holy body to eat, since His flesh is called a mantle in Gen. 49:11.)*

---

* Gerhard gives the impression that he is not particularly sympathetic to this idea. Tr.

CHAPTER 3

BY WHOM THE HOLY LORD'S SUPPER WAS INSTITUTED.

he founder and institutor of the holy Lord's Supper is our Lord and Savior, Jesus Christ, true God and Man. Shortly before His suffering and death, out of carefully considered deliberation and determination, He instituted this Sacrament as His Testament; and, along with the Sacrament of holy Baptism, He bequeathed to His Church also this Sacrament of His true body and blood. That Christ instituted the Lord's Supper is supported as follows:

1. Because the holy evangelists unanimously ascribe the institution of the holy Lord's Supper to Christ the Lord.

Mat. 26:26–28 – **As they then ate, Jesus took the bread, gave thanks and broke it and gave it to the disciples and said: Take, eat, this is My body. And He took the cup and gave thanks, gave it to them and said: All of you drink of this, this is My blood of the New Testament,** etc.

Mark 14:22–24 – **And while they were eating, Jesus took the bread, gave thanks and broke it and gave it to them and said: Take, eat, this is My body. And he took the cup and gave thanks and gave it to them and they all drank from it. And He said to them: This is My blood of the New Testament,** etc.

Luke 22:19–20 – **And He took the bread, gave thanks and broke it and gave it to them and said: This is My body, which is given for you; this do in remembrance of Me. In the same manner also He took the cup after the** evening meal and said: This is the cup, the New Testament in My blood, which is shed for you.

2. Because the apostle Paul, who learned his theology in the third heaven (2 Cor. 12:3), also ascribes the institution of the holy Lord's Supper to Christ.

1 Cor. 11:23, 24, 25 – **I have received from the Lord that which I have given to you; for the Lord Jesus, on the night He was betrayed, took the bread, gave thanks and broke it and said: Take, eat, this is My body which is broken for you; do this in remembrance of Me. In the same manner also He took the cup after the evening meal and said: This cup is the New Testament in My blood; Do this, as often as you drink it, in remembrance of Me.**

3. Because this Sacrament is called the Lord's Supper (as was proved above in chapter 1, no. 1) and which is so because it was instituted by the Lord Christ.

4. Because the institution of the holy Sacrament is vested in none other than God the Lord, as is thoroughly demonstrated in the general article on the Sacraments. But now the holy Supper is also a Sacrament of the New Testament. It follows from this that it could not be instituted by a man, but that it can be and was instituted by the Mediator of the New Testament. It was instituted by Christ.

So then, since the founder of the holy Supper is Christ Jesus, **1.** very Son of God, one essence with the Father and the Holy Spirit; **2.** an almighty Lord, Himself almighty according to His divine nature, to whom according to His human nature has been given all power in heaven and in earth; **3.** a faithful witness, yes, Himself the Truth; **4.** a wise and all-knowing Lord, yes, Himself the Wisdom of God; **5.** our Redeemer, Mediator, and the One who saves us (as has been more fully demonstrated in the article about God and the Person of Christ), it follows that we should without question believe and be assured that what He has prescribed, ordained and instituted, He will and can faithfully fulfill.

CHAPTER 4

THROUGH WHOM THE ADMINISTRATION OR DISTRIBUTION OF THE HOLY LORD'S SUPPER IS NOW PERFORMED.

hrist our Savior instituted and distributed to His disciples this holy Sacrament not only on the night that He was betrayed. Rather, it is He who also today is present when [believers] come together to celebrate His holy Lord's Supper, and it is He Himself who distributes His true body and blood in this worthy Sacrament. For just as no man ever had or has the authority to institute the eating and drinking of the body and blood in the holy Supper, so also no man possesses the ability to distribute Christ's body and blood. Rather, it is Christ who not only originally instituted the eating and drinking of His body and blood, but who there Himself also handed out His body to eat and His blood to drink in the holy Supper. And, just as the Word of God, which in the creation of animals and people provided [the power to]: **Be fruitful and increase yourself** (Gen. 1:22, 28) is still effective today, so that in the power of that very same Word the generations of animals and people increase daily, so also the Word of Christ: **Take, eat, this is My body; take, drink, this is My blood** is still continually effective within the Church of God to the extent that in the power of the very same Word the body of the Lord Christ with the bread, and His blood with the wine, are distributed in the holy Supper. Yet, Christ no longer performs the administration or handles this Sacrament of the holy Supper without intermediary persons, as it happened once at the original institution. Rather, He employs for this the servants of the office of the preaching ministry, i.e., pastors. He is effectual through them, and when they distribute the consecrated bread and consecrated chalice, Christ simultaneously then distributes His true body and blood in, with, and through the distribution of the consecrated bread and chalice. And since Christ and the action of the servant [pastor] cannot and should not be separated, since also the consecrated bread and the body of Christ/the consecrated chalice and the blood of Christ are sacramentally tied together (as shall be demonstrated and clarified later), it follows that the servants of Christ distribute not only bread and wine in the holy Supper, but also Christ's body and blood.

That the administration of the holy Lord's Supper actually belongs to the preachers and servants of the Church is supported as follows:

1. Preaching and the administration of the Sacraments belong together in that the holy Sacraments are nothing else than signs and seals of that which is proclaimed in the Word. Now then, the proclamation of the Word of God actually belongs to the preachers; therefore, they should also administer the holy Sacrament.

2. Teachers and preachers are ordained to be the householders over the fellowship of God. Now, however, among the divine mysteries, the holy Supper is of no mean importance.

1 Cor. 3:9 – **for we are God's helpers.**

1 Cor.4:1 – **Therefore everyone is to regard us, namely, as Christ's servants and householders [managers] over God's mysteries.**

Tit. 1:7 – **For a bishop should be irreproachable as a householder of God**, etc.

3. Since the administration of holy Baptism belongs to the office of the ministry, as indicated in chapter 5 on Baptism, therefore the preachers [pastors] should rightly also distribute the holy Supper, just as they administer other Sacrament of the New Testament.

In opposition to the first part of this chapter, in which is demonstrated that the servant does not act on his own authority, but rather Christ acts through the servant in the holy Supper, there is the apparent point of contention that through these very words: **this is My body, this is My blood,** the priest transforms the bread and wine into the body and blood of Christ. ANSWER: **1.** That in the holy Supper there occurs no essential change of the bread into Christ's body and the wine into Christ's blood will be shown later at the proper place. **2.** That also there is not hidden within the sound and echo of these words: **This is My body, this is My blood,** some sort of secret power through which the body of Christ is sacramentally united with the bread and the blood of Christ with the wine has been previously clarified. Just as the One and only One who instituted this Sacrament is Christ, so also He is the One and only One who in the holy Lord's Supper makes present for reception His true body and His true blood. **3.** Yet it is necessary in the administration of the holy Supper that the Words of Institution be repeated and that in the process the outward elements of bread and wine in this holy Sacrament be set aside and sanctified. Accordingly, when the preacher [pastor] who administers the holy Supper speaks the Words of Institution over the bread and wine in public assembly, it is not a mere historical recitation of what Christ did. Rather, he shows thereby, first of all, that he is not taking action here of his own discretion; instead, as a steward of the divine mysteries, he desires to administer this holy Sacrament according to Christ's ordinance and command. Secondly, therewith he sets aside the bread and wine that is present for this holy Sacrament, so that it no longer shall be simple bread and wine, but the means through which Christ's body and blood are distributed. In the third place, he inwardly prays that Christ would be present in this sacramental action according to His promise, and that along with the present bread and wine He distribute His body and blood. **[4.]** In the fourth place, he testifies that, because of the power of the ordinance and institution of Christ, the consecrated bread is the fellowship of the body of Christ and the consecrated chalice is the fellowship of the blood of Christ. He also testifies that accordingly all those who would receive this holy Sacrament should, with true faith, regard these words of the Testament as true, and, contrary to all doubts of reason, trust what Christ tells them. On account of these four reasons, it is essential that the Words of Institution are repeated articulately and distinctly whenever one administers this Sacrament. And yet it remains true that in no way can or should there be ascribed to the sound or the echo of the words some special, secret, hidden power through which Christ's body and blood are made present.

Against the other portion of this chapter there is the apparent point of contention that not only the preachers [pastors], but also other Christians may administer the holy Supper in case of emergency, in the same way that they are permitted to administer holy Baptism in case of an emergency. ANSWER: Concerning this concluding remark, the issue was dealt with in the article on holy Baptism in chapter 5, contention point no. 5, where it was shown that in this case there is a difference between the Sacrament of holy Baptism and the holy Lord's Supper. For what pertains to holy Baptism, Christ speaks expressly and with great seriousness in John. 3:5 – **Unless then one is born out of water and the Spirit, he cannot enter the kingdom of God.** However, the reception of the holy Supper is not especially necessary for such [entry into the kingdom of God]. Rather, where one cannot have access to an ordained pastor, the spiritual reception of the body and blood of Christ is adequate for salvation if one cannot obtain the sacramental reception.

CHAPTER 5

CONCERNING THE EXTERNAL, VISIBLE ELEMENTS WHICH THE LORD CHRIST USED AND ORDAINED FOR USE IN THIS SACRAMENT.

hen the Lord Christ wanted to institute the fellowship of His body and blood in the holy Lord's Supper, He used external, visible elements, namely, bread and wine. [He did this] so that, just as the water is the external element in Baptism, through which the Holy Trinity is effectual and imparts rebirth and renewal, the bread and wine in the holy Supper are the external elements and means of the fellowship of the body and blood of Christ. That Christ then uses bread and wine for this Sacrament is apparent first of all from the holy evangelists, who have described the institution of the holy Lord's Supper.

Mat. 26:26 – **But when they were eating, Christ took the bread,** etc.

Mark 14:22 – **And while they were eating, Jesus took the bread,** etc.

Luke 22:19 – **And He took the bread,** etc.

In describing the other element, Mat. 26:27, Mark 14:13, Luke 22:20 unanimously state: **In the same way He also took the chalice.** But Matthew, in chapter 26:29, verifies that in that same chalice there was wine: **I tell you** (Christ says to His disciples prior to the Lord's Supper), **from now on I will no longer drink from this vintage of the wine-vine, until the day I will drink it anew with you in My Father's kingdom.** In Mark 14:25, Luke 22:18, it is repeated.

St. Paul repeats Christ's Institution [of His holy Supper] and points it out to the Corinthians.

1 Cor. 11:23–25 – **I received it from the Lord, what I gave to you. For the Lord Jesus, in the night in which He was betrayed, took the bread, etc. In the same way He also took the chalice, etc.**

Thirdly, other places in the Scriptures mention no other external elements than bread and wine; therefore, Christ indeed must have used the same and no other.

1 Cor. 10:16–17 – **The consecrated chalice, which we bless, is it not the fellowship of the blood of Christ? The bread, which we break, is it not the fellowship of the body of Christ? For there it is one bread, so the many of us are one, since we all are recipients of one bread.**

1 Cor. 11:26–28 – **For as many times as you eat from this bread and drink from this chalice, you should proclaim the Lord's death until He comes. Whoever then unworthily eats of this bread and drinks from this chalice of the Lord, he is guilty of the body and blood of the Lord. However, let a person examine himself, and then he should eat of this bread and drink from this chalice.**

Accordingly, since the holy evangelists, like St. Paul, mention no other external elements than bread and wine in describing the institution of the holy Lord's Supper; since Christ used and sanctified no other element for this Sacrament; since no place in the Scripture which treats of the Lord's Supper mentions even a single other element; since it befits the true disciples of Christ to abide by His ordinance and institution (John 8:31); since the promise of Christ concerning the sacramental reception of His body and blood is expressly dependent upon the bread and wine; and finally, since bread and wine are the essential elements of the holy Lord's Supper, it follows that under no circumstances can or should one substitute other elements, which might be comparable, in place of bread and wine.

Here again an apparent point of contention, that one cannot have available bread and wine in every locale. So in Norway one uses dried fish instead of bread; also, there [grapes for] wine cannot be readily grown because of the tremendously cold climate. Hence, it would be better that one use something else similar to bread and wine instead of completely omitting the administration of the holy Lord's Supper. ANSWER: It would be difficult to mention any place on earth where bread and wine would be unavailable. Even though it doesn't grow in every place, yet it is imported. Therefore, one may readily obtain enough bread and wine to administer the holy Lord's Supper. And if, in case of an emergency, one can not obtain bread and wine, then it is better to omit the administration of the holy Lord's Supper than to go against the express institution of Christ. Just as it is not to be regarded as a Baptism when the external element of water isn't used and something else is used in its place, so also it is not a Supper of the Lord, when something else is substituted for the bread and wine.

CHAPTER 6

WHETHER IT IS CONTRARY TO CHRIST'S INSTITUTION FOR A PERSON TO USE LITTLE WAFERS FOR THE HOLY SUPPER.

 enuine natural bread, baked from flour and water, is used for the holy Supper by virtue of Christ's institution. But it is not specified that the bread be large or small, or whether, in preparation for the celebration, one breaks it into pieces prior to, or during, the distribution; in the same way, whether it is baked round or long [loaf], just so it is actually bread. So also, whether the wine is red or white, old or new, nothing depends on that; just so it is the vintage of a wine-vine. We support these contentions as follows:

1. The outward, accidental, and incidental qualities in no way detract from the essence of a thing. Size and shape are incidental to bread in the same way that red is incidental to wine. Through these incidental characteristics, therefore, nothing is detracted from the essence of the bread and wine, nor furthermore, from the essential elements of the holy Supper.

2. Nor is there any divine command in existence as to what kind of bread and wine one should actually use in the holy Supper. Therefore, it is all left up to Christian freedom.

3. Just as there is no directive whether the water in holy Baptism be cold or warm, whether it come out of the sea or well or stream, as shown in chap. 8 in the article on holy Baptism, so also in the holy Supper, nothing is directed whether the bread be small or large, whether the wine be red or white; just so long as it obviously is bread and wine. Accordingly, anyone who would make requirements in these matters fights against the article of Christian freedom, and he causes unnecessary offense to simple hearts within the Christian Church.

Here again are apparent points of contention:

1. That the little, round wafers are merely frothy bread and are not especially nourishing; therefore, it would be better to use a complete loaf. ANSWER: **1.** Whatever is baked from water and flour is indeed genuine natural bread. But now, these little, round wafers are also baked from flour and water. Consequently, they are indeed genuine natural bread, unaffected in this by their little, round form. **2.** Whatever actually is natural bread, as small as it may be, the same also nourishes. But now, these little wafers are truly bread; therefore, they have within them the power to nourish. **3.** The blessed bread in the holy Supper is not used in order to nourish the body (for that's why other common meals are put forth), but rather, that it be a means for the fellowship with the body of Christ (1 Cor. 10:16), which is neither hindered nor promoted by either the quantity or the roundness [of the bread]. Also, the blessed wine in the holy Supper is not used for the purpose that it make glad the heart of man, since usually common wine does that (Psa. 104:15). Rather, it is intended to be a means for the fellowship with the blood of Christ (1 Cor. 10:16), which can take place whether the wine be red or white, whether much or little be received [by the communicant]. **4.** The round wafers are especially suitable for distribution of the holy Supper because they are not unreasonable to stock. Another reason that so little bread and wine are partaken of in the holy Supper is to show thereby that we use the elements not for bodily nourishment, but for sanctification.

2. That a large [loaf of] bread would better signify that Christ's body nurtures us to eternal life; also that we are all one body who all partake of one Bread in the Sacrament (1 Cor. 10:17). Therefore, it would be better to use a big bread instead of little round breads. ANSWER: **1.** This passage of the apostle and of its proper understanding will be dealt with later in chapter 15, point of contention #5. **2.** The blessed bread is used not to represent the feeding of our souls, which takes place through Christ, but rather as a means for the sacramental obtaining of Christ's body. Also, the blessed chalice is used not to represent the shedding of Christ's blood, but rather as a means for the sacramental reception of the blood of Christ (1 Cor. 10:16). **3.** Consequently, it is not necessary that a large bread be used, and in midst of the action of the holy Supper it be broken into pieces, or that the wine be poured out, to thereby indicate one thing or another. Rather, it is sufficient that the bread be eaten and the wine be drunk. **4.** Also, if Christ had used and ordained for usage the bread in the holy Supper for the purpose of such representations, why would St. Paul castigate the Corinthians for their copious eating and drinking at the administration of the Lord's Supper (to the extent that some of them became drunk [1 Cor 11:21]) if such bountiful feeding could much better typify the indulgent, rich [sumptuous] feeding on Christ? **5.** Therefore, it is better that we not take much, but rather very little, since we do not use the holy Lord's Supper to feed the body; rather, to receive, along with the blessed bread, the body of Christ, and, along with the blessed wine, the blood of Christ. More on this later in chapter 11.

CHAPTER 7

WHETHER ONE SHOULD USE LEAVENED OR
UNLEAVENED BREAD
FOR THE HOLY LORD'S SUPPER.

ince [1.] whether bread is leavened or unleavened bread detracts from its essence as little as does whether it is in small pieces, round or long,

2. Since also no divine command exists regarding whether a person should use leavened our unleavened bread in the holy Lord's Supper,

3. Since unleavened can accomplish that for which it is used in the holy Lord's Supper just as easily as leavened, namely, that it be a means for the fellowship with the body of Christ (1 Cor. 10:16),

It follows that the usage of leavened or unleavened bread in the holy Lord's Supper is to be left to the discretion of Christian freedom and that there is to be initiated no unnecessary conflict in the Church of God on account of this. Accordingly, since for the longest time it has been customary in the Christian church to use unleavened bread for the holy Supper, we rightly let the practice continue—not with the intent that it is necessary at all costs to avoid using common leavened bread, but rather for the following reasons.

1. Since Christ used unleavened bread in the first Lord's Supper.

In Exo. 12:8 and Lev. 23:7, God the Lord commands that the Israelites should eat their paschal lamb with unleavened bread and in the days of Passover celebration should use no leavened bread.

Now then, Christ, on the first day of sweetened

[unleavened] bread, shortly after the eating of the Passover lamb, instituted and put into use His holy Lord's Supper (Mat. 26:17–26, Mark 14:22, Luke 22:19, 1 Cor. 11:23–24); therefore, there is no doubt that Christ used unleavened bread for this.

2. Since the unleavened bread can signify that Christ's body—which we receive along with the unleavened bread—is free of the leaven of sin (Isa. 53:9 and 1 Pet. 2:22). [It serves to remind us] that we come to the holy Sacrament with a clean heart, sweep out the old leaven, and desire to be fresh dough.

1 Cor. 5:7–8 – **Therefore sweep out the old leaven that you be new dough, just as you are unleavened**, etc. **Therefore let us not celebrate Easter in old leaven, but rather, in the sweet dough of integrity and truth.** Gal. 5:9 – **A little leaven sours the entire dough.**

Pertinent here is that God the Lord in the Old Testament forbade the bringing of leaven within the offering (Lev. 2:11), a sign that Christ, the true atoning Offering in the New Testament, was free of all the leaven of sin and also that the believers in the New Testament were to bring their spiritual thank-offerings without the leaven of waggishness or hypocrisy.

3. Since the Easter [Passover] lamb, which was a type of the holy Lord's Supper in the New Testament, had to be eaten with unleavened bread.

Exo. 12:8, Lev. 23:7 – **There you shall eat unleavened bread for seven days.**

1 Cor. 5:7, 8 – **For we also have an Easter [Passover] Lamb, that is, Christ offered for us. Therefore, let us celebrate Easter, not in the old leaven**, etc.

Here again is an apparent point of contention, that in all cases it is necessary to use unleavened bread in the holy Lord's Supper:

1. Since Christ used such in the first Lord's Supper. ANSWER: **1.** Christ did not thereby desire to give a law or command that one can actually use only unleavened bread and no other. Rather, He used unleavened bread because it was available. Similarly, He celebrated the holy Lord's Supper in the evening, since the eating of the little Passover lamb had to precede it; yet with this action, He did not establish a law that one must administer this holy Sacrament at night. **2.** The holy apostles used common leavened bread in the administration of the Lord's Supper after Christ's Ascension (Acts 2:42; 20:7). Now then, it would be hard to believe that they would have done so in opposition to Christ's command and ordinance. **3.** Similarly, after the apostolic age, the early church used leavened bread in the Lord's Supper for some time. **4.** Accordingly, when one forces the issue that unleavened bread must be used for the Lord's Supper, one sets *adiaphora* in conflict with Christian freedom, obscures the example of the holy apostles, and burdens the conscience with unnecessary regulations.

 2. Since only unleavened bread provides significant meanings, as related above. ANSWER: Bread is not used in the holy Lord's Supper primarily to indicate or signify one thing or another to us, but rather it should serve the purpose of communicating the body of Christ. Therefore, since one can make a case for the necessity of attaching one meaning or another in such matters of *adiaphora*, by the same token one can say that leavened bread [also] provides a precise significance. For in the same way that leaven permeates and occupies the entire dough, so one could also say that it is thus signified that the body of Christ, received in the holy Lord's Supper, transforms us in a spiritual manner so that we receive from Him new spiritual powers and motivations.

 Job 15:5 – **I am the Vine, you are the branches. Whoever remains in Me and I in him, he brings forth fruit,** etc.

CHAPTER 8

WHETHER THE WINE IN THE HOLY LORD'S SUPPER SHOULD OF NECESSITY BE MIXED WITH WATER.

 hat both bread and wine are to be used in the holy Supper is of course necessary in that the Lord Christ, when He ordained and instituted [the holy Supper] not only gave His body to be eaten with the bread, but also gave His blood to be drunk with the wine.

1. Because the holy evangelists in describing the institution recall no water [being in it], but only wine.

Mat. 26:29, Mark 14:25, Luke 22:18 – **I say to you: I will from now on no longer drink from this fruit of the vine until the day when I will drink it anew with you in My Father's kingdom.**

2. Because the blessed chalice can also be the means for fellowship with the blood of Christ without such mixing.

1 Cor. 10:16 – **The blessed chalice which we bless, is it not the fellowship with the blood of Christ**, etc.

Here again are apparent points of contention:

1. That from the institution of Christ one cannot determine whether the Lord Christ used wine or wine mixed with water, for what is written about the fruit of the vine [vintage of the wine-vine] in Mat. 26:29, etc., refers to the same series of drinks which the Jews were accustomed to passing around after they had eaten the Passover lamb. ANSWER: **1.** [Let it never be said] that one cannot determine from the description of Christ's Institution what kind of external elements Christ used and ordained to be used for the holy Supper. For it would then follow that the essential elements of the holy Lord's Supper have not been expressly and completely revealed. **2.** Granting that Christ spoke these words before the administration of the holy Lord's Supper (as is to be concluded from the evangelist [Luke 22:18]), it is sufficient to understand that the selfsame chalice which Christ shortly thereafter used as the means for administering the holy Supper contained the vintage of the wine-vine, that is, wine.

2. That the context of the [Gospel narratives leading up to the Last Supper] strongly suggests that Christ did not use pure wine, but rather wine mixed with water. For as the disciples went to prepare the Passover lamb, they met a man who was carrying a jug of water, whom they then followed (Mark 14:13, Luke 22:10); without a doubt the wine was mixed with that water. ANSWER: **1.** This water could well have been used for other purposes, particularly for the many cleansings which were customary for the Jews (Mark 7:3, etc.), or also for the preparation of the Passover lamb and the like. **2.** And even if Christ had used wine mixed with water, it still could not be concluded that mixing water with the wine was required as an essential element of this Sacrament, but rather that it was a customary practice in this land of hot climate, as was also the breaking of bread. **3.** Therefore, the question is not whether it is wrong to mix the wine with water for use in the holy Supper (since this was long a common practice in the early church, because at the administration of the holy Lord's Supper they conducted at the same time their common public ἀγάπας [agape] meal [1 Cor. 11:21, Jude 12]. Hence they reduced the strength of the wine with water.) Also it frequently happens today that the wine which is used for the holy Lord's Supper is mixed with water beforehand by the host. Through this practice, then, nothing is taken away from the perfection of this holy Sacrament. Rather, the real question here is if it is necessary that one mix the wine with water in the holy Lord's Supper, and whether it would be of little loss to the Church if it were omitted, since we have already provided grounds for leaving the practice to the discretion of Christian freedom.

3. From the side of Christ on the cross flowed blood and water (John 19:34). By this, is demonstrated that in the holy Supper one should not drink the blood of Christ without water. ANSWER: **1.** From this and similar allegorical interpretations one may not deduce definite, irrefutable arguments for articles of faith when the Holy Spirit Himself does not clarify and reveal the same in the Scriptures. **2.** Now then, nowhere in the holy Scripture is the fact that from Christ's side flowed blood and water applied to the holy Lord's Supper. **3.** One might more properly conclude, however, from the text of 1 John 5:6,8 and from the fathers, that the flow of blood and water applies to both Sacraments of the New Testament—that by the water holy Baptism, and by the blood the holy Supper is indicated, both of which receive all their power from the merits of Christ. **4.** To put it succinctly, Christ intended to teach what external elements were to be used in this Sacrament through the institution of the first Lord's Supper—not from the cross. **5.** Not to mention that it was not wine mixed with water which flowed from Christ's side, but rather just water. Furthermore, it was not blood and water mixed together which flowed forth, but rather first blood, then water. **6.** If then such sophistry spun forth from one's own brain were set forth as articles of faith, then one could conclude that not wine, but rather pure and simple water should be used in the Lord's Supper, since not wine, but only water flowed from Christ's side with the blood.

4. The mixing of wine with water in the holy Supper corresponds well with the types of the holy Lord's Supper in the Old Testament. For example: that water flowed from the rock (Num. 20:10, 1 Cor. 10:4); that the prophet Elijah was fed with water (1 Kin. 19:6). ANSWER: **1.** It is not required that even the essence of what took place in the type must necessarily be used in that which it typifies. Rather, it is adequate that the likeness be found between the picture and that which it portrays. As for example: The water which flowed from the rock is a type of the holy Supper. But even then it is not necessary that water be used in the holy Supper. Rather, it is enough that in certain respects a comparison be found between the water flowing from the rock and the holy Supper—as was shown above in chapter 2. **2.** But if it were required that what is found in the type must also be found in that which it portrays, it would no longer be a type and comparison; rather, in all aspects it would be one and the same thing, and one could draw many absurd comparisons from it. As for example: The Passover lamb is a type of the holy Lord's Supper, which cannot be denied; following the above line of reasoning, one would conclude that one should use not only bread in the holy Supper, but also the flesh of a lamb. **3.** And if one truly scrutinizes the types of the Old Testament, why would one overlook that Melchizedek brought forth bread and wine—without water (Gen. 14:18)? **4.** Not wine and water, but only water flowed from the rock. Elijah was not offered both wine and water, just water. From this it would follow [using the aforementioned skewed logic] that one should use neither pure wine nor mixed wine for the holy Supper, but only pure water.

5. The mixing of water with wine has beautiful symbolism for the uniting of both natures in Christ, as well as indicating the uniting of the Christian Church with Christ, its head. Furthermore, wine that is thus mixed with water is much more suitable for man's nature than is pure wine; hence, the power of the blood of Christ is much better symbolized through it. ANSWER: **1.** The consecrated wine in the holy Supper is used not to signify this or that, but rather that with it Christ's blood be received (1 Cor. 10:16). **2.** Accordingly, the fellowship of the blood of Christ does not consist of mixing wine with water, but rather in the receiving and drinking of the consecrated wine. **3.** Also, in no way is the personal union of the divine and human nature to be confused with the sacramental union of the consecrated bread and the body of Christ, and with the sacramental union of the wine and the blood of Christ. It is true that the sacramental union can be elucidated to a certain degree with the personal union of both natures in Christ; nevertheless, there is a great distinction between the two unions. Also the ancients compared the sacramental union of the wine and the blood of Christ with the union of the divine and human nature, but not with mixing water and wine. **4.** Also, in the holy Supper the wine is not used for the health of the body with the idea that one should mix it with water on that account. Rather, it is used for the fellowship with the blood of Christ. **5.** Not to mention that certain wines spoil and become unhealthy if they are mixed with water. Thus the mixing of wine with water symbolizes the corruption resulting from mixing pure divine teaching with human additives (Isa. 1:22).

CHAPTER 9

WHETHER THE CONSECRATED WINE IS TO BE DISTRIBUTED TO ALL THOSE WHO RECEIVE THE CONSECRATED BREAD IN THE HOLY LORD'S SUPPER.

 he proper administration of the holy Supper consists not only in the offering and the reception of the consecrated bread, but also in the offering and the reception of the blessed chalice, since there is to be no allowance made for extending the consecrated bread* and the consecrated chalice to some, while offering only the consecrated bread to others. We support this position as follows:

1. What Christ, true God and man, has joined and bound together, let no man separate (Mat. 19:6). Christ has instituted His holy Supper in such manner that in it one not only eats the consecrated bread, and along with it His true body, but also drinks the consecrated wine, and along with it His true blood; consequently, no one should make a separation here.

Mat. 26:26, 27, 28 – **But as they ate, Jesus took the bread, gave thanks and break it and gave it to the disciples and said: Take, eat, this is My body. And He took the chalice and gave thanks and gave it to them and said: All of you drink from it; this is My blood of the New Testament,** etc.

Mark 14:22, 23, 24 – **And while they were eating, Jesus took the bread, gave thanks and break it and gave**

---

* The translation "consecrated" for *gesegnete(n)* (blessed) is subsequently favored to reflect Gerhard's "Germanization" of the Latin *consecrare*. Tr

it to them and said: Take, eat, this is My body. And He took the chalice and gave thanks and gave it to them, and they all drank from it. And He said to them: This is My blood of the New Testament, etc.

Luke 22:19, 20 – And He took the bread, gave thanks and broke it and gave it to them and said: This is My body, which is being given for you; this do for My remembrance. In the same manner He also took the chalice after the Supper and said: This is the chalice of the New Testament in My blood, which is being shed for you.

In this institution of Christ, it is to be noted: 1. That Christ joined together the reception of the consecrated bread and His body as well as the reception of the consecrated wine and His blood. Whoever would then desire to receive Christ's blood according to His institution, must not only eat the consecrated bread, but also drink of the consecrated chalice. 2. It should also be noted that the evangelist Luke (22:20) uses the word ὡσαύως ["in the same way or manner"] so that we might be taught that Christ commanded that the consecrated wine is to be drunk in the same manner as the consecrated bread was ordained to be eaten. 3. Furthermore, the evangelist Matthew uses the word "all": all of you drink from this, with which Christ meets head on the [erroneous] thought that it is sufficient to eat only the consecrated bread in the holy Lord's Supper without drinking of the [contents of] the consecrated chalice. 4. Finally, Christ concluded the institution of His holy Lord's Supper by adding: This do, in order to direct us to His institution so that we in responsible continuance of the holy Supper uphold and use the words of institution of our Lord and Master (Mat. 23:8) to whom we listen (Mat. 3:17) and whose voice we should follow (John 10:27) [and] who has ordained that we uphold and use them—namely, that we eat the consecrated bread and drink from the consecrated chalice.

2. Christ has clearly indicated by His example in the administration of the holy Supper that by virtue of His institution we may not eat only the consecrated bread, but rather are also to drink from the consecrated chalice in the holy Lord's Supper, as is plainly perceived from the account of His institution.

3. St. Paul, in writing his epistle, reiterates to the entire Church at Corinth that he was expressly shown that on the strength of Christ's institution they should eat the consecrated bread and drink from the consecrated chalice:

1 Cor. 11:23–29 – **I received from the Lord what I have also related to you. For the Lord Jesus in the night in which He was betrayed, took the bread, gave thanks and broke it and said: Take, eat, this is My body, which was broken for you; do this in remembrance of Me. Also equally in the same way, [He took] the chalice after the supper and said: This chalice is the New Testament in My blood; do this, as often as you drink it, in remembrance of Me. For as often as you eat of this bread and drink from this chalice, you are to proclaim the Lord's death until He comes. Now, anyone who eats of this bread and drinks from this chalice unworthily, he is guilty of the body and blood of the Lord. But a person is to examine himself and then eat of this bread and drink from this chalice. For anyone who eats and drinks unworthily, he thereby eats and drinks to his condemnation, because he does not discern the body of Christ.**

4. The holy apostles demonstrate with their example that in the holy Supper one not only eats the consecrated bread, but one should also drink from the consecrated chalice. It should be noted that this example of the apostles is to be linked with the command of Christ: **This do**, since it is entails the same [and draws upon it].

Mark 14:24 – **And they all drank out of it.**

1 Cor. 11:26 – **For as often as you eat of this bread and drink from this chalice, you shall proclaim the Lord's**

death, etc. (St. Paul here describes for everyone the institution of Christ and directs his Corinthians to conclude from it that they understand the institution of Christ in such a way that in the holy Supper one should eat the consecrated bread and drink from the consecrated chalice.)

5. When a testament is probated following the death of the one who established it, then justly and equitably no part of it can be set aside or nullified. In like manner, the reception of the consecrated chalice is a part of this Testament of Christ, which He has confirmed (probated) with His blood, because at a particular time, with certain words, with a comparable command, He ordained the reception of the consecrated chalice and the reception of the consecrated bread. Therefore, this part of the Testament of Christ may by no means be set aside.

Gal. 3:15 – **One does not disdain a human Testament once it has been confirmed [probated], and also adds nothing to it.**

6. That which deprives a Christian of the comfort which he should receive from the Sacraments is easily repudiated. However, by withholding the chalice, Christians are robbed of the comfort which they should receive from the words of Christ, recorded for the consecration of the chalice. Through these words, He indicates that with the consecrated wine we drink His holy blood and are thus assured of all the blessings promised in the New Testament.

Mat. 26:28, Mark 14:24 – **All of you drink from it; this is My blood of the New Testament, which is being shed for many for the forgiveness of sins.**

Luke 22:20, 1 Cor. 11:25 – **This is the chalice, the New Testament of My blood, which is being shed for you.** (In the holy Lord's Supper the words of Christ apprehend—along with the bread—the consecrated wine, which is the fellowship of the blood of Christ. Through the blood of Christ, the New Testament is sealed; the covenant of the New Testament comprehends/contains within it the forgiveness of sins. Whoever then removes the consecrated chalice from the holy Lord's Supper at the same time takes away this comfort.)

Here again are apparent points of contention:

1. That it is not possible to prove from Christ's institution that the consecrated chalice is to be offered in common to all those who receive the consecrated bread, since Christ is addressing these words to the apostles from whom descended the priests. Hence the reception of the chalice applies only to them. ANSWER: **1.** Christ instituted no other Lord's Supper for the apostles than for His other believers. Rather, Christ's institution is intended for all members of the Christian Church who, in keeping with St. Paul's rule, are able to examine themselves. **2.** Accordingly, what Christ ordained and established with the institution and administration of the holy Lord's Supper applies not only to the apostles or priests, but to all Christians who desire to receive the holy Supper. **3.** As St. Paul teaches without contradiction in 1 Cor. 11:23, 24ff.: When abuses of the holy Lord's Supper began tearing at the Church in Corinth, St. Paul directed them to Christ's words of institution and required that they should judge according to those very words of institution (v. 22). Consequently, Christ's words of institution must indeed be directed not only to the apostles or priests, but rather to all believers. What's more, St. Paul writes not only to the Church officials [lit.=Church servants, i.e., pastors] at Corinth, but to the entire fellowship, those sanctified in Christ Jesus, the called saints, along with all those anywhere who call upon the Name of our Lord Jesus Christ, their Lord and ours (1 Cor. 1:2). **4.** The apostles on that occasion did not consecrate [*consecriret*] nor offer the blessed [*gesegnete*] bread and the blessed chalice; rather, they themselves received it. Therefore it follows that the priests, i.e., church officials, alone do not stand in the place of others, but rather that all who find their way to the holy Supper are to use both. **5.** And, if indeed these words of Christ's institution are not to be applied universally to all Christians, must not evidence be brought forth of a different institution by Christ in which the common Christian is directed to receive only the consecrated bread, but denied the consecrated chalice? Either ordinary Christians must be totally excluded from the holy Supper, or else, on the strength of Christ's words of institution, the entire Sacrament must be offered to them. **6.** Also, the reception of the blood of Christ in the Sacrament must not be denied to those for whom He shed his blood on the cross. For His blood was shed not only for church officials, but for all Christians. Therefore, it should not be denied them in the Sacrament.

 2. That also in no way can a case be made from the restatement of Christ's institution, as related in 1 Cor. 11, that it is necessary to use the consecrated chalice, since nothing more can be derived from the passage than to allow the use of both outward elements, bread and wine, but not that it is necessary to use both. ANSWER: St. Paul directs his Corinthians and all Christians to Christ's [words of] institution. He also directs that one should judge every point of contention which stirs up conflict within the Church on the basis of and according to these same words of Christ's institution. That's why Christ's [words of] institution must indeed apply to all Christians. Since, then, Christ's institution is directed to all in general, this command of Christ: **All of you drink from it, this is My blood, shed for you,** is indeed also meant for and directed to them. St. Paul himself also points out to the Corinthians that he himself received from the Lord what he gave or presented to them (1 Cor. 11:23). He desires that neither they nor others deviate from this *traditione dominica* [divine tradition] and divine ordinance. Also, all the circumstances of chapter 11 indicate that St. Paul is speaking in general of all Corinthians, not only about clergymen; also that he always considers eating and drinking of equal importance.

 3. That Christ's blood is no longer separated from His body; accordingly, anyone who receives the consecrated bread in the holy Supper—and along with it Christ's true body—the same of necessity receives *per concomitantiam* [along with it] the true blood of Christ. Hence it is sufficient to only use the consecrated bread. ANSWER: **1.** If subtilities counted in divine matters, then one could easily do away with the entire Sacrament of the holy Lord's Supper, since those who have been baptized into Christ have put on Christ (Gal. 3:27) and Christ, through faith, lives in our hearts (Eph. 3:17): Why then would it be necessary in such a situation to additionally receive His body and blood in the holy Supper? But as will be properly answered in the concluding remarks, one should regard God's ordinances more highly than our reason's opinions. Furthermore, this [point of contention] is likewise properly responded to by being labeled as a pretext. **2.** Christ, who in the holy Supper has without exception ordained His body to be eaten along with the consecrated bread and His blood to be drunk along with the consecrated wine, is divine Wisdom (1 Cor. 1:24). To Him all human wisdom should justly submit. **3.** Also, if one received with a single external element not only the body but also the blood of Christ, so that one need offer only the consecrated bread to all communicants, it would also follow that the priests (or church officials) should not receive both elements, but only one. **4.** Christ has ordained that under the bread His body is to be eaten, and under wine His blood is to be drunk; thus, one may not say by dint of Christ's institution that under the wine Christ's body is eaten, and neither can one also say that under the bread Christ's blood is drunk. The sacramental benefits of the body and blood of Christ must not be confused; what Christ has ordained for drinking, one should not apply to eating. **5.** In this matter, the question of the essential unity of the body and blood of Christ is not raised or dealt with; also, the personal unity of both Natures of Christ is not being questioned. Rather, the entire question and dispute consists of the sacramental presence of the body and the blood of Christ; that we, in light of the institution of Christ, say that only the body—and not the blood—of Christ is sacramentally united with the consecrated bread in the holy Lord's Supper, and also, that only the blood—and not the body—of Christ is sacramentally united with the consecrated chalice. Every true disciple of Christ truly adheres to this simplicity and disregards any other far-fetched stuff that opposes these clear words of Christ's institution.

4. That even one external element, rather than both, is adequate for the Sacrament, since the feeding of our soul is completely symbolized through the use of one external element. ANSWER: Both external elements of bread and wine should be used in the holy Supper not chiefly so that this or that be symbolized, but rather that the consecrated bread be **the fellowship of the body of Christ** and that the consecrated chalice be **the fellowship of the blood of Christ** (1 Cor. 10:16). **2.** If the reception of only one external element is sufficient for this holy Sacrament, it would follow that Christ instituted two Sacraments and that the holy apostles and contemporary church officials who receive both external elements receive thereby two different kinds of Sacraments. **3.** Therefore, if this sophistry were true, one could turn this conclusion around and say: Since for its proper nourishment the body requires not only food but also drink, and since indeed thirst actually causes more stress and is more harmful than hunger—so also for spiritual nurture. Therefore, not only is the reception of the body of Christ under the bread necessary, but also the reception of the blood of Christ under the wine, so that the feeding might be complete. **4.** It is apparent from the Christ's institution that the reception of the consecrated chalice is an essential part of this Sacrament, because Christ just as much commanded the consecrated chalice to be drunk as He did the eating of the consecrated bread. How then can one external element be enough for this Sacrament? Also, how can Christ's ordinance be complied with if one distributes only the consecrated bread?

5. That one can derive no greater benefit from the use of both elements than from just one element, because the whole Christ is received under [along with] both. ANSWER: **1.** Such a conclusion is concocted from reason, contrary to Christ's institution, **2.** and is based on the *concomitantia* or essential natural unity of the body and blood of Christ, which was briefly dealt with previously (point of contention no. 3 above). **3.** What kind of benefit can one hope to receive from the holy Supper if it is formulated contrary to Christ's institution? But now, Christ has ordained the eating of His body with the consecrated bread, and the drinking of His blood with the consecrated chalice. If one uses only one external element, he deviates from the ordinance of Christ. **4.** Christ has clearly stated concerning the consecrated chalice in the holy Lord's Supper: **Take, eat, this is My blood of the New Testament, which is being poured out for you for the forgiveness of sins.** So that this promise of the forgiveness of sins be confirmed for us, the reception of the consecrated chalice must not be set aside.

6. That the figures of the Old Testament, such as the tree of life, the paschal lamb, the manna, the show-bread, etc., point to only one external element, namely, to the consecrated bread in the holy Supper. Hence, it is sufficient to use only one external element. ANSWER: **1.** The institution of Christ must not be judged according to the types, but rather the types must be applied to Christ's institution and judged according to it; **2.** not to mention that in articles of faith one cannot draw definite conclusions from the figures and types if the Scriptures themselves do not clarify such figures. Also the types in the Old Testament of the holy Lord's Supper must be taken in totality—not half-way—and properly judged on the basis of Christ's institution. Not only are the tree of life, the paschal lamb, the manna, and the show-bread pictures of the holy Lord's Supper, but also the water which flowed from the rock, which St. Paul, as he deals with this in 1 Cor. 10:3, treats as a figure, taking both together, and with his example teaches that we should do the same with other types. **Our fathers** (he says) **have all eaten of the same spiritual food and have all drunk of the same spiritual drink**, etc. **4.** Also, what is to be done with the type of Melchizedek, who presented Abraham and his servants with not only bread, but also wine? (Gen. 14:18) Here one clearly and distinctly finds both external elements together. **5.** Hence, we turn the argument around: Because not only did the tree of life stand in the garden of Paradise, but also a stream watered it (Gen. 2:9, 10); because Melchizedek brought forth not only bread, but also wine (Gen. 14:18); because not only was the flesh of the paschal lamb eaten, but also its blood was smeared over the doorpost (Exo. 12:7); because the Israelites were not only given the bread from heaven, but also were given water from the rock (Exo. 16:15, 17:6); because not only was roasted bread brought to Elijah, but also a can with water in it (1 Kings 19:6)—therefore one should, on the strength of Christ's institution, not only use bread, but also wine in the holy Lord's Supper. In a nutshell, Christ has instituted this holy Sacrament such that one should eat the consecrated bread and drink the consecrated chalice. Against this [command] no types may establish anything else.

7. That Christ has shown with His words and deeds that it is enough to use only one external element in the holy Lord's Supper. In John 6:50, He mentions only the bread, which came down from heaven. He also only multiplied the bread and not the drink. In Luke 24:30, He conducts the holy Supper only with the breaking of bread. ANSWER: **1.** The words of institution are actually the chief foundation upon which the doctrine of the holy Lord's Supper rests. Now then, it is clearly perceived from the institution of Christ how the Lord Christ administered His holy Supper. One should not take one's eyes from this and instead take a stance on other uncertain speculation. **2.** John 6 does not refer to the consecrated bread in the holy Supper, but rather to the Bread of Life, which comes down from heaven. Also it

is not characterized as a sacramental, but rather as a spiritual nourishment from the body and blood of Christ. More on this later. **3.** Christ did not multiply drink in the wilderness as He did the bread because there was no shortage of drink; one should not draw inferences from uncertain figures which oppose the clear institution of Christ. **4.** Christ was definitely not celebrating His holy Lord's Supper in Luke 24, since He did not say of the same bread that it was His body. Therefore it was only an ordinary meal through which Christ made Himself recognizable to them. **5.** And even if He Himself had celebrated the holy Lord's Supper, it would follow that the priests are to receive only one external element, because the two [Emmaus disciples] with whom Christ on that occasion held the evening meal were from the number of the seventy disciples.

8. That, similarly, the holy apostles used only one external element, since after Acts 2:42, 46 the Lord's Supper is called the breaking of bread. ANSWER: **1.** It is not credible that the holy apostles deviated from the ordinance of Christ. But now, Christ commanded them to observe the holy Lord's Supper in and with two external elements. **2.** The holy Lord's Supper is later called "bread breaking," not because in the [celebration of the same] only the consecrated bread was broken, but rather as an exchange of words, implying also the reception of the consecrated chalice; just as in [referring to] ordinary mealtimes, in which there had to have been drink, the holy Scriptures calls them **the bread. 3.** Among these believers in the early church there were present also the holy apostles. But one can indeed not say that because they were priests, they themselves received only the consecrated bread without at the same time receiving the consecrated chalice. **4.** In Acts 20:7 the holy Lord's Supper, which St. Paul administered, is in like manner called the bread breaking; but who would dare say that he did not at the same time consecrate the chalice?

9. That it amounts to just so much rubbish, or it could be so considered, if one wants to offer the holy Supper under both elements to all Christians. ANSWER: How could it be just so much rubbish? Would not Christ who instituted this Sacrament under both elements have known this beforehand? The claim that sometimes there are so many communicants with only one priest, who cannot possibly offer the consecrated chalice to all of them, counts for nothing; for more priests can be provided if necessary. One can take enough time and employ other means to assure compliance with Christ's institution. If one has enough time to hear with his own ears the confession of sins of each person, then can't he also offer both elements of the Lord's Supper to each one? Further they claim: One should guard against carrying the consecrated chalice around with too little respect. But this claim is also without merit, since one must as well equally guard against walking about with the consecrated bread in a disrespectful manner. And the holy Supper must not on that account be neglected. Further they say: There are many who do not drink wine. ANSWER: Why should one for the sake of such few forbid all the rest to receive the consecrated chalice? Also it would be difficult to find someone who could not drink the little bit of wine that is required to be ingested for this Sacrament. Finally they say: Wine is not to be found in every place. ANSWER: It won't be easy to name a single place where there isn't enough wine available as is required for this [holy Supper]. And, how is it that other lands and kingdoms in which there are available massive quantities of wine are nevertheless denied the use of the consecrated chalice? What has happened in this whole matter is the same thing that occurred when our parents [Adam and Eve] took fig leaves to cover themselves after they had deviated from God's Word (Gen. 3:7). In the same manner here, human cleverness hunts for such pretexts after it has deviated in this matter from the clear institution of Christ.

CHAPTER 10

WHY CHRIST THE LORD ORDAINED BREAD AND WINE AS THE EXTERNAL ELEMENTS OF THIS HOLY SACRAMENT.

ven though the truth of the matter is that the works of the Lord are marvelous (Psa. 139:13), and His ways are unfathomable, for who has known His thoughts? (Isa. 40:13, Rom. 11:33, 34), yet it is not improper to ask why the Lord Christ ordained bread and wine for this holy Sacrament of His true body and blood? To this, we answer according to the guidance of the holy Scriptures that it occurred for the following reasons:

1. So that the types of the Old Testament which point to the holy Lord's Supper might be fulfilled.

Gen. 14:18, 19 – **But Melchizedek, the king of Salem, brought forth bread and wine, etc., And blessed him** (Abraham), etc.

In Exo. 25:30, show-bread had to lie before the Lord in the tabernacle at all times.

In 1 Kings 19:6, the angel brought to Elijah in the wilderness bread and a container of water.

2. Because Christ wanted to ordain in His holy Supper the most profound and true (precise) fellowship of His body and blood. Therefore, He takes bread and wine; under it, He gives us His body to eat and His blood to drink, since there is nothing in our natural lives to which we can more closely relate than the plain food and drink which we enjoy.

John 6:51 – **I am the living Bread which comes from heaven. Whoever will eat of this bread, he will live eternally,** etc.

John 15:5 – **I am the Winevine, you are the tendril shoots. Whoever remains in Me and I in him, he brings forth much fruit**, etc.

Gal. 2:20 – **Christ lives in me**, etc.

Eph. 3:17 – **And Christ to live in your hearts through faith.**

Christ wanted to seal this profound, precise fellowship in the holy Lord's Supper. Therefore, He gave under the bread and wine (through which we are sustained in this natural life) His true body and blood to eat and drink for spiritual and eternal life.

3. Because these two external elements, bread and wine, can be likened to the body and blood of Christ in many ways. For, even though the consecrated bread is above all not to be used [merely] to signify the body of Christ, nor the consecrated chalice to signify the blood of Christ (but rather much more that the bread is **the fellowship of the body of Christ and the chalice the fellowship of the blood of Christ** [1 Cor. 10:16]); yet it is definitely not improper that one seek out such symbolism so long as one does not add that therein consists the chief and only *officium sacramentale*, that is, as long as one does not seek or establish the total essence of the holy Lord's Supper in such representations. Of these representations many could be considered*, but we want to recount only the most apparent ones. Bread is prepared from tender wheat grain; so also Christ's body is the noble wheat grain which is extended to us in the holy Supper for the nourishment of our souls.

John 12:24 – **Unless the grain of wheat fall into the ground and die, it remains alone; but where it dies, it brings forth much fruit.**

Just as bread is prepared for food in an oven with heat from fire, so also Christ's body was roasted with love on the tree-trunk of the cross.

In Exo. 12:9, it is written concerning the Passover lamb: **You are not to eat it raw, nor boiled in water, rather**

---

* *Eracht* must be intended here rather than *erdacht*, Ed.

roasted by fire (this points to Christ, etc.)

As the bread sustains and strengthens the heart of man (Psa. 104:15), so also Christ's body nourishes and strengthens us to everlasting life.

John 6:50, 51 – **This is the bread which comes from heaven, so that whoever eats of it shall not die. I am the living bread come from heaven. Whoever will eat of this bread, he will live in eternity, and the bread which I will give is My flesh, which I will give for the life of the world.**

Wine is the most noble juice, which grows from the wine-vine. It comes forth from the dew of heaven and out of the fatness of the land (Gen. 27:18). So also Christ is the noble tendril from whose side flowed His holy blood, which is extended to us in the holy Supper.

John 15:1, 5 – **I am a genuine Wine-vine,etc. ... I am the Wine-vine, you are the tendril.**

Wine quenches thirst and gladdens the heart of man, (Psa. 104:15). So also Christ's blood serves to assuage eternal thirst and quicken the soul.

John 6:55 – **For My flesh is the right food and My blood is the right drink.**

4. Because bread and wine can serve as good reminders to those who find themselves at the holy Supper. For just as bread and wine does not benefit those who have already been satiated, so also the heavenly food of the body and blood of Christ is appetizing only for hearts that are hungry for grace.

Mat. 5:6 – **Blessed are those who are hungry and are thirsty for righteousness, for they will be satiated.**

Rev. 21:6; 22:17 – **I will give the thirsty from the well of living water for free. And he who is thirsty, let him come, and whoever wants to, let him take the water of life for free.**

Like a loaf of bread is made from many little grains and a pitcher of wine from many little grapes, so also in the holy Lord's Supper, all are fed and given to drink of one spiritual body so that we also as members of it should heartily love each other.

1 Cor. 10:17; 12:13 – **For just as there is one bread, so we being many are one body, since we all are partakers of one bread. For we are all baptized into one body through one Spirit – and we all have drunk of one Spirit.** (In holy Baptism, we all were baptized into one spiritual body; in the holy Lord's Supper, we all are given to drink of one Spirit.)

CHAPTER 11

THAT CHRIST'S BODY AND BLOOD ARE TRULY PRESENT IN THE HOLY LORD'S SUPPER.

 hus far the external elements, which are the earthly, visible signs in the holy Sacrament, have been dealt with. Henceforth, we now also deal with the heavenly food in the holy Lord's Supper, which is present as the true body and true blood of Christ. Even though we indeed receive bread and wine in the holy Lord's Supper, yet it is not ordinary bread and wine. Rather, the bread that we bless (received and eaten) is the fellowship of the body of Christ; the chalice which we consecrate in the holy Lord's Supper (received and drunk) is the fellowship of the blood of Christ (1 Cor. 10:16). Therefore, no less than the bread and wine, the body and blood of Christ are present in the holy Lord's Supper, as is generally maintained by Christendom here on earth and which is supported as follows:

1. The words of institution clearly give the understanding that the Lord Christ ordained—on the strength of His institution and promise—not just simple bread and wine to His holy apostles, but [gave them also] with the bread His body to eat, and with the wine His blood to drink. That's why St. Paul expressly announces that the consecrated bread is the fellowship of the body of Christ and the consecrated chalice is the fellowship of the blood of Christ.

Mat. 26:26–28 – **But as they ate, Jesus took the bread, gave thanks and broke it and gave it to the disciples and said: Take, eat, this is My body. And He took the chalice and gave thanks, gave it to them and said: All of you drink from it, this is My blood of the New**

Testament, which will be poured out (spilled) for many for the forgiveness of sins.

Mark 14:22–24 – And inasmuch as they were eating, Jesus took the bread, gave thanks and broke it and gave it to them and said: Take, eat, this is My body; [then He] took the chalice and gave thanks and gave it to them and they all drank from it. And He said to them: This is My blood of the New Testament, which will be poured out for many.

Luke 22:19, 20 – And He took the bread, gave thanks and broke it and gave it to them and said: This is My body, which is being given for you; this do in My memory. In the same way also [He took] the chalice after the supper and said: This is the chalice, the New Testament in My blood, that will be shed for you.

1 Cor. 11:23–25 – I received it from the Lord that which I gave to you. For the Lord Jesus in the night in which He was betrayed, took the bread, gave thanks and broke it and said: Take, eat, this is My body which is being broken for you. Do this in memory of Me. In the same way also [He took] the chalice after the supper and said: This chalice is the New Testament in My blood; do this, as often as you drink it, in memory of Me.

One can take from these words of Christ's institution many arguments to establish the true (real) presence of the body and blood of Christ in the holy Supper. For example: 1. Whatever Christ offered His disciples there to eat and drink, that was truly present in that holy Supper. But now, Christ gave His disciples not only bread and wine, but also His true body and His true blood to eat and to drink, because He spoke and testified about that which He was giving them to eat (that it was His body), and about that which He was giving .them to drink (that it was His blood). Therefore, His true body and His true blood must indeed have been present in the holy Lord's Supper. Since in the first Supper not only bread and wine but also Christ's body and blood were present and distributed to the disciples, the same also occurs now when one, in Christian assembly, celebrates the Supper of the Lord; for the former is the description and model of all others. **2.** Further, since Christ says in the institution that He gives us to drink of His blood of the New Testament (Mat. 26:27, Mark 14:24), it can be concluded that it is not simply a representation of the blood of Christ which is distributed to be drunk in the holy Supper, but rather the true, essential blood of Christ. What's more, since the Law, that is, the Old Testament, contained the shadow of future blessings, the New Testament contains the genuine blessing itself (Col. 2:17, Heb. 10:1).

Accordingly, just as Moses sprinkled the people with the blood of the slaughtered offering (which blood signified the blood of Christ) and said: **See, this is the blood of the covenant which the Lord has established with you**, etc. (Exo. 24:8), so also Christ, in establishing the New Testament, no longer takes the figurative blood of rams and calves. Rather, He takes His own blood and gives us the same to drink in the holy Supper (Mat. 26:27, Mark 14:24). **3.** Furthermore, Christ says that the chalice is the New Testament in His blood, which (chalice) is poured out for us (Luke 22:20). If Christ's blood is not truly present and really drunk from the chalice along with the consecrated wine, how could Christ say that the chalice is poured out for us? But now the words of Christ are clear. The consecrated chalice is poured out for us, namely, because not only wine but also the blood of the New Testament is drunk from it. Concerning this blood, since it is poured out for us, Christ says—as a result of this sacramental union of the consecrated wine and the blood of Christ in the chalice—that **the chalice** is poured out for us. Hence also, the consecrated chalice is of the New Testament, as Christ says in Luke 22:20 and 1 Cor. 11:25. How can that be? The explanation follows soon after; Christ adds that this consecrated chalice is the New Testament in His blood, that is, because therein not only wine, but also His holy blood is actually drunk. **4.** Finally, had Christ, as He instituted this holy Supper in place of the Passover lamb, wanted merely to substitute the external elements and had not wished to ordain a separate eating and drinking (reception) of His body and blood and [also] to ordain a presence of His body and blood (as was the case in the former Old Testament times), it would follow that Christ would have swept aside the clear, symbolic signs. He would instead have established in their place other elements that would by far have been not clearly as symbolic. For the slaughter of the Passover lamb had much more clearly symbolized Christ than the bread and wine in the holy Supper symbolize His body and blood. More about this later.

2. From Christ's institution, St. Paul concluded that the consecrated bread is the fellowship of body and the consecrated wine is the fellowship of the blood of Christ. Not only must bread and wine be present, but Christ's body and blood also must be present in the holy Supper. **1.** The apostle explicitly ascribes to the bread in the holy Supper that it is the fellowship of the body of Christ, and to the consecrated wine that it is the fellowship of the blood of Christ. Hence, he is not speaking of a spiritual fellowship of the body and blood of Christ (which is actually ascribed to faith) but of a sacramental presence and fellowship. **2.** Furthermore, he explicitly writes that the bread is not just the fellowship of Christ's benefits, but of the body of Christ. Therefore, the body of Christ must indeed truly be present in the holy Supper. **3.** Finally, the apostle draws a distinction between the fellowship of the body of Christ and the fellowship of the blood of Christ. Now then, if he were speaking only about the spiritual fellowship of the body and blood of Christ, he would not have done that, because the spiritual fellowship would be directed to the total Christ and not distinguish between His body and His blood.

1 Cor. 10:15, 16 – **I speak as to the wise. You judge what I say. The consecrated chalice which we bless, is**

it not the fellowship of the blood of Christ? The bread which we break, is it not the fellowship of the body of Christ?

3. That through which Christ comes to us, which also testifies upon earth, the same must indeed also be present upon the earth. Now, Christ comes to us through His blood, and His blood witnesses along with the Spirit and the water here upon earth. Therefore His blood must also indeed be present.

1 John 5:6–8 – **This is He who comes with water and blood, Jesus Christ; not with water only, rather with water and blood. And the Spirit is He who testifies that the Spirit is Truth. And three there are who testify upon earth: The Spirit and the water and the blood, and the three are together.** (The spirit is understood to mean the office of the ministry, which is the office of the Spirit [2 Cor. 3:8]; water is understood to mean holy Baptism [John 3:5]; blood is understood to mean the holy Supper, wherein we have present Christ's blood.)

Here again are apparent points of contention:

1. That Christ had a true natural, human body, as the Scriptures attest in several places; but now a true natural, human body cannot simultaneously be at many different places. Therefore, Christ's body cannot simultaneously be present at all the places where His holy Supper is being celebrated. ANSWER: **1.** The Scriptures attest to both, that Christ has a true human body, and that it is truly present in the holy Supper. **2.** Therefore, even though we may not grasp with our reason how this might simultaneously occur, nevertheless we should trust God and, in honor of His Word, believe this. **3.** There are many things which appear impossible to us which for God are very easy, Zec. 8:6 – **Even though before the eyes of the remaining people of this time this appears to be impossible, should it therefore appear to be impossible before My eyes, says the Lord of Sabaoth?** Mat. 19:26 – **For man it is impossible, but with God all things are possible.** Luke

1:37 – **For with God nothing is impossible.** Especially to be noted is the beautiful verse of Eph. 3:20 – **He who can effusively do beyond all that we ask for or can understand**, etc. **4.** Accordingly, the question here is not whether Christ has a true, natural body. Rather, the question is whether it is impossible for Christ to be able to distribute His true natural body to us in the holy Lord's Supper? **5.** If one would say that it "runs against itself" [would be a contradiction to say] that Christ has a true natural body and keeps it in eternity and at the same time gives the same to eat in the holy Supper, then to this the ANSWER is: Since God can do more than we can comprehend—also since something often seems impossible to us which is indeed easy for God the Lord (as we now have demonstrated from the Scriptures)—it thus indisputably follows that He does not have to weigh according to our reason what He may or may not do. Rather, where there is a clear promise, one should acknowledge God's will and, in opposition to all inspirations [bright ideas] of reason, believe it. **6.** That Christ, God's Son, has a true natural body is just as much contrary to reason as Christ's body being received in the holy Supper. Even as we are compelled by Scripture to believe the one, we should also, in reverence of God's Word, believe the other. If one wanted to set the one [article of faith] in opposition to the other, one should show just cause why he would rather deny the true presence of the body of Christ in the holy Lord's Supper than deny the truth of His human Nature. For if it were permissible in articles of faith to decide on the basis of reason and set one article against the other, then one could similarly conclude that since Christ's body is simultaneously present at many places, it no longer is a human body. **7.** Not improperly, philosophy teaches that a natural body cannot simultaneously be present at different locations; but it understands this about the common course of nature, and in no way wants it to be applied to supernatural, divine mysteries. As it would then be improper to say that God the Lord may not do and work anything above and beyond nature, it is equally improper to set this philosophical standard in opposition to Christ's institution and His promises. **8.** If it were permissible to argue from the philosophical standard against the Word of God, one could indeed from philosophy dispute even more strongly against the article of the Holy Trinity and against the resurrection of our bodies than one could possibly argue from philosophical standards against the presence of the body and blood of Christ in the holy Supper. **9.** Why, that Christ's body and blood could be assimilated into the eternal Person of the Son of God is vastly more astounding than that Christ according to His human nature can be present at more than one place at the same time. **10.** In the light of that, I would rather not say that it would be impossible for God to give a glorified body the power to be present at the same time in many places. For since Scripture nowhere denies this about God's almighty power and since we usually do not exhaustively know the nature and distinctive features of glorified bodies, who is to say that this is not totally and completely possible for God? How much more would it not be a sacrilegious conclusion if one wanted to say this about [i.e., apply such a limitation to] Christ's body, which is not only a glorified body, but also is personally united with the Son of God? **11.** In conclusion, that a natural body cannot be present at more than one place at the same time is so ordained by God in nature. But, who will give me the assurance that God cannot work above and contrary to this common ordinance? Such [limitation] is true of an ordinary natural body; but, who can say that Christ's body is herewith prescribed terms and limits—which happens to be God's Son's own body? **12.** Whenever anyone still alleges that it is against nature for a true body to be present at more than one place at a time, a Christian heart should then respond: It is against the nature of the truthful and almighty Lord Jesus Christ to promise that His body and blood is truly present in the holy Lord's Supper and then not to keep that promise.

2. That Christ has ascended to heaven; therefore, His body and blood cannot be present in the holy Supper here on earth. ANSWER: **1.** Both are true. Christ truly ascended to heaven, and at the same time His true body and blood are present in the holy Supper. **2.** The holy Scripture says both. Therefore, we should, in reverence of God and His holy Word, believe both, even though we do not immediately understand how both of these things can occur simultaneously. **3.** The ascension of Christ in no way hinders the fulfillment of His promise regarding the true presence of His body and blood, since He ascended to heaven in a different manner than Enoch and Elijah. This matter will be more extensively discussed at the proper place. Christ ascended to heaven so that He now sits at the right [hand] of God; that is, all things are placed under His feet, all power in heaven and upon earth is given Him, He mightily rules over all creatures, and He fulfills everything in all things—as the holy Scripture explains [the expression] "sitting at the right [hand] of God" (Psa. 8:7; Mat. 28:18; Eph. 1:20, 21; 4:10; 1 Cor. 15:25, etc.). From this it is readily apparent that the ascension of Christ in no way hinders this presence in the holy Supper, since by virtue of the very same power which is given to Him as the Son of Man, He can also make all things be subject to Him (Phi. 3:21). **4.** Also, the presence of the body of Christ in the holy Supper is provided for differently than His (the Lord Christ's) visible presence in heaven—according to which He enables the angels and the elect to recognize His glory. But the former is a sacramental presence, with the provision that we under the bread eat His true body and under the wine drink His true blood, even though we do not see this with our external eyes. **5.** After Christ by all counts had already ascended to heaven, He repeated the words of His institution to St. Paul, and He did not change them in the least. Rather, as they were reported by the evangelists, they were also repeated out of the mouth of Christ by St. Paul (1 Cor. 11:23). Therefore, Christ is in no way hindered in this

His promise by the ascension. **6.** Not to mention, that Christ appeared on earth also after His ascension (Acts 9:5, 23:11). **7.** *In summa*, the advantageous perspective which Christ has from the very heaven to which He ascended, **such no eye has seen, no ear has heard, also has not come into any man's heart** (1 Cor. 2:9). How much less should one set the ascension of Christ in opposition to His promise of the presence of His true body and blood in the holy Supper.

    3. That where a true human body is present, there one can also see it. However, Christ's body and blood in the holy Supper cannot be seen; therefore, they are also not present. ANSWER: **1.** Far be it from us that we no longer believe unless we can see [what we believe in] with our eyes. **Is not faith a certified assurance of that on which one places his hope without doubting, even though one cannot see it?** (Heb. 11:1). Does not the Lord Christ censure Thomas about this, that he didn't want to believe unless he could first see? And, He set this little verse before him: **Blessed are those who do not see and yet believe** (John 20:29). **2.** To be seen or not to be seen is an external, incidental property of a natural body and in no way is its unchangeable, inward attribute. Could not God provide that a genuine body be present and yet not be seen? **3.** Also, who can actually know if we, with our non-transfigured eyes, could see the transfigured bodies of the saints of which St. Paul says that they are **spiritual bodies** (1 Cor. 15:44). St. Matthew in chapter 27:53 says of those who arose with Christ that they came into the holy city [i.e., Jerusalem] and appeared to many. Without a doubt, he thereby indicates that they were not seen by all, but rather [only] by those whose eyes were opened to that end by God the Lord. **4.** How much less can one say that it is by all counts impossible for Christ to be present at a location with His body and not be seen, since His body is not only a transfigured body but also is in personal union with the divine nature of God's Son. **5.** Finally, it cannot be denied that Christ in His state of humiliation walked away from the

Nazarenes as they attempted to topple Him off the hill (Luke 4:30); that He invisibly went out of the temple as the Jews tried to stone Him (John 8:59); that He disappeared from the two Emmaus disciples and became invisible before their eyes (Luke 24:31). How much more is not Christ capable of being present with His body—even though He is not seen—following His state of exaltation in which He is established as the Ruler of everything in heaven and upon earth?

4. That whatever brings no benefit should not be regarded as being promised by Christ; however, one receives no greater benefit from the sacramental presence than the *spiritual* consumption and presence. Yes, Christ expressly says: **It is the spirit which makes alive, the flesh is of no benefit**, etc. (John 23:63). Therefore, one should not accept any other presence of the body of Christ than that the bread is a symbol of His body and that we with true faith eat His body and drink His blood in a spiritual way. ANSWER: **1.** This last statement runs expressly counter to Christ's institution, in which Christ ordained and promised the sacramental presence of His body and blood. **2.** The sacramental presence and reception of the body and blood of Christ is the means and seal of the spiritual reception, which occurs through faith. How can one then say that it is of no benefit? Also, there shall follow a more extensive exposition of the great benefit of the sacramental presence and reception. **3.** And even though we do not immediately see why Christ instituted the sacramental presence and reception of His body and blood, or what benefit they might bring, it still would be incumbent upon us as disciples of Christ to abide by His Word (John 8:31) and to take all our reason captive to the obedience of faith (2 Cor. 10:5). **4.** The Words of Christ: **The flesh is of no benefit** cannot without sin be applied to Christ's flesh, because even at the same spot (John 8:51), Christ testifies that He will give His flesh for the life of the world; and in v. 54 He says: **Whoever eats My flesh and drinks My blood, He has eternal life**, etc. Also, Christ does not say: My flesh is of no benefit; rather, He indicates the opposite, v. 55: **For My flesh is real food and My blood is real drink. 5.** Also, Christ is speaking in terms of a fleshly understanding of His words, as is demonstrated by the contrast and circumstance of the text. For as the Capernaites said in v. 52: **How can this one gives us His flesh to eat?**, meaning that Christ was speaking of a natural eating of His flesh—like one usually eats common food. Christ immediately repudiated such a gross fleshly understanding of His words and taught that He was speaking of a spiritual reception of His body and blood. Here then this rule applies: Whenever flesh and spirit are set against [contrasted with] each other in the Scriptures, by "flesh" is to be understood our old Adam with his lusts and fleshly thoughts; nowhere, however, is it to be understood as referring to the life-producing flesh of Christ.

5. That that which one remembers is not present; Christ, however, instituted the holy Supper for His remembrance (Luke 22:19, 1 Cor. 11:24–25). Therefore, His body and blood are not present in the holy Supper. ANSWER: **1.** From this last remark, it would follow that Christ indeed is not present in and at the administration of the holy Lord's Supper, since He commanded that the same was to be observed in memory of Him. **2.** When Christ says: **Such do to My memory**, He is speaking about the benefit and the result of the holy Supper and not about its essential elements. **3.** Also, this argument can be conveniently reversed: Since Christ instituted the Lord's Supper and commanded it to be observed for His remembrance, He is present in and at the same, for God the Lord says in Exo. 20:24: **For at whichever place I establish My Name, there I will come to you and bless you. 4.** The Ark of the Covenant in the Old Testament was a memorial and remembrance symbol of God. At the same time, God was not absent; rather, He was truly present. **5.** While remembrances [usually] pertain to bygone and invisible matters, it is not necessary that everything which one remembers be absent. I can still remember something that is near beside me. **6.** What kind of remembrance Christ requires in the holy Supper is clarified by St. Paul in 1 Cor. 11:26 – **For as often as you eat of this bread and drink from this chalice, you should proclaim the Lord's death until He comes**. That is, we are to remind ourselves through the use of the holy Supper that Christ gave His body and shed His blood for us so that we in public assembly should thank Him. This remembrance of the suffering and death of Christ does not conflict with the true presence of His body and blood; rather, that's why Christ gives us His body to eat and His blood to drink, so that with His life-producing flesh He might awaken and strengthen such a blessed remembrance within us. Phi. 3:12 – **I am seized by Christ**. **7.** How often are we admonished that in cross and misfortune we should remember God the Lord? And again, how often do the believers petition that God would remember them? But, who would dare say that God is far absent from the believers? Rather it is written: **I am beside** [you] **in tribulation** (Psa. 91:15); **Do not be afraid, for as you go through water, I will be with you so that the streams do not drown you; and if you go into fire, you shall not burn and the flame will not ignite you** (Isa. 43:2). Further, St. Paul says in 2 Tim. 1:6: **For the sake of this matter I remind you that you awaken the gift of God which is in you through the laying on of my hands.**

6. 2 Cor. 5:16: That we no longer are acquainted with Jesus according to the flesh; therefore, we should not be concerned about the presence of Christ's flesh in the holy Supper. ANSWER: **1.** The apostle is speaking here of the carnal delusion which certain ones held about the kingdom of Christ, as if it would be a terrestrial, earthly kingdom. In opposition to this, he writes these words and says in effect: "Even though we indeed at the beginning knew Christ according to the flesh, that is, even though many, including initially the holy apostles themselves, sought earthly, fleshly benefits from Christ because they thought Christ's kingdom would be an earthly, worldly kingdom, we no longer know Him that way. Rather we have laid aside such fleshly delusions about Christ's kingdom and benefits, and from now on seek only heavenly gifts from Him." **2.** If this passage has to be applied to Christ's body, then it would follow that subsequent to His ascension He no longer has a true body. For just as the apostles knew Christ by the enlightening of the Holy Spirit, in the same way we should also know Him. **3.** Consequently, it is one thing to know Christ *according to* the flesh [from a worldly perspective], but it is quite another to know Christ *in* the flesh. In essence, the former refers to having fleshly thoughts about Christ and His kingdom, while the latter means recognizing that Christ took on a true human nature and keeps it in eternity.

7. That one should not believe those who say, **See, there is Christ, or there** (Mat. 24:23). Therefore, one should not believe in the true presence of the body of Christ in the holy Supper. ANSWER: **1.** From this one could also ultimately conclude that Christ is not in heaven, either. **2.** [And could further conclude] that Christ does not dwell in the hearts of believers, even though the Scriptures testify to both. **3.** The correct understanding of these words of Christ is revealed by the circumstances of the text. Christ is here speaking about false prophets and false christs who will present themselves as the true Messiah and mislead many of them. Christ here warns against [such error] and teaches that His kingdom is a spiritual kingdom which does not come with outward trappings. Also, one will not say: **See, here it is, or there it is. For you see, the kingdom of God is inside of you** (Luke 17:20, 21). But who would want to conclude from this passage that the kingdom of Christ is far from us? Thus one should not say: See, here is Christ, see there He is. That is, one should not bind His grace and His kingdom to certain localities. But who would wish to conclude from this that Christ is not present with His true body and blood in the holy Supper?

8. That finally, one might say that, from all the reasons thought through above, no other presence of the body and blood in the holy Supper can be accepted than the *praesentia significativa*, namely, that the bread is a sign of the body of Christ, the wine a sign of the blood of Christ, even though Christ's body and blood are as far from the bread and wine in the holy Supper as heaven is from earth. AN-SWER: What Christ has instituted as a sacramental presence of His body and blood in the holy Supper is to be distinctly and articulately understood from His words of institution: **Take, eat**, He says, **this is My body; take, drink, this is My blood**. Consequently, the sacramental presence of the body and blood of Christ is thus provided for. The bread is not simply a sign of the absent body nor the wine simply a sign of the absent blood of Christ; rather, the institution of Christ makes possible that His body is eaten with the bread and His blood is drunk with the wine. **The bread, which we break** (in the holy Lord's Supper)**, is it not the fellowship of the body of Christ; the blessed chalice which we bless** (in the holy Lord's Supper)**, is it not the fellowship of the blood of Christ?**, says St. Paul in 1 Cor. 20:16. Therefore, the consecrated bread is not just a sign, but the fellowship of the body of Christ, the means through which Christ's body is distributed to us. The consecrated wine in the holy Supper is not just a sign, but the fellowship of the blood of Christ, the means through which Christ's blood is distributed to us. Since we, in simple faith, want to abide by the words of Christ and the apostle Paul, any additional differences which still exist with be dealt with more extensively later on.

CHAPTER 12

WHETHER ONE SHOULD STEADFASTLY REMAIN WITH THE SAME UNDERSTANDING WHICH THE LITERAL WORDS OF CHRIST'S INSTITUTION PRESENT.

s was demonstrated in the previous chapter, the real presence of the body and blood of Christ is founded upon the words of institution—the very presence of which, however, human reason finds to be strange and unbelievable. Thus, some people would rather renounce the clear sense of the words in this holy Sacrament and, through various interpretations, apply a different meaning to these words than to abide with Christ's words in simple and obedient faith. Here again it should be remembered that in no way should or may one deviate from the literal sense of the words of institution, which we demonstrate as follows:

1. The doctrine of the holy Lord's Supper is an article of faith, the proper confession of which is obviously of highest necessity, because those who eat this bread and drink from this chalice unworthily eat and drink condemnation to themselves (1 Cor. 11:29). There can be no doubt that a particular article of faith may be stated in clear, plain words on some point in the Scripture, for how might one otherwise know anything definite about it? Further, it is also undeniably certain that the words of institution are *propria sedes*; [that is], they are the chief basis and the only place in which is described what we should know and believe about this holy Sacrament. Therefore, these very words must of necessity be retained with the same understanding which the letter [literal meaning] actually brings with it.

Mat. 17:5, Mark 9:7, Luke 9:34 – **This is My dear Son. You should listen to Him.**

Mat. 23:8, 10 – **For one is your Master, Christ.**

John 8:31, 32 – **If you keep My words, then you are My disciples and shall recognize the truth and the truth will make you free.**

John 10:27 – **For My sheep hear My voice**, etc.

John 12:48 – **The word which I have spoken, that is what will judge him on judgment day.**

1 Tim. 6:3, 4 – **If anyone teaches otherwise and does not stay with the saving words of our Lord Jesus Christ, he is benighted and knows nothing**, etc.

2. In the holy Lord's Supper, we have the Lord Christ's Testament, as was shown in chapters 1 and 5 above. Now, one abides by the testament of a dying man according to the simple meaning which the words of the testament have. How much less dare one or should one deviate from the same literal sense of the words of Christ's Testament?

Gal. 3:15 – **One does not hold in disdain a person's testament when it has been probated, and also does not add to it.**

3. The words of institution were remembered and recorded from Christ's mouth at different times by three different evangelists and by St. Paul; namely, St. Matthew wrote in the eighth, Mark in the tenth, Luke in the fifteenth, and Paul in the fifty-fourth year after the ascension of Christ. And yet, none of them gave the slightest indication that one should accept a different understanding of Christ's words than what the very letter of the same says. Why would we then want to deviate from the literal understanding of these words? In describing the first element, they all testify: **Take, eat, this is My body**. In describing the other element, St. Matthew and Mark testify that Christ said: **Take, drink, this is My blood of the New Testament**. Luke and St. Paul have also [written]: **Take, drink, this is the chalice, the New Testament in My blood**, which is not contradictory, for the chalice is therefore a New Testament since in it the blood of the New Testament is offered to us to drink.

Mat. 26:26–28 – **As they then ate, Jesus took the bread, gave thanks and broke it and gave it to the disciples and said: Take, eat, this is My body. And He took the cup and gave thanks, gave it to them and said: All of you drink of [from] this. This is My blood of the New Testament, which will be poured out for many for the forgiveness of sins.**

Mark 14:22–24 – **And while they were eating, Jesus took the bread, gave thanks and broke it and gave it to them and said: Take, eat, this is My body. And took the cup and gave thanks and gave it to them and they all drank of it. And He said to them: This is My blood of the New Testament which will be poured out for many.**

Luke 22:19, 20 – **And He took the bread, gave thanks and broke it and gave it to them and said: This is My body, which is given for you; this do in remembrance of Me. In the same manner also** [He took] **the cup after the evening meal and said: This is the cup, the New Testament in My blood, which is shed for you.**

1 Cor. 11:23, 24, 25 – **I have received from the Lord that which I have given to you; for the Lord Jesus on the night He was betrayed took the bread, gave thanks and broke it and said: Take, eat, this is My body which is broken for you; do this in remembrance of Me. In the same manner also** [He took] **the cup after the evening meal and said: This cup is the New Testament in My blood; do this, as often as you drink it, in remembrance of Me.**

4. Whenever Christ held forth in other places about the mysteries of the kingdom of God in parables and veiled (figurative) words, He quickly—with clear, distinct words—clarified the same for His disciples, so that they didn't fall into erroneous interpretations. Now if the words of the holy Supper are to be understood in a figurative manner and differently than they read, then Christ certainly would have explained so Himself, since the danger to salvation hinges upon whether a person eats the consecrated bread and drinks the consecrated chalice unworthily or not (1 Cor. 11:27). But now, nowhere is such an explanation to be found.

In Mat. 13, Mark 4, and Luke 8, various parables are recorded which the Lord Christ spoke to His disciples and to the people. However, the explanation of same follows soon thereafter. Here especially is to be noted what is written in Mark 4:34, that Christ in particular explained everything to His disciples (and those others who were nearby [v. 10]).

In Mat. 15:17, He explains to them how they are to understand that whatever goes into the mouth does not make a person unclean.

In Mat. 16:11 He explains to them how they are to understand that they are to shield themselves from the leaven of the Pharisees and Sadducees.

Also, Christ frequently made clear and intelligible the entire parable by amending a little verse at the end so that one can understand the point of the parable and whereto it is directed.

5. Not only has Christ nowhere implied that the words of the holy Supper are to be understood in any other way than as they read, but rather, in this matter, He has actually stubbornly blocked the way to any interpretation and commentary by which the true presence of His body and blood is removed. So that no one might say that the little words **body** and **blood** are to be understood as the symbol [sign] of His body and blood, He also includes and makes it completely clear as to what sort of **body** and what kind of **blood** He wants to be understood by His words.

Mat. 26:26, Mark 14:22 – **Take, eat, this is My body** (not a figurative, symbolized body, but rather My true, natural body).

In Luke 22:19 it is written next that He was speaking of the same body which **is given** for us, or as St. Paul says in 1 Cor. 11:24 – **which is broken for you**. Now then, this can be understood of none other than the natural body of Christ.

Furthermore, in describing the other part of this holy Sacrament it is written in Mat. 26:27 and Mark 14:22 – **Take, drink, this is My blood of the New Testament which is being poured out for many,** or as related in Luke 22:20 and by St. Paul in 1 Cor. 11:25, the words read: **This chalice is the New Testament in My blood which is being poured out for you** (This chalice is the New Testament. This holy Supper does not belong to the Old Testament, which was surrounded with types and figures. Rather, it is the New Testament in My blood, because My own blood is drunk therein. It is not perchance a prototypical blood, since in former times the blood of rams and calves in the Old Testament signified My blood; rather, My blood is drunk from the consecrated chalice, and indeed even the very blood which is being poured out for you all on the trunk of the cross.)

6. If one abides according to the letter by the simple understanding which the words of institution provide, then one has a peaceful conscience. But if one wants to deviate from the words, then so many various meanings (or rather perversions of the same) crop up that one doesn't know which one should accept. Some take the particle **this** before them and assert that it does not refer to the foregoing, nor does it refer to that which is eaten and drunk in the holy Supper; rather, Christ was herewith referring to His body as He was sitting at the table and was saying of it: **This is My body, which will be given for you.** Others take the **is** before them and want to contend that it means nothing more than **signifies.** Some take the words **body and blood** before them and think they should signify a symbol of the body and blood of Christ. Others interpret the words of Christ as follows: that **body** should be understood as the power [efficacy] and effect of the body of Christ, and the **blood** as the power and effect of the blood of Christ. Others take the word **which** in Christ's words, **Eat, this is My body, which**

is being given for you, and interpret it this way: Eat, this is My body in the very same form as it was given for you into death on the cross. Others allow the words of Christ, **This is My body, this is My blood**, to be understood in the literal sense [according to the letter], and then say that it is figurative language, nevertheless, which then must be understood and interpreted to mean that the bread and wine in the holy Supper not only signify but also seal the fellowship of the body and blood of Christ.

Some take the little word **eat**, as well as the word **drink**, before them and say that both signify the spiritual eating (nourishing) through faith in so far as it applies to Christ's body and blood, and it signifies natural eating with the mouth insofar as it applies to the external bread and wine. More such varied interpretations could be recounted, all of which (even though they boil down to removing the true presence of the body and blood of Christ from the holy Supper) still are not in agreement among themselves. Therefore, it is insufficient for one to say: This or that must be understood in a figurative and allusive (hidden) manner. Instead, if a conscience is to be peacefully grounded upon such [an interpretation], it must be shown from the Scriptures that this or that [word] should be interpreted in a figurative manner. Also, they first must agree precisely upon which word is to be discussed in the figurative sense.

2 Pet. 1:20, 21 – **And you should know this from the first, that no prophecy in the Scripture occurs from one's own interpretation. For there never has been brought forth any prophecy from the will of humans. Rather the holy men of God have spoken, driven by the Holy Spirit.** (The Scriptures must not be interpreted from one's own opinion, since they do not proceed from human opinion, but from the Holy Spirit.)

Here again are apparent points of contention:

1. That understanding the words of Christ in the holy Supper according to the letter (literally) runs contrary to two articles of our Christian faith: that Christ has a true, natural body, and that He has ascended to heaven. Thus, one must search elsewhere in Scripture for a different understanding and not take these words [of the institution] literally. ANSWER: This matter was dealt with extensively in the previous chapter, where it was shown that in no way is our reason to be consulted for advice in matters of what God can and cannot do or in cases in which articles of faith conflict with each other. Rather, where one has a clear and plain-spoken Word of God, there one should in simple faith abide by it and imprison all reason under the obedience of Christ, Rom. 4:18–21 – **And he, (Abraham) believed in hope where there was no hope, so that he became a father of many Gentiles, etc. And he was not weak in faith, did not look to his own body which was already dead** [i.e., infertile], **since he was already one hundred, nor on the dead body of Sarah. For he did not doubt the promise of God through unbelief; rather, he was strong in faith and gave God glory. He knew most certainly that what God promised, that He could also do.** We should set our eyes on this example of Abraham's faith and follow it. There can be no doubt—yes, we even have the circumstances surrounding the text—that, as God gave him the promise about the increase of his seed in Gen. 12:2, 15:4 [sic, 15:5], Abraham had to be adequately satisfied in this conflict with his reason in order to be able to force it under the obedience of faith. Therefore, he also asked if it might not mean that the son of his servant Eleazer was not to be the heir (Gen. 15:3). And even though God the Lord had plainly declared to him that from his body should come an heir, Sarah thought that these words might have a different meaning, as is apparent from her words to her lord, Abraham: **See the Lord has locked me up that I no longer can give birth. Rather, you lie with my maid, so that I might yet possibly increase myself,** etc. (Gen. 16:2). And as God the Lord once more reiterated the promise with plain words (Gen. 17:16), Sarah, your wife, shall bear you a son, in his mind's eye Abraham pictured again his and Sarah's dead [infertile] bodies and asked, v. 17, **Should a child be born to me at age one hundred and Sarah give birth at ninety?** Finally, when God repeated the promise for the last time, Gen. 18:10, **She** (Sarah) **privately laughed and said, Now that I am old, and my lord** [husband] **is also old, am I to cultivate voluptuousness?** God the Lord said, Gen. 18:13, 14: **Why do you laugh, and He said: Are you questioning whether it is true, I shall yet give birth even though I am old? Should anything be impossible for the Lord?**, etc. Thus was Abraham was strengthened in faith. In opposition to all his doubts, he believed the Word of the Lord. And as God later gave him the command to slay his son as a burnt-offering (Gen. 22:2), he obeyed the command of God, even though he did not see how this command could be reconciled with the promise of multiplying his seed. The apostle holds forth this example and desires that we should trust the clear words and promises of God in articles of faith, even though by all counts they appear impossible to our reason [judgment].

    2. That if one wants to abide by the letter of the words in the holy Supper, then it would follow that the bread is changed [transformed, transubstantiated] into Christ's body and the wine changed into Christ's blood. ANSWER: This will be dealt with in detail at its proper place, and it will be shown that in no way can or may one force these words of Christ to mean that this essential change of the bread into Christ's body and the wine into Christ's blood takes place.

    3. That shortly before his departure, the patriarch Jacob established a testament in which he employs many veiled, figurative visionary sayings (Gen. 49). Therefore [by analogy], because the words of the holy Supper are [Christ's] word of testament, it cannot be concluded that one should abide by the letter of same. ANSWER: What the patriarch Jacob discusses with His children on his deathbed was mostly a prophecy about future events, as Moses expressly indicates in v. 1: **And Jacob called his sons and said: Gather yourselves that I might declare to you what you will meet up with in future times.** Such is also evident from the circumstances of the text, since the patriarch declares in advance to each of his sons what will happen to him and his descendants. Consequently, it is no wonder that in keeping with the character of all prophecy that these sayings of the patriarch are somewhat obscure. When he actually establishes his testament in v. 29 and commands that they should bury him in the cave on the acreage of the Hittite Ephron, there he speaks clearly and plainly enough. Accordingly, it remains certain and indisputable that the holy Supper of Christ is the Testament of our Lord. Therefore, we should steadfastly abide by the simple meaning of the words which the letter brings with it; since it is not presumable that He would want to carry on with murky and dubious sayings while wanting to designate the *legata* [*legacy*], that is, the very same heavenly gifts which He had bequeathed His Christians in this Testament.

4. That if there be two disagreeing [different, distinct] matters, of which one [thing] can be stated about the other, such may not occur except in a figurative, allusive manner [i. e., that if one can apply the same term to different or opposite concepts, that term must be used in a figurative sense]. Now it is found in the words of Christ that what is stated about His body is said about the bread, and what is stated about His blood is said about the wine. Now since the bread and the body of Christ are different things, and the wine and the blood of Christ are different things, therefore this [identity] can occur only in a figurative and veiled manner. AN-SWER: **1.** Christ does not say in the holy Supper: The bread is My body, the wine is My blood. Rather He says as follows: **Take, eat, this is My body; take, drink, this is My blood;** the little word **this** points not only to the bread and wine, but it most assuredly refers at the same time to the consecrated bread and to the body of Christ in the first portion of the holy Supper, and then it refers to the consecrated wine and to the blood of Christ in the other portion of the holy Supper. **2.** How this manner of expression is to be employed, [i.e.,] when two contrary things are presented simultaneously, is that a person allows the one visible thing, by which the other invisible thing is presented, to be deferred, and in the predicate (in the other part of the saying) to think only of the invisible and chief [thing]; because, afterwards Christ not only distributed bread and wine to His disciples, but rather at the same time distributed with the bread His true body and with the wine His true blood. That's why He said: **Eat, this is My body; drink, this is My blood.** That Christ distributed bread and wine the disciples could see with their own eyes. That's why Christ did not say: Eat, this is bread *and* My body; drink, this is wine *and* My blood. That, however, with the consecrated bread Christ's true body was distributed to them and, with the wine, His true blood—of this they saw and knew nothing. Therefore, Christ drives home the point with clear words and says: **Eat—this is My body; drink—this is My blood. 3.** Such a mode of speaking is common not only in Scripture, but also in ordinary language usage. In the person of Christ, the divine and human natures are personally united. Whoever saw Christ in such a manner can properly and rightly say that he has seen the Word of Life (1 John 1:1), namely, because the same human nature which he sees before his eyes is personally united with the Word of Life, that is, with the divine nature. So then, just as it is properly stated concerning the personal union of the divine and human nature in Christ, that whoever sees Christ sees the Word of life, so also, because Christ's body is sacramentally united with the consecrated bread and Christ's blood is sacramentally united with the consecrated wine, Christ says as He distributes the consecrated bread, **Eat, this is My body,** and as He distributes the consecrated wine, **Drink, this is My blood.** Here it should be noted that this comparison between the Person of Christ and this holy Sacrament has not been employed on behalf of the argument that, just as God and man are one person in Christ, there is also a personal union in the holy Supper between the consecrated bread and the body of Christ. Rather, this comparison is intended only for the purpose of clarifying the manner of speaking. So then also in John 20:22, 23, Christ blows on His disciples and says to them: **Receive the Holy Spirit**, which means essentially the same as if He had said: Take, this is the Holy Spirit. So then, just as on that occasion the external breath was the fellowship of the Holy Spirit (namely, because by means of the same external breath the Holy Spirit was imparted to the apostles from Christ), so also the consecrated bread in the holy Supper is the fellowship of the body of Christ, [and] the consecrated chalice the fellowship of the blood of Christ. That is, Christ's body and blood [are] distributed by means of the consecrated bread and wine. Thus Christ says: **Eat, this is My body; drink, this is My blood.** Furthermore, as the Holy Spirit descended in the bodily form of a dove at the Baptism of Christ, John the Baptizer said that he saw the Holy Spirit descend (John 1:32), because in that same external form of a dove the Holy Spirit revealed Himself in an extraordinary manner. So also when Christ's body is sacramentally united with the consecrated bread and Christ's blood is sacramentally united with the consecrated wine, one properly states that Christ's body is eaten when the consecrated bread is received (eaten) and Christ's blood is drunk when the consecrated chalice is received (drunk). Furthermore, when the holy angels appeared to the patriarchs and prophets of the Old Testament in the form of vigorous young men or in other outward likenesses, they correctly stated that they personally had seen the angels, namely because the holy angels had revealed themselves in an unusual manner through these very same visible forms, Gen. 32:1, 2 – **And he** (Jacob) **was met by the angels of God. And as he saw them, he said: It is the God's host,** etc. Finally, as Moses properly stated: whenever the Ark of the Covenant is lifted up and carried forth, God the Lord is standing up (Num. 10:35). David says the same in Psa. 68:1, since God the Lord especially testified to and spoke with the children of Israel from this very place (Exo. 25:22). As also Isaiah and other prophets, when the Lord revealed Himself to them through external forms, correctly stated that they had seen the Lord, Isa. 6:1 because God the Lord in a special manner revealed Himself to them through such extraordinary aspects. So then, since Christ by means of the consecrated bread distributes His body to the disciples, and by means of the consecrated chalice distributes His true blood to His disciples, that's why He says: **Take, eat, this is My body; take, drink, this is My blood. 4**. This method of speaking is employed in common language usage whenever two things are presented simultaneously; that is, one expressly names [designates] only the chief and invisible thing, which supersedes the other thing which is visible to the eye. For example, one says: This is the wine which your dear friend admires; this is the money which I owe you; this is the little son of Zachariah. Yet what is referred to is the wine in the [visible] vat, the money in the purse, the child in the cradle, even though the external thing which passes before a person's eyes is not what is assumed in such a conversation. However, it must be remembered that this example in no way is to be used to conclude that Christ's body is [literally] in a spatial manner thus confined inside the bread—like the wine in the vat, the money in the purse, the child in the cradle. Rather, only the manner of speaking is being clarified here—a mode which emanates from the union two different things, of which one is invisible but yet is more worthy than the other. **5**. From all this it is apparent how the little word **"this"** in this saying of Christ—**This is My body, this is My blood**—is in no way to be applied only to the consecrated bread and to the consecrated chalice. The same also becomes obvious from the construction of the [original] Greek: ἄρτος τοῦτο. If Christ with the little word "**this**" was seeing only the consecrated bread and consecrated chalice, He would have had to say: Take, drink, this chalice is My blood; this bread is My body. But such did not take place. Rather, Christ speaks as follows: **Take, eat, this is My body; take, drink, this is My blood**. Thus, with the word "**this**," He expressly indicates that it means the foremost, highest part of what He is distributing to the disciples to eat and to drink. **6**. The same furthermore also becomes apparent from the fact that the evangelist Luke (Luke 22:20) and St. Paul (1 Cor. 11:25) as soon as they—in lieu of the subject (or the first part of the statement)—write the word "**chalice**," they also change the predicate (the other part of the statement), and do not simply say: This chalice is the blood of Christ. Rather, they say: **This chalice is the New Testament in My** (Christ's) **blood.** Therefore, it is apparent that the word "**this**" is by no means to be applied only to the consecrated chalice. Otherwise, Luke and Paul would have recorded the words of Christ as follows: Take, drink, this chalice [i.e., this wine] is My blood; just as by the same measure Matthew and Mark record the words thus: **Take, drink, this is My blood. 7**. What's more, St. Paul (1 Cor. 10:16), as he records in lieu of the subject, **the bread,** does not merely say in the predicate that it [the bread] is the body of Christ and that the consecrated wine is the blood of Christ. Rather, he says as follows: **The bread which we break, is it not the fellowship of the body of Christ; the consecrated chalice which we consecrate** [bless], **is it not the fellowship of the blood of Christ?** From this [evidence] then it is obvious that the words of Christ are not to be interpreted as if He intends the demonstrative pronoun "**this**" to refer only to the consecrated bread and the consecrated wine. **8**. All the same, we do not dispute the statements that the consecrated bread in the holy Supper is the true body of Christ [and that] the consecrated wine in the holy Supper is the true blood of Christ, since these expressions are actually used in the writings of the ancient church teachers. We [insist] only that these words of Christ and St. Paul are interpreted as sacramental utterances in such a manner: The consecrated bread is the body of Christ, not in the sense that the bread has been transformed [transubstantiated] into Christ's body or in the sense that the bread merely represents the absent body of Christ. Rather, it is because the bread in the holy Supper is the fellowship of the body of Christ, since the consecrated bread is not only bread but also the body of Christ on account of the sacramental union and since by means of the consecrated bread Christ's body is received and eaten on the strength of the words of Christ: **Take, eat, this is My body**, and on the strength of St. Paul interpretation: **The bread, which we break, is it not the fellowship of the body of Christ?** The other statement—that the consecrated wine is the blood of Christ—must be interpreted in like manner.

5. That it is common usage in the sacraments that the name of the symbolized and typical thing is attached to the external sign and figure [image]. Hence, circumcision is the **Covenant of God** (Gen. 17:10), that is, a sign of the divine *covenant* (v. 11). The Passover lamb is the **Lord's Passover**, Exo. 12:11), that is, a sign of the passage. **The Rock was Christ** (1 Cor. 10:4, that is, a type of Christ. Here also might be cited all the other similar references in which the name of what is symbolized is applied to the sign, John 15:1 – **I am the legitimate Wine-vine, and My Father is a Vine-dresser;** Mat. 11:14 – **He** (John) **is Elijah**, etc.; Mat. 13:38 – **The field is the world, the good seed are the children of the kingdom, the weeds are the children of evil. The enemy, who sows them, is the devil. The harvest is the end of the world, the harvesters are the angels;** Rev. 1:19 [20] – **The seven lustres** [stars] – **are seven congregations;** Gen. 41:26, 27 – **The seven beautiful cows are seven years, and the seven good ears are also seven years,** etc.; **the seven skinny and ugly cows ... are seven years; and the seven meager and parched ears are seven years of high cost**

of living. In each case, the verb *to be* is used as meaning "signifies" or "represents"; thus one must also understand the words of Christ in the holy Supper **"eat, this is My body"** to mean, this is a sign and symbol of My body. ANSWER: **1.** Even though it might be clearly demonstrated from Scripture that at times the name of what is signified is applied [attributed] to the symbol, yet such would not be sufficient to make the case that one can indisputably conclude from this that the words of Christ in the holy Supper must also be interpreted in this way. Rather, one must prove the same from the very words of Christ themselves, as from the *propria sedes hujus articuli* [*proper seat or basis of this article*]. **2.** Now then, such will never happen because through the words of the Lord's Supper, by all rights, the pathway is closed for all the hair-splitting and sneering remarks by which the real presence of the body and blood of Christ is denied, as demonstrated in sect. 5 [sic, 6] above. **3.** Beyond that, it must be taught and believed about each Sacrament as *in propria sede*, that is, as it is described in the very place where it is actually and completely dealt with. But then, one does not find the least indication in Mat. 26, Mark 14, Luke 22, or 1 Cor. 10:11 that the words of Christ are to be thus understood, even though at these noted places the doctrine of the holy Lord's Supper is specifically and actually dealt with. **4.** Even though the Sacraments of the Old Testament, as well as the sacraments of the New Testament, instituted by God Himself, are powerful means of divine grace and **seals of the righteousness of faith** (Rom. 4:11), yet in no way can it be concluded from this that there is no other presence of the body and blood of Christ in the holy Supper than there was in the sacraments of the Old Testament. In this case, an express distinction has been established by the Holy Spirit between the Sacraments of the Old Testament and those of the New Testament, to the extent that in the Old Testament, and thus also in its Sacraments, is to be found only **the shadow of that which was to come.** In the New Testament, however, and thus also in its Sacraments, **the body itself** [is found] (Col. 2:17). [The distinction is expressed] even more clearly in Heb. 10:1 – **For the Law possessed the shadow of the future blessings, not the essence of the blessings themselves,** etc. **5.** On account of this variation, the Sacraments of the Old and New Testaments cannot be compared with each other as to their essence, especially since the former only signified that which the latter truly have present in reality. **6.** It further follows that the words of Christ, **Take, eat, this is My body; take, drink, this is My blood**, should not and cannot be judged and interpreted according to the same utterances which apply to the institution of the Sacraments in the Old Testament. **7.** Much less may they be compared with and judged according to the same language which the Scripture uses in describing dreams, visions, and other figures of speech, inasmuch as Christ is especially here not speaking figuratively. Rather, He establishes His Testament and describes such an article of faith as has never before been described. Therefore, the words concerning this institution and its description must indeed be understood according to the letter [literally]. **8.** To say nothing of the fact that the entire business of a comparison of the words of Christ in the holy Supper with the passages cited [from the Old Testament] rests on the foundation and ground that the little word "**this**"points only to the bread and wine. Yet just immediately prior something different [the body and the blood] was indicated. Thus, all the apparent irregularities between the propositions cited and the words of Christ in the holy Supper are adequately removed. **9.** Nevertheless, so that therewith the matter be sufficiently laid to rest, we want to deal with and show why the words of Christ in the holy Supper may not be compared to each of the passages cited. The circumcision, which in Gen. 17:11 is labeled a **sign of the divine covenant**, St. Paul in Rom. 4:11 interprets thus: (Abraham) **received the sign of circumcision as a seal of the righteousness of faith.** From this [passage] it is to be concluded that in no way can it be shown by the word **sign** that circumcision only signified God's covenant; rather, on the contrary, [circumcision] **sealed** and ratified [the covenant]. In the same manner, it can also be properly said of the holy Supper (which encompasses within itself not only bread and wine but also Christ's body and blood) that it is a sign, that is, a witness and seal of the forgiveness of sins—[an apt description of] the benefit and fruits of this Sacrament. However, no simile is presented between the earthly and the heavenly as an essential part of this Sacrament. But if one wants to compare the external elements, such as the bread and wine, with the heavenly—that is, the body and blood of Christ—and, in such a simile, call the outward elements *signs* [symbols] ... then, in light of the words of Christ (**eat, this is My body, drink, this is My blood**) and the interpretation of St. Paul (the bread, that we break, is it not the fellowship of the body of Christ? The blessed chalice, which we bless, is it not the fellowship of the blood of Christ?), it must be interpreted in this way: The bread and the wine are symbols not of the absent [body and blood], but of the invisible body and blood of Christ, which [body and blood] by means of the same external elements in the holy Supper are eaten and drunk in an inexplicable, mysterious, incomprehensible manner; and yet they [the body and blood] are not seen. **10.** Of further concern is [the contention] that in Exo. 12:12 the Passover lamb should be called the passage, that is, a symbol of the passage. In addition to the previously noted differences between the Sacraments of the Old and the New Testaments, it is also to be mentioned that these words, "the Passover lamb is the passage," are nowhere to be found in the words of Moses. Much less will be found the [alternative] interpretation of the same words: the Passover lamb is the *symbol* of the Passage. Least of all will you find in the Scripture that the words of Christ in the holy Supper are to be likened to such use of language. Moses, by the command of God, speaks to the children of Israel in this way in vv. 11, 12: **and** (you) **shall eat** [the paschal lamb]**, as those who are hurrying away, for it is the Lord's Passover** [feast]. **For I will go through the land of Egypt on that very night and smite all the first-born**, etc. So then these words—**For it is the Lord's Passover** or **passing-through**—may in no way be applied to the Passover lamb, which pointed not to the Passage of the Lord, but rather to Christ, the Lamb of God (John 1:29, 30; 1 Cor. 5:7). Nor can there be found any simile which relates the Passover lamb and the passing-through of the Lord. However, Moses as much as wants to say: You shall eat the Passover hurriedly, for it is the Lord's passing-through. You will not have much time remaining because the Lord will hastily go over Egypt and smite the first-born. However, if indeed a person wants to apply the word "**Passover**" to the Passover lamb, then the following interpretation may be applied to the text: You shall eat the little lamb with appointed ceremonies and according to prescribed ways, for it is the Lord's **Passover**, that is, it is the paschal lamb of the Lord, ordained by God for the purpose that it be a remembrance that God the Lord went through Egypt and killed the first-born in Egypt. In contrast, He spared the first-born of the Israelites. **11.** When St. Paul says in 1 Cor. 10:4 – **The Rock was Christ,** he is not referring to the stony rock in the wilderness; rather, he understands it as a **spiritual Rock,** which was symbolized by it, that is, Christ. [Such an interpretation] is plainly apparent from the details of the text, since he expressly calls the same rock a **spiritual Rock,** and then adds that he is speaking of such a rock which **followed after** the Israelites in the wilderness. Now then, the same cannot be said about the [actual] rock which remained standing inertly in the wilderness. Some, however, understand the rock which followed the Israelites to mean the water which flowed from the rock. Not only is that a difficult interpretation, but it also conflicts with the fact that the children of Israel shortly thereafter again had no water. This would not have happened had the water from the rock followed after them. Consequently, we maintain that the rock referred to here is to be understood as the Rock of Salvation, Christ, who also on occasion is now and then is called a **Rock** in the Scripture (Isa. 8:14, Mat. 16:18, Rom. 9:33, 1 Pet. 2:8). He Himself is called a Rock, not as [an actual] change in name, but figuratively. He does not symbolize the spiritual Rock, but rather, He Himself was the spiritual Rock—the Rock to whom the rock in the wilderness and other earthly rocks, along with their distinctive features, point. **12.** When Christ says in John 15:1, **I am the true Wine-stalk, and My Father a vine-dresser,** this can by no means be interpreted that Christ symbolizes a wine-stalk (vine), because the text here speaks not of an earthly vine, but of the true, that is, of the spiritual, heavenly Wine-stalk, onto which the apostle and all believers are engrafted as tendril shoots. That very same true, spiritual Wine-stalk does not symbolize Christ; rather He Himself is it. What's more, when Christ says in Mat. 11:14, **He** (John) **is Elias,** in no way may the little word "**is**" in that place be interpreted as John *symbolizes* Elias. No, rather Christ speaks about the very same **Elias, who was to come before.** Thus Elias does not symbolize John; rather he himself is [John]. Also, when sayings are used in parables, such as: **The field is the world, the harvest is the end of the world,** etc., Mat. 13:38; **Seven lustres … are seven congregations,** Rev. 1:20; or also in interpreting dreams: **seven good ears are … seven years,** etc. (Gen. 41:26); these may in no way be applied to the words of Christ in the holy Supper. Neither can the [words of Christ] be judged according to these sayings, not only because Christ presents no parables, describes no visions or trances, nor relates dreams in the holy Supper, but also because the actual words in the dreams, visions and parables are understood as being figurative and not a nominal [literal] exchange. However, He institutes the second Sacrament of the New Testament with deliberate resoluteness and speaks of such an article of faith with which disciples are unfamiliar.

When Christ says, **The seed is the word of God,** He is speaking not about earthly seed in the field, but rather about the heavenly, imperishable Seed in the field of the Lord. This Seed does not symbolize the Word of God, but rather the very same heavenly Seed is [the Word]. When John says, **The seven lustres are ... seven congregations,** he is speaking not of earthly luminaries, but of the very luminaries [stars] themselves, among which the Son of God moves about, and so forth. Not to mention that such parables, visions, and dreams in the Scripture are usually interpreted by the Holy Spirit. Concerning the testamentary words of Christ in the holy Supper, however, one finds no evidence that they should be interpreted in a different way, as though they were allusively and figuratively spoken. In fact, much more [significance] is placed on them than on the interpretation of parables, visions and dreams, because it is stated: **Whoever eats unworthily** (of this bread) **and drinks unworthily** (of this chalice), **he eats and drinks judgment upon himself in that he does not discern the body of the Lord** (1 Cor. 11:29).

6. That the words of Christ in the holy Supper are the specific focus of controversy, i.e., whether they should be understood literally or figuratively. Therefore, they may not be used as the primary evidence [source] in this matter. ANSWER: Indeed, no one can doubt that Christ spoke these very words: **Take, eat, this is My body; take, drink, this is My blood,** in the institution and administration of the first Lord's Supper, because that's how they are recorded by the holy evangelists. Nor can it be denied that the words of institution, *propria sedes* [*proper seat*], are the chief foundation for any discussion of the Supper of the Lord Christ. Why would we want to come to the point that we set this chief foundation from view and instead try to base what is to be held about this holy Supper on other sources, which deal with it only in an incidental way? That would actually be like setting aside the third and fourth chapters of Romans, the second and third chapters of Galatians, and the second chapter of Ephesians, and learning about the article of justification from other sources in the Scripture. And although the words of Christ are interpreted with various loathsome commentaries, or rather are perverted, in that false teachers misuse them for the claims of their preconceived errors, yet nothing is thereby taken away from these words, even as [such perversions] cannot alter [the meaning of] other places (passages) of Scripture. Therefore, we confidently abide by the words of Christ, and precisely by the same understanding which the letter conveys with it for the reasons noted above, and especially since in articles of faith one is to abide by the simple understanding which the words themselves impart, [that is], if the Holy Spirit does not Himself give a different meaning to these words in the Scripture. For otherwise the foundation of our Christian faith would be standing on feeble feet, as, for example, when Moses records the article of faith concerning creation. Hence, one should understand the words literally: By light, firmament, earth, sun, etc., one should understand natural light, firmament, earth and sun. When God the Lord forbade the first parents that they should **not eat from the fruit of the tree in the middle of the garden**, they should have abided by the simple understanding which the letter of these very words conveyed. When, however, Eve began to doubt whether God also meant these very same fruits, whether [the restriction] actually had to do with just one apple [piece of fruit], the fall into sin was not far off. In sum, it is written: **The word which I have spoken to you, that will judge you on the last day** (John 12:48).

7. That if one is to abide by the [literal] words of Christ, why does one say the following: The body of Christ is received in, with, and under the bread; the blood of Christ is received in, with, and under the wine? With these words one not only strays from the words of Christ, but also gives reason to think that there is a spatial locking up of the body of Christ in the bread and the blood of Christ in the wine.

ANSWER: **1.** Regardless of the frequent use of such terms by the ancient teachers of the Church, with clear words we stipulate the following: If the true, essential presence of the body and blood of Christ in the holy Supper is admitted, and it is also allowed that the simple understanding of Christ's words produced by a literal understanding be acceptable, then we in that case gladly cease using those words. And, we will say with St. Paul: The consecrated bread is the fellowship of the body of Christ, the consecrated chalice is the fellowship of the blood of Christ. **2.** However, the words of Christ are interpreted by many to mean either that the bread and wine are to be regarded simply as a symbols for the absent body and blood of Christ or, on the other hand, that an essential transformation of the bread into the body of Christ and the wine into the blood of Christ occurs. For that reason, we shall use these same little words against both perversions, so that thereby we express the essential presence of the body and blood of Christ in the holy Supper while also denying the essential transformation [transubstantiation] of the outward elements. With these and similar words, nothing else is meant than the sacramental union of the consecrated bread and the body of Christ and of the consecrated chalice and the blood of Christ. That is, in the holy Supper, by means of the blessed bread the true body of Christ is received, and by means of the blessed wine the true blood of Christ is received. The bread and wine remain in their natural state and essence, not changed or removed according to their natural state; yet, in the sacramental use and reception, not just common bread and wine, but rather the body and blood of Christ are received by means of the very same external elements. How, then may one differently and more suitably express such sacramental benefit and better guard against all perversions than when one says, the body of Christ is received and eaten in, with, and under the consecrated bread [and] the blood of Christ is received and drunk in, with, and under the consecrated wine? **3.** Also, that these words in no way imply that the body of Christ is spatially encased in the bread and the blood of Christ in the wine may be drawn from the following comparison: The holy Scriptures speak thus of Christ: **God was in Christ** (2 Cor. 5:19); **For God was with Him** (John 3:2, Acts 10:38). But who would say that the divine nature is spatially locked within [encased in] the assumed human nature? Not so, then. Rather, these words go no further than thereby to indicate the personal union of both natures in Christ, that namely, **the Word became flesh** (John 1:14), **that God was revealed in the flesh** (1 Tim. 3:16); that is, God's Son assumed a human nature and personally united Himself with it. Thus, when it is similarly said that the body of Christ is received in and with the consecrated bread, no spatial encasing or hiding is implied by that. Rather, only and uniquely, the sacramental union of the blessed bread and the body of Christ are expressed. The Father is in the Son and the Son is in the Father (John 14:11), not as if the Father is spatially contained in the Son, but because the Father's and the Son's essence is inseparable. So also Christ's body is in the consecrated bread, not as if Christ's body is spatially locked up in it, but rather because Christ's body and the consecrated bread *unum sacramentale*, are one holy Sacrament. The Holy Spirit **lives** in our hearts (Eph. 3:13), but who would say that the Holy Spirit and Christ are spatially locked up within us? Even so, it would not be improperly stated if one said, the Holy Spirit descended upon Christ in the form of a dove (Mat. 3:16, Luke 3:21); with external breathing was given to the apostles (John 20:23); and in the form of fiery tongues was given to the apostles (Acts 2:3). Yet, in no way is thereby implied a spatial locking up [encasement] of the Holy Spirit in the dove's form, the breath of Christ, or the fiery tongues.

4. In summary, these and similar statements—that Christ's body is received in, with, and under the consecrated bread, that Christ's blood is received in, with, and under the consecrated wine—emanate from the sacramental union of the consecrated bread and body of Christ and the consecrated chalice and the blood of Christ. Whoever believes this from the heart will have no second thoughts about employing such forms of expression.

CHAPTER 13

CONCERNING THE CONSECRATION, THROUGH WHICH THE EXTERNAL ELEMENTS AT THE HOLY SUPPER BECOME SANCTIFIED.

oth the earthly material of this holy Supper (namely, bread and wine) as well as the heavenly material (namely, the true body and true blood of Christ) have previously been extensively dealt with. The essential elements of the holy Supper are thus not only bread and wine, but also the body and blood of Christ. At this time must be discussed also the form of this Sacrament, which consists of the action, indeed of such a particular action, that we do what Christ and the apostles did. It will be discovered that Christ and the apostles did a threefold thing, from which emanate three sacramental actions, all of which are essential to the form of this Sacrament. And, if one of them is left out, one does not do what Christ did; consequently then, it also would not be a complete Sacrament. The holy evangelists testify: **1.** that the Lord Christ took the bread and gave thanks; **2.** that He broke the bread, offered it to His disciples and distributed it with the words: **Take, eat, this is My body, which is being given for you**; and **3.** that the holy apostles received and ate the consecrated bread. In the same way, **1.** the Lord Christ took the chalice, which contained the produce of the wine-stalk, and gave thanks; **2.** He offered the same chalice to the disciples and distributed with these words: **Take, drink, this is My blood, which will be poured out for you**; and, **3.** the holy apostles received the consecrated chalice and all drank out of it. For the sake of greater accuracy, we want to deal with these three sacramental actions with discrimination. As regards the first action, the evangelists announce that Christ did take the bread and give thanks (Luke 22:19, 1 Cor. 11:24). In the same way, He did also take the chalice and give thanks (Mat. 26:27, Mark 14:23), which thanksgiving Matthew in 26:26 and Mark in 14:22 call a εὐλογίαν or blessing. It follows that thanking and blessing here are one and the same. Now, it is found in the Gospel histories that when Christ undertook to perform a miracle or some other unusual action, He would lift his eyes toward heaven and give thanks to indicate that He performed such wonders by His divine power, which He in essence had in common with the Father and the Holy Spirit, and which was given to Him as the Son of Man through the personal union.

In Mat. 15:36 and Mark 8:6, when Christ wanted to feed four thousand men with seven loaves of bread, He took the seven loaves and gave thanks.

In John 6:11, when He once wanted to feed five thousand with five loaves, He took the bread and gave thanks.

John 6:23 – ... **where they had eaten the bread through the Lord's thanksgiving.**

In John 11:41, when Jesus wanted to awaken Lazarus, He raised His eyes toward heaven and said: **Father, I thank You, that You have heard Me.**

As the Lord Christ also wanted to have the [disciples drink in turn] following the reception of the paschal lamb (as such was the practice of the Israelites), He likewise gave thanks, that is, He reminded His disciples of the leading out from Egypt, for which remembrance thereof the paschal lamb had been instituted by the Lord God. To that end, He reminded them to thank God for this.

Luke 22:17 – **And He took the chalice, gave thanks and said: Take this and share it among yourselves.**

What then further pertains to the εὐλογεῖν or blessing of Christ, He practiced such also when He wanted to perform miracles or some other extraordinary action.

In Mat. 14:19, Mark 6:41, Luke 9:41, as Christ wanted to feed the five thousand people with five loaves, He looked up towards heaven and blessed.

Christ also used this blessing when He wanted to hand out His heavenly blessings.

In Mark 10:16, the Lord Jesus laid hands upon the children and blessed them.

Luke 24:50, 51 – **But He** (Jesus) **led them** (His disciples) **out up to Bethany and raised up** [His] **hands and blessed them. As He blessed, He departed from them**, etc.

Acts 3:26 – **And** (God) **has sent Him** (Jesus) **to you to bless you**, etc.

Finally, Christ used this blessing also at common mealtime as an example to us that we should receive our daily bread on each occasion with thanksgiving (1 Cor. 10:31, 1 Tim. 4:4, 5).

Luke 24:30 – **And it happened that as He was sitting at the table, He took bread, gave thanks, broke it and gave it to them.**

From all [these examples], but primarily from the circumstances of the institution of the holy Supper, it is to be understood that when Christ in those days took the bread, gave thanks, and blessed, that it is to be understood in the following way:

1. That He was thanking His heavenly Father for the work of redemption which He now was about to perform and that He wanted to institute a constant sign of remembrance of it; also, that He wanted to teach us that we should do the same at the reception of this holy Supper.

1 Cor. 11:26 – **For as often as you eat of this bread and drink from this chalice, you should proclaim the Lord's death until He comes.**

2. That at the same time, He held a counsel of deliberation with the Father and the Holy Spirit about the institution of this holy Sacrament, in the same manner as occurred at the creation of mankind; also, He inwardly longed for a continuing preservation of this Mystery within the Church unto the end of the world.

Gen. 1:26 – **And God said, Let Us make man, an image that is like Us**, etc.

3. That He herewith selected and sanctified the bread and wine present for this holy Supper so that He could by means of these same external elements distribute His true body and blood to the disciples. For in the same way that God the Lord blessed the Sabbath (that is, ordained it as a holy day for dealing with divine matters), even so Christ here also blesses the bread and wine (that is, establishes them as a means and instrument for the fellowship of His body and blood). He sets them aside for this holy Sacrament.

Gen. 2:3 – **And** (God) **blessed the seventh day and sanctified it**, etc.

4. Finally, that through this thanksgiving and blessing He ordains that as often as the holy Supper is celebrated in Christendom according to His ordinance and institution, His true body and blood are being distributed and received by means of the consecrated elements. For in the same way as the blessing of God was once spoken over mankind and the creatures at the first creation, yet still is effectual daily, so also this blessing of Christ in the holy Supper is still effectual every day, so that in the power of the same, His true body—by means of the bread—and His true blood—by means of the wine—are distributed, *dei benedicere est benefacere* [L. for God to bless is to do well]. So then, God does not bless as we humans do. With our blessings we only wish the good. God's blessing, however, is an efficacious act.

Gen. 1:22 – **And God blessed them** (the fish) **and said: Be fruitful and increase yourselves and fill up the waters of the sea, and the birds increase themselves on the earth.**

Gen. 1:38 – **And God blessed them** (the people) **and said to them: Be fruitful and increase yourselves and fill the earth and make it subservient to you,** etc.

Gen. 5:2 – **God blessed humankind**, etc.

Since Christ, then, in the institution of the holy Supper, says that at and with the administration of this holy Sacrament we should do the same thing He did, it follows that the servants of the Church [clergy]—whenever they want to celebrate the holy Supper—should in the same manner take the bread and give thanks [and] after the same manner also take the chalice and give thanks or bless. Such blessing is commonly called the consecration and is accomplished through repeating Christ's words of institution. At the same time, it should be remembered that such a consecration is not to be regarded as a base and simple historical recounting of what Christ did. Rather, as shown in chapter 4 above, it is to be regarded thus: When the preacher who is administering this holy Sacrament repeats, along with the Lord's Prayer, the words of institution, he first of all is testifying that he does not desire to perform, from his own opinion, a human action and institution; rather, as a householder [steward] of the divine mysteries, he is, in accordance with Christ's command, desiring to administer a holy Sacrament. Accordingly, he sets aside visible bread and wine so that it can be the means and instrument for the distribution and fellowship of the body and blood of Christ. Further, he prays that, in accordance with His institution and promise, Christ would be present in this action, and that by means of the consecrated bread wine he might distribute Christ's body and blood. Finally, he testifies that by the power of the institution of Christ, the bread and wine in the holy Supper are not [merely] base bread and wine, but rather that Christ's body and Christ's blood are received sacramentally united and present with the bread and wine. He will herewith then point out this institution and ordinance of Christ to the communicants.

1 Cor. 10:16 – **The blessed chalice, which we bless, is it not the fellowship of the blood of Christ?**, etc.

CHAPTER 14

WHETHER THE EXTERNAL ELEMENTS, NAMELY THE BREAD AND WINE, LOSE THEIR NATURAL ESSENCE THROUGH THE CONSECRATION AND ARE MATERIALLY CHANGED INTO CHRIST'S BODY AND BLOOD.

ven though the true body and the true blood of Christ are truly present in the holy Supper, as is extensively demonstrated above in chapter 11, yet through this very presence of the body and blood of Christ, the essence or nature of the external elements, namely, bread and wine, is in no way annihilated. Rather, the body of Christ becomes sacramentally united with the consecrated bread, the blood of Christ with the consecrated wine. This sacramental unification consists in this: that not only bread and wine are received; rather, by means of the bread, Christ's body and, by means of the wine, Christ's blood are received. It is for that reason an error if one says that through the consecration the bread and wine are materially changed into Christ's body and blood, and that the presence of the body and blood of Christ consists of such an essential transubstantiation. We demonstrate this as follows:

1. Because such essential transubstantiation may not be shown from the words of the institution. For regarding the words of Christ: **This is My body, this is My blood** (upon which this doctrine would establish itself), they present no essential transubstantiation, but rather a sacramental union of the body of Christ with the consecrated bread and the

blood of Christ with the consecrated wine. More about this later.

2. Because the holy evangelists and the apostle Paul call the consecrated bread "bread" not only before, but also after the consecration. Therefore, it is not just in the form of bread; rather, it really is bread.

Mat. 26:26; Mark 14:22, 19; 1 Cor. 11:23 – **However, as they ate, Jesus took bread, gave thanks and broke it and gave it to the disciples and said: Take, eat, this is My body,** etc.

1 Cor. 11:26–28 – **For as often as you eat of this bread and drink from this chalice,** etc. **Whoever then eats of this bread or drinks from this chalice unworthily,** etc. **But a man should examine himself and then eat of this bread and drink from this chalice.**

3. Because St. Paul calls the consecrated bread the fellowship of the body of Christ and the consecrated chalice the fellowship of the blood of Christ, which mode of speaking he would not have employed if the bread had been changed into Christ's body and the wine had been changed into Christ's blood. For, if a thing is changed into something else, then one cannot say that one is the fellowship of the other. For example, one cannot say that the water at Cana, from which wine was made, is a fellowship of the wine. Contrariwise, however, if two distinct things are presented as being united with each other, one enclosed in and with the other, then one says that one is the fellowship of the other. For example, since the Holy Spirit was given in and with the breath of Christ, one thus rightly says that the breath was the fellowship of the Holy Spirit (John 20:23).

1 Cor. 10:16 – **The bread which we break, is it not the fellowship of the body of Christ? The blessed chalice which we bless, is it not the fellowship of the blood of Christ?**

4. Because the essential change of the consecrated bread into Christ's body and the consecrated chalice into

Christ's blood run counter to the rule of faith, indeed, in numerous ways. **1.** It is a common rule concerning the holy Sacraments [that] the Word comes to the element and therefrom it becomes a Sacrament. This rule is set aside through the fabrication of this bread-changing, since it would mean that the Word removes or takes away the external element and changes it into Christ's body and blood. **2.** Just as in the Sacrament of holy Baptism the Word does not remove or extirpate the water in the Sacrament, rather it becomes a saving water bath in the Word (Eph. 5:26, Tit. 3:5), so also the bread and wine in no way [lose] their nature and essence through Christ's words. Rather much more, they are made into a fellowship of the body and blood of Christ. **3.** The bread (not just the outward appearance of bread) is the fellowship of the body of Christ; the chalice (not just the outward appearance of the chalice or wine) is the fellowship of the blood of Christ (1 Cor. 10:16). Should the material essence of bread and wine be removed, how could they remain as means and instruments through which Christ's body and blood are distributed? **4.** By essentially changing the consecrated bread into Christ's body and the consecrated wine into Christ's blood, the analogy which the ancient teachers of the Church sought in this holy Supper between earthly and heavenly food is removed, as related in greater detail above in chap. 10, no. 3. The bread and the wine nourish and strengthen the body. Now then, Christ's body and blood nourish and strengthen the inner man. Just as a loaf of bread is made out of many little kernels and a beaker of wine is made from many little grapes, so also in the holy Supper we are given to eat and drink of one spiritual body so that as members of one body we should love one another. This and other similes are completely canceled (abolished) and "made into water" [come to naught] when one concedes that the bread and wine in the holy Supper lose their essence and no longer remain bread and wine. **5.** The divine blessing does not annihilate that over which it is spoken. On the contrary, it exalts it, as is indicated in all the places in Scripture where the divine blessing is mentioned, especially in Gen. 1:22, 28, where man and beast are blessed, not so that through it they lose their nature, but rather that they receive powers for continuous future propagation. Now then, the bread and wine is made into a Sacrament in the holy Supper through the blessing of Christ. Therefore, one should not think that the bread and wine lose their essence; rather, they are exalted unto a sacramental usage to become a means for the fellowship of the body and blood of Christ.

6. At one time Christ assumed a true human nature from the sanctified lineage of the highly-honored virgin Mary, as holy Scripture testifies; but the Scriptures know nothing of His body and blood being daily made out of bread and wine in the holy Supper.

5. By [the teaching of] the material transformation of the bread into Christ's body and the wine into Christ's blood, all kinds of absurd things are introduced, raising all kinds of questions. For then one would have to say that the incidental properties of the consecrated bread and wine, such as their taste, smell, roundness, and the like remain, while, on the other hand, their fundamental nature (namely, the nature and essence of the bread and wine) are annihilated. Why, this would be as great a wondrous deed [miracle] as if one claimed that a fire has been extinguished and at the same time its ability to burn still remained! One would further have to claim that the priests still daily performed just as great a miracle as Jesus did at Cana (John 2:9), where He made water into wine—to say nothing of the manifold questions and the totally contradictory answers to these questions which are found in such abundance among those who advocate the idea of an essential transubstantiation of the bread into Christ's body and the wine into Christ's blood.

Here again are some apparent points of contention:

1. That the material transformation of the external elements into Christ body and blood is grounded in the words of Christ: **Take, eat, this is My body; take, drink, this is My blood**, because from these words it unequivocally follows that the bread is either a sign of the absent body of Christ or else is in essence changed into same; so also, that the consecrated wine either is a mere sign of the absent blood of Christ or else is in essence changed into the same. Nothing else can be concluded from the words of Christ. ANSWER: **1.** The entire structure of such a conclusion is based on the assumption that the little word "**this**" specifically and only refers to the bread and the wine, and that when Christ says: **Take, eat, this is My body; take, drink, this is My blood**, it is as if He is essentially saying: Take, eat, this bread is My body; the chalice, or wine, is My blood. However, in chap. 12, point of contention no. 4, we have shown with clear, irrefutable proofs that the demonstrative pronoun "**this**" is not to be applied [does not refer] merely to the bread and wine in the holy Supper. Rather, in these words of Christ it is a grammatical mode which a person uses when two separate and yet related things are simultaneously presented, in which one is visible—along with which the other invisible, or higher and more worthy, is presented—so that a person indicates both with the subject in the first part of the saying, or expresses only the chief and invisible in the predicate of the other part of the saying. (Note the various examples of such a mode of speaking in the section cited above.) **2.** If Christ had desired to institute the changing of the essence of the bread and wine into His body and blood, He would have had to use other words and say: This essentially changed bread is My body; or, along with the external form of the essentially changed bread, receive My body; or, out of this bread comes My body; or even, this bread becomes essentially changed into My body. However, one cannot find in any of the evangelists or apostles these or similar sayings from which one could conclude the essential changing of the bread and wine into the body and blood of Christ. **3.** Consequently, if one wanted to thus conclude [when] Christ says: Eat, this is My body, drink, this is My blood, that, therefore, either the bread and wine are essentially changed into Christ's body and blood, or, that the external elements are merely a symbol of the absent body and blood of Christ, the answer is that this conclusion is too mild. For there can be a third conclusion, namely, that by means of the consecrated bread He distributes His body, and by means of the consecrated wine He distributes His blood, and that He wanted to indicate such with the words: **Eat, this is My body; drink, this is My blood. 4.** Thus, this conclusion is indeed also related to what Eutychus in ancient times wanted to infer from Mat. 16:16, where Peter says: **You are the Christ, the living Son of God**: that therefore the assumed human nature had to have been changed into the divine. The true believers of that time would have answered that this saying of Peter is based upon the personal union of the divine and human nature in Christ and was to be understood accordingly, because the little word "**You**" applies to the entire person. So also one must give answer to this objection: Christ says, eat, this is My body; therefore, the bread becomes materially changed into His body, in the following way: Not so! Rather, this saying of Christ originates from the sacramental union of the consecrated bread and Christ's body and is to be understood accordingly, because similarly, the little word "**this**" applies to both of what Christ presents to the apostles in the sacramental union. **5.** Also relevant here is what St. Paul says concerning the consecrated bread in the holy Supper, that it is the fellowship of the body of Christ, and concerning the consecrated wine, (that it is the fellowship of the blood of Christ [1 Cor. 10:16]). He clearly attests that we here should not think about an essential (material) change. Rather, we are to understand the words of Christ as follows: The consecrated bread is the fellowship of His body, that is, that we, on account of the sacramental union of the consecrated bread and the body of Christ, receive the body of Christ by means of the bread. **6.** Would it be improper if John, as he saw the Holy Spirit descend as a dove, had said: That is the Holy Spirit? Or, when the apostles, as the Holy Spirit was given to them through the breath of Christ and in the form of fiery tongues, had said: That is the Holy Spirit? Or, when the lad Elisha, as he saw the fiery wagon and horses, had said, those are the holy angels? How can it be concluded that the dove, the breath of Christ, and the fiery tongues were in essence changed into the Holy Spirit, or that the form of the fiery wagon and horses were in essence changed into the holy angels?

2. That even though after the consecration St. Paul still calls the consecrated bread and wine "bread" and "wine," it may not be concluded that the nature of the bread and wine and their essence does not cease to exist and is not changed into Christ's body and blood. Rather, [Paul still calls it bread] because it previously was bread, or also because it still possesses the outward form of bread, or also because it still has the distinctive features and impressions of bread, or also because according to the mode of sacred speech each nourishing food is called bread. ANSWER: 1. All that would be worth listening to [plausible] if only first of all the essential change [transubstantiation] of the bread into Christ's body were shown [to occur] by the Scriptures. However, that can never happen. 2. In articles of faith one should never in any way deviate from the understanding which the literal meaning of the words conveys, unless perchance the Scriptures themselves require us to do so, or when the rule of faith requires such; otherwise, the entire Christian religion would become doubtful and uncertain. Now, however, it is not contrary to any article of faith if one understands St. Paul's words to mean genuine, natural bread. Also, nowhere has St. Paul declared that he wants his words to be understood in a figurative way. Why would we then want to deviate from the literal and actual understanding of the words? 3. What's more, St. Paul clearly indicates that he wants real, natural bread to be understood; for after he previously had related

the words of institution in 1 Cor. 11:23 – **For the Lord Jesus in the night in which He was betrayed, He took the bread**, etc., he concludes in v. 27 – **Whoever then eats unworthily of this bread**, etc., so that he might clearly show that in these words he is speaking just as much of a true natural bread (which at the same time is the fellowship of the body of Christ) as he was speaking of true natural bread in the previous verse (23). **4.** As a result, the conscience is unable to be pacified nor to be put at ease through such various (and accordingly) uncertain interpretations whenever one deviates from the letter. For it is not enough to say: Because a word in the Scripture is occasionally used in a figurative sense, therefore it must also be understood that way in this place. Not so, rather in articles of faith it must be shown that precisely in this [specific context] a word is used in the figurative sense, or else one must steadfastly abide by the common understanding of the words in their literal sense. **5.** Also, these interpretations contradict each other. For if the bread is to be called bread in a figurative sense by the apostle Paul, it cannot be so labeled because of its nutritious quality; if it is called bread because it was formerly bread, then it cannot for that reason be called bread, because the incidental attributes of bread and the outward form still exist. **6.** Not to mention that these interpretations of the little word "**bread**," if one specifically [individually] accepts them, have as little foundation and basis [for acceptance] as when one compares them side by side [with each other]. They claim St. Paul still calls the consecrated bread "bread" after the consecration, not because it still is bread, but rather, because it formerly was bread, just as in Exo. 7:13 the staff of Aaron—which became a snake—similarly was called a staff, and as in Mat. 11:5 it is stated: **The blind saw and the lame walked, and the lepers were made clean and the deaf heard, the dead arose**, etc., not that they still were blind, lame, lepers, deaf, and dead, but rather because they had been so formerly. But there is a vast difference between these examples and the apostolic text. In Exo. 7:10, it is expressly stated that Aaron's staff was changed into a snake, and in Mat. 11:5 it is similarly stated that such ailing people were healed by the Lord Christ. If it were similarly established that by the words of institution Christ specifically had materially changed the bread into His body, then the comparison with the examples cited might be worthy of consideration. They claim that St. Paul still calls the consecrated bread in the holy Supper "bread" after the consecration of the bread, not because it is bread, but because it retains the external form of bread, just as the brass snake which was raised up in the wilderness was [also] called a "snake" in Num. 21:10, and the carved, artistically drawn lions on the throne of Solomon are called "lions" in 1 Kin. 10:20 because they had the outward form of a snake and a lion. There is, however, a great difference here, for Moses expressly stated that it was only a brass snake, just as in the book of Kings it was simply a lion carved out of wood. But no such thing is written by St. Paul, i.e., that the bread is called such only according to its outward form. It just does not follow that simply because in another place in the Scripture an artistic depiction is called by the name of some natural thing, that the consecrated bread therefore possesses merely the name and not the nature of bread. They claim that the consecrated bread is called "bread" by St. Paul because it possesses the distinctive features and effects of bread, such as giving food and nurture, being round, having a taste, and the like. But, this is even more absurd than if it were true that the consecrated bread loses its nature and essence through the consecration, [for] then also such incidental things which are based solely and alone on the nature of bread and spring directly from it will also be lost. How may that which has totally lost its nature and essence provide nourishment and nurture? One would first have to try this out on these teachers and with its uncovered stench feed it to them for a whole month. Finally, they claim that the consecrated bread is called "bread" by

St. Paul, not because it still is bread, but rather because according to the mode of holy speech any kind of food is called "bread." But it must be shown previously that, precisely for these reasons and for the sake of none other, it is thus called "bread" by St. Paul. The apostle clearly adds, **Whoever ... eats of this bread**, in order to draw on Christ's word and show that he is specifically speaking of such a bread which Christ had taken into His hands, broken, and distributed to His disciples. That, however, was genuine, natural bread. Consequently, this subterfuge also has no status.

Because we have undertaken to speak only about articles of faith from the Scriptures, we will not at this time deal with anything else that is brought forth by the fathers, by the councils or decrees of the Church, and finally by natural reason and miracles regarding the claim of the material change of the consecrated bread into Christ's body and the consecrated wine into Christ's blood. What also pertains to the reinstatement or preservation [of the practice] of carrying around and the adoring of this Sacrament—[a custom] which is based upon this material changing of the external elements into Christ's body and blood—that will be dealt with later along with the clarification of the third sacramental action.

CHAPTER 15

CONCERNING THE BREAKING OF BREAD IN THE HOLY SUPPER, TO WHAT END IT WAS USED BY CHRIST.

 e have until now been dealing with the first sacramental matter, namely, concerning the external elements in the holy Supper, that one specifically consecrate bread and wine in accordance with Christ's command and example, that is, set them aside for this holy Sacrament. The next sacramental matter is the distribution of the consecrated bread and the consecrated wine, for it is not enough that one consecrate bread and wine in the holy Supper; rather, it must also be distributed, as such is apparent from the words of institution.

Mat. 26:26, 27 – **But as they ate, Jesus took the bread, gave thanks, broke it and gave it to the disciples,** etc. **And He took the chalice, gave thanks and gave it to them,** etc.

Mark 14:22, 23 – **And while they were eating, Jesus took the bread, gave thanks and broke it and gave it to them,** etc. **And then took the chalice and gave thanks and gave it to them,** etc.

Luke 22:19, 20 – **And He took the bread, gave thanks and broke it and gave it to them,** etc. **In the same way also the chalice,** etc.

1 Cor. 11:23, 24, 25 – **For the Lord Jesus in the night that He was betrayed, He took the bread, gave thanks and broke it and said: Take, eat,** etc. **In the same way also the chalice,** etc.

Since, however, the evangelists unanimously testify that the Lord Christ not only gave thanks or a blessing and distributed the consecrated bread and the consecrated chalice, but that He also broke the bread, the question thus is raised if then this same breaking of bread does not constitute a special sacramental action, to the extent that the breaking of the bread belongs to the essential parts of this Sacrament no less than the thanksgiving, distribution and reception—since Christ did the one just as much as the other.

Herein lies the solution: Christ obviously broke the bread in the holy Supper, and such bread breaking was also practiced by the early church (1 Cor. 10:16); yet, it is not necessary for the completion of this Sacrament that after the consecration the bread first be broken. Rather, it is sufficient for the bread to be prepared for distribution, whether this occurs before or during or after the consecration. The only reason the Lord Christ [had to break the bread] was that the bread at hand was in a whole piece [loaf], and by this means [He] prepared it for distribution. Accordingly, inasmuch as it is not improper after the consecration to break the consecrated bread (indeed, since it more closely imitates the example of Christ and the early church), yet it is an entirely different matter with the bread breaking when those who do not properly teach about the true presence of the body and blood of Christ in the Sacrament foist upon the Church the assertion that it is a totally necessary ceremony, as if thereby is signified the breaking of Christ's body. Here then we say that such a meaning for the breaking of the bread may by no means be shown from the words of institution. Indeed, they rather demonstrate the contrary, which we establish as follows:

1. If the breaking of the bread in the first part of the holy Supper is stipulated as a special condition for sacramental action, then there would also be something to find in the other part of the holy Supper to correspond with the bread breaking. However, one is unable to bring forth any such thing, since the evangelists in describing the other part do not mention any other action than that Christ took the chalice, gave thanks, distributed it and that the disciples drank from it.

Mat. 26:27 – **And He took the chalice and gave thanks, gave it to them and said: All of you drink from it.**

Mark 14:23 – **And** (He) **took the chalice and gave thanks and gave it to them and they all drank from it.**

Luke 22:20 – **In the same way also the chalice after the supper**, etc.

1 Cor. 11:25 – **In the same way also the chalice after the supper and said: This chalice is the New Testament in My blood**, etc.

2. Is the bread breaking used by the Lord Christ to prepare thereby the bread for distribution, or is the breaking of His body thereby signified and modeled? One cannot say the latter, as will be shown later. Therefore, the former remains, namely, that the Lord Christ broke the bread solely for the purpose that the consecrated bread might be distributed among the disciples. From this it further follows that it is of no consequence whether the bread is broken for distribution either before or after the consecration, just so long as it is followed by the distribution.

3. In the holy Sacraments a distinction is always to be made between distribution and ingestion and the mode or method of distribution and ingestion. The one, namely the distribution and reception, is an essential part of the holy Sacrament; but the other, namely the mode and method of distribution and reception, is left to the discretion of Christian freedom. For example, in the holy Sacrament of Baptism it is essential that a person be washed or wetted with water in the Name of the Father and of the Son and of the Holy Spirit, but whether such washing take place through sprinkling or through dipping-into [immersion] is not elevated to high importance and is left to the discretion of Christian freedom—as was shown above in chapter 12 of holy Baptism.

4. Whatever is *adiaphora*, or an indifferent thing, should not be permitted to be made a matter of conscience.

Rather, much more should one steadfastly cling to the free-dom which Christ has won for us in such matters. Now, however, the breaking of bread is an *adiaphoron* of itself: one can use it or not use it, just so long as the distribution is not omitted. Therefore, one should not make it a matter of conscience whether to use or omit the breaking of the bread.

Gal. 2:4,5 – **For when certain false brothers intrusively crept in beside us to spy upon our freedom which we have in Christ Jesus, in order to take us captive, not for one hour [moment] did we give in to them so that the truth of the Gospel continually endure by you.**

Gal. 5:1 – **So continue then in the freedom with which Christ has freed us, and don't let yourselves be snared once again into the slavish yoke.**

5. Whatever is good in and of itself becomes perverted by means of a false delusion. Consequently, since it is a false delusion that the bread breaking by the Lord Christ was used and is ordained to be used to typify the breaking of His body, the bread breaking, which in and of itself is good, is thereby perverted so that it no longer is broken in accordance of the example of Christ. Instead a new ceremony and teaching, which is contrary to the institution of Christ and the example of the apostles, is labeled as being established. As an example, the giving of alms is a good work in and of itself, commanded by God the Lord, and includes a rich promise. At the same time, this good work is spoiled if a person gives alms with the aim and purpose of being seen by men or thereby atoning for sin, as taught by the Lord Christ in Mat. 6: 2, 3, 4. So also, even though the breaking of bread in the holy Supper is good in and of itself, yet we cannot acquiesce to those who want to force bread breaking on us as a necessary element when the false delusion goes with it that through the breaking of bread is symbolized the breaking of the body of Christ.

Mat. 6:22; Luke 11:34, 35 – **The eye is the body's light. If the eye is innocent, then your entire body will**

be light. But if your eye is a rascal, then your entire body will be dark (for, among other things, a good work entails that one means well by it and has no other goal in mind than to what God has commanded).

Here again are some apparent points of contention:

1. That Christ broke the bread and said: **Do this**; therefore, we also must break the bread if we want to follow Christ's directive and example. ANSWER: **1.** Christ broke the bread so that He might prepare it for distribution; for the Jews used long, thin loaves, which they did not slice. Rather, they broke the loaf in order to eat of it themselves or to distribute it to others, from which comes the saying that with the Hebrews "breaking" means the same as "distribution." Isa. 58:7 – **Break your bread for the hungry**; Gen. 42:1 – **But when Jacob heard that there was much grain in Egypt** (broken, that is, was being sold and distributed); Jer. 16:7 – **And no one will distribute** [bread] **among them on account of the lamentation**, etc. (in the holy language [original Hebrew] it is written, no one will break [instead of distribute] it); Lamentations 4:4 – **The little children beg for bread, and there is no one who breaks it for them** (or distributes it); Mat. 14:19; 15:36; Mark 6:41; 8:6,19; and Luke 9:16 – Jesus broke the bread as He wanted to feed the huge crowd of people; Luke 14:30 – the Lord Christ broke the bread at Emmaus; Acts 27:35 – **And as he** (Paul) **said that, he took the bread, thanked God before them all and broke it and began to eat.** From these testimonies it is to be concluded that for the Jews breaking of bread was customary at ordinary mealtimes, and that also the bread breaking was used for distribution. **2.** Now just because Christ broke the bread in the administration of the first [Lord's] Supper, it does not follow from this that the bread breaking is a special sacramental action (*actus sacramentalis*). Rather, it is an *actus ministerialis*, [i.e.,] the bread breaking was simply and only used for the purpose that the bread might be distributed. **3.** Therefore one may in no way conclude from this that the bread has to be broken after the consecration. Rather, it is sufficient for the perfection [completeness] of this holy Sacrament that the consecrated bread be distributed, just so it is prepared for distribution either before or after the consecration. **4.** The command of Christ, **This do**, applies above all to that which the holy apostles did, namely, that they ate the consecrated bread and drank from the consecrated chalice, as is also shown in 1 Cor. 11:25 – **Such do as often as you drink to My remembrance.** But if one ever wants to refer to the things which Christ did, then one must necessarily make the distinction between those elements which are required for this holy Sacrament (such as thanking or blessing, distributing, eating and drinking) and those which do not belong to the essential elements or fullness (perfection) of this Sacrament. **5.** For otherwise I would want to draw this conclusion: Christ went to the plastered hall [elaborate assembly room] toward evening and sat Himself down with His apostles, *discubuit more veteribus usitato* [*according to the customs used by the ancients*]. Therefore, it is also required that one seat himself at table in such a mode and fashion and celebrate the holy Supper towards evening in a huge assembly room. But [it is] not so; rather, the sitting at the table was an *actus ministerialis*, not *sacramentalis*. Therefore, it is not required that one even sit at a table, just so long as one merely receives the consecrated bread and the consecrated chalice. Also, similarly, in regard to breaking the bread—Christ broke the bread and said: **This do**; therefore, it is required that after the consecration one also break the bread. Not so. Rather, the bread breaking was an *actus ministerialis*; therefore, it is sufficient that the consecrated bread simply be distributed. **6.** In the same way one could also conclude in the article of holy Baptism: Christ says – **Therefore, go forth and baptize all nations** (heathen). Now **to baptize** means to dip into. Therefore, it is required that one dip (immerse) the baptismal candidate [in the water]. Not so. Rather, holy Baptism is a **water-bath in the Word** (Eph. 5:26), and there is no requirement here that one sprinkle (spray) the baptismal candidate or dip him into the water, just so it is done in the Name of the Father and of the Son and of the Holy Spirit. Precisely in this manner is the argument about breaking bread to be answered. 7. Among the evangelists, none describe in what manner Christ actually broke the bread: whether He broke it with His hand, or with a knife; whether he broke a whole bread [loaf] into pieces, or broke the pieces left over from the previous meal. If, however, the bread breaking were a sacramental action (*actus sacramentalis*) and an essential part of the holy Supper, then they certainly would have explicitly described the method of bread breaking.

 2. That the holy apostles also broke bread in the administration of the holy Supper in Acts 2:46; 20:7. Therefore, the breaking of bread belongs to the fullness (perfection) of this Sacrament. ANSWER: **1.** Not to mention that certain of the ancient teachers in the Church apply these verses to the common mealtime, as in the mode of speaking employed in Acts 27:35. **2.** Thus we gladly admit that the apostles broke the bread in the administration of the holy Supper, that is, divided it into pieces; but from this it cannot be proved that bread-breaking is an essential element of the holy Supper, or that they used the bread-breaking to symbolize the breaking of Christ's body. Rather, they used the bread-breaking simply and solely as a preparation for distribution, and herewith by no means command that one must break the bread precisely in the midst of the action and that the breaking of the body of Christ is symbolized.

 3. The bread which we break, is it not the fellowship of the body of Christ (1 Cor. 10:16). That it follows that only broken bread has the promise that by means of same Christ's body is distributed. ANSWER: **1.** Here, by "breaking," distribution can be rightly understood, just as this meaning was shown for the word "breaking" in point of contention 1, above, because in the writings of St. Paul that same mode of expression taken from the holy language is frequently found. Thus, St. Paul also speaks of one such breaking of bread through which we become partakers of the body of Christ. [Such partaking] occurs not through the cutting up but through the distribution of the consecrated bread. Moreover, St. Paul, in describing the institution of the Supper in 1 Cor. 11:24, uses only the word "**breaking**" and omits the word "giving" or "distributing," so that without a doubt he shows that in this matter he understands by the breaking the distribution. **2.** Granted also that if here, by "breaking," the cutting into pieces of the bread is to be understood, then still nothing further can be concluded from this than that the breaking of the bread was practiced by the first apostolic church. Against this we do not argue, in as much as one indeed may well practice the ceremony of bread-breaking, which we also do not deny. But, that it is specifically necessary that one break the bread into pieces after the consecration, and thereby symbolically portray the breaking of the body of Christ, that can indeed not be shown from this text of St. Paul.

    4. That the bread-breaking was used by Christ thereby to portray symbolically the breaking of His body, since Christ speaks of the temple of His body in John 2:19 – **Break** (fracture) **this temple, and on the third day I will raise it.** Since, then, Christ's death and crucifixion are called a breaking, Paul also thus states in 1 Cor. 11:24: Christ's body was broken for us. He thereby indicates the bread-breaking in order to vividly set before our eyes how Christ's body was broken for us. ANSWER: It would really be something if it could be shown from the words of institution that Christ broke the bread for the purpose of setting before eyes [visually demonstrating] the breaking of His body. However, against this fabricated final reason [final cause] for the bread-breaking we set forth the following irrefutable arguments: **1.** The figures and types actually belong to the Old Testament, which had been the period of the shadows; in the New Testament we have the substance of the goods themselves (Rom. 13:12, Col.

2:17, Heb. 10:1). The holy Supper is a Sacrament of the New Testament (Luke 22:20, 1 Cor. 11:25); therefore, we should not think that the Lord Christ instituted the holy Supper only because He wanted to set before the eyes symbols of His body and blood. For how would that be any different then than instituting a new show-bread? **2.** Just as the Lord Christ did not consecrate, and ordain to be consecrated, the bread and wine in the holy Supper simply for the reason that they were signs of His body and blood—but rather because they are the fellowship of His body and blood (1 Cor. 10:16)—so also the Lord Christ broke the bread, not that the bread-breaking was a symbol of the breaking of His body, but rather that by means of the broken bread His true body and by means of the consecrated wine His true blood would be distributed. **3.** Also, the holy Supper was instituted by the Lord Christ not so that by bread-breaking we symbolize His death, but rather, so that we eat the consecrated bread which is the fellowship of His body, and that we drink the consecrated wine which is the fellowship of His blood and in that way should proclaim His death (1 Cor. 11:26). **4.** If Christ broke the bread in order figuratively to portray His crucifixion, then He also would have poured out the wine to demonstrate in the same way the pouring out of His blood. However, one finds absolutely nothing [in Scripture] about such pouring out of the chalice either by the evangelists or by the apostle Paul. Therefore it is not fair that certain ones would use the pouring of the wine into the cup or also the drinking from the cup by the communicants [to convey] such symbolism; for none of these elements may actually be called, so to speak, a "pouring out." Moreover, one finds nothing in the description of the institution that the Lord Christ after the consecration first presented the wine in a beaker and commanded it to be thus presented. Rather, He took into His hands the chalice, in which actually was the produce of the wine-stalk, gave thanks and by means of same distributed His true blood to his disciples. From this, it becomes apparent that the disciples did not, at Christ's command, drink from the consecrated chalice so that the pouring out of Christ's blood would thereby be symbolized, but rather that, in deed and in truth, they drank from the consecrated chalice the blood of Christ, which would later be poured out on the cross. **5.** If Christ used and ordained for use the bread and wine for no other purpose than to symbolize His body and blood, and further, if Christ used the bread-breaking for the purpose of symbolically portraying His death and crucifixion, then He would have been doing away with the clear types and in their place instituting such types which by far would not have been as clear and simple [and] which would then justly be regarded as absurd. The little Passover lamb is a very glorious and clear type of Christ; the slaughter of the little Passover lamb was a clear portent [sign] of His death and the pouring out of His blood (Exo. 12:6, 7). Now if, with the institution of the holy Supper, the Lord Christ had wanted only to signify and figuratively portray to us His death and outpouring of blood, why would He [in so doing] have done away with the figure of the little Passover lamb, since through its slaughter His death and crucifixion is far more clearly [and] gloriously signified than through the breaking of bread? **6.** How may the breaking of bread be used and be ordained for use in signifying the breaking of the body of Christ, since no bone was broken in the death of the Lord Christ (John 19:36), even as the little paschal lamb—the type of Christ—had none of its legs broken (Exo. 12:46)? No solid evidence can be brought forth here by which it might be shown that the body of Christ was, so to speak, actually broken; for the fact that Christ's body was wounded and pierced with nails is not, strictly speaking, a "breaking." Also, the soul's departing from the body of Christ is likewise, strictly speaking, not a "breaking." Therefore, we abide by this conclusion: Something that did not happen to the body of Christ also cannot be pre-figured through bread-breaking. Now then, the body of Christ was not actually broken, so to speak; therefore, the breaking of Christ's body may not be symbolized by bread-breaking. **7.** In John 2:19, Christ is not speaking of such a breaking of His body which would be an actual breaking; rather, He is speaking in a figurative manner, likening His body to the temple at Jerusalem. For just as the glory of the Lord filled the temple at Jerusalem (1 Kin. 8:11), so also the entire fullness of the Godhead resides bodily in Christ (Col. 2:9). Concerning this temple of His body, Christ then says: **Break this temple and on the third day I will raise it up.** In the Greek text it is written λύσατε, which actually means "tear it down, destroy this temple, demolish it." [It is] readily apparent therefrom that Christ is not referring to such a breaking which can, strictly speaking, be called [an actual "breaking"]. **8.** What St. Paul says in 1 Cor. 11:24 about the body of Christ—that it is broken for us—[is also stated in] Isa. 53:5 and Luke 22:19. Phi. 2:8 consequently explains that nothing else can be understood but that Christ's body was given into that shameful death for us, by which declaration of the holy Scripture we certainly abide. It is said of Christ's body that it was broken for us, not as if the bread-breaking signifies the breaking of the body of Christ, but rather because Christ's body was given for us into that shameful death on the timber-trunk of the cross.

5. That if [a single loaf of] bread is not broken, then we cannot partake of the "one bread," which the apostle requires when he says, 1 Cor. 10:17 – **For it is one bread, thus we many are one body, since we all share in the one bread.** ANSWER: The consecrated bread is called "one bread" not because it is a huge portion [loaf] from which each one breaks off a piece, rather **1.** because it is sanctified and used for one Sacrament. Even though St. Paul was in Philippi when he wrote this Epistle to the Corinthians, nevertheless he stated that he becomes a partaker of one bread with the Corinthians in the holy Sacrament, which by no stretch of the imagination can be understood to mean that they all jointly ate from one huge loaf of bread. Rather, he understands it to mean the *unitate sacramentali*, since he together with the Corinthians and all believers in the whole world used the bread for one purpose, namely, that by means of it they became partakers of the body of Christ (1 Cor. 10:16). Thus he similarly also states in Eph. 4:5 that there is only one Baptism, yet not [meaning] that the same water was used for Baptism in various locations. The oneness of Baptism consists in this: that all Christians let themselves be baptized to the end (purpose) that they be washed from sin and be embodied with Christ. The first and foremost reason that St. Paul calls the consecrated bread in the holy Supper "one bread" is this: because it is, to wit, used for one Sacrament and received by all communicants for one purpose so that they become partakers of one body. **2.** One could also say that St. Paul refers to such a oneness of bread: that Christians, when they eat of the consecrated bread [and] celebrate a holy Supper, eat of one bread just as those who sit at table for a common mealtime. Also, just as one bread is baked from many kernels, the communicants are directed towards brotherly love and unity.

CHAPTER 16

WHETHER THE COMMUNICANTS ARE TO HAVE THE CONSECRATED BREAD AND CHALICE GIVEN INTO THEIR HANDS, OR WHETHER THE CONSECRATED BREAD IS TO BE PLACED IN THEIR MOUTH AND THE CONSECRATED CHALICE IS TO BE DRUNK FROM [WHILE HELD BY THE OFFICIANT].

hat the consecrated bread and wine are to be distributed to the communicants in the holy Supper is at all times required. But, whether the consecrated bread and chalice are to be placed into their hands, or whether the consecrated bread is placed into their mouths and the chalice held up to their mouths [by the officiant], is immaterial, which we substantiate as follows:

1. The evangelists mention that Christ gave the consecrated bread and the consecrated chalice to the disciples. But, whether it was given into the hand or into the mouth, about this they give no information, which they certainly would have done if it were a matter high importance.

Mat. 26:26, Mark 14:22 – **But when they had eaten, Jesus took the bread, gave thanks and broke it and gave it to them and said: Take, eat, this is My body.**

Mat. 26:27, Mark 14:23 – **And He took the chalice and gave thanks, gave it to them and said: All of you drink from it.**

Luke 22:19, 1 Cor. 11:23 – **And He** (the Lord Jesus) **took the bread, gave thanks and broke it and gave it to them and said: This is My body,** etc.

Luke 22:20, 1 Cor. 11:25 – **In the same way also the**

chalice, after the supper and said: This is the chalice, etc.

2. In the holy Sacraments a distinction is to be made at all times between the distribution itself and the mode and method of distribution. The one (namely, the distribution) is an essential part of the holy Sacraments. The other (namely, the mode and method of distribution) is left to the discretion of Christian freedom in so far as it is not similarly specified in the institution. Now then, whether the consecrated bread and chalice are to be held to the mouth or placed in the hand pertains to the mode and method of distribution. Also, one does not have an explicit command in the words of institution about this matter; therefore, it is left to the discretion of Christian freedom.

3. Just as it does not matter in the administration of holy Baptism whether the water is poured over the head of the person being baptized or whether the entire body is drenched with it—just so that it takes place in the Name of the Father and the Son and the Holy Spirit (cf. Baptism, chapter 12)—it similarly matters not whether the consecrated bread and wine are given to the communicants in the mouth or in the hand.

Here again are apparent points of contention:

1. That pursuant to the words of institution, the consecrated bread and chalice are to be placed into the hands of the communicants, for Christ used the word λαμβάνεσθαι, which actually means to take in hand. ANSWER: **1.** Even if it were demonstrated that Christ had given the consecrated bread and chalice into the disciples' hands, that still would not prove that such [actions are essential to] this holy Sacrament and that it is thus even wrong to lay the bread into the communicants' mouths and to extend the consecrated chalice for them to drink therefrom. **2.** The word λαμβάνεσθαι or "take" means in general to accept and to receive. Such takes place with the hand, with the mouth, or also with the entire person. John 19:30 – **Now when Jesus had taken the**

vinegar, etc. John 20:22 – **And when He** (Jesus) **said that, He blew on them** (His disciples) **and said to them: Take on the Holy Spirit,** etc. Acts 1:8 – **Rather you shall receive the power of the Holy Spirit,** etc. Rev. 22:17 – **And he who wants to, let him take the water of life for free.**

2. That it stems from superstition that one does not want to give the communicants the consecrated bread and wine into their hands, because their hands might be unholy and unclean and that they thus dare not touch the consecrated bread and the consecrated chalice. ANSWER: We do not prohibit that the communicants be given the consecrated bread and chalice into their hands. Much less do we say that because the communicants' hands are unclean and unholy and that therefore the holy elements are not to be placed in their hands. Rather, we let it remain as *adiaphora*, according to which it should be dealt with so as not to violate Christian freedom. Accordingly, since it has long been the practice in Christendom to place the consecrated bread into the mouths of the communicants and to hold the consecrated chalice to their mouths, we also allow it to continue because it is not contrary to the institution of Christ. Rather, it seems much more convenient for distribution than when one gives the consecrated bread and the consecrated chalice into the hands of the communicants, from which [practice] rubbish* might readily result.

---

* Gerhard may be referring here to such offensive practices as taking home a portion of the host in order to venerate it. Ed.

CHAPTER 17

WHETHER IT BE CONTRARY TO CHRIST'S INSTITUTION FOR ONLY THE PRIESTS TO PARTAKE OF THE CONSECRATED BREAD AND THE CONSECRATED CHALICE, THEREBY TO SERVE OTHERS.

 ince not only the consecration, but also the distribution of the consecrated bread and wine belong to the essential elements of the holy Supper, it is proper to ask whether it is contrary to the institution of Christ that the priest, who in the holy Supper has consecrated the bread and wine, partake alone of it and not distribute it to the others, alleging instead that it redounds to the highest good for those who stand there and merely observe, even also as those for whom the priest then sacrifices. Here we state that this [practice] teaches and deals with falsehood, and we substantiate the same as follows:

1. The Lord Christ, in the institution and administration of the holy Supper not only took the bread, gave thanks and broke it, but He also distributed the same to the disciples and additionally stated: **Such do to My remembrance.** Consequently, if the preacher wants to conduct the holy Supper by only consecrating the bread and wine and not distributing it, he has not done what the Lord Christ did and commanded to be done. What was previously proven is also relevant here: that the distribution of the consecrated bread and wine is a specifically sacramental action which at all times is pertinent for the perfection of this holy Sacrament.

Mat. 26:26, Mark 14:22 – **But as they ate, Jesus took the bread, gave thanks and broke it and gave it to the** disciples and said: Take, eat, this is My body.

Mat. 26:27, 28, Mark 14:23 – **And He took the chalice and gave thanks, gave it to them and said: All of you drink from it; this is My blood of the** New Testament, etc.

Luke 22:19, 1 Cor. 11:23, 24 – **For the Lord Jesus, in the night in which He was betrayed, He took the bread, gave thanks and broke it and said: Take, eat, this is My body, which will be broken for you; such do to My remembrance.**

Luke 22:20; 1 Cor. 11:25 – **In the same manner also the chalice after the supper and said: This chalice is the New Testament in My blood, such do, as often as you drink to My remembrance.**

2. The holy apostles celebrated the holy Supper in such a way that they received the consecrated bread and consecrated chalice not only for themselves; rather, they also distributed it to others. Therefore, it goes against the example of the apostles if the bread and wine are only consecrated in the holy Supper and are not distributed to others.

Acts 2:42, 46 – **But without variance, they remained with the apostolic teaching and with the fellowship and in the breaking of bread and in prayer. And constantly and daily they were of one mind with each other in the temple and broke bread here and there in the homes.**

Acts 20:7 – **On a certain Sabbath, as the disciples came together to break bread** (The bread-breaking is a clear witness that they distributed the consecrated bread; for what purpose would they otherwise have broken it?), etc.

1 Cor. 10:16, 17, 18, 21 – **The blessed chalice, which we bless, is it not the fellowship of the blood of Christ? The bread which we break, is it not the fellowship of the body of Christ?** (Here St. Paul apprehends both sacramental actions of consecration and distribution gloriously together and teaches that one should not take place without the other,

nor would it make for a complete Sacrament.) **For just as there is one bread, so we many are one body, since we all are partakers of one bread. Look at Israel according to the flesh; those who ate the offering, are they not in fellowship with the altar? ... You can not simultaneously drink the Lord's chalice and the devil's chalice. You can not simultaneously be partakers of the Lord's table and the devil's table.** (It is apparent from this that the believers' fellowship in the early church at the table of the Lord consisted of their receiving the consecrated bread and wine. It did not consist in merely standing by and watching what one person did by himself.)

3. The apostle Paul places in opposition the celebrating of the Lord's Supper with one another in open assembly and expressly conducting it in solitude. He thereby proves that it cannot be called a celebration of the Supper of the Lord if one wants to receive the consecrated bread and wine alone for the benefit of others.

1 Cor. 11:17, 20–23 – **I cannot laud the fact that you do not assemble in a respectable manner but in an irritating way. When you then come together, one is not celebrating the Lord's Supper. ... As one then would celebrate the Supper, each of you takes his own in advance, and one is hungry, another is drunk. Don't you have homes where you might eat and drink? Or do you despise the fellowship of God and embarrass those who have nothing? What should I tell you? Should I praise you? About this I do not praise you. I received from the Lord what I have given you. For the Lord Jesus in the night that He was betrayed took the bread ...** (The apostle here again wants to correct the abuses that had ripped apart the administration of the holy Supper among the Corinthians. That is why he directs them to the institution of the Lord Christ).

4. Just as one cannot be baptized for someone else, that is, if it is going to do some good for the other person, so also no one else can receive the blessing of Christ's body and blood in the holy Supper [on behalf of someone else]; rather, one must in true faith individually come forward and participate in this heavenly mealtime.

Here again are apparent points of contention:

1. That even though Christ instituted the holy Supper and the apostles in the early church administered it by distributing the consecrated bread and wine to others, yet they nowhere forbade that one should not consecrate even though no communicants are present. ANSWER: Christ's institution is rightly to be regarded as a rule and form which we are to observe and according to which we are to conduct ourselves in administering the holy Supper; and it has a much different connection with the distribution of the consecrated bread and wine than with external circumstances of the time, the place, and other incidental things. [I.e., Christ's institution relates much more to the distribution itself than to other external matters.] As pertains to external circumstances, it is apropos to conclude that Christ conducted the first holy Supper in the evening at the place of lodging, and yet nowhere forbade holding it in the early morning in the churches, etc. To take such a position is therefore not of itself wrong, nor is it contrary to Christ's institution. However, as previously stated, the distribution of the consecrated bread and wine is an entirely different matter. For, it is even as much an essential part of the holy Supper as is the consecration. Therefore it cannot be omitted without destroying the perfection of this Sacrament. The command of Christ: **This do** in the holy Supper applies as much to the distribution as does the giving of thanks.

2. That the holy Supper is the kind of action in which the priest sacrifices for the entire Church. Therefore it serves not only those who eat this offering, but also those for whom it was offered; just as in the Old Testament, the offering was consumed only by the priests and yet was for the good of others. ANSWER: Whether the Lord Christ ordained a sacrifice with the institution of the holy Supper will be dealt with later, and the opposite will be proven. Accordingly, since the basis for this conclusion is faulty, what is built upon it cannot stand, to say nothing of the fact that concerning certain sacrificial offerings in the Old Testament, not only the priests and Levites ate of them, but also others. In 1 Sam. 16:5, Samuel invited the sons of Jesse to the sacrifice.

CHAPTER 18

CONCERNING THE SACRAMENTAL EATING AND
DRINKING OF THE TRUE BODY AND BLOOD OF
CHRIST IN THE HOLY SUPPER.

 hus far the first two sacramental actions have been dealt with; namely, concerning the consecration and distribution of the consecrated bread and wine in the holy Supper. Now follows the third sacramental action; namely, concerning the sacramental eating, drinking and reception of the consecrated bread and wine, which is no less an essential part necessary for the perfection of this holy Sacrament and which we substantiate as follows:

1. The Lord Christ used the kinds of words in the institution of this holy Supper that expressly require the sacramental eating, drinking and reception of the consecrated bread and wine.

Mat. 26:26, Mark 14:22 – **But when they ate, Jesus took the bread, gave thanks and broke it and gave it to the disciples and said: Take, eat, this is My body.**

Mat. 26:27, Mark 14:23 – **And He took the chalice and gave thanks, gave it to them and said: All of you drink from it.**

Luke 22:19, 1 Cor. 11:23,24 – **For the Lord Jesus, in the night that He was betrayed, took the bread, gave thanks and broke it and said: Take, eat, this is My body, which will be broken for you. Such do,** etc.

Luke 22:20; 1 Cor. 11:25 – **In the very same way also the chalice after the supper and said: This chalice is the New Testament in My blood; do this, as often as** you drink it, to My remembrance.

2. The holy apostles and the believers in the early church celebrated the holy Supper in such a way that they ate the consecrated bread and drank from the consecrated chalice.

Mark 14:24 – **And they all drank from it.**

1 Cor. 10:21 – **You cannot simultaneously drink from the Lord's chalice and from the devil's chalice. You cannot simultaneously be partakers of the Lord's Table and the devil's table.**

1 Cor. 11:26–29 – **For as often as you eat of this bread and drink from this chalice, you should proclaim the Lord's death until He comes. Now anyone who unworthily eats of this bread or drinks from this chalice of the Lord, he is guilty of the body and blood of the Lord. Let that person examine himself and then eat of this bread and drink of this chalice. For whoever eats and drinks unworthily, he eats and drinks judgment to himself,** etc.

3. Since the distribution of the consecrated bread and wine belongs to the essential elements of the holy Supper, it thus follows *ex vi et natura relationis* [*from living and natural relationships*] that also the consumption of the consecrated bread and wine belongs to the essential elements of the holy Supper. For that reason the consecrated bread and wine are distributed to the communicants is that they receive it and be fed by it.

CHAPTER 19

THAT NOT ONLY BREAD AND WINE, BUT ALSO THE TRUE BODY AND BLOOD ARE RECEIVED AND CONSUMED IN THE HOLY SUPPER; ALSO, OF WHAT THIS SACRAMENTAL CONSUMPTION CONSISTS.

n the holy Supper it is not that the consecrated bread is simply and separately eaten and, again, that the body of Christ is [also] separately eaten, but that by means of the consecrated bread we eat the body of Christ. Nor is it that the consecrated wine is simply and separately drunk and, again, that the blood of Christ is [also] separately drunk. Rather, by means of the consecrated wine we drink the true blood of Christ. This consumption of the body of Christ along with the consecrated bread and the blood of Christ along with the consecrated wine is in no way to be regarded as a natural eating and drinking, much less as a Capernaitish eating and drinking, since Christ's body and blood are not eaten and drunk as one usually receives and uses other food and drink, [i.e.], in a natural manner for the nurture of the body. Rather, such an eating and drinking takes place in a highly incomprehensible mystery, [in an] unfathomable and genuinely spiritual manner. However, it is called a sacramental eating and drinking because it occurs only in this Sacrament and is due to the sacramental union of the true body of Christ with the consecrated bread and the true blood of Christ with the consecrated wine. However, it consists, as stated, in this: that by means of the consecrated bread, Christ's body is eaten and received, and also by means of the consecrated wine, Christ's blood is drunk, which we substantiate as follows:

1. These very same words of institution, in which are named the essential elements of the holy Supper, must be accepted and retained with the presented literal understanding, as was established in chapter 12, above. Now then, in the very same words—as the Lord Christ says: **Take, eat; take, drink**—such a sacramental action is named which belongs to the essential elements of this holy Sacrament, as was shown in the previous chapter. Therefore, these words must be accepted and retained with the same understanding which the letter brings with it [i.e., literally]. From this, it further follows that the eating and drinking are here again not to be understood in a figurative sense, but rather, the eating and drinking must be understood in the literal sense: eat, drink, and receive with the mouth.

Mat. 26:26, Mark 14:22 – **But as they ate, Jesus took the bread, gave thanks and broke it and gave it to the disciples and said: Take, eat, this is My body.**

Mat. 26:27, 28, Mark 14:23 – **And He took the chalice and gave thanks, gave it to them and said: All of you drink from it; this is My blood of the New Testament**, etc.

2. Just as by the sacramental union the body of Christ is furnished with the consecrated bread and the blood of Christ with the consecrated wine, so also by the sacramental eating, the body of Christ is furnished with the bread, and by the sacramental drinking, the blood of Christ is provided with the wine. This is because the eating and drinking originates in (arises from) the sacramental union, and the sacramental union takes place at the sacramental consumption [and is] also directly focused on it. For, in the holy Supper Christ is not present with His true body and blood for the sake of the bread and wine; rather, He is present with His true body and blood for the sake of people. Now, however, the sacramental union of the body of Christ with the consecrated bread and of the blood of Christ with the consecrated wine does *not* consist in this: that the bread and wine are merely symbols of the absent body and blood of Christ. Rather, Christ is truly and essentially present in the act of the holy Supper with His true body and true blood, as was established above in chapter 11. Therefore, the sacramental eating and drinking does *not* consist of this: that only bread and wine are eaten and drunk in the holy Supper and that the spiritual consumption of the body and blood of Christ are thereby figuratively portrayed and empowered and sealed. Rather, the oft-mentioned sacramental consumption consists of this: that by means of the consecrated bread, Christ's body and, by means of the consecrated wine, Christ's blood are truly and in point of fact received, eaten, and drunk.

1 Cor. 10:16 – **The consecrated chalice which we bless** (distribute and drink from – 1 Cor. 11:27)**, is it not the fellowship of the blood of Christ? The bread which we break** (distribute and eat)**, is it not the fellowship of the body of Christ?**

3. When the eating and drinking of real, natural food and drink are spoken about, then it cannot be understood in any other way than according to the letter [literally], since figurative eating and drinking would have status only if it were referred to as a figurative food and drink.

Now, however, the words of Christ: **Eat, drink**, refer to natural food and drink, namely to the consecrated bread and wine (although not only to the external elements, but at the same time to the true body and the true blood of Christ, which are sacramentally united with the same external elements). Therefore, these words of Christ: **Eat, drink**, may not be understood in any other way than literally. To demonstrate and properly understand these closing words [of Christ], it is to be noted that every time the Scriptures mention figurative eating and drinking, a figurative eating and drinking is therewith brought to mind.

John 4:32 – **I have a food to eat about which you do not know.** Thereupon Christ quickly clarifies this in v. 34 – **My food is this, that I do the will of the One who has sent Me.**

John 6:27 – **Work not for food that is perishable, rather for that which remains for eternal life**, etc.

John 6:35 – **I am the Bread of Life. Whoever comes to Me, such a one will not hunger; and whoever believes on Me, such a one will nevermore thirst.**

John 6:50 – **This is the Bread which comes from heaven, so that whoever eats of it will not die.**

John. 6:51 – **I am the living Bread come from heaven. Whoever eats of this bread, he will live eternally. And the bread, which I will give, is My flesh, which I will give for the life of the world**, etc. v. 52–58.

Rev. 2: 17 – **Whoever overcomes, him I will give to eat of the hidden Manna,** etc.

In these and similar places, it is easy to perceive from the circumstances of the text and the enlightenment of the Holy Spirit that by the eating and drinking some other figurative and allusive manner [of speaking] is to be understood than what the words mean literally. But, in the words of the institution, the Holy Spirit gives no such explanation.

4. The manner in which the apostles ate and drank at the administration of the first Lord's Supper was also the meaning intended by the words of the Lord Christ: **Eat, drink**—especially since it is implausible that Christ would have commanded one thing and the apostles would have done another.

Now then, the apostles understood and carried out Christ's directive [in such a way] that they ate the consecrated bread and drank from the consecrated chalice. Therefore, they comprehended the eating and drinking to be according to the letter and not according to a figurative or allusive manner. Thus, we should similarly understand Christ's words literally.

Mark 14:23 – **And they all drank from it** (not figuratively or in an allusive manner, but actually drank—[and] not just with the mouth of faith, since Judas also with the others drank from the consecrated chalice. Judas had no faith and consequently was unable to drink with the mouth of faith. Rather, with their mouths they received the consecrated wine and, by means of same, the true blood of Christ; which then in the same manner is to be applied to the first part of the holy Supper [i.e., the eating of the bread].).

5. The words "**eat**" and "**drink**" in the institution of the holy Supper cannot be understood to mean the same kind of spiritual consumption of which Christ is speaking in John 6. This [statement] is to be clearly supported with many arguments. In the holy Supper, Christ established one such eating of His body. 1. It is distinguished from the drinking of His blood (Mat. 26:26, 27; Mark 14:22; Luke 22:19, 20; 1 Cor. 11:23, 24, 25). 2. It takes place for all who eat the consecrated bread, including also for the unworthy (1 Cor. 11:27). 3. Through it the spiritual nourishment is sealed and strengthened as a fruit of the holy Sacrament (Luke 22:19, 20; 1 Cor. 11:24, 25). 4. It is a means through which Christ wants to work the spiritual nourishment in the hearts of the believers. 5. It is done by means of the consecrated bread (Mat. 26:26, Mark 14:22, Luke 22:19, 1 Cor. 11:23). 6. It does not always take place for salvation, but rather to the judgment of the unworthy guests (1 Cor. 11:29). 7. It was first instituted in the New Testament (Mat. 14:26, Mark 14:22, Luke 22:19, 1 Cor. 11:23). 8. Some often do without it and yet are saved (1 Cor. 11:28).

On the other hand, the spiritual consumption (nourishment) of which Christ speaks in John 6: 1. is not distinguished from drinking of the blood of Christ, since faith simultaneously eats Christ's body and drinks His blood, that is, it appropriates Christ's merits for itself (John 6:53); 2. takes place only for those who truly believe in Christ (v. 35); 3. is confirmed by the sacramental consumption; 4. and to the same purpose, Christ instituted the sacramental eating and drinking. **This do**, He says, **for My remembrance** (Luke 22:19, 1 Cor. 11:26); 5. takes place without the means of external elements; 6. is entirely and solely for salvation,

[and] in no way for judgment (v. 54); **7.** has taken place for the believers of the Old Testament as well as for the believers of the New Testament (v. 53); **8.** is necessary for all who would be saved (v. 53). **Truly, truly, I say to you: If you don't eat the flesh of the Son of Man and drink His blood, then you have no life in you.** Hence, it follows indisputably that these words of Christ in the institution—**eat, drink**—may in no way be understood to mean the same spiritual consumption which is referred to in John 6 and elsewhere in Scripture.

Here again are apparent points of contention:

1. That Christ's body and blood are a spiritual food (John 6:55, 58); therefore they cannot be received any other way but spiritually. ANSWER: **1.** If by spiritual reception is understood the same spiritual consumption of which Christ speaks in John 6, [i.e.,] that we in true faith appropriate for ourselves the merits of Christ as He with the offering of His body and pouring out of His blood on the timber-trunk of the cross redeemed us, then we say that the sacramental consumption of the body and blood of Christ in the holy Supper is truly distinguished from the spiritual consumption, and as a result one cannot be mingled with the other. The sacramental consumption is an essential part of the holy Supper and takes place for all those who receive the consecrated bread, be they worthy or unworthy. The spiritual consumption, however, is a fruit of the holy Supper and takes place only for the believers and worthy guests. **2.** If by spiritual consumption is understood that the mouth receives only bread and wine, while faith, on the other hand, swings itself up to heaven and there receives Christ body and blood, then we say that it must be shown from the words of institution that Christ by the words "**eat**" and "**drink**" had established such a consumption. But that can hardly be the case. Rather, the words of institution give [us] clearly to understand that Christ not only distributed bread and wine to His disciples, but that, by means of the consecrated bread, His true body, and by means of the consecrated wine, His true blood. What the Lord Christ distributed to the disciples, which they also ate and drank, [was], namely, not only bread and wine, but also the true body and true blood of Christ. **3.** If however, by spiritual consumption it is understood that the Lord Christ, in a secret, hidden, supernatural, heavenly and incomprehensible manner, offers to us at the time of the holy Supper along with the consecrated bread His true body to eat and with the consecrated wine His true blood to drink, then we say that certainly by such an understanding the sacramental consumption is a true spiritual consumption. For even if we, to be sure, by means of the consecrated bread eat Christ's body and by means of the consecrated wine drink His blood, such indeed does not occur in a natural manner like other common natural food and drink is usually received. Rather, [it occurs in] a mysterious, supernatural, and in such a spiritual manner that our external man—our flesh and blood—does not comprehend how it takes place or even can take place. Instead, our inward man has to perceive and comprehend it through faith. **4.** Accordingly, we gladly confess that Christ's body is a spiritual food for the following reasons: First of all, because it is not a common natural food by which we are sustained in this natural life. Also, because it is a spiritual, glorified body (1 Cor. 15:44, Phi. 3:21). Furthermore, because through it we are fed (nurtured) for spiritual and eternal life. Finally, because it is received in the holy Supper in a supernatural, incomprehensible, and spiritual manner. **5.** However, the allegation that Christ's body may be received in no other way than through the mouth of faith, and that by no means can the body of Christ be received with the mouth by means of the consecrated bread—since it is a spiritual body—runs counter to the institution of Christ; for there, in the distribution of the consecrated bread to His disciples, Christ said: **Take, eat, this is My body.** He thereby testifies that by means of the consecrated bread His body is truly (actually) received. **6.** Is not the Holy Spirit a spiritual Essence who also resides in our hearts? Yes indeed, our bodies are the **temple of the Holy Spirit** (1 Cor. 3:16, 6:19). Is not rebirth a spiritual work, and yet does not the entire person also and not just the soul become reborn? (John 3:6) Is not the Word of God a spiritual, imperishable seed, and yet it is in our mouths and in our hearts? (Rom. 10:8) Is not eternal life a spiritual blessing, a spiritual, eternal treasure, and yet not just our soul but also our body will become a partaker of it? **7.** If, without a single contradiction, it is true that a spiritual food may not be received with the mouth, then it would also be true that a genuine body could not be received with the mouth of faith *propter eandem vim relationis* [*because of the same power of relationship*]. Where then would that leave the spiritual reception of Christ's body? **8.** Therefore, it is agreed that a spiritual food cannot be received by mouth, that is to say, not without some kind of means. But [when] Christ's body and blood are received in the holy Supper, it does not take place without means; rather, it occurs by means of the consecrated bread and the consecrated wine in a sublime, incomprehensible mystery.

2. That the Lord Christ Himself revealed in John 6 what kind of eating and drinking of His body and blood He instituted in the holy Supper, namely, a spiritual eating and drinking. Therefore, it is not necessary to consider a different sacramental eating and drinking. ANSWER: **1.** It was previously adequately [explained] in proof 5, above, that there is a vast difference between the spiritual consumption about which Christ speaks in John 6 and the sacramental eating and drinking which He established and instituted in His holy Supper, thereby to confirm that one must not be confounded with the other. **2.** The sermon which John describes in [chapter] 6 was formulated by the Lord Christ at least an entire year before He entered His suffering, as testified to by the Gospel history. However, He instituted the Sacrament of the holy Supper on the night in which He was betrayed (Luke 22:19, 1 Cor. 11:23). How can it be said that Christ in John 6 is revealing to us the sacramental consumption of

His body and blood since it had not been preceded by the institution of same? That would mean allowing commentary and interpretation to step in before the [existence of] the text [itself]. **3.** It is certain and irrefutable that the institution of the holy Supper is actually described in Mat. 26, Mark 14, Luke 22, and in 1 Cor. 11. Why would we want to remove from sight as the chief foundation of this matter (*propriam hujus doctrinae sedem*) these same references and search in the sixth chapter of John (or other places in Scripture) for what we should believe about this Sacrament or for what kind of eating and drinking it is which Christ speaks of in the institution of the holy Supper, since it can nowhere be found in John 6 that Christ is dealing with the kind of eating and drinking which occurs by means of consecrated bread and wine? **4.** Finally, were the words "**eat**" and "**drink**" in the institution of the holy Supper to be understood as in John 6 (namely, in an allusive and figurative manner), it would unequivocally follow that the little word "**bread**" would also then be understood in the same way as in John 6 (namely in an allusive and figurative manner), and it would thus readily [lead to the conclusion] that one dare not use natural bread for this holy Supper. **5.** Yet we herewith by no means forbid one to proclaim from chapter 6 of John the spiritual eating and drinking which is a fruit of this holy Supper.

3. That if the word "**eat**" and the word "**drink**" are to be understood literally in the words of institution, then it would follow that the body of Christ would be eaten in a natural manner, just like other common food. ANSWER: **1.** In no way does it follow that every consumption that takes place by mouth (orally) occurs in a natural, common manner. Did not the holy angels, when they appeared to the men of God, truly eat and drink? At the same time, it was not a natural, ordinary eating. In Tobit 12:19 the angel says, It appears as if I am eating with you, but I am using invisible food which no man can see. The holy angels truly ingested food and drink with their mouths as they appeared in the assumed human form, and it was no sham or delusion; however, they did not chew and digest the food like we human beings do. Thus also Christ ate and drank with the holy apostles after His resurrection in Acts 10:41, where the words "**eat**" and "**drink**" are to be understood literally, namely, that Christ truly ingested food and drink with His mouth; for otherwise Christ would not have demonstrated thereby that He actually was risen from the dead (Luke 24:42,43; John 21:15). But who would dare say that Christ ate and drank in a natural, ordinary manner as we human beings commonly use natural food? **2.** Accordingly, a distinction must at all times be made between the thing itself and the mode of a thing. The Son of God was truly begotten by the Father in eternity, and the word "beget" or give birth must be taken in a literal sense and in no way in a figurative sense. But who would say the Son of God was born of the Father in a natural way as people are usually begotten and born? God's Son was born of Mary (Gal. 4:4). From this it follows that Mary herself carried the Son of God, nursed Him, and reared Him, since the words "carry," "nursing," and "rearing" have to be understood literally. Yet it does not follow from this that the Son of God was carried in the body [womb] of the virgin Mary in a natural, common manner; rather, it is and remains a **great mystery** (1 Tim. 3:16). The Holy Spirit descended in a true form of dove in Mat. 3:16, Mark 1:10, and Luke 3:21, since the word "**descended**" is to be understood in the literal sense. And yet, it does not follow that He descended in a spatial, natural way as other natural things are accustomed to doing. **3.** Accordingly, just as it is an incomprehensible mystery that Christ's body with the consecrated bread and Christ's true blood with the consecrated wine are united in the holy Supper in a sacramental manner, so also the sacramental consumption of the body and blood of Christ in the holy Supper is and remains a highly incomprehensible mystery, which we, in honor of Christ, believe and which we, with our disputations drawn from our reason, shall be unable to dislodge (change) or comprehend. Why, we don't even understand how it could happen that the holy angels ate and drank when they appeared in the form of men and also that Christ ate and drank with the apostles after His resurrection. There are also many other mysteries which we cannot comprehend. Why would we then deny the sacramental consumption [eating and drinking] of the true body and blood of Christ even though we cannot immediately understand it? **4.** If we were to say that Christ's body and blood are received in the holy Supper by mouth without means, then it could be concluded that it has to occur in a natural, common manner. But then, Christ's body and blood are not eaten and drunk in the holy Supper without means; rather, His body is received by means of the consecrated bread with which it is mysteriously united in a sacramental manner, and His blood is drunk by means of the consecrated wine with which it is sacramentally united in a mysterious way. Therefore, from this it cannot be concluded that it takes place in a natural, common way; rather, just as the sacramental union of the body of Christ with the consecrated bread and the blood of Christ with the consecrated wine is an incomprehensible mystery, so also it is to be said—and thus to be held—that the sacramental eating and drinking of the body and blood of Christ in the holy Supper takes place in a mysterious, incomprehensible manner.

4. That if the word "**eat**" should be understood literally, then it would follow from this that Christ's body is bitten into with the teeth, and what could be more absurd than that? ANSWER: **1.** When one approaches God, one should take off his shoes (Exo. 3:4); when one would think about or speak of divine mysteries, then gross thoughts which spin out from reason must be set back (placed aside). **2.** Did not Christ eat after the resurrection? But who would dare conclude from this that He chewed the food, swallowed it, digested it, and changed it into blood? **3.** Since the body and blood of Christ are therefore not a common, natural food which we use for the proper sustenance of the body and for this natural life, but are rather a heavenly, spiritual food, therefore we should not think that it thus happens with the consumption of the body and blood of Christ as it customarily occurs when one uses natural, common food. Christ's body does not through natural digestion become changed in our body. On the contrary, our inner man is nurtured through it for eternal life, and indeed also through this life-producing food our bodies become partakers of immortality. **4.** Christ's body is not simply eaten without a means; rather, it is eaten by means of the consecrated bread in the holy Supper. Therefore, in no way can it be concluded from the eating of the body of Christ that it has the distinctive features of natural eating; otherwise, I would want similarly to conclude: The Holy Spirit descended in the form of a dove in Mat. 3:16, Mark 1:10, and Luke 3:21; therefore, this descent occurred, step by step, in a spatial, natural way.

5. Wouldn't it be conformable to the institution of Christ if one said that the word "**eat**" is to be understood literally in so far as it applies to the consecrated bread, whereas it is to be understood in a figurative, allusive manner in so far as it applies to Christ's body? ANSWER: It matters not if one concocts this or that meaning from the word "**eating**" (and "**drinking**"); rather, the same meaning has to be shown from the words of institution. **2.** Who is going to convince me that Christ's body can be eaten in no other way than in a spiritual, figurative manner, since this conclusion rests simply and solely upon this: Shall it be impossible for God, by means of the consecrated bread and wine, to extend in the holy Supper Christ's body and blood, truly present for eating and drinking, since in the holy Supper, with clear words, such consumption is established, instituted, and promised by Christ? **3.** It is impossible that a single word in a particular utterance is capable of two meanings and be simultaneously understood in both the literal and the figurative sense. **4.** Also by such designs two Sacraments and two sacramental consumptions would be created out of one Sacrament, out of one sacramental union, and out of one sacramental eating and drinking, which would be absurd. For just as the holy Supper is a Sacrament simply because Christ's body is sacramentally united with the consecrated bread and Christ's blood is sacramentally stipulated with the consecrated wine, so also these same words, in which the essential elements of this Sacrament are named, have only one meaning which is appropriate to the sacramental unity and oneness of the Sacrament. **5.** In the holy Supper it is not that the consecrated bread is [first] individually and separately eaten, and that then once more Christ's body is separately eaten; nor is it that the consecrated wine is [first] individually and separately drunk, and then once more is Christ's blood drunk separately. Rather, Christ's body is eaten by means of the consecrated bread and Christ's blood is drunk by means of the consecrated chalice. This single, indivisible sacramental eating and drinking would indeed be ripped apart, in opposition to Christ's institution, if one purported that the consecrated bread was eaten with the physical mouth [and that] Christ's body was eaten with the mouth of faith. Further [false teachings]: that there are many of those who eat the consecrated bread who yet do not sacramentally eat Christ's body. In other words, the bread would be received here upon earth, while Christ's body would be received in heaven. Finally, that those who eat the consecrated bread indeed first receive Christ's body much later; why, this is tantamount to saying that Christ's body would be separated from the consecrated bread and the blood of Christ from the consecrated wine, while obviously Christ in His institution very precisely bound them together in one Sacrament. **6.** To say nothing of the fact that previously it has been demonstrated with many arguments that the very same eating and drinking of His body and blood, which Christ instituted in the holy Supper, must of necessity be distinguished from the spiritual eating and drinking, and in no way are they to be confused with each other. **7.** Therefore we conclude as follows: In the article of the Person of Christ, concerning the personal union of His divine and human natures, the attributes of both natures are predicated to the entire person because the words are understood literally, and by no means both literally and figuratively at the same time. In like manner, Christ's body is sacramentally bound [united] with the consecrated bread and Christ's blood with the consecrated wine. Because of this sacramental union, these very words—in which the essential parts of this Sacrament are named—must be understood literally, and by no means should such a distinction be made that they are simultaneously interpreted in both the literal and the figurative senses.

6. That if a person wants to understand the word "**eat**" and the word "**drink**" literally, then it would follow that a Capernaitic eating and drinking has been introduced, yet Christ indeed rejects such a notion in John 6. ANSWER: Far be it that we should introduce a Capernaitic eating and drinking of the body and blood of Christ. The Capernaites regarded Christ as merely a man. Therefore they thought that the eating of His flesh as an ordinary man would be of little benefit to them. We, however, know and believe that Christ's flesh is a life-giving flesh because it is the flesh of the Son of God (John 6:55). Therefore He also gave this flesh for the life of the world (v. 51). And whoever eats of it has eternal life (v. 54). The Capernaites, with their minds of flesh, fall into these kinds of thoughts: that Christ spoke of a natural eating and drinking, just as common food is usually taken, chewed, and digested. We, however, believe and confess that Christ's body by means of the consecrated bread and His blood by means of the consecrated wine are received in the holy Supper in a mysterious, hidden, spiritual, super-natural, and incomprehensible manner. The Capernaites thought everyone received a piece of Christ's body until He was totally consumed, to the extent that they readily expose their gross fleshly thoughts by saying: **How can this one give us His flesh to eat** (John 6:52). But Christ censures this fleshly thought and says in v. 63: **It is the Spirit that makes alive, the flesh is of no benefit**, etc. Consequently, we cast aside and condemn the fleshly thoughts of the Capernaitic consumption as we plainly confess: Christ's body by means of the consecrated bread and His blood by means of the consecrated wine are with a high mystery received in a supernatural, heavenly, incomprehensible and spiritual manner.

7. That if Christ's body is received by means of the consecrated bread and His blood is received by means of the consecrated wine, it would thus follow that Christ's blood becomes separated from His body. ANSWER: **1.** As in everything else, so also in this mystery, our reason must be taken captive to the obedience of Christ (2 Cor. 10:5); if we could comprehend it with our reason, what would be mysterious about that? **2.** By no means do we say that Christ's blood becomes separated from His body, nor do we say that the natural union of the body and blood of Christ or the personal union of the divine and human nature in Christ are dissolved. Rather, we simply abide by the institution of Christ, that by means of the consecrated bread His true body is received in a distinctive [different] way, and that by means of the consecrated wine His true blood is also received in a distinctive manner. How something like this happens or can happen, however, that we commend to the Originator of this holy Supper. **3.** The natural, personal, and sacramental unions must be spoken about [dealt with] separately. Christ's body and blood are and remain naturally united into eternity so that a true, natural humanity emanates therefrom. Christ's body and blood are personally united with God's Son, that is, with His assumed humanity so that from the divine and human natures in Christ came forth one Person who will also exist in eternity. In the holy Supper, Christ's body and blood are, not naturally or personally, but rather sacramentally

united with the consecrated bread and wine. These three kinds of unions must be spoken about and dealt with separately. Also, one must not be set against the other, or one rejected because of the other. **4.** If we cannot fathom how it happens that the assumed human nature is personally united with the divine nature of Christ and at the same time retains its essential attributes and does not become changed into the unending divine nature, why is it surprising that we cannot understand how it happens that Christ's body is eaten along with the consecrated bread and His blood drunk along with the consecrated wine, while at the same time not in the least separating the body and blood of Christ? Christ is the true, almighty God; His body is the Son of God's own body. Therefore, He can do and accomplish more with that body than we ever might understand (Eph. 3:20).

8. That the promises of the Gospel are received only by faith. Because the consumption of the body and blood of Christ belongs to the promises of the Gospel, it will happen only through faith. ANSWER: **1.** A distinction has to be made between the promise itself and the promised blessings. The promise is received through faith, but many times we receive the promised blessings in our bodies; health, daily bread, and the like are also promises of God, and at the same time we receive them into our bodies. **2.** The sending of the Holy Spirit is called the promise of the heavenly Father (Acts 1:4); nevertheless, as this promise was fulfilled, one could see the tongues on the apostles as if they were fiery [tongues] (Acts 2:3). **3.** Rebirth, the indwelling of the Holy Spirit, and eternal life are all Gospel promises. Even so, the entire person is reborn; the Holy Spirit lives also in our bodies; our bodies and souls become partakers of eternal life. **4.** That Christ's body is received by means of the consecrated bread and His blood by means of the consecrated wine originates in the initiation, ordinance, and institution of Christ, which cannot be invalidated by man's unbelief (Rom. 3:3). The spiritual eating and drinking, the forgiveness of sins, and salvation are actually Gospel promises which apply solely to the believers. But there is a different situation (state) with the sacramental consumption of the body and blood of Christ, which also, to be sure, can take place to the judgment of the unworthy (1 Cor. 11:27). Pertaining to the latter, it matters not if one believes or does not believe. **5.** Therefore, what some thus would conclude may likewise not be supported, [to wit]: Christ's body and blood cannot be received in the holy Supper other than through the evangelical promise; but then in the promise of the Gospel, Christ's body and blood are received only in a spiritual manner. Thus, no other kind of eating and drinking has been instituted in the holy Supper. Not so! Rather, the holy Sacraments are seals of the Gospel promise, but to the essential elements of the holy Supper belong not only bread and wine, but also the body and blood of Christ, as was established above in chapter 11. Accordingly, the sacramental eating and drinking of the body and blood of Christ, which He instituted in the holy Supper, can by no means be excluded from the Gospel. Christ, the trustworthy witness of Rev. 1:5, not only wanted to strengthen us and seal to us in the holy Supper the divine promises of the Gospel with bread and wine; rather, He employed the highest pledge for this promise, namely, precisely the very body which He gave for us into death on the timber trunk of the cross, and the very blood which He shed for our sin, and thereby won for us the heavenly blessings, as they are presented in the Gospel, so that by this pledge our faith might be mightily strengthened and the promise of the forgiveness of sins might be sealed to us with an adequate precious price. Concerning this matter, a more detailed presentation will follow.

9. That in Mat. 15:17 Christ says: **That which enters into the mouth goes into the belly and is through the natural course totally expelled.** But who would want to say or think anything like that about Christ? Therefore, one should not say that the reception occurs by mouth (orally) in the holy Supper. ANSWER: **1.** Christ is speaking there of common, natural eating and drinking of common, natural food, which is used for the proper sustenance of the body. How dare one apply something like that to this heavenly meal and great mystery of the holy Supper in which we do not eat Christ's body and blood in a natural, common manner, but in a heavenly, supernatural, incomprehensible manner? **2.** Not to mention that not a single time can Christ's speaking about natural food be construed in a vulgar manner, since the best part of food is that it serves the body for nurture. How much less should this be applied to the lofty, heavenly food in the holy Supper, which is not transformed within our body. Rather, we are much more made alive through it and are thereby nurtured for eternal life.

CHAPTER 20

WHETHER THE BLESSED BREAD IS TO BE PRESERVED AND LOCKED IN THE LITTLE SACRAMENTAL HOUSE [TABERNACLE].

ince until now the third sacramental action—namely concerning the eating and drinking of the consecrated bread and wine in the holy Supper—has been dealt with, it is in this connection to be asked whether the consecrated bread should not be picked up [elevated] and preserved so that hereafter it might be carried around in open procession and be revered. To this we respond that such [an action] should by no means take place, which we substantiate as follows:

1. The Lord Christ took bread in the holy Supper, gave thanks, and thereupon distributed it to His disciples to receive and eat. He did not lift up [elevate] the bread, nor did He command the disciples to lift up the bread; rather, as He distributed it to the disciples, He said: **Take, eat, this is My body.** Thus He did not first delay for a lengthy period to distribute the consecrated bread to the disciples; rather, as soon as He had given thanks He proceeded with the distribution. Accordingly, if it is to be called the Lord's Supper, the distribution is to take place shortly after the blessing or consecration, and the distribution is to be shortly followed by the communicants' eating of the consecrated and distributed bread.

Mat. 26:26, Mark 14:22 – **But as they ate, Jesus took the bread, gave thanks and broke it and gave it to the disciples and said: Take, eat, this is My body.**

Luke 22:19, 1 Cor. 11:23 – **For the Lord Jesus, in the night in which He was betrayed, took the bread, gave** thanks and broke it and gave it to the disciples and said: This is My body.

2. The disciples of the Lord Christ did not lift up (elevate) the blessed bread; rather, as soon as they had received it from the Lord Christ, they ate it. So that no doubt remain, this [conclusion] is not only derived from the fact that they immediately put into effect the command of Christ their Lord as He said: **Take, eat**, but rather, it is also clearly apparent (because St. Mark clearly testifies to this) that they all immediately drank from the chalice. Just as it then happened with the drinking from the consecrated chalice, so also, beyond any doubt, with the eating of the consecrated bread; it took place immediately.

Mark 14:23 – **And they all drank from it.**

3. In the early church at the time of the apostles, the believers celebrated the Supper as follows: They blessed the external elements, bread and wine, distributed them, and immediately ate of the consecrated bread and drank from the consecrated chalice. Accordingly, if one wants to conduct the holy Supper after the example of the first apostolic church, then the blessing, distribution, and the eating and drinking must take place at the same time.

1 Cor. 10:16,21 – **The blessed chalice which we bless, is it not the fellowship of the blood of Christ? The bread which we break, is it not the fellowship of the body of Christ? You cannot simultaneously drink the Lord's chalice and the devil's chalice; you cannot simultaneously be partakers of the Lord's Table and the devil's table.**

1 Cor. 11:26, 28 – **For as often as you eat of this bread and drink of this chalice, you should proclaim the Lord's death until He comes. A man should examine himself, and then he should eat of this bread and drink of this chalice.** From this source it is to be definitely concluded that in the early church one celebrated the holy Supper by eating the consecrated bread and drinking from the consecrated chalice.

4. If the consecrated bread is to be elevated, much rubbish follows from [the practice]: **1.** One does it in order to carry it around in a procession and adore it, even though Christ did not bless the bread in the holy Supper for that purpose and did not ordain that it should be so used. **2.** It gives occasion to mutilate the Sacrament, since one elevates only the bread and not the consecrated wine at the same time. **3.** By this [practice] more is done than what Christ did in the administration of the holy Supper. He only took the bread, gave thanks, broke it and distributed it to the disciples. **4.** Also, this preservation of the consecrated bread conflicts with the same rule which is taken from the words of institution: *nihil habet rationem sacramenti extra usam a Christo institutum*; [i.e.] if one changes or omits a sacramental action, then it can no longer be called a celebration of the holy Supper according to divine institution; **5.** to say nothing of the fact that such consecrated bread, when damaged by mice or other means, is thus not dealt with respectfully.

5. Finally, this setting-aside and preserving of the consecrated bread conflicts with the types of the Old Testament.

In Exo. 12:10, God the Lord expressly commands: **And should not leave any of it** (the Passover lamb); **but whenever some is left over until morning, you should burn it with fire** (but now the Passover lamb is a type of the holy Supper, as was established above in chap. 2).

Lev. 7:15 – **And the meat of the praise offering in the sacrifice of thanksgiving is to be eaten the very same day on which it is offered, and nothing is to be left over into the morning.** In the holy Supper we receive the true body of Christ which He offered for us on the timber trunk of the cross; therefore, the consecrated bread, with which the body of Christ becomes united in correct sacramental usage, should not be elevated nor preserved.

Here again are apparent contradictions:

1. That the bread in the holy Supper is essentially changed into Christ's body; therefore, it cannot be improper that after the consecration of same one lay it aside, carry it around in a procession, and fall down before it to adore it. ANSWER: **1.** It was established in chapter 14 above that bread and wine are by no means changed into the body and blood of Christ. On the contrary, in the holy Supper, Christ's body is sacramentally united with the consecrated bread and is received by means of the same. Thus also is Christ's blood sacramentally united with the consecrated wine and is drunk by means of the same. Since, therefore, the foundation and basis for the [practice of] preserving, carrying around, and adoring of the consecrated bread is dilapidated and worthless, it is easy to conclude how it is to be regarded when the consecrated bread is laid aside, carried around, and adored.* **2.** Also, even less may this preservation be [based upon] the sacramental union of the body of Christ, since this sacramental union consists of this: that it occurs only when a person eats the consecrated bread according to Christ's command and institution. If one, however, uses [the bread] for a purpose other than for which it was instituted by Christ, then it is no more Christ's body than baptismal water is a Sacrament if one uses it for a different purpose than pouring it upon a person in the Name of the Father, the Son, and the Holy Spirit for rebirth and renewal.

2. That sometimes people who unexpectedly come down with an illness require this Sacrament; therefore, it cannot be wrong that one lay aside and preserve the consecrated bread for such a purpose. ANSWER: It is not wrong to distribute this holy Supper to the sick for the strengthening of faith. However, aside from that, it is superstitious if one means that the bread must of necessity be blessed and elevated in a church for this purpose. For even Christ did not institute and celebrate His first Supper in the temple, but in a house in Jerusalem; there He Himself at the same time blessed the bread, broke it, and then distributed it

---

* I.e., if the reason for doing it is faulty, the action itself is worthless or even harmful. – Ed

to the disciples. Also, by the words of the holy Supper the glorious comfort is held up to the communicants that they actually are receiving the body which Christ gave into death for them and actually are drinking the blood which Christ shed for them on the timber-trunk of the cross. Therefore, it is indeed very comforting, when, in the presence of the sick, the words of institution are repeated and thereby the external elements for this holy Sacrament are [specifically] set aside [for this purpose].

CHAPTER 21

WHETHER THE BLESSED BREAD IS TO BE CARRIED ABOUT IN THE PROCESSION.

t can be proven with nearly the same arguments which were marshaled against the preservation and setting aside of the consecrated bread that it is wrong to carry the same bread around in the procession with great festivity and with cymbals and lights in order thereby to achieve one thing or another before God. For:

1. The Lord Christ did not carry around the consecrated bread in the holy Supper, nor did He direct His disciples to carry it around in a procession.

2. Also, the disciples did not carry the consecrated bread around; rather, in keeping with Christ's command, they ate it.

3. The early church at the time of the apostles knew nothing of such carrying around of the bread; rather, it was first introduced into the Church long after the time of Christ and the apostles.

4. By such carrying around of the consecrated bread an excuse is given for worshiping it, resulting in the mutilation of the Sacrament and in false worship and various superstitions. Also, it uses the consecrated bread for a different purpose than was instituted by Christ.

5. In the same way that it did not please God that the Ark of the Covenant be carried out of the camp except by His command—so that the Israelites could the better protect themselves against their enemies (1 Sam. 4)—so also, since Christ nowhere has commanded that the blessed bread is to be carried around in such a procession, neither will such [an action] in any way please Him.

1 Sam. 4:3, 4, 5, 10, 11 – **And as the people came into the camp, the elders of Israel spoke: Why did the Lord allow the Philistines to strike us today? Let us get for ourselves from Shiloh the Ark of the Covenant of the Lord, and let it come among us that it help us from** [give us a hand against] **the hand of our enemies. And the people sent to Shiloh and allowed for the Ark of the Covenant of the Lord Sabaoth, who sits over the cherubim, to be brought from there,** etc. **And as the Ark of the Covenant of the Lord came into the camp, the whole of Israel cheered with a great jubilation so that the earth echoed. Then the Philistines fought, and Israel was defeated and each one fled to his hut. And it was a very huge slaughter so that thirty thousand men of Israel's infantry were felled. And the Ark of God was captured and the two sons of Eli, Hophni and Phinehas, died.**

Here again, an apparent point of contention:

That by this carrying around of the consecrated bread, people are admonished to thank Christ for the work of redemption and for instituting this holy Sacrament. ANSWER: Christ, in the institution of the holy Supper, has adequately taught us how we are to thank Him for the work of redemption and for the institution of the holy Sacrament, namely, in this way: that according to His command we are to eat the consecrated bread and drink [from] the consecrated chalice, and thereby also to proclaim His death (1 Cor. 11:26). Consequently, we are not allowed the freedom to use the consecrated bread according to our own discretion; rather, the Lord Christ has ordained in the institution of the holy Supper that we eat the consecrated bread and thus should proclaim His death. But how can it agree with the institution of Christ that one carry around the consecrated bread with cymbals and lights, thereby to avert conflagrations and other mishaps, and along with this purport that one just as readily becomes a partaker of the benefits of the holy Supper of Christ through the consumption of the consecrated bread and wine if one falls down and worships before the consecrated bread, which is being carried around with in such a festive spirit, and helps to celebrate such festivity?

CHAPTER 22

WHETHER ONE SHOULD ADORE (WORSHIP) THE BLESSED BREAD IN THE HOLY SUPPER.

he question here is not whether the adoration is to be directed towards the Lord Christ, who is truly present in the holy Supper and distributes His true body and blood; for [on that point] we expressly say that Christ, as God and Man, is to be worshiped (adored). For without the same worship which takes place in Spirit and in Truth (John 4:23, 24), one cannot properly proclaim His death, that is, correctly give thanks for the work of redemption, which of course belongs (is essential) to the salutary use of this Sacrament (1 Cor. 11:26). Also, the question here is not whether the consecrated bread and chalice are to be distributed and received with all deference, so that with external respect one testifies that one is sure in his heart that Christ, true God and Man, is Himself present in the action of this holy Supper and through it imparts His true body and His true blood by means of the consecrated bread and wine. Whoever believes this from his heart will not approach this table of the Lord without reverence; rather, he will distinguish between the body of the Lord and other common food (1 Cor. 11:29); that is, he will remember that the consecrated bread is not simply and only bread, but that by means of same the true body of His Savior Christ is imparted to him.

Regarding this matter, the question actually is whether the worship is to be directed only towards the Lord Christ or also towards the consecrated bread in the holy Supper in such a way that when the consecrated bread is carried around one adores it and outwardly manifests such inward adoration. To this we then say that such [behavior] is wrong and to be cast aside.

1. God nowhere has commanded that one should give the consecrated bread in the holy Supper the honor of being adored. Therefore, it is a self-selected worship and cannot please God. That such self-chosen holiness does not please God will be shown in its proper place.

2. After the consecration, the bread still remains as bread and thus a creation of God. Consequently, when the adoration is directed not only to Christ but at the same time also towards the consecrated bread, then it is not only a dead worship but also a damnable idolatry.

Rom. 1:23, 25 – **And [they] have changed the glory of the imperishable God into a form of perishable mankind,** etc. **They have changed the truth of God into lies and have honored and served the creature more than the Creator,** etc.

That the honor of adoration is due only and solely to God the Lord shall be established in detail at the proper place.

3. As the Lord Christ said to His disciples in the holy Supper: **Take, eat, this is My body; take, drink, this is My blood,** they did not get up from the table and adore the bread and the chalice. Rather, in accordance with Christ's command, they ate the consecrated bread and drank from the consecrated chalice.

Mark 14:24 – **And they all drank from it.**

4. Through the action of carrying around and adoring the consecrated bread, the holy Supper becomes perverted into something which Christ by no means instituted, since in the words of institution there are to be found only three actions: that Christ first of all took the bread and gave thanks; that He then broke and distributed it; and thirdly, that the disciples received and ate the consecrated and distributed bread.

Here again are apparent points of contention:

1. That after the consecration bread and wine are no longer present in the holy Supper, since the bread becomes essentially changed into Christ's body and the wine into Christ's blood. ANSWER: It has already been established that this material change in no way can be proven from the words of institution, but rather conflicts with same. Whoever then adores the consecrated bread commits idolatry; to say nothing of the fact that those who avow this material change must themselves admit that there is a great danger in this adoration which is directed towards the consecrated bread, for no one can actually know whether the priest also properly baptizes and properly dedicates, whether he also has consecrated with due intention and devotion, whether he diligently took note of everything that belongs to the essential parts of this Sacrament, etc.

2. That Christ is truly present in the holy Supper and by means of the consecrated bread hands out His body and by means of the consecrated chalice His true blood. Therefore, this holy Sacrament is indeed to be adored (worshiped). ANSWER: Obviously the Lord Christ is present in the holy Supper with His true body and blood; but it by no means follows that the entire Sacrament is to be adored [worshiped], since to the essential parts of this Sacrament belong not only the true body and the true blood of Christ, but also bread and wine. Worship belongs solely and alone to Christ as God and Man. By no means, however, is it to be directed towards bread and wine, for **1.** the Lord Christ indeed established in the holy Supper a sacramental arrangement of His body with the consecrated bread and of His blood with the consecrated wine, but at the same time ordained that the consecrated bread was to be eaten and the consecrated cup was to be drunk; if this sacramental eating and drinking is neglected and the consecrated bread is joined to the purpose of being carried around to be worshiped by everyone, then that does not constitute celebrating the Lord's Supper because something of that which the Lord Christ prescribed for the essential elements of this Sacrament has been omitted. **2.** Also, by no means is the body of Christ personally united with the bread and the blood of Christ with the wine so that on the strength of such a personal union the bread and wine would be worshiped no less than the human nature is worshiped by virtue of its personal union with the divine nature. Instead, it is and is called a sacramental union, which is completely and solely directed to this end: that by means of the consecrated bread the true body of Christ be received, and by means of the consecrated chalice the true blood of Christ be received. **3.** Accordingly then, just as the Israelites in no way worshiped the Ark of the Covenant or the column of cloud-and-fire, even though they were external symbols and signs of the wonderful presence of the grace of the Lord God, but completely and solely directed their prayers and petitions towards the true God of Israel, who went before them in the pillar of smoke and fire (Exo. 13:21), and spoke to them from between the two cherubim that were upon the Ark of the Covenant, thus also prayer in the holy Supper should be wholly directed to Christ, who by means of the consecrated bread and wine actually distributes His true body and blood. **4.** And if it were valid to conclude that because Christ is present in the holy Sacrament of the Supper, therefore the entire Sacrament should be adored, then one could also conclude that because Christ's body lay in the crib as the shepherds came towards Bethlehem (Luke 2:16), therefore they should not only have adored Christ but also the crib; that because the Wise Men from the East found the little child Jesus on the lap of Mary, His mother (Mat. 2:11), therefore they should have adored not only the little child but also Mary. *Item:* Christ's body is in heaven; therefore, one should not only adore Christ but also heaven. Who doesn't see that these are all absurd conclusions? **5.** Consequently, it remains thus: Whoever wants properly to adore Christ in the holy Supper should not direct his adoration to the consecrated bread, but rather (as St. Paul prescribes this rule) proclaim the Lord's death. That he first of all believes from the heart that Christ is truly present in the holy Supper and distributes His true body and His true blood and, along with the same, distributes to the believers the gift of heavenly blessings. Secondly, that with heartfelt devotion he think on the merits of Christ, the Mediator, Who for the sake of mankind came from heaven, took on a true human nature, gave His life into death for us, poured out His blood for our sin, and also in the holy Supper distributes to [us] His body and His true blood for the strengthening of our faith. Thirdly, that he inwardly thank the Lord Christ for this great grace and thus proclaim His death. Fourthly, that he thereupon heartily petition that Christ would also be His Mediator, Advocate, and Savior, that Christ would cover all sins with the grace-mantle of His merits and make him into a worthy guest for this heavenly meal, that Christ would work true repentance in his heart and increase in him faith and love, etc. See, this is the correct inward and Christ-pleasing adoration which is required for the wholesome (beneficial) use of this Sacrament. Whereupon, it self-evidently follows that one also outwardly present himself in an honorable manner in the partaking of this most holy Sacrament. The outward without the inward cannot please God.

CHAPTER 23

FOR WHAT PURPOSE THE LORD CHRIST INSTITUTED THE HOLY SUPPER AND WHAT KIND OF BENEFIT THE BELIEVERS RECEIVE BY A SALUTARY (WHOLESOME) USE OF SAME.

p to this point, we have dealt with the Founder of the holy Supper, as well as with the material and form, that is, with its essential elements. At this time, the ultimate reasons for the sake of which Christ instituted this Sacrament must be further dealt with. From these it will be easy to perceive what a great benefit and fruit the believers receive from a salutary use of same. At the same time, it is to be noted that not all those who attend the holy Supper obtain from it the same benefit, but only those who partake of this Sacrament wholesomely and worthily, namely the believers; that is, those who, upon prior confession of sins and heartfelt contrition over same, hold on to Christ in true faith and also have the steadfast intention to serve God the Lord and to protect themselves from sins against conscience. Regarding the latter, it will be dealt with extensively later under the title: "Concerning the Proper, Salutary Preparation for Partaking of the holy Supper." It is indeed the intention of Christ the Lord to impart these heavenly gifts and blessings to all those who appear at the holy Supper, and these He offers to them. However, that not all become recipients of these blessings occurs because of impenitence, unbelief, and godlessness—or, in a word, because of unworthy reception. Regarding the fundamental reasons for which the Lord Christ instituted this Sacrament, as well as the benefits which we receive through a salutary use of same, the Lord Christ alone has briefly summarized them in the words of institution when He says: **Eat, this is My body which is given for you; drink, this is My blood of the New Testament which is poured out for you. Do such to My remembrance.** But [these words] must be further explained and interpreted. Accordingly, we say that by virtue of the institution, the holy Supper was established by Christ and was used by the believers chiefly to this end: that the promise of the gracious forgiveness of sins should be sealed and our faith should thus be strengthened. Then too, we are incorporated in Christ and are thus sustained to eternal life; in addition, subsequently, other end results and benefits of the holy Supper come to pass. Yet, both of the fruits indicated above always remain the foremost. First of all we say: Christ instituted His holy Supper (also it is used by believers for this purpose) because the promise of the gracious forgiveness of sins is sealed to the believers and thereby their faith is strengthened. For all that, the following considerations are to be well noted:

1. The holy Scriptures testify that on the timber-trunk of the cross Christ gave His body into death for us poor sinners and poured out His blood for our sins. This *precium nostrae redemptionis*, that is, this His true body, which He gave into death for our redemption, and this His true blood, which He poured out for our redemption, the Lord Christ takes and distributes to us by means of the consecrated bread and wine so that thereby we might be strengthened and made sure in faith and so that also to us applies the promise of the gracious forgiveness of sins. For since we eat Christ's body, which He gave into death for us, and drink His blood, which He shed for us, we thus can be assured that He will by grace give us what He won for us with the offering of His body and the shedding of His blood on the timber-trunk of the cross, namely, the forgiveness of sins, God's grace, and eternal life.

Luke 22:19, 1 Cor. 11:24 – **This is My body, which is being given** (broken) **for you.**

Mat. 26:28, Mark 14:24, Luke 22:20 – **This is My blood of the New Testament, which is being poured out** (for you) **for many.**

2. The promise of the Gospels in general truly testifies that all those who believe in Christ shall not be lost, but shall have eternal life. Since, however, unworthiness and weakness often hovers before the eyes of a weak and anxiety-ridden conscience, so that it begins to doubt whether this promise applies to it in particular—whether it can truly trust it and may stand before the judgment of God—see then how the Lord Christ distributes His true body and His true blood especially to it [the weak and anxiety-ridden conscience], and as the faithful Witness (Rev. 1:5) herewith wants to convince it—against all doubts and weakness—that certainly the comforting promise of the Gospels applies especially to it.

Mat. 26:26, Mark 14:22, 1 Cor. 11:24 – **Take, eat, this is My body.**

Mat. 26:27, 28 – **All of you drink from it, this is My blood,** etc.

3. Our body is dead, that is, it is subjugated to death on account of sin (Rom. 8:10) which still resides in us (Rom. 7:17) and strives against the law in our mind (v. 23), so that it is said of us **that flesh and blood cannot inherit the Kingdom of God** (1 Cor. 15:50). So that we now do not become too despondent on account of our misery and our sin that is hidden in our flesh, Christ lays His true body and His true blood (through which He won forgiveness of sins and salvation) into our mouth by means of the consecrated bread and wine so that our flesh's weakness, unworthiness, and uncleanness do not topple our faith; rather, that we be made certain that before God's throne our flesh's weakness and uncleanness will be covered with the most holy flesh of Christ and with His most priceless, precious blood.

Mat. 26:26, Mark 14:22, Luke 22:19, 1 Cor. 11:24 – **This is My body,** etc.

Mat. 26:28, Mark 14:24 – **This is My blood**, etc.

4. We are indeed taken into the grace-covenant of God through holy Baptism (1 Pet. 3:21) and are washed of all sin (Eph. 5:26). But since we often transgress such a covenant, we begin to doubt whether through genuine repentance we can again have access to that same grace-covenant and obtain forgiveness of sins. Now, so that this doubt be overcome, Christ instituted this holy Sacrament of the [Lord's] Supper in which He gives us to drink of His holy blood, which He shed to establish and reinforce this new covenant; and He herewith testifies that through true repentance we have access anew to this grace-covenant of God and can receive the forgiveness of sins, since this very same new covenant consists of this, that God the Lord never again will remember our sins (Jer. 31:34).

Mat. 26:28 – **This is My blood of the New Testament**, etc.

Luke 22:20, 1 Cor. 11:25 – **This chalice is the New Testament in My blood.**

5. If we are to become partakers of Christ's merits, we must lay hold of Him in true faith; but, since we cannot come to Him in heaven because of being weighed down with the burden of sin and the weakness of the flesh, nor tolerate His heavenly glory, see then how He comes to us and gives us His true body to eat and His blood to drink and does such under bread and wine so that He may at the same time lay hold of us (Phi. 3:12). Thus we need not say: **Who will ascend up to heaven?** (Rom 10:6), but instead be assured that in the holy Supper He truly is beside us and accordingly wants to be sought and found by us.

Mat. 26:26, 28; Mark 14:22, 23; Luke 22:19; 1 Cor. 11:24 – **Eat, this is My body; drink, this is My blood**, etc.

6. We are unable to deal with pure Divinity in our lives, for it is for us a consuming fire, in the face of which we are nothing but stubble (Deu. 4:24, Heb. 12:29). Accordingly, Christ assumed our flesh and bone, that is, our true human nature, so that through Him we are reconciled with God, and thus **all things were constituted together** in Christ (brought under One Head), **both that which is in heaven and that which is on earth** (Eph. 1:10). Since, however, Christ has ascended to heaven—and we may consequently think that we here on earth must deal solely with pure Divinity and will be consumed like stubble—see how Christ feeds us with His body and blood here upon earth in the holy Supper, thereby testifying that His flesh is the means through which we come to God and are united with Him.

Mat. 26:26, Mark 14:22, Luke 22:19, 1 Cor. 11:24 – **Eat, this is My body.**

Mat. 26:28, Mark 14:23 – **Drink, this is My blood,** etc.

7. Since our faith is often weak and we so easily forget the Lord Christ and His merits, Christ wanted to establish this holy Supper to His remembrance; and, consequently, alongside of the Word, He instituted the fellowship of His body and blood so that He may stir us with His life-producing flesh and through it awaken in us the proper, living remembrance of His death—all this, of course, to increase and strengthen faith. For how might we be awakened more strongly to remember the death of Christ than if Christ actually gives us to eat of the same body which He gave into death and actually gives us to drink of His blood which He shed on the cross?

Luke 22:19, 1 Cor. 11:24 – **And He took the bread, gave thanks and broke it and gave it to them and said: This is My body which is being given for you; this do to My remembrance.**

1 Cor. 11:25 – **In the same manner also** [He took] **the chalice after the supper and said: This chalice is the New Testament in My blood, do such, as often as you drink it, to My remembrance.**

8. Finally, because the first Adam lost the gift of the heavenly blessings which had been entrusted to him by eating of the fruit from the forbidden tree in Gen. 3, therefore has this other heavenly Adam (1 Cor. 15:47, 48) wanted to ordain His true body and His true blood—through which He has once again rescued the lost blessings—to be eaten and drunk in the holy Supper, so that we thus in faith may be assured and reassured that we, through Christ, once again richly obtain all that we previously lost through [the first] Adam.

Mat. 26:26, Mark 14:22 – **Take, eat, this is My body.**

From all this [testimony] it is apparent in what manner our faith is strengthened in the holy Supper and how the promise of the forgiveness of sins is made certain to us. At this time, we must demonstrate in what manner we are incorporated in the Lord Christ in the holy Supper and how we are fed for eternal life. Here the following views (considerations) are to be noted:

1. Nothing is more intimately related to the Lord Christ than His assumed human nature, His flesh and blood, with which He has personally united Himself; however, nothing comes closer to us humans than what we eat and drink, since it permeates our innermost being. Accordingly, since the Lord Christ wanted to unite us with Himself to the deepest and most precise degree, to that end it pleased Him that we receive His true body and blood by means of the consecrated bread and wine.

Mat. 26:26, Mark 14:22, Luke 22:19, 1 Cor. 11:24 – **Take, eat, this is My body.**

Mat. 26:28. Mark 14:23 – **Drink, this is My blood**, etc.

John 6:56 – **Whoever eats My flesh and drinks My blood, He remains in Me and I in him.**

2. Christ's flesh is a life-producing flesh, which He has assumed into the unity of His Person through the personal union and [which He] has filled with the treasure of eternal, heavenly blessings without measure. So that we, who are by nature dead in sins (Col. 2:13, Eph. 2:1), might now dip from this flowing Fountain of Life the legitimate spiritual life and be nurtured for eternal life, Christ desired to ordain His life-producing flesh to be eaten and His blood to be drunk for this very purpose in the holy Supper.

John 6:32, 33, 35, 48, 50, 53, 54, 55, 57, 58 – **Rather, My Father gives you the true bread from heaven. For this is the bread of God which comes from heaven and gives life to the world. I am the Bread of Life. Whoever comes to e, such a one will not hunger; and whoever believes on Me, such a one will never, ever thirst. I am the Bread of Life. This is the bread which comes from heaven, so that whoever eats of it will not die. And, the bread, which I will give, is My flesh which I will give for the life of the world. If you will not eat of the flesh of the Son of Man and drink His blood, then you have no life in you. Whoever eats My flesh and drinks My blood, such a one has eternal life,** etc. **For My flesh is food indeed and My blood is the drink indeed. Just as the living Father sent Me, and I live by the will of the Father, so also whoever eats Me, the same will also live because of Me. This is the bread which is come from heaven.** — **Whoever eats this bread, such a one will live in eternity.**

John. 15:4, 5 – **Remain in Me and I in you. Just as the tendril can produce no fruit of itself unless it remains on the wine-vine, so neither can you unless you remain in Me. I am the wine-vine, you are the tendrils; whoever remains in Me and I in him, such a one produces much fruit, for without Me you can do nothing.**

3. The Lord Christ has been established as the head of His Christian Church (Eph. 1:22), to which the entire body is joined and one member attaches to another (Eph. 4:16). In that we too have become members of this spiritual body and have received from Him spiritual life and spiritual movement, He has desired to institute in the holy Supper the fellowship of His body and blood and thus bring it to the fellowship of the spiritual body.

1 Cor. 12:13 – **For through one Spirit we all have been baptized into one Body,** etc., **and all have drunk into**

one Spirit. (We drink one and the same Sacrament so that we also receive one and the same Spirit; just as we receive one and the same Baptism, so that we be one body.)

4. The Lord Christ imparts to us His Holy Spirit through the Word of the Gospel (Gal. 3:2), so that we may thereupon confess that we abide in Him and He in us, since He has given us of His Spirit (1 John 4:13). But many times we do not feel the movement of the Spirit as we would well like to, especially in temptations; and it can often be said of us [that] **The spirit is willing, but the flesh is weak** (Mat. 26:41). Accordingly, so that the gifts of the Spirit are increased in us and the movement of the Spirit for all good be strengthened in us, Christ gives us His body (which was endowed with the Holy Spirit without measure, John 3:34) to eat and His blood to drink so that we might partake of His fullness (John 1:16).

John 6:56 – **Whoever eats My flesh and drinks My blood, such a one abides in Me and I in Him.** John 15:5 – **Whoever abides in Me and I in him, such a one bears much fruit.**

5. Our sinful flesh is subjugated to death (Rom. 8:10) and in Adam we all die (1 Cor. 15:22). So that we might now have a certain comfort, namely this, that our bodies someday shall be awakened from the dust of the earth and go forth to eternal life, see how Christ feeds us with His life-producing flesh so that we may be certain that our bodies, which are fed with the life-producing flesh of Christ in the holy Supper, shall not and cannot eternally remain in death.

John 6:54 – **Whoever eats My flesh and drinks My blood, such a one has eternal life, and I will awaken him on the Last Day.**

6. In Paradise, God the Lord had planted the tree of Life (Gen. 2:9), by whose fruit the man could have been sustained in incorruptible and constant blooming youthfulness had he not by the Fall into sin cut himself off from God. So that we again might be brought to the true life which is from God (Eph. 4:18), Christ, the Tree of Life, ordained His flesh (which is the Bread of Life) to be eaten and His blood to be drunk in the holy Supper.

Rev. 22:2 – **And on both sides of the stream there stood** [a tree] **of life which bore fruit twelve-fold and produced fruit every month, and the leaves of the trees provided health to the nations.**

John 6:35.48, 51: **I am the Bread of Life.**

Here may also be cited the other Old Testament types of the holy Supper which have been examined in the other chapter of this *Tractate*.

7. Bread and wine not only give a fine indication and admonition to love—that we, through loving one another, should be one body and similarly be one cake, just as one bread [loaf] is made from many kernels and one beaker of wine is made from many grapes (cf. chap. 10, no. 4, above); but, since Christ unites Himself with us according to the very same nature with which He is related to us and is our Brother, in that He feeds us with His body and blood, He thus—through His assumed, kindred human nature—works in the hearts of the believers also this: that we, as members of One Body, heartily love one another since He, as our Head, is and lives in us.

1 Cor. 10:17 – **For it is one bread; so we many are one body, as we all are partakers of one bread.**

1 Cor. 12:13 – **And** (we) **all have been given to drink of one Spirit.**

These, then, are the foremost, basic reasons for Christ's instituting His holy Sacrament and the foremost profits [benefits] which we receive from the salutary use of this Sacrament; namely, that our faith be strengthened, that the promise about the gracious forgiveness of sin be assured to us, that we also have Christ live within us, and that we be fed for eternal life. In addition, there are other reasons for which the holy Supper was instituted by Christ and is used by us:

1. That we be awakened heartily through it to thank Christ for the work of redemption.

1 Cor. 11:26 – **for as often as you eat of this bread and drink from this chalice, you should proclaim the Lord's death until He comes.**

2. That we herewith demonstrate our obedience towards Christ's command and do what He has commanded us out of indebted love and obedience.

Luke 22:19, 1 Cor. 11:24 – **Do such to My remembrance.**

1 Cor. 11:25 – **Do such as often as you drink it to My remembrance.**

3. That we herewith testify how we would patiently carry our cross according to Christ's example and, if necessary, shed our blood for the sake of His Word, just as we drink the blood which He has shed for us.

Luke 14:27 – **And whoever does not carry his cross and follow after Me, such a one cannot be My disciple.**

4. That we, with our example, help maintain the public assembly of which this holy Supper is the bond (binding tie).

1 Cor. 11:20 – **When you then come together, you do not** (properly) **observe the Lord's Supper** (as indeed it should be conducted in your assembly).*

5. That we hereby indicate our genuine repentance and godliness, since only the repentant are admitted to this holy Supper.

1 Cor. 11:28, 29 – **But a person** [should first] **examine himself and then he eats of this bread and drinks from this chalice. For anyone eating and drinking unworthily, such a one eats and drinks the judgment on himself, in as much as he does not discern the body of the Lord.**

6. That we publicly confess that we are one in religion and confession of faith with the same Church in which we celebrate the holy Supper.

---

* A negative example; Paul is here admonishing the Corinthians for their unloving practices. Ed.

1 Cor, 10:17, 18, 20 – **For it is one bread, so we many are one body, as we all are partakers of one bread. Observe Israel according to the flesh. Those who eat the offering, are they not in the fellowship of the Altar? But I say that what the heathen offer, they offer to the devil and not to God. Now I do not wish that you be in the fellowship with the devil. You cannot simultaneously drink the Lord's chalice and the devil's chalice. You cannot at the same time be partakers of the Lord's Table and the devil's table.**

7. That by the celebration of the holy Supper we publicly testify that we pardon [our] neighbor's failures, counsel and help him according to our ability, and also that we want to accept each other as brothers [and sisters] and fellow members in Christ.

Mat. 5:23, 24 – **Therefore when you offer a gift upon the altar and there happen to remember that your brother has something against you, then leave your gift there before the altar and go to him and reconcile yourself with your brother; and after that come and offer your gift.**

1 Cor. 10:17 – **For it is one bread, so we many are one body, since we all are partakers of one bread.**

In this connection, it is to be noted that the present enumerated ultimate reasons [for] and fruits of the holy Supper are not the foremost ones for which Christ instituted [the Supper] and on account of which we celebrate it. Rather, as mentioned above, the foremost fruits of the institution and the foremost profits (benefits) of a salutary reception are that we be strengthened in the faith, have Christ dwell in us, be fed and sustained for eternal life—which God the Lord through Christ and for His sake bestows on all of us who crave this from the heart. Amen.

CHAPTER 24

WHETHER THE LORD CHRIST INSTITUTED THE HOLY SUPPER SO THAT UNDER THE BREAD AND WINE HIS TRUE BODY AND BLOOD WOULD BE OFFERED TO GOD THE LORD BY THE PRIESTS.

 p to this point the reasons for which the holy Supper was instituted by Christ and used by us have been dealt with. Now the question arises whether the Lord Christ, among other things, instituted this holy Supper so that in it the priests should with pomp, words, vestments and other ceremonies offer to God the Lord, under the form of the bread and wine, the true body and blood of Christ in order to benefit the living and the dead. To this we say that such a Mass-offering (sacrifice) is false and fabricated, since not only does it not have any foundation in the words of institution and other Scripture passages, but it is directly in opposition to them. That the sacrifice of the Mass has no foundation in the words of institution or in other places in the Scriptures will become apparent when we later interpret and untangle the very pretexts which are directed to this conjecture. That [the sacrifice of the Mass] is, however, contrary to the Scriptures, we demonstrate as follows:

1. The holy Scriptures testifies that the Lord Christ solely and alone is the High Priest of the New Testament. This [testimony] runs directly contrary to [the practice] of having many Mass-priests who daily bring before God the Lord no fewer external, visible sacrifices (*repraesentativa sacrificia*) than did the high priests in the Old Testament.

Psa. 110:4 – **The Lord has sworn and He will not**

regret it: You are a Priest forever after the order of Melchizedek.

Zec. 6:12, 13 – **See, there is a man, whose name is Zemah***, etc. **He ... also will be a Priest upon His throne,** etc.

Heb. 4:14 – **Since we then have a great High Priest, Jesus, the Son of God,**etc.

Heb. 5:5, 6 – **So also Christ did not set Himself in honor, so that He became the High Priest; rather, He who said to Him: You are My Son, today I have begotten You. As He also said in another place: You are a Priest into eternity according to the Order of Melchizedek.**

Heb. 7:11 – **Now if perfection could have taken place through the Levitical priesthood ..., why is it necessary further to say that another Priest should arise according to the Order of Melchizedek,** etc.? In vv. 15, 17, 21 it is repeated.

Heb. 7:23, 24, 26 – **And of those who became priests, there were many because death would not allow them to remain. This One, however, because He abides eternally, has an imperishable priesthood. For we were to have such a High Priest who would be holy,** etc.

Heb. 8:1 – **We have such a High Priest who sits at the right hand upon the stool** [throne] **of majesty in heaven.**

Heb. 10:21 – **And** (we) **have a High Priest over the house of God.**

2. The holy Scriptures testify that Christ offered Himself once and for all upon the timber-trunk of the cross for the sin of the world as a sweet smell for His heavenly Father. It is contrary to this when one says that Christ has offered His body and blood not only on the timber-trunk of the cross but also in the institution of the holy Supper and [that it] is still also offered daily by Mass-priests.

---

* Gerhard here uses the Hebrew for branch or offspring, i.e. of God, an elliptical name for the Messiah. Tr..

Heb. 7: 26, 27 – **For we need to have such a High Priest, one who would be holy, guiltless, unspotted, separated from sinners, and is higher than the heaven; One who does not—like the other high priests—need daily first to make an offering for His own sin and then for the sin of the people; for this He did once and for all when He sacrificed Himself.**

Heb. 9:12, 25, 26, 28 – **Rather, He** (Christ) **entered into the holy place through His own blood once and for all and established an eternal redemption. Nor also did He frequently sacrifice Himself, like the high priest who each year went into the holy place with foreign blood. Otherwise He would have had to suffer often from the beginning of the world on. But now at the end of the world He as appeared once to lift up sin through His own sacrifice. Christ was sacrificed one time to take away the sin of many.**

Heb. 10:10–14, 18 – **By whose will** (Christ's) **we have been made holy, taking place through the once and for all sacrifice of the body of Christ. And each priest is installed so that he daily take care of service to God, and frequently make a simple offering which never could take away the sins. This One however, since He offered one sacrifice for sin which avails eternally, now sits at the right** [hand] **of God and from now on waits until His enemies are laid down as His foot-stool. For with one sacrifice He perfected forever those being made holy. For where for the same** (sins) **there is forgiveness, there no longer is any more sacrifice** [offering] **for sin.**

3. The holy Scriptures testify that Christ, with His one sacrifice, accomplished on the timber-trunk of the cross, won an everlasting redemption. It is contrary to this [testimony] when one says that Christ's body and blood, under the form of the bread and wine, must still be daily sacrificed for the sins of men and to acquire God's grace.

In John 19:30, Jesus says on the cross: **It is finished,** etc.

Heb. 1:3 – **Who, since He ... has accomplished the cleansing of our sins through Himself, has seated Himself at the right hand of the majesty, etc.**

Heb. 5:9 – **And since He is perfected, He has become for all those who obey Him the cause for their eternal salvation.**

Heb. 10:14, 18 – **For with one sacrifice He perfected into forever those being made holy. But, where there is forgiveness of same** (sins), **there no longer is any sacrifice for sin.**

4. The holy Supper is a Sacrament in which Christ's body and blood are distributed by means of the consecrated bread and wine; therefore, it cannot be a sacrifice through which we there bring something to God the Lord. The *forma sacrae coenae* consists of this, that we receive something; therefore, it cannot be a sacrifice by which we present something to God the Lord.

Mat. 26:26, Mark 14:22, Luke 22:19, 1 Cor. 11:23, 24 – **For the Lord Jesus in the night in which He was betrayed took bread, gave thanks and break it and said: Take, eat, this is My body which is broken for you; such do to My remembrance.**

Mat. 26:27, 28; Mark 14:23, 24; Luke 22:20; 1 Cor. 11:25 – **In the same way also** [He took] **the chalice after the evening meal and said: This chalice is the New Testament in My blood; such do, as often as you drink it, to My remembrance.**

5. The reason that Christ instituted the holy Supper is so that, through it, we be awakened to the remembrance His death and the sacrifice which He accomplished on the cross; therefore, [the holy Supper] cannot itself be an atoning sacrifice in which Christ actually is sacrificed anew.

Luke 22:19, 1 Cor. 11:24 – **Such do to remember Me.**

1 Cor. 11:25, 26 – **Such do, as often as you drink it, to remember Me. For as often as you eat of this bread and drink of this chalice, you should proclaim the Lord's death until He comes.**

6. Whenever the holy Scriptures in the New Testament mention sacrifices other than the sole atoning sacrifice of Christ, which He accomplished on the timber-trunk of the cross, at all times they are understood as inner, spiritual sacrifices. It flies in the face of this [principle] if one alleges that in addition to the sacrifice of Christ on the cross there is to be found in the New Testament yet another external, visible, and sin-atoning sacrifice. The spiritual, inner thank-offerings which are mentioned in the New Testament and are designated in a figurative manner, are these:

1. The spreading of the Gospel.

In Rom. 15:16 St. Paul says: **That I should be a servant of Christ among the Gentiles, to offer the Gospel of God, so that the heathen become a sacrifice acceptable to God, made holy through the Holy Spirit.**

2. The conversion of the Gentiles [heathen].

Rom. 15:16 – **So that the Gentiles might become a sacrifice acceptable to God,** etc.

Phi. 2:17 – **And even if I am sacrificed on account of the sacrifice and divine service of your faith,** I still **rejoice,** etc.

3. Prayer.

Heb. 5:7 – **And He** (Christ)**, in the days of His flesh, offered up prayers and petitions with loud screams and tears,** etc.

Rev. 5:8 – **And the twenty-four elders each had a golden vessel full of incense which are the prayers of the holy ones** [saints].

Rev. 8:4 – **And the smoke of the incense of the prayers of the saints went up from the hand of the angel before God.**

4. Thanksgiving.

Heb. 13:15 – **Now then, let us at all times offer through Him** (the Lord Christ) **the praise-offering to God, that is, the fruit of the lips which confess His name.**

5. Good works towards the needy.

Phi. 4:18 – I am fulfilled since I received through Epaphrodites that which came from you, a sweet scent, an acceptable sacrifice, pleasing to God.

Heb. 13:16 – Forget not to do the beneficial and to share, for such sacrifices please God well.

6. The killing off and crucifixion of the old man.

Rom. 12:1 – That you give over your lives for a sacrifice that is living, holy and well-pleasing to God, which happens to be your sensible service [divine service].

7. Suffering death for the sake of Christ and His Word.

Phi. 2:17 – And though I be sacrificed (killed) for the sake of the sacrifice and divine service [worship] of your faith, etc.

2 Tim. 4:6 – For I am already being sacrificed and the time of my departure is near.

Here it is also pertinent to note that at times the word "sacrifice" [offering] in the Old Testament is used in this way, [namely,] that by it is to be understood the inner, spiritual sacrifice.

Psa. 4:6 – Offer righteousness, etc.

Psa. 50:14,23 – Offer God thanks, etc. Whoever offers thanks, such a one glorifies Me, etc.

Psa. 51:17, 19 – The sacrifices which please God are a stricken-with-fear spirit ... Then the sacrifices of righteousness will please You.

Psa. 54:6 – Thus I will do a joy-offering for You, and thank Your Name, Lord, etc.

Psa. 107:22 – They should offer thanks.

Psa. 116:17 – I will offer thanks to You.

Psa. 141:2 – My prayer must be fit before you as an incense-offering [sacrifice]; my hands lifted up as an evening-sacrifice [offering].

Mal. 1:11; 3:3, 4 – In all places incense and a pure food-offering should be sacrificed to My Name. ... Then they shall bring the Lord food-offerings in righteousness,

... and the food-offerings of Judah will please the Lord,
etc.

Here again are pparent points of contention, that
the sacrifice of the Mass can indeed be demonstrated from
the types and verses of the Old Testament, as well as from
many testimonies of the New Testament.

1. That in Gen. 14:18 it is announced that Melchizedek,
king of Salem, brought out bread and wine (for an offering)
because he was a priest of God. Now then, Christ is a priest
after the order of Melchizedek (Psa. 110:4); therefore, He
has also instituted a sacrifice under the bread and wine.
ANSWER: **1.** In articles of faith one may not conclude with
certainty anything from the types and figures if such is not
first shown with clear, distinct verses from the Scriptures;
therefore, the sacrifice of the Mass would first have to be
established from the institution of the Supper, as from the
propria sede [L. – *proper seat*], before one would look back on
the types and figures. **2.** If it were proper to conclude that
Christ had to institute the sacrifice of His body under the
form of bread and wine, since Melchizedek (who was a type
of Christ) offered up bread and wine, then one could similarly
also conclude that [because] Aaron and other Levitical priests
sacrificed rams, calves and other animals, Christ therefore
had to institute the sacrifice of His body under the form of
rams and calves, since Aaron and other Levitical priests were
no less types of Christ than was Melchizedek. **3.** It is not
necessary that exactly the same thing which is found in the
type be found in what is portrayed; rather, it is enough that
in a few elements a comparison between the type and what
is being portrayed be indicated. The bread and wine which
Melchizedek carried forth points to this: that Christ in the
holy Supper distributes His true body and blood by means of
the consecrated bread and wine; but it does not follow that
under the form of the bread and wine the body and blood of
Christ are sacrificed, even if it were previously established
that Melchizedek sacrificed bread and wine. Rather, it would

be enough that in a few elements a comparison be indicated between Christ and Melchizedek. **4.** It may not be shown from the Scripture that Melchizedek in those days sacrificed bread and wine; for in the holy language [the original Hebrew] there is such a word which actually means he had carried it forth, namely to Abraham and his people who were coming out of the slaughter (battle) in order to renew them. Even though Abraham and his fellow travelers had substantial booty with them, Melchizedek no less wanted herewith to demonstrate his good will towards them by bringing them bread and wine. And even though Melchizedek was a priest, it does not follow that at that particular time he sacrificed (offered) bread and wine, though it could have occurred at other times. Even could it also be shown that Melchizedek had sacrificed bread and wine on that occasion, yet by the wildest stretch this would not establish the sacrifice of the Mass, for it does not follow that precisely (*idem numero*) what Melchizedek used for his offering had to be in Christ's sacrifice. Rather, it would be enough that a comparison could be found in a few elements, as for example these: Melchizedek offered up bread and wine and thereupon distributed same to Abraham and his servants. So also Christ sacrificed His body and blood on the timber-trunk of the cross to God; in the holy Supper He gives us to eat and drink the very same body and blood. **5.** The Epistle to the Hebrews has indeed painstakingly interpreted the type of Melchizedek, especially in chapter 7, and yet has nowhere implied that in it a comparison between Melchizedek and Christ is to be sought, [to wit], even as Melchizedek sacrificed bread and wine, so also Christ, under the form of bread and wine, sacrificed His body and blood in the holy Supper. Not so! Rather, in the Epistle to the Hebrews a comparison between Melchizedek and Christ is employed in the following elements: First of all, Melchizedek was simultaneously a king and a priest; so also Christ. Secondly, Melchizedek was the King of Salem, that is, of peace; so Christ is the true Prince of Peace.

Thirdly, Melchizedek blessed Abraham, and he also took the tenth [the tithe] from him and from the Levites that were in his land; so also is Christ higher and greater than all the Levitical priests of the Old Testament and through Him we are blessed. Fourthly, Melchizedek is presented without father or mother or ancestor [i.e., family], and had neither a beginning nor an end of life. Thus also Christ, according to His divine nature, had no mother; according to His human nature, had no father; and, according to His divinity, had neither beginning nor ending to His days. Fifthly, in his priesthood Melchizedek had no descendants; so also, Christ is the sole Priest of the New Testament and abides into eternity. **6.** Also, it does not follow that since Christ is an eternal Priest after the order of Melchizedek that therefore He must have a daily atoning sacrifice; for in that Christ is called an eternal Priest, the Scriptures (and particularly the Epistle to the Hebrews) give the following reasons: First of all, because His personage exists eternally, Heb. 7:24 – **This One, however, in that He remains eternally, has an imperishable priesthood.** Subsequently, because the power of His atoning sacrifice, which He accomplished on the cross once and for all, endures eternally, Heb. 5:9, 10 – **And in that He was perfected, He became for all who are obedient to Him a cause for eternal salvation, called by God a High Priest according to the Order of Melchizedek** (cf. also Heb. 7:25, 10:14). Finally, because He there continually intercedes for us, which intercession (no less than the sacrifice) is a part of His High Priestly office, Heb. 7:24, 25 – **This One, however ... has an imperishable priesthood. As a result, He also continually can make saved those who come to God through Him, and He continually dwells there to make intercession for us.** These reasons concerning why Christ will be called an eternal Priest after the order of Melchizedek, the Scripture itself gives us. Concerning this matter, however, should it be necessary for the eternal priesthood of Christ that He conduct a daily atoning sacrifice, then it would follow that such a sacrifice would also be necessary in eternal life; *item* [furthermore], that Christ would have to perform such a sacrifice by Himself and not through the Mass-priests. **7.** To say nothing of the fact that there is a marked distinction between the sacrifice of Melchizedek (if it indeed was a sacrifice) and the sacrifice of the Mass: Melchizedek brought forth bread and wine, but in the sacrifice of the Mass there no longer is bread and wine according to its nature and essence but merely the form of bread and wine. Melchizedek gave Abraham and his servants such [real] bread and wine. In the sacrifice of the Mass, only bread and not wine is given to the laity; indeed, often the bread is also not distributed but laid aside and later adored in the procession. Melchizedek wanted to feed bread and wine to the living; in the sacrifice of the Mass, [however,] one wants to sacrifice, under the form of bread and wine, for the living and the dead. **8.** To say nothing also of the fact that the distinction between Melchizedek and the Aaronite priests may not be looked for [found] in this case—that only Melchizedek, and by no means the Aaronites, had sacrificed bread and wine—since in the Aaronitic sacrifice the bread and wine were also used, Exo. 29:38, 40 – **Every day you are continually to offer two year-old lambs on it. ... And with one lamb a tenth of meal cake mixed with a fourth of a Hin** [Hebrew – ca. a liter] **of crushed oil and a fourth of a Hin of wine for a drink offering. 9.** If the sacrifice of Melchizedek were also still to be observed daily in the Christian Church of the New Testament, then it would follow that Christ has not fulfilled and abolished [i.e., fulfilled] all the figures and types of the Old Testament—which is contrary to the Scriptures (Col. 2, Heb. 10).

2. That the Passover lamb is a type of the holy Supper, but then the paschal lamb had [also] been a sacrifice; therefore, the holy Supper is also a sacrifice. ANSWER: **1.** In articles of faith one cannot draw any certain conclusions from types/figures if they are not previously established by

clear texts of Scriptures; therefore, the sacrifice of the Mass would have to first be established from the words of the institution. **2.** But, on what basis will one prove with certainty that the Passover lamb was a sacrifice? It is the same little lamb [which] was slaughtered by each head of household in the community of Israel and eaten with special ceremony in remembrance of the Exodus from Egypt; and the post of the door along with the top beam of the doorway was smeared with its blood (Exo. 12). However, sacrifices were not to be performed in houses, but upon the altar of the Lord by the Levitical priests. Consequently, the Passover lamb was actually a Sacrament of the Old Testament and not a sacrifice. One would be unable to produce anything certain from the holy Scriptures which might prove that the Easter-lamb was sacrificed. **3.** The little Passover lamb points not only to the holy Supper, but rather, in general, to Christ, who was slaughtered on the timber-trunk of the cross as the innocent Paschal Lamb and who feeds us in the holy Supper with His flesh—just as the Passover lamb was slaughtered and was eaten by the children of Israel. The holy apostles ate the true body of Christ in the holy Supper; however, it does not follow that Christ first sacrificed His body; for the offering up of His body, which was signified by the slaughtering of the Passover lamb, occurred later on the timber-trunk of the cross. By all rights, Christ was the Lamb of God before His slaughter on the cross (John 1:29), **that was slain before the beginning of the world** (Rev. 13:8). Therefore, He very well could distribute His true body to the disciples in the first Supper, even though the slaughter and sacrifice actually took place afterwards on the timber-trunk of the cross. **4.** If the Passover lamb was indeed sacrificed, it would, however, have been a bloody offering. Consequently, such sacrifice would not have pointed to the sacrifice of the Mass (in which they say that Christ is sacrificed in an unbloody manner). Rather, it would have pointed to the bloody sacrifice upon the timber-trunk of the cross, in which the Lord

Christ gave His life as a sacrifice and shed His blood, just as the little Passover lamb in former days was slaughtered and its blood smeared on the [door] posts, [and] just as it is also adequately attested to in John 19:36 that the figure in the slaughter of the little Passover lamb is presented in such a way as to be fulfilled on the timber-trunk of the cross. **5.** If then, from the way in which the type of the Easter lamb is presented the Lord Christ still had to be sacrificed daily, it would follow that with His death the Lord Christ had still not fulfilled and abolished all the types of the Old Testament. It would also follow that Christ still is being daily sacrificed in a bloody manner just as the little Easter-lamb was sacrificed in a bloody manner; *item* [furthermore], that the sacrifice of the Mass could also be performed by the laity just as the little Passover lamb was slaughtered by each head of household. **6.** In Exo. 8:26, Moses expressly says that the Israelites could not sacrifice in Egypt. However, the little paschal lamb was slaughtered in Egypt; therefore, it would not be a sacrifice. Also, nothing is mentioned there about the little Passover lamb of God the Lord; rather, it was completely devoured by the Israelites. In Exo. 12:27 it is written, it is **a Paschal-offering** [sacrifice] to the Lord; yet, it is to be noted that the word **Zebach**, which in that very place is used in the holy tongue [i.e., Hebrew], in general denotes a slaughter (Deu. 12:15, 22; 1 Sam. 28:24; 1 Kin. 19:21) and is applied to spiritual sacrifices which are thus designated in a figurative manner (Psa. 50:14, Psa. 51:19). Thus it is also written in Mark 14:12 – **And on the first Day of the sweetened** [unleavened] **bread, when one sacrifices the Easter lamb,** etc.; in that very place, the Greek text once again uses the word θύειν, which in general means "to slaughter" (Mat. 22:4, Acts 10:13, etc.). Finally, it is written in 1 Cor. 5:7 – **For we also have an Easter Lamb, which is Christ, sacrificed for us,** which declares Christ as being the blameless Lamb of God, sacrificed for us. It does not establish, however, that Christ is to be sacrificed daily in the Mass in an unbloody manner;

rather, He was sacrificed for us once and for all time on the timber-trunk of the cross. **7.** But, as [previously] mentioned, we would not strongly advocate that the little Passover lamb actually was, so to speak, a sacrifice; for if that much is permitted, then it still cannot be shown therefrom that Christ is to be daily sacrificed in the Mass offering. Rather the type of the slaughtering and sacrificing of the Passover lamb is by all rights fulfilled by Christ on the timber-trunk of the cross no less than other types of the Old Testament [were fulfilled by Him].

3. That in Exo. 24:6–8 the Old Testament was established with the blood of the slaughtered sacrifice [offering]; therefore it follows that Christ's body and blood also had to first be sacrificed before He could institute His body and blood to be received in the holy Supper and thereby establish the New Testament. ANSWER: **1.** From this, it would follow that Christ would first have had visibly and in a bloody manner to sacrifice Himself and shed His blood (just as the Old Testament sacrifices were slaughtered in those days) before He could institute His holy Supper. What would that be other than vindicating divine Wisdom? (Mat. 11:19) **2.** The entire New Testament testifies that the sacrifices of the Old Testament were directed to Christ to the extent that they were fulfilled by Him on the timber-trunk of the cross; but nowhere can it be found that Christ was also sacrificed in the holy Supper in fulfillment of such types.

4. That in 1 Sam. 2:35 God the Lord says to Eli – **But I will raise up for Myself a faithful priest who shall do what pleases My heart and soul; him I will build a permanent house so that he there may always walk before My Anointed.** This is to be understood as [referring to] the daily sacrifice of the Mass in the New Testament. ANSWER: **1.** From the succeeding words it appears that this text literally means that instead of Eli, God the Lord wanted to choose a different, faithful, and diligent high priest (not [waiting until] the New Testament, but soon thereafter) who would walk before His anointed (that is, the King) according to His good pleasure; for thus it soon follows in v. 36 – **And whoever is left from your house will come and fall down before him for a silver penny and a piece of bread and will say: please allow me a part of the priesthood that I might eat a bit of bread. 2.** And this prophecy was directly fulfilled when Zadok became high priest at the time of King Solomon as a replacement of Abithar in 1 Kin. 2:27. **3.** Even if this text were to be applied in a spiritual manner to the sacrifice of Christians in the New Testament, the sacrifice of the Mass could still not be drawn from it, because in the New Testament—aside from the atoning sacrifice of Christ on the cross—no other sacrifice could be thought of other than the spiritual, inner sacrifice of Christians.

5. [That the words of] Pro. 9:1, 2 (**Wisdom built her house and raised up seven columns. She slaughtered her cattle and carried forth her wine and prepared her table.**) also point to the sacrifice of the Mass in the New Testament. ANSWER: **1.** An article of faith may never be proven from such allegorical interpretations if such did not first occur in a clear Scripture reference. **2.** How may the words which follow in v. 3 be applied to the sacrifice of the Mass: **And** (she)[Wisdom] **sent out her maids to invite the city from the top of the palace,** etc. ? **3.** If one would interpret this text in a spiritual manner, then it must in general point to the blessings of the Gospel. **4.** Even if we allow that it applies specifically to the holy Supper, yet it still does not follow that in the holy Supper Christ's body and blood are actually sacrificed; rather, it is sufficient that the same body and the same blood of Christ with which we are nourished in the Supper was actually sacrificed on the timber-trunk of the cross.

6. That Isa. 19:21 (**For the Lord will become known to the Egyptians, and the Egyptians will be acquainted with the Lord at that time and will serve Him with sacrifice and food offerings,** etc.) is, again, understood as the sacrifice of the Mass. ANSWER: **1.** The prophet is here prophesying about the calling of the Egyptians and other Gentiles into the fellowship of the kingdom of Christ in the New Testament. Accordingly, what is said in this verse about sacrifice is to be understood as referring to the spiritual, inner sacrifice which is mentioned only in the New Testament. For it is common practice of the prophets that they, with such words, which are taken from the Old Testament situation, describe the circumstances of the Church in the New Testament. **2.** If on this account one wants to allegorize this text, then, according to the interpretation of the New Testament, the Lord Christ has to be understood as the altar (on which spiritual sacrifices are pleasing to God). By sacrifices are to be understood the spreading of the Gospel, prayer, thanksgiving, the killing off of the old man, kindness, etc. **3.** But if one insists that such prophecies of the Old Testament be interpreted literally and to show from this that Christians in the New Testament must have (no less than the Israelites in the Old Testament) an external, visible, daily atoning sacrifice, then one could similarly show that, according to the letter, there is even greater reason for billy-goats, calves, rams, and other [animals] be sacrificed in the New Testament (Psa. 51:21, Isa. 60:7, etc.).

7. That Isa. 66:21 (**And from among them** [from the children of Israel] **I will take priests and Levites, says the Lord)** [and] Jer. 33:18 (**There shall never fail to be such, priests and Levites before Me who do burnt offerings and ignite food offerings and slaughter sacrifices**) point to the Mass-priests in the New Testament, who daily sacrifice Christ's body and blood in an unbloody manner. ANSWER: **1.** If one wishes to understand this and similar prophecies literally, then one would conclude with good Jewishness that in the New Testament one should elect priests from the tribe of Levi, slaughter young bulls and calves, and erect only one altar. **2.** But if one would understand this in a spiritual manner (which of necessity must be the case), then one must understand the priests to be all the true Christians in the

New Testament, for that is how it is interpreted in 1 Pet. 2:9, Rev. 1:6, 5:10, 20:6. By "sacrifice" one must understand only spiritual thank-offerings, as there is no other sacrifice by Christians mentioned in the New Testament. **3.** Moreover, it is to be noted that nowhere in the New Testament is the name "priest" to be understood as referring only to teachers and preachers; rather, this name in general designates all Christians. **4.** And if indeed the Mass-priests want so eagerly to be understood as being referred to by the designation of priests and Levites, then they may also apply to themselves what is written in Luke 10:31, 32, that the priest and the Levite passed by the poor wounded one and did not take care of him.

8. That the Antichrist's taking away of the daily sacrifice in Dan. 8:12 refers to the sacrifice of the Mass. ANSWER: **1.** Literally, only Antiochus, who had forbidden and hindered the Jews in their worship, is meant here (1 Macc. 1:47). **2.** In a spiritual manner [the passage] refers to the Antichrist, who obscures the teaching about the atoning sacrifice of Christ, which He accomplished on the cross, and who pathetically perverts true worship, which is the spiritual daily sacrifice of the New Testament.

9. That Mal. 1:10, 11 (**And the food-offering from your hands is not acceptable to Me. But from the rising of the sun until its setting My Name will be glorified among the Gentiles, and in all places incense and pure food-offerings shall be sacrificed to My Name,** etc.) once more signifies the sacrifice of the Mass. ANSWER: **1.** From the words of the prophet which follow: **For My Name shall be glorified among the heathen, says the Lord of Sabaoth,** and especially from St. Paul in Rom. 15:16, there is enough to conclude that [the text] is here speaking of the spiritual sacrifice of the common call to the Gentiles; for St. Paul there says: **For the sake of the grace which is given me from God that I should be a servant of Christ among the Gentiles, to offer the Gospel of God so that the Gentiles**

become a sacrifice acceptable to God, etc., which words are gloriously parallel to the words of the prophet Malachi. **2.** It is indeed the common practice of the prophets to describe with the words of the Old Testament the worship of the New Testament, as can be shown from many references, especially from Joel 2. Therefore, then, in such prophecies the explanation should not be forced upon the letter [literally], but rather the interpretation should be taken from the New Testament. Thus, if one presses for a literal [interpretation] of this prophecy of Malachi and would force an external, visible sacrifice from it, then one would also have to say that in the New Testament such an outward burning of incense must also be practiced, just as was customary in the Old Testament. Isa. 66:20 speaks of this food offering in the New Testament, that it should be sacrificed upon the holy mountain in Jerusalem. If one insists on a literal understanding of such [a passage], it would follow that also in the New Testament there is to be sacrifice only in the temple in Jerusalem.

10. That in John. 4:21, 23, [when] Christ says to the woman of Samaria: **The time is coming when you will worship the Father neither on this mountain nor at Jerusalem; but the time is coming and already is when genuine worshipers will worship the Father in spirit and in truth,** already here by "worship" is understood a special worship, namely a sacrifice, the sacrifice of the Mass in particular. ANSWER: Nothing is being said here about sacrifice, but rather about prayer. The woman of Samaria asked the Lord Christ at which place one should worship, for the Jews had the custom from divine command that in prayer they turned their face towards the tabernacle and later towards the temple at Jerusalem; contrarily, the Samaritans worshiped on the Mount of Gerazim. And so this woman asked the Lord Christ which party was correct. To answer this question, the Lord Christ instructed this woman that in the New Testament prayer and divine service was no longer bound to a particular spot or place as in the Old Testament. Rather, the true worshiper would worship in spirit and in truth; but how can the sacrifice of the Mass be forced from this?

11. That in the institution of the Supper the Lord Christ, under the form of bread and wine, offered Himself in an unbloody manner to His heavenly Father and thereupon commanded that the apostles and all their successors (the priests) should do the same, for He says, **do this**; that is, also sacrifice as I have done. That Christ sacrificed Himself to the Father in an unbloody manner is proved by His statement that His body is being given into death and His blood is being shed. [These words] cannot be applied to His subsequent giving of His body into death and the shedding of His blood on the cross because Christ is speaking *in praesenti* [*in the present*]; His body **is being** given now into death and His blood **is being** shed now. ANSWER: For once this matter is beginning at the proper place—that one shows from the words of the institution, as from the chief foundation of this article, whether the holy Supper is a sacrifice or not. From there it will receive authoritative credit and worth. However, the entire conclusion rests upon these two reasons: First of all, because Christ speaks *in praesenti* that His body **is being** given at that time, [that] His blood **is being** shed, [and] simply because the word **do** sometimes means to sacrifice, therefore, Christ sacrificed Himself in the holy Supper. Concerning the first, this very reason is quite uncertain, for it is quite common in the Scripture that future matters are described with such words as though they are occurring now or are ready to happen, not to mention the Old Testament prophecies in which the same [mode of speaking] is commonly used. Thus, the following places are to be noted: Mat. 26:24 – **The Son of Man indeed goes there, as is written about Him; yet woe to the man through whom the Son of Man will be betrayed**; John 13:31 – **Now is the Son of Man transfigured**; John 17:11 – **And now I am no longer in the world;**

1 Tim. 4:6 – **For I am being offered up and the time of my departure is here.** Accordingly, since the beginning had already occurred through Judas' betrayal and through the inner sufferings of Christ, note that Christ speaks there *in praesenti*: His body **is being** given into death and His blood **is being** shed. Thus, St. Paul points to [that text] when He says that the Lord Christ instituted the holy Supper in the night in which He was being betrayed (1 Cor. 11:23). Now then, so that there is no room for doubt whether this giving of the body of Christ and the shedding of His blood took place on the cross or in the holy Supper, it is especially to be noted that the Epistle to the Hebrews (7:27, 9:12) testifies: The Lord Christ sacrificed Himself one time and through a single sacrifice He won an eternal redemption. If, then, Christ became a one-time sacrifice for our sins while on the cross (as the entire Scripture testifies and no Christian can deny) then He did not sacrifice Himself in the holy Supper; otherwise, it would be untrue that He sacrificed Himself only one time. If Christ already sacrificed Himself in the holy Supper, what would be the need for Him to sacrifice Himself again on the timber-trunk of the cross? Moreover, had Christ sacrificed Himself to His heavenly Father in the holy Supper, under the form of bread and wine, it would have occurred in order to portray the bloody sacrifice on the timber-trunk of the cross; and in such a form the holy Supper would still belong to the Old Testament, to which such figures and types are proper (peculiar). Finally, if the words of Christ were to indicate that even on that occasion His body was given into death and His blood was poured out, it would follow that in the holy Supper He was not sacrificed in an unbloody manner (as the defenders of the sacrifice of the Mass purport), but rather that He truly did pour out His blood, which, of course, could not have taken place in an unbloody manner. [Furthermore], it is not valid for one to say that the blood of Christ was poured out under the form of the wine, for the consecrated chalice was not poured out by Christ; rather He

distributed it to the disciples. Concerning the other claim, namely, that [the Hebrew word for] **do** sometimes means as much as to sacrifice, this claim is as weak as the first one; for **1.** it is not sufficient for this matter that **do** is at times used to mean sacrifice. Rather, it must be shown that it is also used in this way in the words of institution of the holy Supper. **2.** However, such may not be demonstrated; on the contrary, [from the context] the opposite can be adequately established, [i.e.,] that it does not especially mean so much "to sacrifice"; for Christ does not simply say, **Do**, that is, "sacrifice." Rather He adds: **This do**, thereby pointing to the foregoing; namely, that they should eat the consecrated bread and drink of the consecrated chalice, and do this to His remembrance as thereafter He additionally states. **3.** So that we do not have to doubt this interpretation, it is to be noted that St. Paul in 1 Cor. 11:25, in describing the other part of the holy Supper, especially adds: **Do this, as often as you drink it, for My remembrance**, so that he clearly testifies that the word "**do**" in the holy Supper means nothing else than eating the consecrated bread and drinking [from] the consecrated chalice to the memory of Christ. **4.** When the word "**do**" in the holy language (Hebrew) is applied to mean sacrifice, there is always something [in the context] from which such can be clearly and distinctly concluded; but such is not to be found in the words of the institution. **5.** Also, that with the words, "**this do**," Christ did not really intend to say, "Sacrifice My body and blood in the holy Supper, just as I have now done," we establish as follows: If Christ, in the institution of the Supper had, under the form of bread and wine, offered up to His heavenly Father His body and blood with clear words, gestures, and ceremonies, then either it would have occurred with audible words and visible ceremonies and actions, or it would have taken place quietly and in secret so that none of the apostles either saw or was aware of anything of the kind. But of this nothing is mentioned. Yet, had Christ offered Himself to His heavenly Father with clear words and visible, special actions, how could this have escaped the notice of the holy evangelists to the extent that they passed over it in silence, even though one would assert the sacrifice the Lord Christ instituted thereby as an article of faith, in fact, as a chief article of faith? Were, however, the sacrifice to have taken place quietly and in secret, how could Christ with the words, "**This do**," have indicated such a sacrifice, since the apostles saw or noticed nothing of what the Lord Christ did? Which conclusion is justly to be drawn?

12. That in Acts 13:2 it is announced that the holy apostles served the Lord, that is, in open fellowship performed the sacrifice, for the word λειτουργεῖν actually means to perform divine worship in public assembly. ANSWER: **1.** The word λειτουργεῖν or "to serve," is used in certain distinct ways in the holy Scriptures and in general means nothing more than performing the duties of a public office. In Rom. 13:6 political authorities are called by this name since the are servants of God; in Heb. 1:14, the holy angels are called λειτουργικὰ πνεθματὰ [or] "serving spirits." Otherwise, this word also means as much as demonstrating service and helpfulness (Rom. 15:27, 2 Cor. 9:12, etc.). **2.** What sort of divine service the holy apostles carried out in public assembly in those days is to be concluded from the foregoing [verses]; for in the first verse the prophets and teachers are referred to. From this is to be concluded that they would have preached the Word, administered the holy Supper, prayed and given thanks to God—just as all these things still happen today in the assembling of Christians. Such service, although it is directed towards the salvation of people, nevertheless is principally performed for God, since everything jointly is meant to glorify God—for the sake of which political authority is labeled as a servant of God (Rom. 13:6) because in all its governance it should rule to the glory of God. **3.** And even if the Greek text had used a word which actually meant "sacrifice" and nothing else, it still would have to be understood as referring to no other sacrifice than a spiritual sacrifice—specifically the spreading of the Gospel, even as St. Paul says in Rom. 15:16, that he offers/sacrifices for the Gospel.

13. That in 1 Cor. 10:18 ff. the apostle compares the table of the Lord (upon which the holy Supper is administered) with the altars of the Gentiles (heathen) and with the altar of the Jews. Because sacrifices were made upon these altars, so also sacrifices are to be made upon the table of the Lord.

ANSWER: **1.** Actually the apostle is there not speaking about altars of the heathen, but about the public meals which they held in honor of their idols and in which they gorged themselves on what they had previously sacrificed to their idols, as the context of the text adequately shows. The Christians at Corinth did not sacrifice alongside the heathen on their altars; rather, they partook with them of the idol sacrifices. [Paul] warns against this practice and indicates that they cannot simultaneously be participants of the Lord's table and of the devil's table, as well as not simultaneously drink from the Lord's chalice and from the devil's chalice (vv. 20, 21). 2. Accordingly, we turn this conclusion around in this way: Just as at that time those who, along with the heathen, ate from the idol sacrifices did not themselves sacrifice, but even so participated in the idol sacrifice and thus became participants of the devil's table, so also Christians who make their way to the table of the Lord and eat of the consecrated bread and also drink from the consecrated chalice do not indeed sacrifice; even so, they become participants of the body and blood of Christ which were sacrificed on the cross. The idol sacrifice of which certain Christians at that time ate with the heathen had not been sacrificed on the same table at which they found themselves; rather, it took place prior on the altar, as can be deduced from verse 28. Thus, if one ever wanted to stretch the apostle's comparison this broadly, it would follow that Christ's body and blood, which we receive in the holy Supper, is also a sacrifice; however, it would not be sacrificed there, but rather this offering up willingly occurred previously on the timber-trunk of the cross. **3.** When the apostle says in v. 18: **See the Israelites after the flesh. Those who ate the sacrifice, are they not in the fellowship of the altar**, in essence he wants to say: "Just as some of those who ate of what the Israelites had previously sacrificed came into the fellowship of their altar and were regarded as their fellow believers, thus some of those who knowingly and deliberately eat of what was previously offered to idols by the heathen come into the fellowship of the table of the devil, because the very same food had been previously sacrificed to the heathen idols, that is, to the devil; and these very meals were held to honor the idols, that is, the devil."

14. That when a people are to be brought together through a special religion or worship, then such must be accomplished through an outward, visible sacrifice, as one can see from the fact that not only the Israelites in the Old Testament, but also the heathen at all times sacrificed in their worship. It follows therefrom that reason teaches that also Christians must have an outward sacrifice through which their religion becomes drawn together. ANSWER: **1.** Articles of faith must be established from the clear Word of God, not from the opinions of reason. **2.** The Israelites in the Old Testament sacrificed because they had a clear command from God the Lord, and these very offerings pointed to Christ. Moreover, since He has now come, such types of sacrifice are held up in the New Testament as shadows.* **3.** That the Gentiles sacrificed is not [an action] inspired by reason; rather, it comes from superstitious mimicry. For since they heard that the Israelites sacrificed in the worship, they wanted to imitate them, or rather to ape them. **4.** Consequently, just as the Jewish sacrifice in the New Testament, as well as the sacrifice of the heathen, did not please God (namely, because they did not have a command to sacrifice) it will thus obviously

---

* "*Aufheben*," translated here as "held up," also means "repealed" or "abolished," terms which also readily apply to types which have been replaced by the Real Thing. Ed.

not please God when the Christians in the New Testament want to bring to God the Lord an outward, visible atoning sacrifice, since they also have no divine command to do so. 5. In the New Testament, the outward, Levitical worship, and thus also the type of the daily visible sacrifice, is abolished; however, [it still serves] to direct Christians to offer up inner, spiritual thank-offerings to God the Lord and daily to remember in true faith the atoning sacrifice performed on the timber-trunk of the cross, especially through the reception of the holy Supper, which holy Supper now in the New Testament is, along with other motives (grounds), also the *nervus* [sinew, tendon, i.e., that which ties together] and bond for the public gathering of Christians.

15. That no flesh (meat) may be eaten and no blood may be drunk if it is not first slaughtered and thereby prepared for consumption. Now then, not only in these days is Christ's body and blood distributed to us in the holy Supper after He gave His body and shed His blood on the cross; but the Lord Christ, in the first Supper, actually distributed His body and blood to be eaten and drunk by His disciples. Therefore, a slaughter (even though in an unbloody manner) must have preceded it. ANSWER: **1.** This conclusion originates from a strong Capernaism, for the Capernaites understood Christ's proclamations (John 6) to refer to natural consumption of His body and blood, as one eats and ingests other common, natural food—which food, of necessity, had to be previously prepared for consumption. **2.** But far be it from us to think of the high and holy Supper of the Lord Christ in such a Capernaitish manner. In the holy Supper we do not receive common, natural food; rather, the life-creating body of Christ. We do not eat and drink of it in a common, natural manner, but in a mysterious, supernatural manner. Through the consecrated bread and the consecrated chalice we receive the true body and the true blood of Christ, which requires no slaughter or sacrifice; rather, it is sufficient for this sacramental consumption that Christ's body is sacramentally united with the blessed bread and Christ's blood with the consecrated chalice. **3.** Also, had it been necessary for some sort of slaughter to precede the institution of the holy Supper, then it would no longer be an unbloody sacrifice, as they usually [call it]. For what does that mean: an unbloody slaughter, an outpouring of blood without bloodshed, etc.?

Thus far we have heard how if one wants to prove the sacrifice of the Mass from Scripture, there is little solid evidence for it to be found there. We have put off (deferred) other pretexts taken from reason because they are readily answered from the same. Furthermore, we also want to see how the proponents of the sacrifice of the Mass set out from the Scriptures to respond to the above proposed arguments and think to defend themselves against them, in that they say:

1. That a distinction must be made between the highest High Priest of the New Testament (namely, Christ) and the other subordinate priests, just as between the bloody and the unbloody sacrifice. That Christ is called the only High Priest of the New Testament is to be understood [as meaning] that He solely and alone is the highest High Priest; herewith, however, nothing is taken away from the Mass priests, who are the subordinate priests. That when the Epistle to the Hebrews also states Christ sacrificed Himself one time, such is to be understood as the bloody offering up on the timber-trunk of the cross; herewith, however, is nothing taken away from the sacrifice of the Mass, in which Christ is sacrificed in an unbloody manner. ANSWER: **1.** If one could first have proven the sacrifice of the Mass from clear and plain passages of the Scripture, one might thus devise such a distinction that he could compare with other passages of Scripture; [such support], however, is completely lacking, for one can produce nothing certain from the Scriptures to support this sacrifice of the Mass, as we have thus far seen. **2.** The holy Scripture in general speaks to this, that the Lord Christ is the only High Priest of the New Testament and that He sacrificed Himself one time on the timber-trunk of the cross; so then, one should not produce such fabricated distinctions from outside the Scripture. Otherwise, nothing can any longer remain certain in the Scriptures, for one could knock it all down with contrived distinctions. **3.** That one would create many subordinate priests in the New Testament, who no longer offer God the Lord external, visible sacrifices—as did the Levitical Priests in the Old Testament—runs counter to Scripture; for it places the Levitical priests, who were many in the Old Testament, in opposition to the one and only Christ, Hebr. 7:23, 24 – **And there were many who became priests, because death did not allow them to remain; but this One, because He abides forever, has an imperishable priesthood.** From this, we conclude that many Levitical priests were ordained because death would not allow them to live, but Christ, the High Priest of the New Testament lives forever; therefore, He does not require any subordinate priests in the New Testament. **4.** What pertains to the high priestly office of the Lord Christ, He accomplished Himself without the assistance of any human being, since that very same high priestly office encompasses within itself the atoning sacrifice for all of mankind. He is the sole Atoner and Mediator; therefore, no other man may be exalted to such honor. **5.** The Lord Christ required no subordinate priests for His sacrifice; instead, as the Epistle to the Hebrews clearly states (7:27) – **For it was not necessary, as with those high priests, ... to make a daily sacrifice; ... for that He did once and for all when He sacrificed Himself.** Heb. 9:12, 14, ... **Rather He with His own blood entered the holy place one time and established an eternal redemption. ... Who sacrificed Himself to God ... by the Holy Spirit,** etc. Here again a clear contradiction if one alleges that Christ is sacrificed daily through the subordinate priests; whatever He does through others, that He does not do Himself without means [i.e., He does it with means]; and, whatever He Himself does without means, that He does not do through others (John 4:1, 2). **6.** The Scriptures nowhere call the Church's servants (clergy) specifically "priests," but rather "shepherds," "teachers," "preachers," etc. However, when Christians are called priests in the New Testament, it is because of the spiritual, inward sacrifice of thanksgiving which they offer to God the Lord; accordingly, since the clergy are nowhere specifically called priests, other than the same name which they have in common with other Christians, they do not possess any special sacrifice. Rather, their sacrifices are to be spiritual thank-offerings, the same as the sacrifices of other Christians. **7.** The holy Scriptures frequently describe the office, as well as the ordination, of the clergy, especially in 1 Cor. 12, Eph. 4:1, 1 Tim. 3, Tit. 1, etc., but nowhere is it ascribed to them that they should sacrifice for the people's sin or raise up among themselves special Mass-priests. It is easy to comprehend therefrom what is to be [understood] when they say that Christ is the only Master and the chief Shepherd and yet has undershepherds; thus, He can, all the same, have underpriests and still remain the [unique] High Priest, [which is to say] that there is a considerable difference between the office of a teacher and the high-priestly office of Christ. He has commissioned His apostles to the office of teacher, but not to the works which belongs to the high-priestly office, as that consists of the offering up of His body and blood; for He Himself performed the elements of His high priestly office without means and required no subordinate priests for that. The sacrifice of Christ took place for the atoning of sin, but then He alone is the One who purchased the atonement for us. **8.** In like manner, we respond to the distinction made between the bloody and unbloody sacrifice of Christ, that this distinction is not only never made in the Scriptures, but that this distinction also runs counter to Scripture; for the Scriptures testify in general that Christ sacrificed Himself only one time (Heb. 7:27; 9:12, 25, 28; 10:10). If, however, Christ is still being sacrificed daily by the Mass-priests, then it would no longer be a once-and-for-all accomplished sacrifice, whether such a sacrifice occurs in a bloody or an unbloody manner. **9.** Beyond that, the sacrifice of Christ is always described in the Scriptures as a bloody sacrifice, Heb. 9:22, 25, 26 – **And without pouring out of blood no forgiveness takes place. ... also not that He** (Christ) **offers Himself often, as the High Priest enters into the holy place every year with strange blood** [i.e., not his own]; **otherwise He would have had to suffer often from the beginning of the world on. Now however, at the end of the world, He appeared one time, to abolish sin through His own sacrifice.** In this and similar passages of Scripture, the **sacrifice** and Christ's **pouring out of His blood** are at all times set side by side. That's why no unbloody sacrifice can be fabricated; rather, if Christ were being sacrificed by the priests in the holy Supper, such would have to occur with the shedding of blood. In addition, if Christ still were to be sacrificed daily, then He still daily would have to make satisfaction for sin; for the Scripture at all times sets side by side His **offering up** and His **adequate satisfaction** for the sins of the world (Heb. 9:26, etc.). If, however, Christ still had to make daily satisfaction, then the satisfaction and atonement of Christ which took place on the cross would not be complete—which expressly runs counter to the passage from Heb. 10:14 – **For with one sacrifice He has eternally perfected those who are sanctified. 10.** If Christ in the holy Supper actually had sacrificed Himself in an unbloody manner, that would indeed have taken place for the reconciliation with God and for the payment of the sin of all mankind; but then why would it have been further necessary that Christ later on offered Himself up once more in a bloody manner on the cross? **For where there is forgiveness of sins, there is no longer any sacrifice for sins** (Heb. 10:17).

    2. That if the Supper already is a Sacrament, then it can still indeed be a sacrifice at the same time, namely, to the extent that Christ's body under the form of the bread and wine is first sacrificed to God and thereafter is received by the communicants—just as in the Old Testament the Israelites made a sacrifice to God the Lord and thereafter ate the offering. ANSWER: Because of the institution of Christ, the form of the holy Supper consists of this: that we eat the consecrated bread and drink [from] the consecrated chalice. This action is totally perverted if one wants to make the holy Supper into a sacrifice; for the form of the sacrifice consists of giving, that we offer something to God the Lord. The form of the Sacrament consists of receiving—that we receive something from the hand of the Lord. However, giving and receiving are opposites. Also, it is not enough to assert that Christ's body and blood first be sacrificed before it can be received; rather, it must be clearly established from Christ's institution.

CHAPTER 25

WHETHER THE SACRIFICE OF THE MASS IS AN
ATONING SACRIFICE
FOR SIN AND FOR THE PUNISHMENT OF SIN.

 lthough there is enough information in the previous chapter regarding the answer to this question—for if the holy Supper is not such a sacrifice in which Christ under the form of bread and wine is sacrificed in an unbloody manner, then it is easy to conclude that it also is not an atoning sacrifice—yet, we still want to deal specifically with this question and establish that the sacrifice of the Mass is by no means an atoning sacrifice.

1. The Lord Christ has once and for all provided such an atoning sacrifice on the timber-trunk of the cross, which is eternally effectual; therefore, it is not necessary that He still be daily sacrificed in the holy Supper to atone for the sin of mankind.

Heb. 5:9 – **And since He was perfected, He has become for all who are obedient to Him a source for eternal salvation.**

Heb. 7:26, 27 – **For we should have such a High Priest, ... who unlike any other high priest did not need daily to first make a sacrifice for his own sin, [and] thereafter for the people's sin; for this He did one time when He sacrificed Himself.**

Heb. 9:12, 26, 28 – **Instead He** (Christ) **went into the holy place [and] by His own blood and established an eternal redemption.... But now at the end of the world He** (Christ) **has appeared one time to lift away sin through His own sacrifice.... Thus Christ was sacrificed once to take away many sins.**

Heb. 10:12, 14, 18 – **But this One** (Christ), **in that He offered up for sin one sacrifice which is valid eternally, now sits at the right of God... . For with one sacrifice He eternally perfected those being sanctified... . But where there is forgiveness for the same** (the sins), **there no longer is sacrificing for sin.**

Pertinent here are all the passages of Scripture which address the atoning sacrifice of Christ for the sin of the world, for they all speak about the atoning sacrifice which He accomplished on the cross.

2. Were Christ still being sacrificed daily in the holy Supper under the form of bread and wine for the atonement of mankind's sin, then it would follow that the atoning sacrifice on the cross was not complete; hence, it would be incorrect that He said from the cross—**It is finished!** (John 19:30). Far be it [from us] to say or even think that.

Heb. 10:1–3, 11, 12 – **Every year one had always to sacrifice the same offering, and those who made the sacrifice could not make it complete. Otherwise the sacrificing would have ceased where those who are worshiping no longer had a** [guilty] **conscience concerning sins once they were cleansed. Instead each year** [the sacrifice] **took place only as a remembering of sins. And a particular priest was designated to serve in worship and often make the same sacrifice every day—which never could take away the sins. But this One, in that He offered up one sacrifice for sin, which is valid forever, now sits at the right of God.**

3. If Christ would be sacrificed for atonement in the holy Supper, then such would occur in a bloody manner, since without shedding of blood no reparation or payment for sin can take place.

Heb. 9:22, 25, 26 – **... And without shedding of blood no forgiveness takes place. Also, not that He** (the Lord Christ) **frequently sacrificed Himself, just as the High Priest went into the holy place every year with blood not** his own. Otherwise He would have had to suffer from the beginning of the world on, etc.

4. The holy Supper was instituted by the Lord Christ for a remembrance of His atoning sacrifice, which He accomplished on the timber-trunk of the cross; therefore, it can itself not be an atoning sacrifice, for why would it be necessary to remember with a thankful heart the previously accomplished atoning sacrifice if in the holy Supper an atoning sacrifice to God the Lord was still offered each day?

Luke 22:19, 1 Cor. 11:24 – **Do such for My remembrance.**

1 Cor. 11:25,26 – **Do such as often as you drink it, to My remembrance. For as often as you eat of this bread and drink from this chalice, you should proclaim the Lord's death until He comes.**

Here again are apparent points of contention:

1. That in the holy Supper to each person in particular is bequeathed what Christ has won on the timber-trunk of the cross with His atoning sacrifice; therefore, to such a degree and with such an understanding it can properly be called an atoning sacrifice. ANSWER: **1.** If the true body and the true blood of Christ is received with true faith in the holy Supper, then we indeed become beneficiaries of the merits which Christ won with the sacrifice of His body and blood on the timber-trunk of the cross; but it does not follow that the holy Supper is an atoning sacrifice. **2.** With His own atoning sacrifice on the timber-trunk of the cross, the Lord Christ completely paid what was required—and all that was required—to purchase us from sin and to reconcile us to God the Lord, so that these very merits of Christ are bequeathed to us. [The latter] does not take place through a fictitious sacrifice of the Mass; rather, from God's side, through the Word and holy Sacraments—from our side, through a true faith.

2. That because the believers in the Old Testament were made partakers of the merits of Christ (which He would accomplish by His bloody atoning sacrifice on the timber-trunk of the cross) through the sacrificial offerings, such would such take place also in the New Testament through a sacrifice. ANSWER: **1.** The Levitical sacrifice in the Old Testament pointed to the atoning sacrifice of Christ on the timber-trunk of the cross; since this has now been accomplished, [the Levitical sacrifice] has also ceased. **2.** Accordingly, if in the New Testament, no less than in the Old, one wants to sacrifice outwardly and visibly, thereby to prefigure the death and suffering of Christ, what would that be other than once again searching for the shadow after the body has already appeared? **3.** Also, the Levitical sacrifices by no means pointed to the sacrifice of the Mass, but to the bloody sacrifice of Christ on the timber-trunk of the cross; therefore, [their purpose] was ended long ago by Christ's death. **4.** In the holy Supper, the true body and the true blood of Christ (and thus all benefits which He purchased by the offering of His body and pouring out of His blood) are distributed, in addition to which distribution no new, outward, atoning sacrifice is required.

3. That in the first Supper, the Lord Christ sacrificed Himself for the sin of the apostles in an unbloody manner, for He says: **This is My blood, which is being shed for you for the forgiveness of sins**; but now the sacrifice of the Mass is in all aspects the same thing as the sacrifice of the Lord Christ in the first Supper. ANSWER: **1.** It has been sufficiently established in the previous chapter that with these words Christ pointed to the shedding of His blood on the timber-trunk of the cross. **2.** And how could Christ's blood have been poured out in an unbloody manner in the first Supper? Can one also shed blood in an unbloody manner? More on this above. **3.** Even though the chalice is called the New Testament in Luke 22:20 and 1 Cor. 11:25, it is not for the sake of asserting that the holy Supper is a sacrifice; rather, as Christ Himself explains, it is because from it Christ's blood (with which the New Testament is ratified and sealed) is distributed to us. **This is the New Testament in My blood,** says Christ. **4.** Just as the heir does not give anything to the testator who has established the testament, but, on the contrary, receives the goods which are bequeathed and allotted to him, so also we bring nothing of a sacrifice to God the Lord in the holy Supper. Rather, we receive in it—as from Christ's Testament—His true body and blood for the strengthening of our faith and for the reassurance of the gracious promise of the forgiveness of sins.

4. That the chief office of a priest is to sacrifice for sin (Heb. 5:1); and since we also have priests and sacrifice in the New Testament, they shall also sacrifice for sin. ANSWER: **1.** This [passage] is actually speaking of the Levitical priests of the Old Testament, who were established by God for the purpose of sacrificing for the people's sin. **2.** Christ is the only High Priest of the New Testament prefigured by the Levitical priests; He, with a single sacrifice, eternally perfected those being sanctified (Heb. 10:14). **3.** On this account, it is not necessary that Christ be daily sacrificed anew for the sin of mankind; rather, it is sufficient that the forgiveness of sins, purchased once and for all, be distributed to the believers and to the penitent through the Word and the holy Sacraments. The gift has been prepared long ago; it is only necessary that it be distributed.

CHAPTER 26

WHETHER THE HOLY SUPPER IS THE KIND OF SACRIFICE THROUGH WHICH SPIRITUAL AND PHYSICAL MERITS, INDEED, EVEN DELIVERANCE FROM AFFLICTION, MIGHT BE ACQUIRED.

 nce again, there is sufficient [evidence] in chapter 24 to establish that the holy Supper can by no means be such an *impetratorium sacrificium* [a sacrifice by which one obtains a request], yet we further demonstrate the same to the point of overflowing [superfluity]:

1. The Lord Christ instituted the holy Supper for the purpose that by means of the blessed bread and wine He distributes His true body and blood in it; therefore, it could not have been instituted for the purpose that we sacrifice in it, and by it through such sacrifice acquire spiritual and bodily merits.

Mat. 26:26, Mark 14:22, Luke 22:19, 1 Cor. 11:23, 24 – **For the Lord Jesus in the night in which He was betrayed took the bread, gave thanks and broke it and gave it to the disciples and said: Take and eat, this is My body which is being broken for you.**

Mat. 26:27, 28; Mark 14:23, 24; Luke 22:20; 1 Cor. 11:25 – **In the same way He also took the chalice after the supper, gave thanks, gave it to them and said: All of you drink out of it; this chalice is the New Testament in My blood which is being poured out for you for the forgiveness of sins.**

2. In order that we might be strengthened in faith and fed [nourished] for eternal life in the holy Supper, Christ instituted the eating and drinking of His body and blood; but in no way did He command the sacrificing of His body and blood, by virtue of which spiritual or bodily merits might be obtained.

Mat. 26:26, Mark 14:23, Luke 22:19, 1 Cor. 11:24 – **Eat, this is My body which will be broken for you, do this to My remembrance.**

Mat. 26:27, 28; Mark 14:23, 24; Luke 22:20; 1 Cor. 11:25 – **Drink, this is My blood, which will be poured out for you; do such as often as you drink it, to My remembrance.**

3. If the sacrifice of the Mass also obtains something for the unrepentant and begs something from God for them, then it would be more effective than the atoning sacrifice of the Lord Christ on the timber-trunk of the cross, which only brings benefit to the repentant believers.

Heb. 6:4–6 – **It is impossible that those should again be renewed to repentance who once were enlightened and tasted the heavenly gifts and became recipients of the Holy Spirit and have tasted the benevolent Word of God and the power of the world to come, since they have fallen away and have for themselves once again crucified the Son of God and hold Him in contempt.**

Heb. 10:26 – **Were we thus to sin deliberately after we have received the confession of Truth, we no longer have any sacrifice for sin, rather a horrible awaiting of judgement and ardently zealous fire,** etc.

Here again are apparent points of contention:

1. That although the sacrifice of the Mass does not obtain forgiveness of sins, yet it still secures (obtains) repentance [for sin], through which [sinners] subsequently come to [obtain] the forgiveness of sins. ANSWER: **1.** The holy Supper was not instituted for the sake of the unrepentant, so that through it they might be helped to repentance, but for the sake of the repentant and believing, so that they be strengthened in their faith and assured of the promise of the gracious forgiveness of sins. **2.** Repentance does not originate in the sacrifice of the Mass; rather, the first part of repentance, namely genuine contrition, originates in the preaching of the Law, through which, as with a hammer, the heart is shattered. The other element of repentance (namely, true faith in Christ) originates in the preaching of the Gospel, through which the broken and shattered heart once again is lifted up [comforted] in true confession and contrition over sin; then also, out of true faith arises the serious intention to better one's life.

 2. That in the Old Testament one had not only burnt offerings and sin-offerings, but also thank-offerings through which one obtained something from God. Thus in 2 Sam. 24:25 David sacrificed to God the Lord so that the pestilence might be averted; therefore, the sacrifice of the Mass in the New Testament is likewise not only an atoning sacrifice but also serves the purpose of acquiring from God thereby all kinds of gifts and benefits. ANSWER: **1.** God expressly commanded in the Old Testament to bring Him such thank-offerings. He also prescribed the form and manner of such thank-offerings; but, in the New Testament one does not have any such command from God for outward thank-offerings. **2.** The thank-offerings of the Old Testament were a type of the spiritual thank-offerings of the New Testament, which consist of praise and thanksgivings to God (Heb. 13:16). The outward Levitical worship (divine service) which was customary in the Old Testament is done away with in the New Testament and changed into spiritual, inner worship. **3.** The thank-offerings in the Old Testament were distinguished from the burnt-offerings; for that reason, the sacrifice of the Mass may not be simultaneously prefigured by the burnt-offerings and the thank-offerings; rather, if it truly were an atoning sacrifice, then it could not be a thank-offering.

CHAPTER 27

WHETHER THE SACRIFICE OF THE MASS DOES
ANY GOOD FOR THE DEAD IN PURGATORY.

 ince the holy Supper is not such a sacrifice through which one may obtain atonement with God for others, dispensation for punishment, or other spiritual or bodily merits, it is thus easy to conclude that it is wrong to sacrifice for the dead in purgatory.

For, **1.** There is no divine command to sacrifice for the dead, nor is there any promise that God the Lord would view such a sacrifice [favorably]. In the Old Testament, God the Lord prescribed various sacrifices for His people, but none for the dead are found among them.

2. The Lord Christ instituted the holy Supper, not for the dead, that one should therein make sacrifice for them, but for the living, that by means of the consecrated bread and wine they receive His true body and His true blood, and thereby be strengthened in faith and be reassured concerning the gracious promise of forgiveness of sins.

Mat. 26:26, Mark 14:22, Luke 22:19, 1 Cor. 11:24 – **Take eat, this is My body, which is being broken for you; such do to My remembrance.**

Mat. 26:27, 28; Mark 14:23, 24; Luke 22:20; 1 Cor. 11:25 – **All of you drink from this, that is, the chalice, the New Testament in My blood, which is shed for you for the forgiveness of sins; do this, as often as you drink it, in memory of Me.**

3. The holy Scriptures know as much about purgatory as they do about the sacrifice of the Mass, as shall be established at the proper place. After their departure from this life, the believers and righteous souls come from their bodies into the hand of God; the unbelieving and godless souls come to the place of excruciating torment. Nowhere does the Scripture give thought to a third place.

4. The Lord Christ instituted His holy Supper so that in it one should think about His death and thank Him for it, which the deceased are not able to do. Thus, the holy Supper was not instituted for the departed.

Luke 22:19, 1 Cor. 11:24 – **This do to My remembrance.**

Luke 22:20; 1 Cor. 11:25, 26 – **Do this as often as you drink it to My remembrance. For as often as you eat of this bread and drink from this chalice, you should proclaim the Lord's death until He comes.**

Here again is an apparent point of contention:

That in 2 Macc. 12:43 ff. it is announced that Judas Maccabeus permitted a sin-offering to be made for the dead, and he is praised for it; thus the Mass sacrifice will also benefit the dead. ANSWER: **1.** This book is not in the Canon; that is, it is not counted among the books about which one knows without a doubt that they are written by the men of God by the inspiration of the Holy Spirit. For that reason, one cannot base articles of faith on the testimony of this book. **2.** Also [this passage] is not to be held up (presented) to us as a command of God, but rather as relating an undertaking by Judas. That God the Lord was not pleased with it is readily to be concluded in that God nowhere in the Law has commanded to sacrifice for the dead. **3.** What is written here about the sacrifice for the dead is recounted neither in 1 Macc. 5 nor by Joseph Ben Gorian nor by the Greek Josephus, and yet these have recorded this history. It is thus to be concluded that this [passage] must have been added later. **4.** At the time of the Maccabees, the Israelite religion was actually quite obscured and corrupted through heathen abuses; therefore, if Judas did permit sacrifices for the dead, it still would have to be regarded as wrong and pagan. **5.** Is it not extolled in the fourteenth chapter of this book that Rhazis committed suicide? Who, then, would want to glorify such a deed? **6.** The same soldiers for whom Judas Maccabeus ordained a sacrifice died in an accursed mortal sin, for they had taken something from the exiles and hidden it under their garments. However, the defenders of the sacrifice of the Mass themselves say that the Mass sacrifice does not avail for the good of those who die in an accursed mortal sin; therefore, this example of Judas makes no sense for purposes of their argument. **7.** Not to mention that in the New Testament there no longer is any external, visible sacrifice. So then, even if it were shown that Judas Maccabeus did the right and proper thing by permitting a sin-offering for those who were slain, it would still, however, not be proven that one should or may similarly in the New Testament conduct an atoning sacrifice for the dead, since one has neither a command nor an example—not even a single promise—concerning this [practice]. **8.** Finally, one will not find, from the time of the Maccabees until the time of Christ, that this procedure of sacrificing for the dead was ever performed [or] that the example of Judas Maccabeus was ever followed. Why, then, would one want to follow it in the New Testament?

CHAPTER 28

WHETHER CERTAIN MASSES SHOULD OR MAY BE CONDUCTED IN HONOR OF THE DEAD SAINTS,THEREBY TO OBTAIN THEIR INTERCESSION.

 That special Masses are conducted in honor of the dead saints, thereby to obtain their intercession, is **1.** Contrary to the institution of the holy Supper, for the Lord Christ did not command celebrating it to revere the dead, but to remember His death therein and to thank Him for it.

Luke 22:19, 20; 1 Cor. 11:23, 24 – **This do as often as you drink it to My remembrance.**

1 Cor. 11:26 – **For as often as you eat of this bread and drink from this chalice, you should proclaim the Lord's death until He comes.**

2. Contrary to the example of Christ, of the holy apostles, and of the early church, who in the administration of the holy Supper commemorated no dead saints, much less conducted Masses to revere them.

3. Contrary to the high priestly office of Christ, who has entered into heaven, appearing on our behalf before the presence of God to intercede for us; that, however, the beloved saints should know of a particular need and should be making specific intercessions for a particular person—of this nothing certain can be brought forth [produced] from the Scriptures.

Rom. 8:34 – **Who (Christ) is at God's right hand and acts on our behalf.**

1 Tim. 2:5, 6 – **For there is one God and one Media-**

tor between God and man, namely, the man Christ Jesus, who gave Himself for all for rescue, etc.

1 John 2:1, 2 – **And if someone sins, then we have an Advocate with God the Father, Jesus Christ, who is righteous, and He is the reconciling atonement for our sins,** etc.

Heb. 7:24, 25 – **But because this One** (Christ) **remains forever, He has an imperishable priesthood, so that He can also always save those who come to God through Him, and He always lives there and intercedes for them.**

Heb. 9:24 – **For Christ is ... entered ... into heaven itself, in order to appear before the presence of God for us.**

Here again are apparent points of contention:

1. Even though Christ had not commanded in the institution of the holy Supper that the sacrifice of the Mass should be performed to honor the saints, yet He did not forbid it; thus, it is not contrary to the institution of Christ. ANSWER: **1.** That one should conduct special Masses to honor the beloved saints is presented by the advocates of the sacrifice of the Mass as an article of faith. Against this, we justly say: If such Masses conducted to revere the saints were to be made necessary and accepted as an article of faith, it would have to be able to be established from the Scripture; for even as we want to hear where it is recorded, no article of faith is to be accepted if it cannot be clearly and distinctly proven from the Scripture. **2.** In the same way, could not one then also thus conclude: Christ indeed has commanded to baptize in the Name of the Father, the Son and the Holy Spirit, but He does not forbid baptizing in the name of the saints? Therefore, doing that would not be wrong. **3.** Actually, concerning this matter, the passage of St. Paul in Gal. 3:15 is to be heeded: **One does not disregard a human testament if it has been ratified and does not add anything to it.** How much less should we add to the Testament of Christ itself that we would perform the sacrifice of the Mass to honor the saints in order to obtain their intercessions?

2. That the saints in heaven intercede for us in 2 Macc. 15:12, 13 and in Rev. 5:8, etc.; therefore, it cannot be wrong to revere them with sacrifices in order to obtain their intercessions. ANSWER: **1.** Whether the beloved saints in heaven know specifically of one's special needs and pray for him, of this nothing certain can be produced from the canonical books of the Scriptures to prove it. More about this at its proper place. **2.** And even if the saints in general pray for the church militant, it still does not follow that sacrifices of the Mass are to be held to honor them; rather, it would at the same time also have to be shown from God's Word that such sacrifices please God and the saints.

3. That St. Paul admonishes in 1 Tim. 2:1 – **That one ... ask, pray, intercede, and give thanks for all people**; therefore, it would not be wrong to sacrifice to honor the saints. ANSWER: **1.** St. Paul is speaking here of living people, not about the deceased, whom he deals with extensively in 1 The. 4, and yet mentions no prayers or sacrifices for them. **2.** Also there is another **sacrifice**, another prayer, which we rightly are to pray for all people, but it does not follow that an external, visible atoning sacrifice is to be performed for the dead. **3.** In the early church one remembered the martyrs and the deceased saints during the action of the holy Supper, not as if one wanted to sacrifice in the holy Supper in order to honor them and thereby obtain their intercession, but rather thereby to exhort the living toward the example of their virtues.

CHAPTER 29

THAT THE HOLY SUPPER WAS INSTITUTED ONLY FOR AND IS TO BE ONLY OFFERED TO CHRISTIANS.

 hus far we have dealt with extensively all the *causis*, that are concerning the Founder, the essential elements, and the fruits (effects) of the holy Supper. Here follows a further treatment of the question regarding for whose good and benefit the holy Supper was instituted and should be offered; namely, solely and only to Christians, that is, to those who confess the teachings of Christ and are members of the Christian Church, which we substantiate as follows:

1. In the administration of the first Supper, Christ instituted and distributed this holy Sacrament to His beloved disciples. Here, then, the disciples were a picture [representative] of the entire Christian Church and of all disciples of Christ—in the same manner as in former times, when the names of the twelve tribes of Israel on the breastplate of the high priest represented the entire nation of Israel.

Mat. 26:26, Mark 14:22, Luke 22:19, 1 Cor. 11:23, 24 – **For the Lord Christ, in the night in which He was betrayed, took the bread, gave thanks, and broke it and gave it to His disciples and said: Take it and eat, this is My body,** etc.

It is apparent from the following passages that in the Old Testament the entire nation was prefigured and represented by means of the twelve tribes of Israel:

In Exo. 28:9, 10, 12, God the Lord says to Moses: **And You shall take two onyx stones and engrave upon them the names of the children of Israel, six names upon each** one, in order of their age. And you shall attach (sew) them to the shoulders of the body-robe so that they be stones of remembrance for the children of Israel, so that Aaron bear upon his two shoulders their names for a remembrance before the Lord.

Jos. 3:12, 4:1–3 – And the Lord said to Joshua: Take twelve men, one from each tribe, and command them and say: Pick up out of the Jordan twelve stones from the place where the feet of the priests are standing and bring them over with you, etc.

2. The holy Sacraments are actually the possession of the Church; thus, whoever is outside the fellowship of the Christian Church should also not be admitted to the use of the Sacraments, of which the holy Supper is one.

Mat. 7:6 – You shall not give the sacred thing to dogs, and you shall not throw your pearls in front of sows.

Rev. 22:15 – For outside (the heavenly Jerusalem) are the dogs and sorcerers and the whoremongers and murderers and the idolaters, etc. 1 Cor. 5:12,13 – For what do I have to do with those outside that I should judge them? Don't you judge those who are within? But God will judge those who are outside, etc. (From this is to be seen that those who are outside the Church are compared to dogs; accordingly, the holy thing of the Sacrament should not be given to them).

Eph. 2:12 – That you at that time were without Christ, strangers and outside the citizenship of Israel and strangers to the Testament of Promise. (Those who are outside the Church are strangers to the Testament of Promise; therefore, they should also not be admitted to the Sacrament and grace-seal of the Testament.)

3. The Passover lamb had been a type of the holy Supper, as shown above in chapter 2. Just as no one was allowed to eat of the paschal lamb unless he first had been taken into the fellowship of the Israelite Church through circumcision, so should no one be welcomed to the holy Supper unless he first be taken into the Christian Church through holy Baptism.

Exo. 12:43, 44, 48 – **And the Lord said to Moses and Aaron: This is the way to conduct the Passover: No stranger shall eat of it. But whoever is a bought servant should first be circumcised, and then [may] he eat of it. But if a stranger lives with you and wants to observe the Lord's Passover, he should circumcise everyone that is male; then let him prepare [to celebrate the Passover] and be like a native of the land, for no uncircumcised person shall eat thereof.**

4. In the holy Supper, we are fed with Christ's body and blood for eternal life, as was shown above in chapter 23. Now, just as it is necessary first to be born into this life before one can have earthly food administered to him, so also it is necessary that we first become born again (John 3:5) before we can be fed for eternal life with Christ's body and blood in the holy Supper.

It follows therefrom that the heathen, Turks, and Jews are not be admitted to the holy Supper until they let themselves be baptized and receive the Christian faith.

CHAPTER 30

THAT THE HOLY SUPPER IS TO BE OFFERED ONLY TO CHRISTIANS WHO EXAMINE THEMSELVES.

ince the apostle Paul expressly requires in 1 Cor. 11:28, 29 that a person first examine himself and then eat of the consecrated bread and drink of the consecrated chalice, so that he does not become guilty of the body and blood of the Lord through an unworthy reception, it thus indisputably follows that not only Christians (that is, those who confess the Christian faith and are in the fellowship of the Church) are to be admitted to the holy Supper, but specifically only those who examine themselves, that is, those who judge themselves (1 Cor. 11:31), discern the Lord's body (v. 29), and proclaim His death (v. 26). Therefore, the following are herewith excluded:

1. The dead—for since the Lord Christ ordained His body to be eaten by means of the consecrated bread and His blood to be drunk by means of the consecrated wine and, in addition, His death to be proclaimed in the holy Supper, and since such cannot be done by the dead, it is thus improper for one to put the bread and pour the wine into the mouth of the dead.

Luke 22:20, 1 Cor. 11:25 – **This do, as often as you drink it, in My remembrance.**

1 Cor. 11:26 – **For as often as you eat of this bread and drink from this chalice, you shall proclaim the Lord's death until He comes.** (However, it is written in Psa. 115:17 – **The dead will not praise You, Lord, nor those who descend into the stillness**).

2. Wicked, unrepentant sinners, who against all admonition and warning sin against their consciences and give no indication that they are straightening up, that is, confess themselves to be poor sinners before God the Lord, humble themselves from the heart and become an enemy of sin—such will receive the holy Supper to their judgment [condemnation].

In Num. 9:6, no unclean person is permitted to observe the Passover. (The Passover lamb pointed to Christ, who in the holy Supper gives us to eat of His body and to drink of His blood. Just as those who had not yet been cleansed from their bodily uncleanness were not allowed to eat of the Passover lamb, how much less should those be granted admission to the holy Supper who lie in sin's gross, outward uncleanness.)

Mat. 7:6 – **You shall not give holy things to dogs, nor hurl your pearls before sows.** (Before the Lord, dogs and sows are those who are always wallowing in sin's muck and do not want to repent. Pro. 26:11 – **As a dog eats his vomit again, so is the fool who continues in his foolishness.** 2 Pet. 2:20, 22 – **For in that they escaped from the filth of the world through the confession of the Lord and Savior, Jesus Christ [and] were once again won back to what they had fled, the last became more scandalous than the first.** It is the experience of the true word of Scripture: The dog gobbles up again what he has regurgitated, and the sow wallows again in the muck after swimming.)

1 Cor. 5:11 – **If there is anyone who allows himself to be called a brother, and is a whoremonger or avaricious or an idolater or a slanderous back-biter or a sot or a robber, with him you should not eat.** (How much less should one allow such to come to this heavenly meal?)

1 Cor. 11:27, 29 – **Whoever eats of this bread and drinks from this chalice of the Lord unworthily, such a one is guilty in respect to the body and blood of the Lord. For whoever eats and drinks unworthily, with that**

such a one eats and drinks judgment to himself in that he does not distinguish (discern) the body of the Lord.

3. Those who have been excommunicated, for that [ban] also encompasses their exclusion from the fellowship of the holy Sacraments.

Mat. 18:17 – **If he** (the sinner) **doesn't listen to the Church, then regard him as a heathen and a sinner.**

4. Those who deliberately persist in an error which is contrary to the chief foundation of Christian teaching, ignoring every instruction and admonition, thereby sever themselves from the fellowship of the true Church. Therefore, they also cannot be allowed to have the benefits of the Church. [In this category] especially belong those who deny the true presence of the body and blood of Christ in the holy Supper and look upon it as nothing higher than a common meal.

Mat. 7:6 – **You shall not give holy things to the dogs,** etc. (The holy Scripture also calls misleading teachers "dogs," Phi. 3:2 – **Watch out for the dogs, look out for the workers of evil,** etc.)

1 Cor. 11:29 – **For whoever eats and drinks unworthily, therewith eats and drinks judgment to himself, inasmuch as he does not distinguish (discern) the body of the Lord** (that is, he does not believe nor remember that Christ's body, by means of the blessed bread, is being distributed in the holy Supper).

Tit. 3:10 – **If he has been admonished again and again, steer clear of a heretical person.**

2 John 10, 11 – **If someone comes to you and does not bring this teaching, don't take him into your home, neither greet him. For whoever greets him makes himself a participant in his evil deeds.**

5. The possessed, the insane, the raving mad, the halting idiots, and the like, who are unable to use their mind, for they cannot perceive the body of Christ, nor examine themselves.

1 Cor. 11:28, 29 – **But let a person examine himself and thus eat of this bread and drink from this chalice. For whoever eats and drinks unworthily, therewith eats and drinks judgment to himself, inasmuch as he does not distinguish (discern) the body of the Lord.**

6. The *infames personae*, that is, those who carry on the kind of dealings and works to which a person may not obligate himself without mortally sinning, such as necromancers, a proprietor of harlots, a public usurer, a fencer who duels to the death, and the like; for as long as they do not refrain from these their deeds, they are not truly repentant.

1 Cor. 11:31 – **For if we judge ourselves, we shall not be judged.**

7. The mutes who are unable to indicate with outward signs to us about their faith, for of those one cannot know if they have examined themselves.

1 Cor. 11:28 – **But [let] a man examine himself and thus eat of this bread and drink from this chalice.**

8. Those who are unable to drink any wine, for since the wine is an essential element of the holy Supper—as was shown above in chapter 9—it is thus better that such persons completely refrain from the Lord's Supper, so that no action is taken contrary to Christ's institution.

9. The minor children, who have not yet arrived at the age of understanding, for they cannot examine themselves and discern the body of Christ.

1 Cor. 11:26, 28, 29, 31 – **For as often as you eat of this bread and drink from this chalice, you should proclaim the Lord's death, until He comes. But [let] a person examine himself and thus eat of this bread and drink from this chalice. For whoever eats and drinks unworthily, therewith eats and drinks judgment to himself in that he does not discern the body of the Lord. For if we judge ourselves, we will not be judged.**

Here again are apparent points of contention:

1. That although the dead don't eat the consecrated

bread nor drink the consecrated wine and thereby are unable to proclaim Christ's death, even so the fruit of the Supper, as a sacrifice, can serve to their benefit. ANSWER: It was previously established that the Supper is not a sacrifice, nor is there a sacrifice for the dead in it; rather, it is a holy Sacrament instituted for the living, that they eat Christ's body and drink His blood by means of the consecrated bread and wine and therewith should proclaim Christ's death with thankful, believing hearts.

2. That [in addition] to the other disciples, the Lord Christ distributed the holy Supper to the betrayer Judas, as is to be concluded from Luke 22:20,21; therefore, the unrepentant wicked are not to be excluded from the holy Supper. ANSWER: Even though Judas had already resolved in his heart to betray Christ—indeed, had also taken thirty pieces of silver for this purpose—his gruesome sin was still not apparent to the other disciples, for they asked among themselves who was going to do it (Luke 22:23). Since, therefore, his murderous intentions then were known only to the Lord Christ, but became known to the apostles only at a later time, the Lord Christ thus allowed him to celebrate the holy Supper alongside the other disciples but faithfully admonished him that he confess his sin and that he should abstain from it. **But see, the hand of My betrayer is with Me on this table**, He says in v. 21. **And indeed, the Son of Man goes forth, as it has been determined; but woe to that person by whom He shall be betrayed** (v. 22). Accordingly, a distinction is to be made among sinners. Those who fall into sin unknowingly or in weakness and are overtaken with by failure (Gal. 6:1)—but who confess their sin, trust in the Lord Christ, and promise to amend [their ways]—such [sinners] one should not exclude from the holy Supper, for Christ instituted it for the sake of tormented [anxious] sinners. Also, if the sin is secret, that is, known only to the preacher or indeed only to a few others, thus in the same way one should not exclude the sinner, but faithfully admonish him and allow him, on his conscience, to attend the Supper. However, if the sinner lies in public and known sin, promises no amendment, and by deed indicates none, one should by no means admit him to the holy Supper.

3. That it sometimes happens that those who have been excommunicated are overtaken by sudden illnesses and desire the Sacrament before they can be publicly reconciled with the Church; should one also exclude such from the holy Supper? ANSWER: In such an instance one should not deny the Supper. If they testify beforehand that they are heartily sorry for their sins and promise amendment and reconciliation with the Church, thus by God's grace they shall again be restored to health.

4. That there are many who err because of weakness and don't know any better; should one deny them the holy Supper just because of that? ANSWER: A distinction is to be made between the errors which go contrary to the foundation of faith and salvation and the schisms that arise on account of certain questions which do not sever the unity of the chief articles of faith. Accordingly, a distinction is to be made between those who err out of ignorance and weakness and those who willfully, in spite of all moderate instruction and admonition, persist in their errors. Regarding those who retain the foundation of faith and salvation [and] who also offer to refrain from the errors, as they are shown the better way from the Word of God, they should be instructed in a gentle spirit (Gal. 6:1) and not so hastily be excluded from the fellowship of the holy Supper and the Church.

5. That one also finds certain insane and mindless ones who at certain times are sane and desire the holy Supper; should one refuse it to them? ANSWER: In such a situation, one should not deny them the holy Supper, provided that they can with express word give confession that they can examine themselves and distinguish (discern) Christ's body.

6. That the world also regards as *infames* [infamous] spies, executioners and those who have been condemned to

die; should these absolutely be excluded from the holy Supper? ANSWER: By no means. Rather, if they are otherwise irreproachable in faith and life, then, like other Christians, they, too, are admissible to the Supper. Regarding the criminals who have been condemned to die, if they have heartfelt sorrow over their sins and with true faith trust in Christ's payment and with patience receive the justly earned punishment for their misdeeds, then they can no more be excluded from the celebration of the Supper than was the repentant malefactor on the cross excluded from paradise by Christ (Luke 23:43).

7. That one finds some mutes, who with wonderful gestures (signs) acknowledge their repentance, faith, and devotion—yes, even the desire for the holy Supper; should one deny such? ANSWER: If they possess a sound mind and by such signs indicate that they examine themselves and distinguish (discern) the body of Christ, then one should not wantonly exclude them from the holy Supper; for the Holy Spirit can just as readily do His work on them as He can on the children in their mothers' womb.

8. That it would actually be better if one gave only the consecrated bread to the *abstemiis* [the abstainers], who can drink no wine, instead of completely excluding them from the holy Supper. ANSWER: One actually finds few people who cannot ingest the [small] amount of [wine] required for use in the holy Supper. However, if they indeed cannot ingest even a tiny droplet of wine, then it is more advisable that they abstain from the holy Supper rather than have one undertake to do something contrary to Christ's institution. And, such persons are to be instructed that it is not the *deprivation* of the Sacrament because of a case of necessity, but rather the *despising* of the Supper which is damnable.* Such persons are also to cling to this: that they all the more frequently and with intense devotion appear at the administration of the holy Supper and alongside the communicants lift up their

* Emphases by translator.

sighs [groaning, Spirit-offered prayers] to God in order to share in the spiritual consumption of the body and blood of Christ.

9. That Christ says in John 6:53 – **If you don't eat the flesh of the Son of Man and drink His blood, then you have no life in you.** According to this, one should also offer the holy Supper to the minor children so that they not be excluded from eternal life. ANSWER: Christ is speaking there not about the sacramental, but rather of the spiritual consumption of His body and blood—without which one cannot do without losing salvation. However, one can dispense with the sacramental eating and drinking in case of necessity without the loss of salvation—as witnessed by the example of the malefactor on the cross (Luke 23:43). Accordingly, even though the minor children should not be offered the holy Supper, since they cannot examine themselves (nor can they perceive [discern] Christ's body), nevertheless, they are not thereby excluded from the Church or from salvation. Rather, it is sufficient for their salvation that they have been born again by the Holy Spirit in holy Baptism (John 3:5) and have been washed of their sins through the blood of Christ (Eph. 5:26). Nevertheless, we do not wish wantonly to condemn the early church, which for some time practiced the offering of the holy Supper to minor children.

CHAPTER 31

CONCERNING THE PROPER, SALUTARY PREPARATION FOR PARTAKING OF THE HOLY SUPPER.

nasmuch as the apostle expressly and with great seriousness describes in 1 Cor. 11:29 – **For whichever person eats and drinks unworthily, he eats and drinks judgment on himself,** etc., and again in v. 27 – **Whoever then eats from this bread or drinks from this chalice of the Lord unworthily, he is guilty of the body and blood of the Lord,** it is thus sufficient to conclude therefrom how highly necessary it is to deal with the proper, salutary preparation for participating in this holy Supper, so that one does not approach it unworthily and receive that which was instituted by the Lord Christ for life to one's death and judgment. Of what such due preparation consists, St. Paul himself teaches with one word when he says in v. 28 – **But a man examine himself, and thus let him eat of this bread and drink from this chalice.** However, in the Scriptures the word "**examine**" means to ponder with precise and extraordinary diligence what it is one is dealing with.

Psa. 11:5, Psa. 17:3, Psa. 139:1, Jer. 17:10, 1 The. 2:4 – **Thus the Lord examines the heart** (He sees the hidden bottom of the heart and considers what is in it).

Rom. 2:18 – **And since you have been instructed from the Law, you consider what is the best thing to do.**

Rom. 12:2 – **Rather change yourselves by renewing your minds, so that you may consider what is the good thing, that which pleases and completes the will of God.**

2 Cor. 13:5 – **Try yourselves if you still are in the faith, examine yourselves,** etc.

Gal. 6:4 – **However, each one of you examine his own work.**

Eph. 5:10 – **And examine what there is which is pleasing to the Lord.**

Phi. 1:9, 10 – **And concerning this very thing, I pray that your love indeed become more and more rich in all kinds of confession and experience, that you might examine what is the best,** etc.

1 The. 5:21 – **But examine everything and retain the good.**

1 John 4:1 – **Examine the spirits,** etc.

Accordingly, when St. Paul admonishes a person to examine himself prior to approaching the holy Supper, he in essence wants to say that one should with intense diligence examine (scrutinize) first himself, and thereafter, this precious food which he would receive.

A man should undertake the examination of his own person according to the rule of divine Law; the examination of this precious food, which one desires to receive, should be undertaken according to the rule and norm of the institution—just as St. Paul himself further clarifies this examination and encompasses it in the following three points:

1. That we should ponder and proclaim Christ's death, (v. 26). This contemplation of the death of Christ will remind us of our sins, for Christ died on account of our sins. Accordingly, the contemplation of the death of Christ will bring us to the point of confessing the huge burden and horror of our sins before God, for in no other way can we be rescued from them except through the painful death of the Son of God.

Isa. 43:24 – **Yes, indeed, with your sins you have caused Me work, and with your transgressions you have caused Me painful exertion.**

Isa. 53:5 – **But for the sake of our transgressions He was wounded, and on account of our sins He was battered,** etc.

Rom. 4:25 – **Who** (Christ) **is given up for the sake of our transgressions,** etc.

Rom. 6:10 – **In that He** (Christ) **died, He died for sin one time.**

1 Cor. 15:3 – **That Christ has died for our sins according to the Scriptures.**

Gal. 1:4 – **Who** (Christ) **has given Himself for our sins.**

1 Pet. 2:24 – **Who on account of our sins did sacrifice Himself in His body upon the timber-trunk,** etc.

If we contemplate Christ's death in this manner—that He died for the sake of our sin—thus will spring forth therefrom genuine confession of sins and heartfelt contrition because the bright glare of divine Law will hit us between the eyes so that we will clearly see our uncleanness and hidden sin and be terrified by it. Relevant also to this matter is what St. Paul himself adds (v.34) that we should judge ourselves, that is, accuse ourselves as poor sinners before God and regard ourselves as guilty of God's strict judgment and eternal damnation.

Psa. 51:4 – **Against You alone have I sinned and done evil before You, so that in the end You are right in Your Word and remain pure* when You are judged.** (The hypocrites always want to judge God, who in His holy Law accuses them of being sinners, so that as a consequence they actually all the more judge themselves), etc.

Isa. 1:16,18 – **Wash yourselves, clean yourselves up, put away your evil ways from Mine eyes,** etc. ... **Thus come now and let us dispute with each other, says the Lord.** (The people were saying: God always does the unjust

---

* The Septuagint Greek may be translated "pure (blameless) when You [God] are judged" as well as "blameless (or justified) when You judge." The Hebrew text used for modern translations must be rendered as the latter. Gerhard, however, using Luther's German translation, makes a relevant point about man's propensity for judging God. Ed.

thing, even though we are pious; why do You punish us?), etc.

So that a person may come to such a genuine confession of, and godly contrition for, his sin, it is advisable, indeed also necessary, that he take before him the holy Ten Commandments [and] consider them with all diligence for the kind of obedience God requires. Also, [he should] next ponder his nature, his life and doings, so that to some degree he might detect and recognize the multitude and gravity of his sins, be humble before God, and sigh to God for forgiveness from an anxious heart; for where there is true confession of and contrition for sin in the heart, it will break forth and visibly manifest itself in words and gestures—as [for example], through sighs, tears, humble demeanor, and the like, as is dealt with more extensively in the article on true repentance.

2. Further, for an appropriately performed examination, St. Paul requires that one distinguish (discern) Christ's body (v. 29); that is, one should ponder from the words of institution that this is not an ordinary meal, but that it is the Lord's Supper in which He Himself feeds us with His body and blood by means of the consecrated bread and wine, so that He may seal and impute (ascribe) to us His gracious promise of the forgiveness of sins, strengthen our faith, and unite Himself with us. Through such meditation faith is awakened and increased in our heart so that not only are we sure that in the holy Supper Christ's body and blood are truly distributed for us to eat and drink, but also that we firmly believe that, above all, the benefits which Christ won for us with the offering of His body and the shedding of His blood are distributed and sealed to us in the holy Supper; as a result, the debt of gratitude will follow on its own wherever faith is properly constituted.

1 Cor. 11:20–24, 26, 29 – **Now whenever you come together, is it not to celebrate** (with proper and due reverence) **the Lord's Supper. For as one celebrates the Supper,**

each one takes his own ahead of the others; and one remains hungry—the other is drunk. (You regard the Lord's
Supper no higher than an ordinary meal, not considering
that it is the Lord's Supper). **Should I praise you? In this I
do not praise you. I received from the Lord that which I
gave to you. For the Lord Jesus, in the night in which He
was betrayed, took the bread, gave thanks and broke it
and said: Take, eat, this is My body which is being broken
for you** (I must direct you to the institution of Christ, from
which you can distinctly and clearly understand that the
true body and the true blood of Christ are distributed in the
holy Supper), etc. **For as often as you eat of this bread and
drink from this chalice, you should proclaim the Lord's
death until He comes.** (The holy Supper was instituted by
Christ so that we should thereby ponder His death—the
death by which he paid for sin so that we by this means
may thus be strengthened in faith). **For whoever eats and
drinks unworthily, therewith eats and drinks judgment
on himself, in that he does not distinguish (discern) the
body of the Lord.**

It is also relevant here that in the institution of the
holy Supper Christ expressly states that in it He is giving
us the very same body to eat which He gave up for us into
death, and the very same blood to drink which He shed for
our sin; for we are thereby being admonished to come to this
table in true faith and to clutch these words tightly within
our hearts so that we do not doubt the gracious promise of
the forgiveness of sins.

3. Finally, for a salutary celebration of the Supper
and a proper examination, St. Paul requires that a person
should proclaim Christ's death (v. 26); that is, in public assembly, to thank Him from our hearts that He has loved us
so much and that He has given Himself for us into death (Gal.
2:20); for the word "**proclaim**" actually means this kind of
heartfelt, public thanksgiving (Psa. 9:11; 19:1; 51:15; 96:2, 3
etc.).

However, it is not sufficient to thank Christ for His death only with words; rather, if the thanksgiving flows from the heart, the following will also accompany it:

1. That from the heart one becomes an enemy of sin, since it cost the Lord Christ so much to pay for it; but whoever would deliberately and against conscience continue in sins, and continue in them without fear of God, in cocky self-assurance and godlessness, such a one has shown evidence enough that he has not yet properly taken to heart the death of Christ.

Heb. 10:26–29 – **For if we deliberately sin after we have received the confession of the truth, there is no more sacrifice for our sins, rather a horrible awaiting of judgment and the fiery zeal which will consume the wicked. When someone broke the Law of Moses, he had to die without mercy through [the word of] two or three witnesses. How much worse punishment do you think that a person deserves who with his feet treads on the Son of God and regards as unclean the blood of the Testament by which he was sanctified, and reviles the Spirit of grace?**

2. That one forgives the neighbor and reconciles himself with him; for if one considers and believes in his heart that God the Lord has pardoned our great debt of sin, how would one not forgive the neighbor his insignificant sin?

Mat. 5:23, 24 – **Therefore, if you sacrifice your gift upon the altar and there happen to recall that your brother has something against you, then leave your gift there before the altar and first go away and reconcile yourself with your brother, and after that come and sacrifice your gift.**

Mat. 6:14, 15 – **If then you forgive people their shortcomings, your heavenly Father will thus also forgive you. But if you do not forgive people their failings, then your Father will also not forgive you your faults.**

Col. 3:13 – **And put up with each other and forgive one another if someone has a complaint against another; just as Christ has forgiven you, so also you forgive.**

3. That one have the heartfelt intention to honor God and henceforth to conduct oneself in the best manner of living towards the neighbor; moreover, heartily to sigh and plead that Christ would live within us, rule us with His Holy Spirit, produce the fruits of the Spirit within us, [and] uphold us steadfast in faith and love unto our end to eternal life.

2 Cor. 5:15 – **And that is why He** (Christ) **died for you all, so that those who live do not henceforth live for themselves, but rather for Him who died for them and rose again.**

1 Pet. 2:24 – **Who** (Christ) **Himself sacrificed our sins in His body on the timber, so that we die to sin** [and] **live for righteousness.**

1 John 3:5, 6 – **And you know that He has appeared to take away our sins,** etc. **Whoever remains in Him, does not sin; whoever then sins, has not seen Him nor known Him.**

Rev. 1:5, 6 – **Who** (Christ) **has loved us and has washed us from sins with His blood, and has made us into kings and priests before God** (so that we **willingly sacrifice** to Him **in a holy garment** [Psa. 110:3], and subjugate our flesh, etc.).

Such then are the elements that constitute a proper examination and God-pleasing proclamation of the death of Christ which are necessary to a salutary observance of this Sacrament. For this reason, it was the practice of the early church that those who desired to attend the holy Supper had to announce themselves beforehand to the preacher [pastor], so that one might know whether they also had properly examined themselves, [to wit:] a true confession of sins in their hearts, humble contrition over them, a true faith in Christ, and a heart-felt intention to amend their lives, so that the unrepentant might be converted, the weak be comforted, the injudicious be instructed, the lax be aroused, and above everything else, that the unworthy reception of the holy Supper be prevented. Further, it was also customary that those who wanted to attend the holy Supper some days prior be obliged to turn from all other affairs and turn their thoughts and devotion solely to this their intention [to attend the holy Supper]. On the day before, they also fasted or surely interrupted [eating] so that they might be the more humble in the confession of sins, and on the following day be all the more devotional and adept in prayer during the celebration of the Supper. Finally, it is not to be viewed as a bad idea that in the general prayer of the Church one specifically pray for the communicants that God the Lord would through His Holy Spirit by His grace work in their hearts true reclamation and salutary preparation for this worthy food and that none among them receive this holy Supper to their judgment. Each church will reasonably take heed and, as opportunity presents itself, retain all this as a useful aid and guide for a blessed preparation [for partaking of the holy Supper].

Here again is an apparent point of contention:

That we all must confess that we are not worthy enough to receive this precious food—the body and blood of the Son of God; therefore, we all will be unworthy guests at the holy Supper. ANSWER: No one can make himself so pure and worthy before God the Lord, that a comparison may be found between one's worthiness and this heavenly meal. Rather, from a humble heart we all must confess our unworthiness and say: **Lord ... I am not worthy of all the mercy and faithfulness which you have bestowed on your servant** (Gen. 32:10). **Lord, I am not worthy that You come under my roof** (Mat. 8:8); ... **and henceforth am not worthy any longer to be called your son,** etc. (Luke 15:19). According to St. Paul, for one to attend the holy Supper worthily means to approach it not just with true repentance and proper examination, but to judge oneself, discern the body of Christ, and with a thankful heart proclaim His death. The word "**worthy**" is used in the same way in Luke 20:35 – **But those who are considered worthy to achieve that world,** [and in] Luke 21:36 – **And pray, that you might be worthy to escape all this which will happen and to stand before the Son of Man.** Acts 5:41 – **They joyfully went away from the presence of the counsel in that they had been worthy to suffer disgrace** [insult] **for the sake of His Name.** 2 The. 1:5 – **And you shall become worthy for the kingdom of God.** Rev. 3:4 – **And they will walk with Me in white garments, for they are worthy of it.**

CHAPTER 32

WHETHER ALSO THE UNWORTHY SACRAMENTALLY RECEIVE THE TRUE BODY AND THE TRUE BLOOD OF CHRIST.

t can readily be understood from the previous chapter who the unworthy guests at the Heavenly Meal are, namely, those who do not examine themselves, that is, those who do not confess their sins nor are grieved by them so that they would judge themselves; also, those who do not believe that Christ gives them His true body and blood to eat and drink to affirm to them the promise of the forgiveness of sins; those who have no sincere intention to better their lives; those who do not forgive their neighbor; and, in a word, those who do not discern the body of Christ. It is asked concerning these unworthy guests at the holy Supper whether they receive only bread and wine, or whether by means of the bread and wine they receive in a sacramental manner the true body and blood of Christ. It is here to be noted that one by no means would deal with the unworthy for the purpose of speaking the Word to them to strengthen them in their unworthy reception; rather, the unworthy are to be dealt with because they receive the holy Supper to their judgment. First of all, that they be hereby admonished to refrain from an unworthy reception and be admonished towards a sincere examination and worthy preparation. Next, that the God-fearing be aroused so that they in a salutary preparation also be all the more earnest and zealous in contemplation of the serious judgment of God against those who eat and drink unworthily. Finally, the real presence of the body and blood of Christ in the holy Supper is herewith confirmed, since it is established from St. Paul that not only the believers spiritually eat the body and drink the blood of Christ in the holy Supper to their salvation, but also that the unrepentant and unbelievers sacramentally receive Christ's body and blood—yet to their judgment—inasmuch as by the word "**sacramentally**" is understood that they receive not only bread and wine as symbols of the absent body and blood of Christ. Rather, this word is set in contrast to the spiritual eating and drinking which occurs in believers for life. Accordingly, it is herewith announced that the unworthy indeed eat Christ's body by means of the consecrated bread and drink His blood by means of the consecrated wine, but not for life and salvation, but to their own judgment and damnation, which is established as follows:

1. Because in 1 Cor. 11 St. Paul expressly teaches that the unworthy eat and drink Christ's body and blood, but to their judgment. For as he castigates the Corinthians for regarding the holy Supper no higher than a common meal, and directs them to the words of institution, he includes this warning:

1 Cor. 11:27–32 – **Whoever then eats of this bread and drinks from this chalice unworthily, he is guilty against the body and blood of the Lord. [Let] a person examine himself, however, and thus eat of this bread and drink from this chalice. For whoever eats and drinks unworthily thereby eats and drinks judgment upon himself in that he does not distinguish [discern] the body of the Lord. That's also why so many among you are weak and sick and a good portion are asleep [dead]. But if we judge ourselves, then we will not be judged. But if we end up being judged, then we will be chastised by the Lord so that we do not become damned with the rest of the world.**

In these words of the apostle it is to be noted **1.** That he proves these statements about the heavy guilt which the unworthy lay upon themselves from the preceding words of institution. He says, **Whoever then eats unworthily,** as if to say: "Because the Lord Christ expressly testifies that in His holy Supper He distributes not common bread and wine, but, by means of these same external elements, distributes His true body and His true blood. [As a result] the unworthy guests at the holy Supper become guilty of the body and blood of Christ and eat and drink judgment upon themselves." **2.** That the apostle does not merely say: Whoever eats the bread and drinks from the chalice unworthily; rather, he states: **Whoever eats of this bread and drinks from this chalice unworthily,** so that he once again may direct our attention back to the words of institution, from which we are able to conclude that the consecrated bread in the holy Supper is the fellowship of the body of Christ and the consecrated chalice is the fellowship of the blood of Christ (1 Cor. 10:16). From thence it comes to pass that the unworthy become guilty of the body and blood of Christ, since by means of this consecrated bread Christ's body and by means of this consecrated chalice Christ's true blood are distributed in the holy Supper. **3.** That the apostle says [that] the unworthy become guilty not, say, in respect to the holy symbol, but in respect to the body and blood of the Lord, in that he then describes the guilt and cause for which the unworthy incur divine judgment, [i.e.] because they do not properly deal with the body and blood of Christ. Deu. 19: 4–10: You shall establish sanctuaries to which may flee those who have unintentionally committed a homicide so that the avenger in his initial wrath does not seize him and kill him, that is, so that you do not become guilty of innocently shed blood. Jam. 2:10: **For if someone keeps the entire Law and sins against one, he is wholly guilty;** that is, he is guilty of transgressing the Law. In the same manner of speaking, St. Paul thus states: The unworthy become guilty over against the body and blood of the Lord, that is, Christ's body and blood is precisely the same against which the unworthy sin and make themselves guilty of divine judgment. **4.** That the apostle expressly sets down in what manner the unworthy become guilty over against the body and blood of Christ, namely, by their unworthy eating and drinking; [1 Cor. 11:] 27, 29 – **Whoever then eats of this bread and drinks of this blood unworthily, such a one is guilty against the body and blood of the Lord. For whoever eats and drinks unworthily, such a one eats drinks judgment upon himself.** From this, it irrefutably follows that the unworthy eat and drink Christ's body, because through unworthy eating and drinking they become guilty over against Christ's body and blood. **5.** It is likewise to be noted, then, that the apostle employs this peculiar form of speaking which is otherwise not often employed in the Scriptures (namely, that the unworthy eat and drink judgment to themselves) so that we thereby do not doubt that the unworthy eating and drinking is precisely the same through which they become guilty over against the body and blood of Christ and thus draw down upon themselves the severe judgment of God. **6.** Moreover, it is to be carefully considered that the apostle says that the unworthy eat and drink judgment to themselves in that they do not discern the body of Christ, since he then proclaims what it is that the unworthy eat and drink unworthily, namely, not only the consecrated bread, but the true body of Christ. That's why he would say the unworthy incur such a heavy judgment upon themselves, because they do not consider that Christ's body and blood are distributed to them in the holy Supper, but [partake of] this heavenly meal as only an ordinary meal. **7.** Finally it is to be noted that St. Paul distinctly says that the unworthy become guilty over against the body and blood of the Lord and indeed by unworthy eating and drinking; therewith he clearly attests that he is speaking of the kind of guilt and the kind of unworthy eating and drinking which does not *uno actu* [*in one action*] at the same time apply to the entire Christ, rather it is done specifically against His body and blood through unworthy eating and drinking. What the apostle understands in this text by "the unworthy," as well as by "judgment," will be made known later in the explanation of the points of contention.

2. The betrayer Judas was no less present at the first Supper than the other apostles and had eaten the consecrated bread and drunk the consecrated wine along with the other apostles. But now Christ speaks as much to Judas as to the other apostles: **Take and eat, this is My body, take and drink, this is My blood**, for one does not read that the Lord instituted for, or celebrated with Judas, a different Supper; rather, He distributed His true body and blood by means of the consecrated bread and wine to Judas at the same time as to the other apostles. It follows therefrom that Judas, despite his unbelief and his godlessness, also sacramentally ate and drank Christ's body and blood, but to his own judgment.

In Luke 22:19, 20 are described the institution and administration of the First Supper, and then immediately follow v. 21, 23 – **Yet behold, the hand of My betrayer is with Me at this table. ... And they began to ask among themselves who it might be among them who would do this.**

3. The faith or worthiness of the recipient does not belong to the essential elements of this holy Sacrament; therefore, the consecrated bread does not cease to be the fellowship of the body of Christ if the recipient does not believe or worthily celebrate this holy Supper. That again the faith of the recipient does not belong to the essential elements of the holy Supper may be demonstrated in many ways. For, **1.** it is undeniable that the holy Sacraments are institutions and ordinances of God the Lord; now, however, nothing is taken away from the institution of God by man's unbelief.

Rom. 3:3, 4 – **Should their** (mankind's) **unbelief invalidate God's faithfulness? Far be it**, etc.

Rom. 11:29 – **God's gifts and calling cannot cause Him to repent.**

2 Tim. 2:13 – **If we don't believe, He still remains faithful; He cannot disavow Himself.**

2. Accordingly then, nothing more is essential to the holy Supper than that the bread and wine be consecrated, and thus by means of the consecrated bread and wine Christ's body and blood be distributed and received. **3.** Faith is not an essential element of the holy Supper, but rather to the salutary use of same [and] to a proper and worthy preparation. **4.** Indeed, faith is strengthened and empowered through the holy Supper; therefore, it will indeed never be an essential element of [the Sacrament]. **5.** Just as faith is not an essential element of holy Baptism, although without faith Baptism benefits nothing. **6.** Indeed, as little as the faith or the opinion of those who distribute this Sacrament is essential to it, so also is the faith of him who partakes of it not required as an essential element, even though [the Sacrament] is of no benefit without it, but rather is received to [his] judgment. **7.** Finally, that which belongs to the essential elements, particularly to form of a thing, is that by which it is distinguished from all other things; however, the holy Supper is not distinguished from other Sacraments by the faith of the recipient. Instead, just as with the other Sacraments, faith is required for its salutary use. Therefore, one may not say that faith belongs to the essential elements of the holy Supper.

4. In the holy Supper, by virtue of the institution of Christ, the bread and wine are sacramentally united with the true body and blood of Christ, so that not only bread but rather along with the bread Christ's body is eaten, [and] that not just wine but rather by means of the wine Christ's blood is drunk, as shown above in chapters 11 and 19. Now, however, the unworthy indeed receive the consecrated bread and the consecrated chalice; therefore, they will also, through the same, receive Christ's body and blood.

1 Cor. 10:16 – **The consecrated chalice which we bless, is it not the fellowship of the blood of Christ? The**

bread which we break, is it not the fellowship of the body of Christ?

Here again are apparent points of contention:

1. That the unworthy certainly can become guilty over against the body and blood of the Lord even if they do not receive Christ's body and blood, namely, because they push aside Christ's body and sin against the holy symbols—not unlike a disobedient subject who disgraces the coat of arms or the image of his prince. ANSWER: **1.** The apostle has not allowed us the freedom to bring forth according to our own thinking the particular mode and manner by which the unworthy become guilty of the body and blood of Christ; rather, he himself has expressly set forth the *modum*: that it takes place through unworthy eating and drinking. **2.** And indeed, not only through the unworthy eating of the bread and the unworthy drinking of the wine, but through the unworthy eating of this bread of which the Lord has stated that it is His body, and through the unworthy drinking of this chalice of which the Lord has stated that it is His blood. **3.** Furthermore, he states that the unworthy thereby eat and drink judgment upon themselves in that they do not distinguish (discern) the body of Christ. He then expresses both [concepts], namely, that the unworthy invite God's judgment upon themselves precisely through unworthy eating and drinking, and then that not only bread, but also the body of Christ is received by the unworthy. For should the unworthy discern Christ's body in the holy Supper, that is, if they distinguish the worthy food which is distributed to them in the holy Supper from other ordinary food, then obviously Christ's body is also truly present and received. **4.** If the unworthy were guilty over against the body and blood of Christ in the manner in which a subject offends against his prince's coat of arms or image, then it would have been sufficient had the apostle stated that the unworthy sin against Christ; however, he specifically mentions the body and blood of Christ, [and] he also specifically mentions the eating and drinking through which the unworthy then invite this onerous guilt upon themselves. **5.** Also, just as Christ's body and blood by means of the consecrated bread and wine are distributed to the unworthy, it follows therefrom that they also receive Christ's body and blood; for the evangelists testify that not only did the Lord Christ give His apostles (by means of the consecrated bread and wine) His body and blood, but that they also received in the [bread] His body and in the [wine] His blood. Just as the Son of God on that occasion gave His body and blood as much to Judas as to the other apostles, and they (the apostles) had received the same body and the same blood of Christ, He still today says to all who attend the holy Supper, be they worthy or unworthy: **Take, eat, this is My body; take, drink, this is My blood.**

    2. That perhaps the apostle understands the unworthy to mean those who are weak in faith, who indeed have a faith, but yet, at the same time, are burdened with many weaknesses and do not adequately reflect on the great mystery of the holy Supper, which can accordingly be proven because the apostle says that many among the Corinthians are weak and a goodly portion sleep (v. 30). Therefore, one cannot prove from Paul that the unbelievers also receive Christ's body and blood. ANSWER: **1.** Since the Lord Christ accepts the weak in faith (Rom. 14:3) and acknowledges being their Physician (Mat. 9:12); since His power is mighty in the weak (2 Cor. 12:9); since He promises renewal to the burdened (Mat. 11:27); and finally, since the holy Supper was even instituted for the purpose of strengthening the weak in faith, therefore these sharp words of the apostle may not be applied to the weak in faith. **2.** Whoever believes does not come into judgment (John 5:24), for such a one spiritually and fruitfully consumes the body of Christ (John 6:54). How, then, can it be said of believers (even though they are weak in faith, for weak faith is also faith) that they eat and drink judgment to themselves, indeed also that they become guilty of the body and blood of the Lord? **3.** Also, if [the term] "**unworthy**" in this apostolic text were to be understood as the weak in faith or those who have not worthily enough prepared themselves, then would we forever have to go to the holy Supper in fear and doubt, for then no one could ever know if he possessed the kind of faith that would be strong enough or whether he had adequately prepared himself. **4.** By "the weak" the apostle does not refer to those who are weak in faith, but those who are inflicted by God with bodily weakness, as is sufficiently apparent from the words that immediately follow: **And a goodly portion are asleep. 5.** In as much then by "are asleep" is understood the sleep of death, and even though the Scripture commonly uses this way of speaking about the death of believers in that it calls their death a sleep, so also at times the death of the unrepentant is referred to in this manner—as can be seen from 1 Kin. 14:16 and 22, Dan. 12:2, and in many other places. **6.** Not to mention that without any doubt, many among the Corinthians, as they were chastised by the Lord, and on account of their desecration of the holy Supper were visited with bodily weakness, were converted to the Lord and are thus blessedly are asleep in Christ.

3. That from the evangelist John (chap. 13:30), it is to be well nigh concluded that Judas was not present at the institution and distribution of the holy Supper, but he immediately left after he received the morsel (sop) from Christ. ANSWER: **1.** John does not announce that the Lord Christ had distributed this morsel to Judas before the institution of the holy Supper, nor that he thereupon immediately went out. **2.** However, from the evangelist Luke, who **describes everything with diligent orderliness** (Luke 1:3), it is easily to be concluded that the Lord Christ first extended the morsel to Judas after the Supper and thereby revealed his betrayal to the disciples. For as the disciples already had celebrated the holy Supper with Christ, they began to question among themselves who indeed would be the betrayer (Luke 22:21, 23); if, however, by this morsel the betrayer Judas had already been revealed, why would there have been a need for all this questioning?

4. That Christ's body is a life-giving flesh (John 6); how, then, can it be received by the unbelievers for judgment? ANSWER: **1.** Christ's flesh at all times is and remains in and of itself a life-giving flesh; but, if we are to dip life from this well of life, then it is not enough that we sacramentally by means of the consecrated bread eat Christ's body; rather, to this must be added the spiritual consumption which occurs through faith and of which Christ speaks in John 6. John 5:21: **Thus also the Son makes alive whomever He desires**; now, however, only those shall have life from Him who cling to Him in faith, as the entire Scriptures testify. **2.** From the fact that the unbelievers and unrepentant are not made spiritually alive in the holy Supper, one should by no means conclude that they do not receive Christ's body in a sacramental manner; rather, from this it can only be concluded that they not do eat Christ's body nor drink His blood in a spiritual manner and that they are lacking (deficient) in the salutary use of this worthy food. **3.** Christ is not only the Life of the believers, but He is also the Judge of the unbelieving and unrepentant. Therefore His body and blood is received by the believers to their life and salvation, but by the unbelievers to their judgment and damnation. **4.** Is not the Word of the Gospel in itself a Word of Life and yet becomes to some a stench of death for death (2 Cor. 2:14–16), namely, on account of their unrepentant stand? Is not God the Lord the essence of Life, and, at the same time, there are many who are not made alive in a spiritual manner, even though they already in God live, move, and have their being (Acts 17:28)? **5.** [Did not] many people crowd around Christ in Mark 5, and yet no power went out to them from Christ—with the sole exception of the woman with the blood flow who touched Christ with true faith? Did not the accursed Jews crucify Christ and yet through the handling of this life-producing flesh were not made alive in a spiritual way?

5. St. Paul says in 1 Cor. 10:21: **You cannot at the same time drink of the Lord's chalice and the devil's chalice; you cannot at the same time be a partaker of the Lord's table and the devil's table;** however, the unrepentant are in fellowship with the devil and therefore do not become partakers of the body and blood of Christ. ANSWER: **1.** The apostle himself chastises the Corinthians that they together ate of that which had been offered to idols, that is to the devil. Hence he is by no means speaking about something that [literally] cannot occur, but rather about something that cannot occur in a proper, God-pleasing manner. **2.** The table and chalice of the Lord in the holy Supper includes not only Christ's body and blood, but also bread and wine. Accordingly, if the apostle is speaking specifically here about the kind of eating and drinking which by no means can exist together with the fellowship of the devil's table and chalice, it would thus follow that they also had not received the consecrated bread and wine, even though he yet expressly states in the following chapter that they drink from the chalice of the Lord (1 Cor. 11:27). **3.** It therefore remains irrefutably true that the apostle is not speaking here of that which by no means can take place, but about that which cannot occur with a good conscience and without sin, as such a mode of speaking is used in the Scriptures in Gen. 34:14; Deu. 16:5, 17:15, 21:16; Acts 4:20; 8[:18–23]; Gal. 4; etc.

6. That receiving and rejecting run counter to each other. Now, however, the unbelieving push away from themselves Christ and His benefits; therefore, they will also not receive His body. ANSWER: **1.** As far as the spiritual, fruitful consumption and reception of the flesh of Christ is concerned, it is obviously in respect to that that the unbelievers reject Christ with all His benefits; however, it may not be concluded therefrom that they do not in a sacramental manner, by means of the consecrated bread, receive Christ's body. **2.** For the same sacramental consumption originates from the institution of Christ, that He in the holy Supper desires to distribute His body by means of the consecrated bread. This foundation is not removed by the unbelief of men. The unrepentant and unbelieving reject the Word of God (Acts 13:46), but even so they hear it with their ears, yet without benefit and to their greater damnation (Heb. 4:2).

7. That only those receive the body of Christ for whom He gave Himself into death and for whose sake He shed His blood; now, however, Christ gave Himself into death only for the believers to wash them of their sins. Therefore, also only the believers will eat Christ body and drink His blood. ANSWER: At its proper place, it will be made as clear as daylight that Christ gave Himself into death for all mankind and is the Atonement for the sin of the entire world; therefore, no conclusions may be drawn from such a false foundation against the true presence of the body and blood of Christ in the holy Supper. We would much rather turn this closing argument around and say: Since Christ gives His body to eat and to drink in the holy Supper also to the unrepentant, He therewith makes it clearly to be understood that He also paid for their sins [and] that God has no desire for their death. Rather, [He] desires that they confess their sins, repent, and in true faith should possess for themselves the benefits which Christ has won for them by the offering of His body and the shedding of His blood. Therefore, this matter of the eating and drinking [on the part] of the unworthy gives a clear testimony that Christ died for all people, and that God the Lord from the heart calls all mankind to repentance and to the fellowship of Christ's kingdom.

8. That no one may come to possess the legacy of a testament (will) if he is not expressly and by name included as an heir in the testament; now, however, the unbelievers and unrepentant are by no means included as heirs of the heavenly blessings in the grace-covenant of God. Therefore, they will also not receive the precious legacies in the testament of the holy Supper, namely Christ's body and blood. ANSWER: The Lord Christ has promised and established the

sacramental eating and drinking of His body and blood for all Christians who eat the consecrated bread and drink from the consecrated chalice; but the spiritual consumption of the body and blood of Christ pertains only to the believers who in true faith productively receive the body and blood of Christ in the holy Supper. From this it is to be observed that actually, so to speak, forgiveness of sins, God's grace, and the inheritance of eternal life are the same legacies and heavenly blessings which the Lord Christ promises to believers in His testament. His body and blood are the seal with which He empowers this promise; and if one wanted to say with a proper understanding that Christ's body and blood are the true legacies of this testament, thus one still may not conclude therefrom that the unrepentant do not also receive them in a sacramental manner. For just as it might happen that someone takes (receives) a legacy from a testament that has not been bequeathed to him, so also do the unbelievers receive (to their judgment and damnation) Christ's body and blood, which, for true Christians, are actually blessings.

CHAPTER 33

CONCERNING THE TIME WHEN CHRIST INSTITUTED THE HOLY SUPPER AND WHEN IT IS TO BE USED [PARTAKEN OF] BY US.

aving to this point dealt with the Founder, the essential elements, and the purpose of this holy Supper, as well as with the questions of to whom this Sacrament of the holy Supper is to be offered and how one is to prepare for it, it is still necessary that the details themselves be dealt with; namely regarding the time, the place, the ceremonies, and similar matters, which are to be taken into account in the observance of the holy Supper. Concerning the time, the question first of all arises, at which time the holy Supper was instituted by Christ and when we are to partake of it, since it is evident from the account of the institution that Christ, on the evening of the very same day which immediately preceded the day of His suffering, or Good Friday, instituted this holy Supper and distributed it to His disciples.

Mat. 26:26–28 – **But as they were eating** (as they ate together the Passover lamb, which according to God's command had to be slaughtered in the evening and shortly thereafter be consumed, Exo. 12:6)**, Jesus took the bread, gave thanks and broke it and gave it to the disciples and said: Take, eat, this is My body. And He took the chalice and gave thanks, gave it to them and said: All of you drink therefrom; this is My blood of the New Testament, which is shed for many for the forgiveness of sins.**

Mark 14:17, 18, 22, 23 – **However, in the evening He arrived with the twelve. And as they sat at table and** ate, etc. Jesus took the bread, gave thanks, etc. And took the chalice, etc.

Luke 22:7, 14, 19, 20 – **Now the day of sweet** [unleavened] **bread arrived, on which one had to sacrifice the Passover** (paschal) **lamb. And as the hour arrived, He sat Himself down and the twelve with Him. And He took the bread, gave thanks, and broke it and gave it them and said: This is My body,** etc. **In the same manner also** [He took] **the chalice after the Supper and said: This is the chalice, the New Testament in My blood,** etc.

1 Cor. 11:23, 25 – **I have received from the Lord that which I have given to you. For the Lord Jesus, in the night in which He was betrayed, took bread, gave thanks,** etc. **In the same way also** [He took] **the chalice following the Supper and said: This chalice is the New Testament in My blood,** etc.

That the Lord Christ desired to institute and observe this holy Supper precisely on the very day shortly before His suffering therefore occurred [because]:

1. The Passover lamb, which was a type of the holy Supper and was replaced by the institution of the holy Supper in the New Testament, had to be slaughtered and consumed with special ceremonies according to the command of God—even though the Jews at the time of the Lord Christ [and] around the writings of the Fathers deviated from this ordinance of God and slaughtered the Passover lamb on the following day.

Exo. 12:6, 8 – **On the fourteenth day of the moon of Abib** (or the March moon) **you shall betwixt the evening slaughter the Passover lamb. ... and should thus eat meat in the same night,** etc.

Mark 14:12, Luke 22:7 – **And on the first day of the sweet** [unleavened] **bread, when one sacrificed the Passover lamb, the disciples spoke to Him** (Christ): **Where do you want us to go and make preparations so that You may eat the Passover lamb?**

2. Furthermore, Christ wanted to institute this holy Supper precisely in the same night in which He was betrayed and was soon to embark on His suffering, because it was to be His holy Testament in which He bequeaths to us the highest blessings and heavenly benefits, and we are thus to be inspired to accept as true with greater devotion and zeal His endowment as a testamentary endowment; also that we let this holy Supper be all the more commended to us. For just as a husband, prior to his death, by means of a well-thought-out testament, once more assigns the wedding dowry he received from his bride back to his spouse, so has Christ, our heavenly Bridegroom, desired to assign anew (again) to us His true body and blood (which He had assumed from us) by means of this testament of His holy Supper prior to His returning to His Father through His suffering and death.

Mat. 26:27, Mark 14:23 – **This is My blood of the New Testament.**

Luke 22:20, 1 Cor. 22:25 – **This is the chalice of the New Testament in My blood.**

Now, although Christ wanted to institute this holy Supper at the time of Passover, and indeed in the evening, yet He did not want to give any law thereby that one had to partake of this holy Supper precisely at this time and in the evening; rather, each Christian may and should partake of it as often as he thinks that he needs the comfort which is presented in it, and as often as he can be prepared and fit for it. That now the administration and the use of this Sacrament are not bound to any certain time of the year or to any certain hour, we substantiate as follows:

1. Because there is no command of the Lord regarding this matter in the words of institution; for inasmuch as the evangelists record that Christ conducted this Supper with His disciples in the evening, such belongs to the historical account and by no means includes a divine command that one must conduct this Supper at precisely the same time.

2. Because Christ states in the words of institution that we should partake of this holy Supper as often as we do it to His memory, in that He then contrasts the word ὁσάχις (as often as) to the celebration of the little Passover (pascal) lamb, which had to be slaughtered precisely between the evening on the fourteenth day of the March moon (Exo. 12:6). Now, since the little Passover lamb was a type of the holy Supper, [and] also because Christ instituted this holy Supper shortly after the observance of the little Passover lamb (and one might be inclined to think that the observance of the Supper was bound to a certain time of year and hour of the day no less than [was] the observance of the little Passover lamb) the Lord Christ thus wanted to confront this delusion [and thus] commands that we should [celebrate] the Supper, as often as we do it, to His remembrance.

1 Cor. 11:25, 26 – **Do such, as often as you drink it, to My remembrance. For as often as you eat of this bread and drink from this chalice, you should proclaim the Lord's death**, etc.

3. Because time, place, and similar details do not belong to the essential elements or the perfection (completeness) of the Sacramental action, in as much as they are not thereby bound to it by any express divine directive.

4. It is to be concluded from Acts 20:7 that the disciples of the early church observed the holy Supper on the first day after the Sabbath, that is, on Sunday.

Here again are apparent points of contention:

1. That Christ's example is held up to us in order to be emulated; however, Christ instituted this holy Supper at the time of Easter and, indeed, in the evening. Therefore we should rightly make use of [observe] it at the same time. ANSWER: **1.** The question here is not whether it is correct to [celebrate] the holy Supper during Easter time and in the evening, but rather whether it is necessary that it occur precisely at this time and, moreover, whether it is incorrect if it occurs at a different time. **2.** With His example, Christ did not wish to give a commandment regarding these external circumstances; rather, with the words "as often as" He sufficiently indicated that we are to have access to this heavenly medicine at any time when need and the devotion of our conscience require it. **3.** By no means are all the works of Christ presented for our emulation if we do not also have the Word and command of God; therefore, we are directed more to His Word than to His example. **4.** Christ conducted the Supper while seated. On that account, should it be wrong that one conduct it standing or kneeling? Christ had only twelve disciples with Him and distributed the holy Supper to them; because of that should it be incorrect to conduct the same in a larger assembly of Christians? Christ conducted the Supper in a home at Jerusalem; because of that should it be wrong to conduct it in the church? **5.** It therefore remains that the administration of the holy Supper is not bound to any particular time; and since it is customary in the Christian Church that the holy Supper, in an orderly manner, is administered in the early morning, one thus rightly abides by such an order (with the exception of an emergency) because one is in a state of fasting and better fitted to all affairs in the morning.

2. This Sacrament is called the holy Supper [lit., evening meal]; therefore, it is necessary that it be conducted in the evening. ANSWER: This Sacrament is not called the holy *Evening* Meal as if for that reason it were necessary that it must at all times be conducted precisely in the evening, but rather because the Lord Christ instituted and celebrated it with His disciples in the evening. Thus it is similarly called the **bread-breaking** (see above in chap. 2), not as if it were necessary that precisely in midst of the action the bread be broken, but rather because the Lord Christ, in the administration of the holy Supper, broke the bread and thereby prepared it for distribution.

CHAPTER 34

HOW OFTEN ONE SHOULD MAKE USE
OF THE HOLY SUPPER.

 t is not enough that one partakes of this Sacrament only one time in his life, the same as one is baptized only once; rather, the holy Supper is to be made use of many times and often by the Christian, which is accordingly to be demonstrated:

1. Christ our Lord has not given us the freedom to use the holy Supper or not use it; rather, He has expressly set down the command: **Do such to My remembrance,** which command all obedient disciples of Christ, as His servants, should justly follow.

Luke 23:19, 1 Cor. 11:24 – **This do to My remembrance.**

1 Cor. 11:25, 26 – **Do such as often as you drink to My remembrance. For as often as you eat of this bread and drink from this chalice, you should proclaim the Lord's death,** etc. (It is to be especially noted here that the apostle Paul sets down Christ's Word thus: **Such do as often as you drink it,** etc.; for from [these words] it is easily to be understood that it is not enough to make use of the holy Supper only one time; rather, if Christ's command is to be satisfactorily carried out, it must be done often).

2. If we truly also want to take our Christianity seriously and ponder from our heart how grossly and how often we have acted against the Commandments of God, and thereby have transgressed the covenant of our Baptism, then our own need would of itself drive us to make use of this holy Supper for the strengthening of faith.

3. By the same token, if we remember the great benefit and glorious comfort which we receive from the consumption of the holy Supper (providing we precede it with true repentance and approach in faith), we will all the more be attracted thereby to receive this holy Sacrament frequently and many times. Relevant here also is the foregoing twenty-third chapter of this treatise, in which the fruits (benefits) of this holy Supper were expressly dealt with.

4. Finally, before our eyes stands the example of the holy apostles and the early church, who not just once, but often and many times made use of the holy Supper.

Acts 2:42,46 – **They, however, persistently remained in the apostolic doctrine and in the fellowship and in the bread-breaking and in prayer. And they daily and constantly were of one mind in the temple and broke bread back and forth in homes.**

Acts 20:7 – **But on a certain Sabbath, as the disciples were coming together to break bread, Paul preached to them,** etc.

It can be readily seen therefrom that the holy Supper should be frequently and regularly made use of (after proper prior preparation) by true Christians who are serious about their godliness and Christianity, not merely because of their own need and for their own benefit, but so that herein they might also show themselves [in contrast to] others as members of the Church (1 Cor. 10:16). However, at what time of the year and how often during the year the same should occur, about this one cannot give definite, general rules; rather, such has to be left to the personal discretion of each person, in as much as the need of conscience, the zeal for godliness, the guilt about obedience to Christ's ordinances, and especially the motivation of the Holy Spirit can best be able to give the best counsel to each person in particular. That is precisely why Christ did not wish to bind the use of this holy Sacrament to a specific time, so that at any time, whenever we might have need for this great gift and find ourselves properly prepared for it, we may have a sure access to it. "Live every day," said an ancient teacher, "so that you may each day be a worthy guest of Christ." *Item*: Avail yourself hourly of the spiritual consumption of the body and blood of Christ, of the Sacramental nourishment, as often as it is necessary and (after prior preparation) helpful for the strengthening of your faith.

John 14:15 – **If you love Me, then keep My commandments.**

John 15:14 – **You are My friends if you do what I command you to do.** Rom. 8:15 – **Those whom the Spirit of God motivates are God's children.**

Here again is an apparent point of contention: That one lets himself be baptized only once; therefore, one should avail himself of the holy Supper only one time. ANSWER: This conclusion is dealt with extensively in chapter 28 of the treatise on holy Baptism, and the distinction was clearly shown as to why one allows himself to be baptized only one time as opposed to availing one's self frequently of the holy Supper. For, **1.** in the institution of holy Baptism it is not revealed nor required that one should be baptized more than one time; but in the institution of the holy Supper stands the clear, express command of Christ: **This do, as often as you drink it. 2.** One has no example that the apostles ever baptized a person more than once, but the apostles and the Christians of the early church frequently celebrated the holy Supper. **3.** Circumcision in the Old Testament was received only once by each, but the eating of the Passover (paschal) lamb was repeated annually. Now in the New Testament, holy Baptism comes in place of circumcision [and] the holy Supper in place of the little Passover lamb. **4.** Through holy Baptism we are born again; in the holy Supper we are fed for eternal life. Just as a natural person is born only once but later is often fed and given drink, so it is sufficient to be born again once through holy Baptism and later to be fed often with Christ's body and blood. **5.** Through holy Baptism we are simultaneously installed (invested) into Christianity and taken into the fellowship of the Church; through the Sacrament of the holy Supper we are sustained therein. Therefore, the repetition of the holy Supper is necessary, but not the repetition of Baptism. **6.** In the Sacrament of holy Baptism, God the Lord establishes a grace-covenant with us that from God's side remains constant and irrevocable; consequently, the repetition of Baptism is not necessary. We, however, often times violate the covenant of holy Baptism; therefore, it is necessary that through genuine repentance we be once again received back into this grace-covenant, and that we be reassured of it through the salvation-restoring participation in the holy Supper. **7.** Holy Baptism testifies about the gracious will of God the Lord towards us; now, since His gracious will is unchangeable (Rom. 11:29), therefore Baptism does not need to be repeated. Contrariwise, since our faith at times becomes weak, it must be strengthened through the use of the holy Supper.

CHAPTER 35

AT WHAT PLACE [LOCALITY] THE HOLY SUPPER SHOULD AND MAY BE ADMINISTERED.

 oncerning the [specific] location for administering and receiving the holy Supper, there exists no express command of the Lord in the holy Scriptures, for even though Christ instituted the holy Supper and conducted it with His disciples in a private home in Jerusalem and not in the temple, He still did not thereby intend to give any specific rule and command that the holy Supper was to be specifically administered in homes and not in the church. Accordingly, since it is customary in the Christian Church that the holy Supper is administered and received in public assembly after the hearing of the Word, one thus rightly abides with this practice and does not deviate from it except in cases of emergency, which we substantiate as follows:

1. The holy Sacrament is simultaneously a visible Word and a seal of the that which is promised in the Word. Now then, the proclamation of the divine Word is carried out in public assembly; therefore, this holy Sacrament should there also rightly be administered.

2. Since holy Baptism is performed in public assembly, except in cases of emergency, therefore the holy Supper should rightly also be conducted in public assembly.

3. Since the practice in the early church was to celebrate this holy Supper in public assembly of the Christians, one rightly continues with this practice without any further thought.

Acts 20:7 – **But on one Sabbath, as the disciples came together to break bread, Paul preached to them,** etc.

1 Cor. 11:20,33 – **When you then come together, does not one then observe the Lord's Supper** (They had not been celebrating it properly and in accordance with Christ's institution as it should have been.)**? Therefore, my dear brothers, when you come together, do wait for each other.**

Even though it is now a fine arrangement that the holy Supper is administered and received in church in the general public assembly of Christians, yet this does not mean that it would be wrong to distribute the holy Supper to the sick in private homes for the strengthening of their faith. We substantiate this as follows:

1. Christ did not institute His holy Supper in the temple at Jerusalem; rather, He Himself instituted it and celebrated it with His disciples in the home of a citizen. How, then, could it be wrong and contrary to Christ's institution to similarly celebrate it there in case of an emergency?

Mat. 26:17–20, 26 – **But on the first day of sweet [unleavened] bread the disciples approached Jesus and said to Him: Where do you wish us to prepare for the eating of the Passover lamb? He said, Go into the city to a certain person and say to him: The Master wants it said to you: My time is here; I want to celebrate the Passover with My disciples at your place. And the disciples did just as Jesus instructed them and prepared the Passover (paschal) lamb. And in the evening He sat down at table with the twelve. But as they ate, Jesus took the bread, gave thanks and broke it and gave it to the disciples and said: Take, eat, this is My body,** etc.

Mark 14:12–17, 22 – **And on the first day of the sweet [unleavened] bread, at the time one sacrificed the Passover lamb, the disciples spoke to Him (Jesus): Where do You wish for us to go and make preparations so that You can eat the Passover lamb? And He sent two of His disciples and said to them: Go forth into the city, and a man will meet you carrying a jug of water; follow after him. And where he enters, you say to the householder:**

The Master wants us to say to you: Where is the guest house in which I will eat the Passover lamb with My disciples? And he will show you a large hall which is plastered and prepared; make the same ready for us. And the disciples went out and came into the city and found it as He had said, and they prepared the Passover lamb. But in the evening He came with the twelve. And inasmuch as they were eating, Jesus took the bread, gave thanks and broke it, and gave it to them and said: Take, eat, this is My body.

Luke 22:7–14 – Now the day of the sweet [unleavened] bread had arrived, on which one had to sacrifice the Passover lamb. And He sent Peter and John and said: Go forth and prepare the Passover lamb so that we may eat it. But they said to Him: Where do you want us to prepare it? He said to them: As you come into the city, see, a man will meet you who will be carrying a water jug; follow after him into the house into which he enters. And say to the landlord: The Master wants us to tell you: Where is the lodging in which I may eat the Passover with My disciples? And he will show you a large plastered hall. There make the preparations. They went forth and found like He had said, and they prepared the Passover lamb. And when the hour came, He sat down and the twelve disciples with Him.

2. The holy apostles, as also the first churches, celebrated the holy Supper in private homes, without giving it a second thought, whenever their persecutors wouldn't allow them to administer it in churches and in open [public] assembly.

Acts 2:46 – And daily and constantly they were of one mind with each other in the temple and broke bread back and forth in homes. (They said their prayers in the temple at Jerusalem, but since they were not allowed to celebrate the holy Supper in it, they performed its celebration in the homes.)

3. Since in the institution of the holy Supper no particular place is designated, it thus cannot be contrary to Christ's ordinance to administer the holy Supper in private homes.

4. If the circumstance of time, place, and the like are not bound to the administration of the holy Sacrament by a clear, divine command, then they do not belong to the essential elements or to the perfection of same.

5. In the Old Testament, the worship and the Levitical sacrifices were bound to a certain place, but in the New Testament this distinction of place is lifted along with other Levitical ceremonies; and just as one should pray in all places, so also one may in case of emergency also administer and celebrate the holy Sacrament in all places.

In John 4:21, Jesus says to the Samaritan woman: **Woman, believe Me, the time is coming when you will worship the Father neither here on this mountain nor in Jerusalem. But the time is coming, and has already arrived, that the true worshiper will worship the Father in Spirit and in truth,** etc.

1 Tim. 2:8 – **So I now would that men pray in every place and lift up holy hands without wrath and doubt.**

6. The sick are indeed comforted in their anxieties of conscience by the evangelical promises; why should it then be wrong that one extend to them the seal of the evangelical promises in their private homes? Sometimes the sick are much more fit for such a heavenly meal than the able-bodied, since they through their illness are reminded of their sin and find themselves in heartfelt contrition over sin.

In Mat. 11:28 Jesus says: **Come here to Me, all of you who struggle with difficulties (problems) and are loaded down; I will reinvigorate you.**

John 6:37 – **And whoever comes to Me, such a one I will not kick out.**

Rom. 14:1, 3 – **Take in the weak in faith,** etc. **For God has received them.**

Here again are apparent points of contention:

1. That the administration of the holy Supper is the kind of celebration which really belongs in the church; therefore, it should not be changed into a private celebration. ANSWER: **1.** If the holy Supper were the kind of ecclesiastical celebration which could only be performed at a prescribed public assembly of the congregation, why would Christ not much rather have instituted and celebrated the holy Supper in the temple at Jerusalem than in a private home? Why did not the apostles and the early church celebrate it in the same way? **2.** In the New Testament, [the word] "Church" is understood not as a pile of rocks or a stone building, but rather the assembly of Christians; accordingly, wherever Christians assemble themselves in the Name of Christ, there He is among them (Mat. 18:20). Therefore, the same must also constitute a proper church; and St. Paul also mentions congregations or churches in the homes (Rom. 16:4, Phm. v. 2). **3.** In accordance with congregational order, the holy Supper is certainly to be administered in the church; but in case of emergency the circumstances of the place are indeed not to be so highly overrated that one would rob an anxious heart of this great comfort.

2. That the Passover lamb is a type of the holy Supper; however, it was slaughtered and consumed by the assembly of the Israelite Church. ANSWER: **1.** Why would one much rather regard the type than the institution of the holy Supper itself? It cannot be denied that Christ celebrated the holy Supper with His apostles in a private home. **2.** From what source would one show that the Passover lamb was at all times consumed either in the ark of the covenant or in the temple at Jerusalem? It is much rather to be concluded from Exo. 12:4 that [the lamb] was slaughtered and consumed by the Israelites in their homes; if it also of necessity had to be consumed in the temple, then Christ certainly would not have celebrated [the Passover] with His disciples in a private home. **3.** In Deu. 16:6, God expressly ordained a specific place for the paschal lamb; one can show no such a command concerning the administration of the holy Supper. **3.** That nowhere has Christ commanded that one should distribute the holy Supper to the sick in the privacy of their homes; therefore, it is wrong and forbidden. ANSWER: In *adiaphora* the conclusion does not apply that what God does not command, therefore He has also just as soon forbidden. For otherwise, by this [way of thinking] every ceremony and indifferent thing (*adiaphoron*) would be abolished. So also it does not apply concerning external matters that what God has nowhere commanded is specifically forbidden as well. For otherwise I too would in like manner surely infer that because Christ has nowhere commanded that one administer and celebrate the holy Supper in the early morning, it would thus specifically be forbidden and be wrong. Not so! Rather, in the New Testament the Levitical specification of time and place has been abolished, so that the holy Supper is now not bound to a certain place and time, as was the paschal lamb in the Old Testament. By the same token, it is fine and beneficial that the holy Supper be administered in keeping with congregational order in the church on Sundays in a large assembly of Christians.

4. That if the holy Supper had to be administered at home for all the sick, it would be too much of a burden for the preachers [pastors]; or, if one is visited and not another, it would raise the suspicion that one regarded the person [i.e., discriminated on a personal basis]; therefore, the practice would be best that it be totally omitted. ANSWER: Experience testifies that such assertions are completely invalid and irrelevant, for faithful pastors and soul-stewards will by no means allow themselves to be discouraged from visiting the sick, from comforting them out of God's Word, and (upon prior, proper, genuine repentance) from feeding them with the holy Supper; whereas the sick especially require this comfort, and in general they recognize the sickness of their soul more so than in prior healthy days. Isa. 38:13, 14 – **But**

he broke all my bones, as a lion. I whined like a crane and cooed like a dove.

5. That the holy Supper is called a *synaxis*, since it was, to wit, celebrated in the early church as the Christians came together (1 Cor. 11:20); therefore, it should not be celebrated in private homes. ANSWER: **1.** We gladly agree that in keeping with the congregational order the holy Supper should be celebrated in the public assembly of Christians; however, it does not follow that it may not be celebrated at home in a house in case of an emergency. **2.** Even though this Sacrament is called the Supper, who would or could conclude therefrom that it must thus be celebrated precisely in the evening. **3.** When the fathers of the early church call the holy Supper *synaxin*, they are primarily referring to the fellowship of saints in the entire Church, as far and wide as they are scattered in all the world, since Christians are collectively one body because they all partake of one bread, (1 Cor. 10:17); they all drink of one Spirit (1 Cor. 12:13). For this to happen, it is not necessary that all Christians from the entire world come together and eat from one piece of bread and drink out of the same chalice; rather, it is sufficient that the consecrated bread and the consecrated chalice be received by Christians according to Christ's command so that they become partakers of the body and blood of Christ.

CHAPTER 36

CONCERNING THE CEREMONIES WHICH ARE OB-SERVED AT THE ADMINISTRATION OF THE HOLY SUPPER.

till remaining to be dealt with in the final chapter of this treatise are the ceremonies which should or may be observed in the celebration of this holy Sacrament. So then, the following rules are to be taken into consideration:

1. In the institution of the holy Supper, those ceremonies which were employed by Christ as special sacramental actions must also of necessity be used by us and are by no means to be omitted. These are the necessary ceremonies: **Taking the bread, blessing it, distributing it, and eating it; in the same manner, taking the chalice, blessing it, distributing it, and drinking it, and thereby to proclaim Christ death.**

Luke 22:19, 1 Cor. 11:24 – **This do to My remembrance.**

1 Cor. 11:25 – **Do this, as often as you drink it, to My remembrance.**

2. Those ceremonies which serve the purpose of awakening in one a grateful remembrance of Christ's death and a salutary examination (even though they are not required for the holy Supper through an express command of the Lord) should thus by no means be omitted or done away with. Such ceremonies include the following: effecting prior Christian admonition of the communicants, reading the Lord's Prayer or other little prayers, singing of Christian Psalms by the communicants, thanking God the Lord after

performing the act of this Sacrament, and speaking the divine blessing over the communicants.

1 Cor. 11:26, 28 – **For as often as you eat of this bread and drink from this chalice, you should proclaim the Lord's death until He comes. A person** [should] **examine himself, however, and then eat of this bread and drink from this chalice.**

3. Such ceremonies which of themselves are *adiaphora*, which do not contradict the faith, and which serve a purpose in awakening proper devotion towards this holy Sacrament can be retained without damage to the faith, under the following conditions: **1.** that they are not made equal to the foregoing ceremonies, much less that they supersede them, but that by them the teaching is promoted and upheld that it is best to administer the holy Supper plainly and simply according to the example of Christ and the apostles. **2.** That they do not heap on too much and thereby suppress other beneficial [actions]. **3.** That they do not result in the false delusion that such ceremonies are necessary or are an essential part of the worship service. **4.** That the hearers be instructed that a worthy preparation and reception of this holy Supper is by no means dependent on these ceremonies, but rather that one go to it in genuine repentance and true faith. Such ceremonies include the following: using gold or silver patens and chalices, covering the altar or table [with paraments], wearing a surplice [or cope—*Chorröcke*], kindling lights, striking up the organ, singing the words of institution, and the like.

Gal. 5:1, 13 – **Thus now stand in the freedom with which Christ has freed us. But you, dear brothers, have been called to freedom,** etc.

4. Those ceremonies which serve little or no purpose for edification, which present this holy Sacrament as an external drama, or also those which are ascribed a special power and a part of the worship service apart from God's Word, such may properly be done away with, and upon prior instruction from God's Word, be discarded. Such ceremonies are as follows: The priest's lifting up the chasuble and ringing a bell under it, breathing on the bread, consecrating in an unfamiliar language, secretly murmuring the words of Christ: **This is My body, this is My blood,** throwing the arms up high and then quickly dropping them down again, and whatever additional similar practices there might be.

1 Cor. 14:26, 40 – **Let everything occur for the betterment. Let everything take place honorably and orderly.**

5. Such ceremonies that of themselves are idolatrous and superstitious [and] are contrary to God's Word and Christ's institution, should by no means be tolerated; rather, regardless of all offense to the simple folk, they should be eliminated as soon as possible. Such ceremonies include the following: offering the laity only the bread, perverting the holy Supper into a sacrifice for the living and the dead, calling upon [praying to] the saints, conducting private masses, and the like.

1 Tim. 6:3, 4 – **If someone teaches differently and does not remain with the salutary Words of our Lord Jesus Christ, and with the teaching concerning divine salvation, such a one is in darkness,** etc.

John 17:17 – **Make them holy (and uphold us) Lord with Your truth. Your Word is the Truth. Amen.**

Made in the USA
San Bernardino, CA
09 May 2017